The secret of Israel's Power | Uzi Eilam

THE SECRET OF ISRAEL'S POWER

UZI EILAM

Contents

ACRONYMS OF ISRAELI ORGANIZATIONS AND TITLES

PALMACH
Hebrew acronym for Plugot Machatz (impact companies), the elite force of the pre-state Haganah fighting force.

GADNA
Hebrew acronym for Gdudei No'ar Ivri (Hebrew youth battalions), a pre-army training framework for high school teenagers.

IDF
Israel Defense Forces.

CGS
Chief of the General Staff, the commanding officer of the IDF with a rank of Lieutenant General.

OC
Officer in Command.

Sayeret Matkal
Transliteration of the elite special force unit under direct command of the General Staff.

IMI

Israel Military Industries, an Israeli weapons systems company.

R&D

Research and Development, also the name of the combined IDF/Defense Ministry Unit that preceded MAFAT. IAI Israel Aerospace Industries.

RAFAEL

Hebrew acronym for Authority for the Development of Armaments, a government agency that became a government owned weapons systems company.

MAFAT

Hebrew acronym for the Administration for the Development of Weapons and Technological Infrastructure.

IAEC

The Israel Atomic Energy Commission.

PREFACE

Celebrating my 70th anniversary brought together hundreds of friends that were with me along the way I served my country. Childhood in the Kibbutz, paratroopers in the 50's, Six Days War in Jerusalem, R&D for the IDF in the 70's, the Israeli Atomic Energy Commission, Defense R&D and international cooperation in developing technologies. These formed a kaleidoscopic picture that persuaded me to write.

Not being sure of my memory I turned to the IDF archive where all my notes, diaries, lectures and timetables book-notes were kept. This treasure, thanks to the outstanding help of the Archive team, was a key to success and I thank the IDF Archive team for that.

For 18 months I could not stop writing and as it went on I acquired insight and the whole Defense Technology scene was revealed.

Many former colleagues and friends were at my side to help and I remember all of them with deep gratitude.

Battalion 890 fighters from the era of the military activities in the 50th, my soldiers from battalion 71 who fought in Jerusalem in 1967, fellow R&D people of the whole Defense community in the I.D.F, in M.O.D and in the Industries...m indebted to all of you!

The way the book attracted so many Israeli readers encouraged me to think of translating it to English. I thank Jeremy Forman, who did an excellent diligent work of translation. Michael (Mike) Eilan took upon himself to edit the book and did an invaluable job.

Sussex Academic Press with Anita and Anthony Graham were a good support from the outset and I feel privileged that the book has been published by Sussex.

My dear family, Naomi my wife and my children Osnat, Nimrod

and Noah deserve a big thank you. My family was with me all along the tough and demanding duties that I had in my career but also along the process of writing this book, patiently encouraging and supporting. Thank you my family!

1

Childhood

My earliest childhood memory is of my maternal grandfather, Shlomo Kovelman, when he came to visit Kibbutz Tel Yosef where I was born and raised. As a two-year-old sitting on his lap, I can still recall his long white beard tickling my face. His eyes were bright and his hands were soft and gentle — the hands of a scholar. Grandpa spoke only Russian and Yiddish, and I can still recall the musical sound of his tenor voice. Before they immigrated, Shlomo Kovelman spent most of his time in the court of his rabbi in the town of Skvira, south of the Ukranian city of Kiev. It was Grandma Miriam who ran the household and the family flour and grain business.

The anti-Jewish pogroms in the Ukraine began after World War I. One evening, Grandpa Shlomo returned home from the rabbi's court injured and bleeding. His clothes were torn and half his beard had been shaved off. Grandma Miriam...mall, strong, and practical woman — understood exactly what had happened and decided they should leave at once. So began their exodus from the Ukraine that very night. My mother Shifra and her sister Chava immigrated to Palestine to join the pioneers of the modern wave of Jewish-Zionist immigration to Palestine known as the 'Third Aliyah'.

My grandfather on my father's side was named Yehoshua Trachtenberg, but I never knew him. All that remains of Grandpa Yehoshua in the family photo album is a single picture of a lifeless, badly beaten body. From the bits and pieces of information provided by my father,

I understood that his town of Kalinovka had also suffered a Ukrainian anti-Jewish pogrom during which my grandfather was killed.

Yehoshua Trachtenberg was a blacksmith, an unusual occupation for a Jew in those days. My father was also a blacksmith, and as a boy I spent many magical hours with him in his smithy shop on the kibbutz, surrounded by the smell of smoking coal and white hot iron, captivated by the art of producing metal fixtures and accessories and the fascinating work of making horseshoes and placing them with nails that were also forged by hand especially for that purpose. My father's hands were rough, black, and strong. In my eyes, he was the strongest man in the world.

My father Baruch left home in 1916 at the age of 16, to join the Red Army. However, he quickly became involved in the Zionist movement, which was then operating underground. He was subsequently arrested and, after a quick trial, sent to Siberia. One day in 1924 he was informed that they were being exiled to Palestine. Immediately upon his arrival he joined the Labor Battalion (Gdud Ha'avoda), whose members were then engaged in quarrying and paving roads.

And so it came to pass that I bear not only the legacy of my learned Grandpa Shlomo and my Grandpa Yehoshua, with his hands of iron, but also a memory of the pogroms, instilled in me when I was very young. The image of Grandpa Yehoshua's desecrated dead body remains ingrained in my memory like a mysterious and foreboding brand. For some people the words "never again" may have lost some of their intensity from overuse, but that photograph made them an integral part of my legacy. Growing up, I was imbued with the strength and moral fiber of the legacy of the Jewish people, as well as the physical strength and wisdom of my grandfathers. I have carried this spirit with me my entire life.

My parents' home on Kibbutz Tel Yosef was the closest house to the fence that encircled the kibbutz. To the east, just over the fence, were fields that belonged to Arab farmers. One afternoon when I went to my parents' 'room', as we called our parents' homes on the kibbutz, I found my father and our neighbor pouring cement into large metal containers and placing them on the patio facing the fence to the east of the house. Arabs had come close to the kibbutz fence during the night, and I could see bullet holes on the interior wall of the room that served as both a living room and a kitchenette. This was the beginning of the eruption of Palestinian violence that historians refer to as the Arab Revolt of 1936–1939. It was during this period that Charles Orde Wingate, the British intelligence officer who established the Special Night Squads in 1938, first encountered Palestine.

As children on the kibbutz, we were naturally curious. We knew that the Night Squads' headquarters was the basement of the theatre that stood between Tel Yosef and Ein Harod, a central venue for the cultural events of all the Jewish settlements in the area. We admired Wingate's courage and that of his men, who regularly ventured outside the kibbutz fence to launch night operations.

Toward the end of 1941, tents were pitched in the northern section of the kibbutz. They were quickly filled with young men and women, marking the arrival of the Palmach — the elite fighting force of the Haganah — the pre-state Jewish military force. Palmach members spent half their time training and the other half working. As children, we kept a close eye on their activities, especially hand-to-hand combat training using clubs and grenade throwing. The grenades they used in training were "friction grenades", which were ignited by striking them against a matchbox. We watched each grenade-throw with bated breath, unable to take our eyes off the exercise and wondering if the grenade would go off. Even at that early age I took a special interest in weapons systems.

One day I was summoned in complete secrecy to meet with one of the Palmach commanders in the Jezreel Valley. He asked me to bring my trumpet, which I had been playing since I was eight years old, and to travel with a group of Palmach members to a secret event. In those days Kibbutz Tel Yosef was known for its wind orchestra, which was the extraordinary project of one extremely enthusiastic and dedicated man — Shimon Shadmi — who had played in a wind orchestra in Russia before immigrating to Palestine. I was eight years old when I received my first trumpet, which I still have today. It was only after we left the grounds of the kibbutz that the Palmach member told me that we were on our way to the groves surrounding the Harod Springs for an induction ceremony of a new Palmach unit, and that I was to play the trumpet as the flag was raised at the beginning of the ceremony. Electrified by the secrecy, the quiet issue of terse commands, and the magnitude of the event, I played with emotion and excitement, and without missing a note. I returned home with a great sense of pride that I could not share with anyone. My lips were sealed.

In those days kibbutz children did not live with their parents but in separate children's houses. On Saturday June 29, 1946, all the children in our house were woken up early in the morning and told to move into one room and lie down on the floor. The British, we were told, had surrounded the kibbutz, and there was concern that the British soldiers, who were already positioned next to the kibbutz fence, would open fire on anything that moved. The operation, which the British codenamed Operation Broadside, was undertaken a few months after the Haganah had embarked upon a policy of active opposition to British policy in Palestine. The British operation was meant to break the Palmach, imprison the Haganah leadership, and to confiscate the weapons and ammunition that had been stockpiled throughout Palestine in clandestine caches in kibbutzim, groves, and forests.

Rumors spread through the kibbutz like wildfire: "All the adult members are being arrested and driven to an undisclosed place... Whoever resists is beaten with rifles and stabbed with bayonets. Kibbutz member Haim Harodi has been shot to death..." By evening, we knew that most male kibbutz members had been jailed indefinitely and that we were now responsible for caring for the crops and livestock of the kibbutz. We were eleven and twelve-year-old children, but we took ourselves and the jobs to which we were assigned very seriously.

Israel's War of Independence actually began with the UN General Assembly's plan to partition Palestine, which was passed on November 29, 1947. On that night everyone on the kibbutz congregated in the dining room and joined the concentric circles of dancers who spun round and round for hours in joyful celebration.

The UN resolution also led to a wave of violent Arab attacks on the Jewish community in Palestine, and everyone was concerned for their safety. During the months preceding David Ben-Gurion's Declaration of Independence on May 14, 1948, the battles in the Jezreel Valley began to intensify. The large Arab village of Zir'in that controlled the main road that ran lengthwise through the Jezreel and the Harod Valleys was a permanent source of sniper fire on Jewish vehicles. One March morning a rumor spread through the kibbutz that a battle was being fought at the Arab village of Nuris (today, the site of Moshav Nurit, on the slopes of Mt. Gilboa), which was known to have a large number of people who were involved in anti-Jewish violence. We closely followed the condition of the wounde, who were brought to the kibbutz's infirmary in the pine grove between Tel Yosef and Ein Harod. Not long had passed until rumors started about fatalities as well. The funeral of Tel Yosef native Dan Tzvik, held the following day, was my first real encounter with the War of Independence. It effectively brought home the painful realization that, in war, people die and suddenly cease to exist — not just anonymous souls, but people who are close to you.

In the spring of 1949, as the War of Independence was drawing to a close, I was chosen to attend a fitness coach's course. The course was held by the Hapoel organization and was held in Holon over Passover vacation. The course participants came from both kibbutzim and towns, and included Amitzur Shapira, an athlete of international standing who was well known as a sprinter. Shapira had blond hair and an Aryan face, and wise green penetrating eyes that sized you up immediately. Shapira and I had a special relationship, perhaps because we both specialized in sprints. Shapira would later go on to coach Esther Shahamorov, one of the greatest Israeli athletes of all time. Shapira was one of the eleven athletes murdered in the attack carried out by the Palestinian terrorist group Black September on September 5, 1972 at the Munich Olympic games. For Israelis like me with lifetime of relationships intertwined with our country's defense, the most dramatic events often involve people one knows well from the past.

It was pure chance that on May 30, just a few months before Shapira was murdered, I was in Lod airport (which had not yet been named after Ben-Gurion). By that time I was already a colonel in the IDF with extensive combat experience and was currently serving as deputy director of military R&D. Airliner hijacking was rife and Israel had adopted a policy of placing armed guards on all El Al flights. These guards had to look like normal passengers in every way, and the question was how to best conceal their weapons in a way that allowed instant response in emergencies. That day I had come to the airport with a young officer to assess the situation and to advise El Al's security unit on how the on-flight security guards should hide their weapons. As we assessed the various options, the sound of explosions and gun shots suddenly erupted. We rushed to the arrivals terminal and found a horrific massacre. Three members of the Japanese Red Army had landed at Lod airport, pulled out assault rifles, sub-machine guns, and hand grenades from their suitcases and opened fire on travelers who had just landed. Dozens of people lay on the floor. Some were injured and groaning, others were already dead. Next to one of the bodies sat an open bag, a Kalashnikov assault rifle, and a few hand-grenades. The upper part of one body had been blown to pieces by the grenade blast, and we later realized that it was the body of one of the Japanese terrorists who had taken his own life with a hand grenade after thinking he had completed his mission. I sent the border guards to locate and capture the terrorists and began organizing an evacuation of the wounded. Twenty-four people were killed in the attack and 78 were wounded. One of those killed was Prof. Aharon Katzir, a world renowned scientist and director of the Weizmann Institute's Polymer Department, who had been returning from an academic conference abroad. His brother was Efraim Katchalksy, with whom I had worked when I was director of the Weapons Development Branch. Efraim later went on to become President of Israel.

I of course knew nothing about the coming lifetime of defense relationships when we began Gadna (the Hebrew acronym for "youth battalions"), a preliminary military training course for youth run by IDF soldiers. I was chosen to take part in the Gadna squad commanders' course held at IDF Camp No. 80 near the town of Hadera during summer vacation of 1949. It was a military training program of the highest quality, with demanding physical training, weapons training, and strict order and discipline.

Throughout my entire tenth-grade year I also served as a Gadna instructor, as well as a fitness instructor for the morning exercises of the Tel Yosef children's society. For me the greatest challenge was training my own classmates from Tel Yosef—Ein Harod high school at Gadna. I enjoyed positions of command and leadership. Had I not, I doubt whether I would have been able to cram so many activities into my daily schedule. I also had to find time for my schoolwork and for practicing the trumpet to play with the adult orchestra, as it took time for me to reach the musical level I demanded of myself. I also worked in the kibbutz's dairy — an integral part of kibbutz life and of young people's training for work.

When my father died of a heart attack in 1951 on the day before Purim, I quickly went from being a teenager to being a man. From that moment on I knew I would need to provide for myself and to forge my own path in life, and that I would receive no substantial support from anyone else.

I wanted to change my life by moving from the kibbutz dairy barn to work outside with the field crops, but my efforts were unsuccessful and I was stuck working in the dairy barn all summer long until the beginning of my senior year of high school. I felt trapped, like a fish in a net...amiliar image from my father's work in the kibbutz fish ponds. Desperate to change my circumstances I began to prepare myself for the high school matriculation exams, which most kibbutz teenagers did not take in those days. This decision was a vague, internal declaration of divorce from kibbutz life, although I was not aware of it at the time. During most of the summer, until the beginning of the school year, I spent my free time alone, studying English with the diligence and determination that stemmed from my inclination to leave the kibbutz and be free to pursue a wider range of activities and work.

As the beginning of the school year approached, I asked a girl in my class if she wanted to study for the matriculation exams with me. At that time kibbutz high schools did not usually prepare their students for the matriculation exams because the exams were viewed as a door to the effete values of non-kibbutz life. So it was clear that we would have to take the exams outside the kibbutz. After speaking with a few other classmates I quickly emerged as the leader of a group of eight students who were determined to take the matriculation exams. Although the school's initial response to our plan was decisively negative, we refused to give up. In fact, we even told our teachers we would stop attending class and pursue an independent program of study instead. A few weeks later the teachers relented and we suddenly had teachers for maths, physics, chemistry, and English. The fact that we were a tightly knit group of students who supported one another played a major role in our success.

English was our major weak point, and I worked hard to improve my language skills by reading books in English with the help of an English language dictionary. I continued reading books in English during my military service as well. My fellow soldiers and, later, the soldiers in my charge, liked to say that instead of cigarettes and sweets my "elephant pack" — the heavy pack each soldier carried during marches and exercises — was filled with English books.

At the end of the school year we took the external matriculation exams with a great sense of excitement and trepidation. After a tense period of waiting we received our test scores just a few days before being drafted into the IDF. I had passed all the exams — even English — the subject that gave me most concern.

My father, Baruch Trachtenberg, and mother, Shifra Kovelman, in their Saturday best when they moved into Kibbutz Tel Yosef in 1932

Proudly wearing a broad belt on my Bar Mitzva just before the State of Israel was declared in May 1948. The height of the celebration was pistol practice.

2

From Gadna to Academia

Our IDF enlistment procedure began before the matriculation exams. The first stage was a medical examination, where I was dealt an unexpected blow. After being called back for a second test I was diagnosed with a cystic heart murmur that was audible when my heart contracted. I couldn't believe that as an athlete who was constantly exercising and working out that I had a heart defect. The additional examination I requested changed nothing, and with a heavy heart I prepared for my enlistment knowing that I would not be accepted to serve in a combat unit. At first I considered trying to get accepted into the Academic Reserves, a recently established program in the IDF that allowed people to complete a first degree before their military service. My plan was to study mathematics and physics — my

With his trumpet at the Hapoel convention in Tel Aviv where Uzi Eilam
and the kibbutz band performed

two favorite subjects — at the Hebrew University in Jerusalem. But I submitted my application after the deadline and was not accepted into the program.

After I my initial induction into the army I reported to the Gadna training base on the grounds of the old British police station at Givat Olga, on the Mediterranean coast. At the end of a training course we were awarded the rank of corporal and began our service as Gadna instructors.

WHY I DIDN'T MAKE IT TO UNIT 101

At the beginning of August 1953 a rumor spread that a secret incursion unit was being set up within the Jerusalem Brigade. Volunteers from other IDF units and various kibbutzim and moshavim were recruited for the new unit through an informal network of friends. The volunteers assembled for a meticulous selection process carried out by Shlomo Baum and Arik Sharon at the unit's base near the ruins of the Arab village of Sataf. Eventually, approximately 50 men were selected to begin training, which involved long-distance reconnaissance, shooting and target practice while running in mountainous areas, sabotage, and the use of explosives and hand grenades. The personal weapons issued to soldiers in the unit were different than standard IDF issue. Each soldier in the unit carried a Thompson Submachine Gun (a Tommy Gun) and a commando knife, typically wore civilian dress (short pants and sandals), and displayed little regard for military discipline, rank or chain of command. Instead of these traditional aspects of military culture, unit 101 soldiers were imbued with combat values such as courage, steadfast focus on the goal of a mission, and flawless implementation. In January 1954, Unit 101 merged with the 890th paratroop battalion, and Sharon was appointed as battalion commander.

Many of my classmates from Ein Harod and other kibbutzim joined the unit, including the famous scout Meir Har-Tziyon and

Yair Tel-Tzur of Afikim, a close friend who was later killed when his jeep drove over a landmine in the Sinai desert whilst in command of the 890th paratroop battalion. I was keen to join the unit and rather naïvely requested a formal transfer. After getting no response my patience reached its limit and I requested an interview with my commander, only to learn that he simply had not bothered to pass on the transfer form. I was furious, and the experience brought back the trapped feeling I had on the kibbutz after my father's death — the feeling that had motivated me to rebel against the kibbutz and begin preparing for the matriculation exams.

I decided to leave Gadna and reverted to the plan of joining the Academic Reserves. By then, however, I had begun thinking about what I would do after my military service, and this time I requested to study electrical engineering at the Technion in Haifa instead of mathematics and physics in Jerusalem. Engineering seemed like a solid profession to me. I passed all the tests, and my application to study at the Technion was accepted.

STRUGGLING WITH THE KIBBUTZ TO STUDY AT THE TECHNION

A week later I was summoned to the IDF's Induction Base to be discharged and transferred to the Academic Reserves. I left the base feeling free but deep in thought about how to broach the subject with my kibbutz, which had to approve my studies. I met the kibbutz secretary and told him that I had been accepted to the Academic Reserves to study electrical engineering at the Technion. He promised to raise the issue before the central committee and told me that it would have to be decided by the kibbutz general meeting. I began working on the kibbutz as was expected of me, but this time I insisted on working in the field crops.

From the moment the general meeting came to order I could feel opposition to my academic career plan growing. One of the main opponents was Shmuel Hefter, a founder of Tel Yosef and a veteran of the Hashomer Jewish self defense force. This short, sturdy man, with a wrinkled sun darkened face, spoke out against studying in general and academic study in particular. He argued that learning how to operate a Caterpillar D-2 tractor required no more than nine lessons and that this should be the basis of all kibbutz study programs. After discussion the secretary announced that another general meeting would be called to consider the subject and vote.

The day of the second meeting arrived. I was filled with anxiety, and I dreaded the prospect of having to endure another session of ridicule against higher education. The kibbutz secretary, however, led the discussion wisely. When he saw how determined I was, he let me speak first in order to explain to the members that the academic year was already underway, that the army had released me specifically in order to study, and that this was what I wanted to do more than anything. The meeting voted to approve my studies — and I was finally able to breathe easily.

THE TECHNION

I immediately travelled to Haifa, where I used my first days to make up for lost time by concentrating hard on my studies. I passed all my exams at the end of the academic year, which for me was actually only a six-month period. Serving in the Academic Reserves entailed going through a three-month officers' training course in the summer. In the meantime I met with the kibbutz secretary who told me that the kibbutz would most likely make me study agriculture instead of engineering because that was a skill that the kibbutz considered useful. With this new information I decided it would be best for me to complete my military service and to put off all decisions about academic studies for the time being. I informed the Technion of my decision, and was told that that I would be able to continue my studies at any time of my choosing in the future.

COMBAT FITNESS!

I was happy to take part in the officers' training program, and even happier to find out that there was no combat fitness requirement. Toward the end of the course I had another meeting with the medical committee. I was set on serving in the paratroops, and combat fitness was one of the requirements. I told the doctors who examined me that I was about to complete officers' training, that I regularly took part in all the long runs, and that I would carry my friends' rifles when they get tired. I argued that there was no way that my fitness was inadequate. This time the doctors agreed.

3

At the Forefront with the Paratroops

MY FIRST MEETING WITH ARIK SHARON

I was tremendously pleased when my request to serve with the 890th paratroop battalion was granted at the Induction Base at Tel Hashomer. When I arrived at the Tel Nof base, where the 890th Battalion was stationed at the time, I had an interview with battalion commander Arik Sharon.

In a voice we all quickly learned to imitate, Sharon asked me my name and where I came from. He already knew everything about me: that I had come from the Gadna program, that I had grown up on Kibbutz Tel Yosef, and that I had been a classmate of the young men who had served under him in Unit 101. "I asked the guys," he told me, referring to my classmates. "They told me that you're alright." Because of my training experience from my service in Gadna, Sharon assigned me to A Company as a squad commander under the command of Sa'adia Alkayam, who we all called Supapo.

SUPAPO

The atmosphere in the paratrooper base was very different from that of other military units. To me, it seemed less like a military unit and more like a group of irregular guerilla fighters. I bunked in the officers' quarters, along with company commander Supapo and his deputy Moshe Yanuka.

As for weapons, the Uzi submachine gun that Israel Military Industries (IMI) had just started to produce was not yet widespread, and fighters were proud to carry heavy submachine guns. I too received a Tommy Gun, with the high caliber 11.43 millimeter ammunition, as opposed to the 9 millimeter ammunition used by Uzis. Tommy Guns were also heavy, weighing almost 5 kilograms compared to the 3.5 kilogram Uzi with its wooden butt.

After completing paratroop training, I started training with A Company. We were working in an area close to the border, which today is known as Hevel Lakhish in the foothills southwest of Jerusalem. On one particular day soldiers were training as squad commanders, and it was Ze'ev Sverdlik's (today Sever) turn to take the lead. He was walking at the head of the squad when we suddenly saw two armed men sitting on a hill some 300 meters away, extremely close to the border. I am still not certain whether they were on our side of the border or the Jordanian side. In any case, we outflanked them, crept up close, opened fire, and charged their position, killing one of the Jordanians and making the other to drop his weapon and flee. We took the body and the two weapons back to our company encampment.

This incident set off a long series of inquiries with the UN armistice agreement inspectors, to whom the Jordanians submitted a formal complaint. Sharon arrived on the scene to verify what had taken place during the skirmish. After asking a few questions and being told of the circumstances of the engagement, he continued on his way. Later, I was required to accompany our liaison officers to a meeting of the Israeli— Jordanian Armistice Committee, and to take the UN observers to the location of the skirmish to convince them that it had actually taken place on the Israeli side of the border.

What happened afterwards was typical of the way Sharon worked. There had been no reprisal operations and no hostile encounters for weeks leading up to the skirmish. However, a hostile encounter had just taken place, and, sensing the potential for more, Sharon instructed our company and two other companies, including D company under the command of Motta Gur, to place ambushes all along the border with Jordan in the hope of sparking more skirmishes. That was how he did things — inciting contact with the enemy in ways that created pretexts for military action and ensured both the General Staff backing and political authorization needed for reprisal operations.

Shortly after the skirmish infiltrators who had come across the Jordanian border carried out an attack on Israeli territory. In response a reprisal was planned against the Surif police station, which was located on a ridge across from the region of Mavo Betar and Nes Harim, also southwest of Jerusalem, but closer to the capital and higher in the hills. I was selected to command the forward squad in the operation. We set out in a long line after nightfall, and my heart fluttered as we crossed the border. Not only was it my first time crossing the border, but I was leading the entire force, with the battalion commander's radio operator at my side. Soon after we crossed the border, the radio operator told me that we had been ordered "to move the wagon backwards," a somewhat silly code for retracing our steps back across the border. "Arik," I said to Sharon, who was walking just a few meters behind me, "we received an order over the radio to move the wagon backwards."

"You heard nothing," Sharon told me in a whisper.

We continued walking, and a few minutes later we received another transmission: "Move the wagon backwards — confirm execution." When we received the third transmission Sharon understood that we had no choice, and we began to retrace our steps toward the border. When we arrived back at base we learned that the Jordanians had somehow learned of the impending operation, either from an observation post or via intelligence, and had prepared a decidedly unpleasant reception for us. A few weeks later another operation was planned, this time against an Egyptian military command post in Gaza.

Since the end of the War of Independence, the Gaza Strip had been a constant point of origin of cross-border infiltration operations. The operations were carried out primarily by the population of Gaza (most of whom were refugees) at the explicit encouragement of Egyptian intelligence, which had an office in the Gaza Strip. A few months earlier, in August 1954, the IDF conquered and destroyed an Egyptian border post across from Kibbutz Kisufim in an attack known as Operation Kisufim. On February 28, 1955, we embarked upon a larger operation, which would subsequently be called "Operation Black Arrow." It was only later, when I had the opportunity to work alongside Sharon as his intelligence officer, that I learned how he went about convincing his superiors — the regional command and the General Staff — to authorize such operations.

THE GAZA OPERATION — OPERATION BLACK ARROW

We knew that something was about to happen because a few days earlier a jeep from the battalion's C Company detonated a mine while driving on the patrol road that ran along the border of the Gaza Strip. Sharon managed to convince Ben-Gurion and the General Staff of the logic of a broad-scale reprisal attack on the headquarters of the Egyptian military forces in the Strip, which was located north of Gaza city. Supapo, who had not been assigned a major role in the aborted attack on the Surif police station, was compensated with the highly coveted role of leading the attack on the Egyptian base.

According to the plan, five groups would take part in the operation: a platoon-sized force from A Company under the command of Supapo; a platoon-sized force from D Company under the command of Motta Gur; a force charged with blocking the road to the south of Gaza city under the command of Danny Matt, with a reconnaissance platoon consisting primarily of former soldiers of Unit 101; a small force charged with blocking the road to the north; and a small platoon-sized reserve force under the command of deputy company commander Moshe Yanuka.

Supapo chose three commanders for the three forces, each of which consisted of approximately 10 soldiers. One force was commanded by Hillel, my platoon commander, the second force was commanded by Tuvia Shapira and I was selected to command the third force. Sharon took part in the operation with a small staff that included deputy battalion commander Aharon Davidi. The overall force that took part in the operation was the size of a paratroop company, about 70 soldiers and officers.

We began by driving south in trucks along with a few parachute folders, women soldiers mainly from kibbutzim, in order to conceal the true aim of the trip. We sang songs and had a good time, and for a moment even forgot that we were on our way to battle. Supapo was in high spirits, for he had finally received a major command position in an operation of the battalion. Our company was charged with leading the force and, as in the Surif operation, Supapo chose me for the front squad.

After nightfall we were served the traditional pre-operation meal, consisting of inedible meat and potato stew that often caused diarrhea, which resulted in considerable problems during the operations themselves. Before such a major and intimidating operation, our appetites were not that great. Sharon said his final words to us before the operation, and we set out between the fields of the kibbutzim along the Gaza Strip until we reached the border, which was marked by a deep plow-made furrow. We climbed down into the furrow and out the other side, and our hearts skipped a beat as we crossed the border.

Our progress was slow, steady, and quiet. After advancing approximately two kilometers into the Strip in an area between Egyptian positions where it was the safest to walk, a voice called out in Arabic: "Min hada?" (Who's there?) We did not answer and kept on walking. Suddenly, a single shot broke the silence of the night, and then another one. The shots were not aimed at us and seemed to have been shot in the air. Without asking questions and without wasting a moment, I charged ahead with my force and entered the post. It turned out to be a small external post of one of the bases with a few Egyptian soldiers, and we cleared the trenches with bursts of gunfire as we ran. Suddenly, a dark figure appeared in the trench right in front of me. It was the first Egyptian I had ever encountered, and he was aiming a rifle directly at me. Before he could get off a shot, I shot him from close range and he collapsed in the trench. After searching all the trenches in the post, we concluded that some of the Egyptians had been killed and that the others had fled — most likely back to the primary base. However, no shots were fired from the primary base, and everything was soon quiet again.

After the firefight ended we were joined by Sharon, and I was there to witness his consultation with Supapo. The dilemma was not easy: our target was still a long way off and our presence had already been discovered as a result of the skirmish. Sharon decided to continue anyway, and his decision was supported by the two observers accompanying the force: Lieutenant Colonel David Elazar and Major Michael Kartin. Elazar, who would later serve as Chief of General Staff (CGS) during the Yom Kippur War, was then serving in the IDF's Training Department. In those days it was the custom to give General Staff officers the opportunity to take part in operations to generate lessons based on their own first-hand impressions.

We continued moving, with my force still leading and Supapo right behind me, until we reached the area surrounding the Egyptian command center, the target of the operation. Sharon positioned his staff at the corner of an orange orchard north of Gaza city just a few hundred meters north of the base.

Supapo began moving his men toward the target. Our plan was to attack the base from the west with two forces: my force from the left and Shapira's force from the right. The force led by Hillel, my platoon commander, was meant to serve as an offensive reserve, and his men carried bags of explosives to blow up the buildings in the camp after we conquered it. We now followed Supapo, passing the railroad tracks that ran north from Gaza and walking along them to the west. We kept moving, and at a certain point Supapo started to pull the line eastward. "There's the base!" Supapo whispered, pointing toward a road with fences just beyond it. We ran toward the fence, using our Bangalore Torpedoes (explosive charges in a long pipe) to blow open the gate, and then shot bursts of automatic weapons fire as we fanned into the base. At one point during the battle I felt a razor-sharp pinch in my right arm and knew I had been injured. When the gun-fire died down I asked one of the soldiers to bandage my hand. Then, without paying much attention to the pain, I moved on.

Suddenly we heard deputy battalion commander Davidi call out: "Supapo, it's not here!" Supapo understood that he had mistaken the base we were supposed to attack for a water pump installation. "Follow me," he called out after regaining his composure. We left the pump installation and walked quickly in single file along the road to the south. To our right were illuminated fences lined by Egyptian positions. Supapo walked quickly along the illuminated fence, but the entire line of his small force (machine-gunner Uri Spector and two bazooka operators) and my force were then exposed to the sight-line of the Egyptian soldiers in their positions. We were sitting ducks, and we suffered heavy casualties when the Egyptians began to pour down heavy fire upon us. Less than a minute later I heard Supapo cry out in pain and saw him collapse. I reached him in a sprint, and I saw that Uri the machine-gunner had also been hit and was lying injured on the ground next to him, with his stomach blown open. One of the bazooka operators was also down. Calls for a medic rang out from my force and as I bent down over Supapo and saw a gaping hole in his forehead. Seeing that he was dead I asked a medic to tend to the wounded lying in the trench. I climbed down into the trench and tried to engage the Egyptian positions that had attacked us and somehow extract ourselves from the enemy fire that was keeping us pinned down.

As if out of nowhere, Aharon Davidi suddenly appeared. He was standing by one of the eucalyptus trees right next to the road, and I stood up too, feeling uncomfortable sitting down when the deputy battalion commander was standing so close to me. "What's happening here?" he asked.

"Supapo's been killed and a lot of men are injured."

"And what are you doing," Davidi continued questioning me unhurriedly, as if he did not notice the heavy enemy fire pouring down around us.

"We're returning fire, trying to take out the Egyptian forces in their positions inside the base," I answered. Davidi pulled out a grenade from his belt and threw it toward the closest Egyptian position. I also pulled out a grenade and threw it toward one of the positions beyond the base's fence. And then, without him saying another word, a voice deep inside me implored me to start moving.

"So, what are you going to do?" Davidi asked, and I told him that my plan was to enter the base through its northern perimeter. The wounded were already bandaged and relatively well-protected in the trench by the road. I called out to all those in my force who were still in good shape to come with me. Four soldiers got up and followed me to the northern perimeter of the base. There, we found entangled barbed wire. We cut through with wire cutters and entered the base. I ran ahead, first to clean out the positions within the camp, then to take over the building, and finally to mop up the headquarters. When I reached the center of the camp, Micha Livni, a native of Kibbutz Ginnosar, was shot dead right next to me. I kept running, and my men behind me kept passing me grenades and magazines for my Uzi. Completely focused on the task of taking over the base, I ran ahead without thinking about the dangers. By the time I reached the headquarters building I only had two other soldiers with me, one of whom was Ze'ev Saverdlik.

The headquarters building had been abandoned and suddenly everything was quiet. The silence was eerie, almost deafening after all the gunfire, explosions, and screams of pain. I sent Saverdlik to Davidi to inform him that the entire base had been cleared and that we could now begin blowing up the buildings. I do not remember a great deal about the mad dash taking over the bunkers and the buildings. I can still smell the gunpowder and the explosives of the grenades we threw into each bunker and each building. It was the smell of war. I can still hear the groan of Micha Livni as he was hit with a burst of gunfire and fell to the ground beside me.

A feverish discussion among Sharon, Gur, and Davidi was now underway. The dilemma was whether to withdraw ourselves and all our casualties by truck and to use the vehicle to break through the Egyptian border crossing near Kibbutz Kisufim or to return to Israeli territory by foot, carrying our casualties ourselves. They decided to return by foot on a route that was shorter than the one we had used to reach the base, which passed between the large Egyptian positions. We fashioned improvised stretchers out of shirts and rifles to carry the eight dead and 12 wounded.

In addition to the two stretchers my force carried, I was also assigned the point position on the way back to the border.

Fully aware that all the Egyptian forts in the area were now on alert, we began a slow and exhausting march carrying the stretchers. We again made our way between Egyptian positions but now under fire. Fortunately, the Egyptians used tracer ammunition, so we were able to see from where the bursts came and take cover. When a burst ended, we would start walking again. Some of our men were wounded by the Egyptian fire on the way back as well. As we neared the border we found a deep riverbed to walk in, which provided protection from the Egyptian gunfire and enabled us to reach the border with all our stretchers.

I was now able to tend to the wounded and make sure they received medical attention. The battalion had been allocated one ambulance and a doctor, Dr. Shlomo Shibolet, who was waiting for us on the Israeli side of the border. After I made sure that all my men were accounted for and that all the wounded were being tended to, I walked over to the ambulance and told the doctor that I was also injured. "Where have you been this whole time?" he shouted at me. "Go straight to the hospital!"

I arrived at Tel Hashomer hospital early in the morning. Now that the fighting was over I was able to feel my badly injured hand, but it was extremely painful. They immediately transferred me to an operating room, and placed me in the capable hands of Professor Weisman, director of the Orthopedics Unit, who confidently and skillfully stitched me up. I was then transferred back to the ward.

In the late morning, Defense Minister and Prime Minister David Ben-Gurion arrived at Tel Hashomer hospital along with Sharon and Davidi to visit the soldiers who had been wounded in the operation. "Uzi, what are you doing here?" asked Sharon with surprise when they reached my bed.

"I'm wounded," I said, somewhat seriously and somewhat in jest.

"When were you injured?" asked Davidi.

"Back at the water pump," I told them.

Davidi looked shocked. "We had no idea," he said.

For all of us, the Gaza operation was an important test of how we functioned under fire, our dedication to the mission, our determination during combat, and our camaraderie of arms. I received a citation from CGS Moshe Dayan, which was converted to a Medal of Courage after the enactment of the IDF Decorations Law of 1970.

Second Lieutenant Eilam Uzi 245829
ACCOUNT OF THE ACT:

During a battle in Gaza on February 28, 1955, after breaching an enemy base into which his force fled after disengaging from the enemy, Second Lieutenant Uzi Trachtenberg (Eilam) led his force in storming an enemy base, in conjunction with the other forces, and completed his mission despite being injured. After conquering one part of the base, he was directed — at the head of his force and in conjunction with the other forces — against the second part of the base, which he stormed quickly and decisively, including a zone that had been assigned to a different sub-force. Despite his injury, he displayed initiative and exemplary leadership, including the task of preparing the conquered base for demolition. Second Lieutenant Uzi Trachtenberg remained in command of his squad during the retreat and completed the mission assigned to him in an exemplary manner.

For this act, he is awarded the Medal of Courage, April 1973

LIEUTENANT GENERAL DAVID ELAZAR,
CHIEF OF GENERAL STAFF

A few days later I was discharged from the hospital with my arm in a cast. I stopped by Training Base 12, a base near Tel Aviv where women did their basic training where my girlfriend Naomi was serving as an instructor. The base was closed to visitors in general and male visitors in particular, but I used my red beret, my rank of lieutenant, and my arm cast to persuade the guards to let me in.

I first met Naomi a few weeks earlier under musical circumstances. After I completed my paratroop training course and before I began training A Company, I received a few days of leave which I used to play a few concerts as a trumpet soloist with the kibbutz movement orchestra. I had suggested that I perform Joseph Haydn's Trumpet Concerto, and I still cannot understand what possessed the orchestra to take me up on my rather audacious offer. In any event, they did. The first concert was held in the dining hall of Kibbutz Usha. I stood at the front of the stage before the orchestra and surveyed the audience. At the back of the room I spotted a woman soldier with green eyes, and during the intermission at the end of the concerto I went straight over to her. I did not say anything, but I did notice that she was wearing squad commanders' training tags. A few days later, I learned from a young woman from Tel Yosef, who was also taking part in the course at Training Base 12, that there was in fact a young woman from Kibbutz Usha in her course, and that her name was Naomi Meir. I went to the end-of-the-course celebration, and, in the chronicles of the Eilam family, the rest is history.

With my arm in a cast I returned to my battalion, which was now in the final stages of the squad commanders' training course. I reported to Captain Danny Matt, who had in the meantime been appointed to replace Supapo as company commander. The parents of the trainees and instructors were invited to the final ceremony of the course, and my mother also came. During the review Matt surprised me by asking me to stand before the battalion and then read aloud the citation I had received. I had no idea that they were cooking up such an acknowledgment of my role in the operation, but I realized that it must have been connected to Sharon and Davidi's look of surprise when they found me wounded in Tel Hashomer hospital.

FROM SQUAD COMMANDER TO COMPANY COMMANDER — THE BIG LEAP

When I returned from leave Aharon Davidi called me in for a meeting. "We're building a company out of the remaining soldiers of A Company and the remaining reconnaissance platoon of Unit 101," he told me "You'll be in command." I was speechless. Although my new assignment clearly reflected their faith in me, I was nonetheless consumed by worry in light of the importance of the position. When

I told deputy battalion commander Davidi what was bothering me, he told me in his quiet, voice — the same voice I heard during the Gaza operation — "Don't worry, I'll guide you."

The company had two platoons which were commanded by Shapira, who had until that point been a squad commander in A Company, and Oved Ladizinski, a former Palmah member who resumed his military service; both were older and more senior. For me it was the beginning of a challenging and difficult period, but Davidi was always there to advise me. With his help and encouragement I gained the confidence necessary to acquire the standing of a company commander with authority.

A Company of the 890th Battalion was the forerunner of Sayeret Tzanhanim, the paratroop reconnaissance unit that also specializes in special-forces operations. Its natural commander was Meir Har-Zion, but at the time he was working as a sheep herder on his kibbutz, Ein Harod. We shall return to Har-Zion later.

Between Operation Black Arrow and the Khan Yunis Operation, which took place in February and August 1955 respectively, we carried out cross-border reconnaissance patrols with select teams from the company. We also carried out a major battalion-wide training program — the first of its kind — in the Negev desert near the town of Yeruham. Suddenly, I found myself serving as a company commander alongside such well-known leaders as Motta Gur (D-Company commander), Rafael Eitan (E-Company commander), and Danny Matt (B-Company commander).

The 890th Battalion continued to grow stronger during the years that Davidi and Sharon were in command, as its ranks expanded with new companies of new inductees. Training on the company level was almost completely in the hands of the extremely independent company commanders. The battalion command staff spent much of its time planning reprisal operations and cross-border incursions and patrols. The almost automatic response to attacks from across the border — from the Gaza Strip, Jordan, and Syria — was to declare an alert for an operation. The process of convincing the regional command OCs and, with their help, the General Staff and the country's political leadership often lasted a few days. Sharon wasted no opportunities to carry out reprisal operations, and for this reason he preferred the battalion's companies to be on stand-by at the base so that he would never need to go through the trouble of calling them back early from remote training areas. We knew what the battalion command had recommended and after getting preliminary orders, spent entire days just waiting around on the base for the plans to be approved. Authorizations for such operations were issued sparingly.

MEIR HAR-ZION RETURNS TO THE SAYERET

In late 1955, Meir Har-Zion returned to the battalion after a few months of suspension. In 1954, Meir's sister Shoshana had taken a hike in Jordanian territory through the Judean desert from Jerusalem to Ein Gedi with her boyfriend Oded Wagmeister. When the two entered Jordanian territory they were captured by Bedouin and murdered. Meir, along with four recently discharged friends from Unit 101, returned to the area where the abduction had taken place, murdered four Bedouin, and sent back the fifth to convey the message that vengeance had been taken. The murders were quickly discovered and the Jordanians filed a complaint with the UN. Ben-Gurion told Sharon that the incident was something that needed to be dealt with, and when the five returned they were arrested by the police. Ben-Gurion ordered that Har-Zion be suspended and sent back to his kibbutz for a few months.

When his suspension ended Har-Zion returned to the battalion to assume command of A Company, the Sayeret, a position which until that point I had held in his stead. I was relieved when Har-Zion returned to assume command. He had been my classmate in the Tel Yosef—Ein Harod joint high school, and I knew that neither I nor anyone else could compete with his navigating skills or his combat experience. In the summer of 1951, while on a hike in northern Israel, Har-Zion and his sister Shoshana crossed the border and were taken prisoner by the Syrian army. Although he never told me about his difficult experience as a prisoner in Syria, I had no doubt that it had a profound influence on him.

Meir and I slipped easily into the non-routine routine of the reconnaissance company: Meir as commander and I as his deputy. We continued to work with our soldiers on navigation and combat training in teams, including reconnaissance work across the border. Initially as part of the 890th Battalion and subsequently as part of the paratroop brigade, the Sayeret set high standards for navigation skills and the precise execution of small-team cross-border operations.

INJURY AND THE DIFFICULT ROAD TO RECOVERY

During night-time orienteering training in the Galilee I passed by a settlement populated by Jewish immigrants from North Africa. I said hello to the armed guards at the gate, and they responded in kind. However, after I walked another twenty or thirty meters they apparently changed their minds and concluded that I was actually an infiltrator. They began shooting, and the bullets struck me in my arm and my leg. I fell to the ground and lay there bleeding until the security officer of the settlement arrived. The security officer was a young native-born Israeli. He understood that the guards had erred and called an ambulance. I was taken to Military Hospital 10 in Haifa, where an orthopedist from Rambam Hospital stitched up my wounded arm and leg quickly, but, unfortunately, not very professionally.

I returned to active duty in my battalion before I was fully healed and again got injured, this time during a night-time parachute drop. My leg had still not healed, and the impact of the landing and the blow I received to my leg caused me to lose consciousness. A few months later we embarked upon a five-day trek through the Judean Desert toward Ein Gedi carrying the very heavy "elephant packs" on our backs. After two days of walking, my leg gave out.

When I returned from the exercise, battalion commander Sharon took me to task. "I won't let you put your health in jeopardy," he said. "You can't go on like this. You have to recover, and until you do you will be my intelligence officer." I told Sharon that I had not yet completed intelligence officers' training, but he dismissed my concern: "No, no, no," he said, "You'll learn with me." I never imagined the level of schooling that awaited me, not just in intelligence, in which Sharon was a master, but in tactics and the meticulous and creative planning of military operations.

For almost a year and a quarter I attended what I like to call the "Arik Sharon school of intelligence and operations" where every day had its new lesson. At first I was the intelligence officer of the 890th Battalion, and when the framework of the paratroop brigade was established, I became the brigade intelligence officer.

The brigade staff worked as a small, tightly knit, harmonious, well-focused, and extremely active unit that produced an abundance of plans and commanded a large number of reprisal operations, all from the school of Arik Sharon. Every once in a while I found myself lagging behind Sharon in the acquisition of new intelligence information. He had the benefit of his experience in intelligence, having served in this capacity in the Southern Command, and also knew how to obtain new information directly from sources in the upper echelons of the General Staff's Intelligence Branch.

SHARON EYES MY TRUMPET

Being Arik Sharon's intelligence officer in the Paratroop Brigade required planning at a dizzying pace. I needed to read his thoughts and prepare intelligence information for operations that I believed he was hatching. It also gave me a clear appreciation of some of Sharon's less positive qualities. As the commander of the 890th Battalion, Sharon was interested in neither training nor what was happening in his companies. His primary focus was to obtain more and more authorizations for carrying out reprisal operations. Davidi was the one who weighed in on the training programs and kept abreast of the mood within the battalion. I also began to realize that Sharon invested great effort in gathering information about other senior officers. Later, I understood that this stock of personal information played an important role in the kind of manipulation in which he became a virtuoso. After a year and a quarter of serving alongside Sharon as his intelligence officer I knew exactly how his mind worked.

Regardless of whether they were ultimately executed or cancelled at the last moment, the long list of operations that Sharon planned constitutes an incomparable source of material for the study of military tactics. Each of Sharon's plans was a work of craftsmanship, based on his understanding of the field, his precise knowledge of the enemy's forces, and a wise assessment of the strengths and weaknesses of their defenses. But in addition to the typical military situation assessment regarding the field, the enemy forces — and our forces — every Sharon-made plan had a twist of some kind that made it special. In some cases it was the unique way the forces were organized; in others it was an unexpected route to the target or the way we went about sealing off the area of operations from the possible intervention of external enemy forces. Sharon was obsessive when it came to integrating variety and innovation into planning his operations, and this enabled him to continue surprising the enemy with new tactics every time.

One day during the planning of an operation to conquer Fort 108 in the Gaza Strip, Sharon's creative spirit latched on to my silver trumpet. During the long days and nights of waiting before operations, when we would assemble in the officers and sergeants' canteen and sing Israeli folksongs, I would accompany the men with my trumpet. "Why don't you take your trumpet with you and take up a position with a team behind the fort," Sharon suggested. "The moment you let out a blast, we'll attack." This time I was taken aback thinking that Sharon had reverted to some kind of Napoleonic War fantasy. I told Sharon that I preferred my Uzi as a weapon and that, in any event, my trumpet belonged to the kibbutz and could not be placed in such a high-risk situation. When he heard my response, he gave up on the idea.

THE HUSAN OPERATION

In September 1956 I decided that I had gotten all I could get out of serving as intelligence officer of the Paratroop Brigade. Sharon honored my request to be discharged, and Gideon Mahanaymi, who had been transferred to us from the Givati Brigade, was named as my replacement.

I was now able to report for another complex operation on my arm. But my knowledge of Sharon's modus operandi was always at the back of my mind. After leaving hospital I was again assigned to Convalescent Home 3 on the slopes of Mt. Carmel where I found myself with Micha Kapusta from the paratroop reconnaissance unit. We somehow got wind of the plan to attack the Jordanian fort at Husan (September 25–26, 1956). We couldn't phone anybody and the planning and timing of operations were kept completely secret. But I knew Sharon, and we knew just when to take unofficial leave of absence from the convalescent home and reach the staging area. I came to Sharon with my entire arm in a cast, and it was clear to both of us that I would not be able to join the fighting force. But Sharon came up with a solution: "Go to Tel Nof and fly a Piper above the area of the operation," he said. "After all, you know the area and the plan well. Look out for any reinforcements that the Jordanians try to bring into the area, particularly from the direction of Hebron, and report in to us."

As I flew elliptic routes from Hebron to Bethlehem, the operation began. Soon enough, I was able to hear the far off sounds of gunfire and the explosion of grenades coming from the battle being fought at the Jordanian fort. A convoy of vehicles left Hebron with their headlights on, but quickly turned them off. I immediately warned Sharon, who asked me if I could direct the artillery fire of the relatively meager 25 pound cannon at our disposal at the convoy. I established communication with the artillery battalion and, based on an estimate of the rate of travel of the reinforcements, who were now driving without headlights, I provided the gunners with waypoints along the route of the convoy where they could aim their salvos. The next day, we learned that the artillery fire had been accurate and that the convoy had been brought to a halt by direct hits. Years later, this episode became a formative legend of the Artillery Corps.

THE QALQILIYA ACTION — OPERATION SHOMRON

I returned to Convalescent Home 3 to continue my medical treatment, which lasted much longer than I had patience for. Two weeks after the Husan operation, Israel suffered another attack that came out of Jordanian territory — the murder of workers at the town of Even Yehuda. It was clear that Israel would show no restraint after such an act, and that Sharon was already busy persuading the General Staff and the political leadership to authorize the brigade to carry out a reprisal operation. I again slipped out of the convalescent home without asking anyone's permission, put on my paratroop dress uniform, and hitchhiked to Kfar Saba. My instincts and experience after more than a year as Sharon's intelligence officer again brought me directly to the location where the forces were assembling. Again, I reported to Sharon, my entire left arm still in a cast. Sharon remembered my role in the Husan operation and without delay told me to go to Tel Nof, and to fly a Piper above the area of the operation, the police station in the West Bank town of Qalqiliya just a few kilometers east of Kfar Saba in Israel's coastal plain.

This time Motta Gur, with the 88th Battalion, was assigned the coveted mission of attacking the operation's main target — the police station. Eitan's 890th Battalion was designated as a reserve force, and his flushed, wrinkled face revealed his displeasure with this supporting role. The large reserve and rescue forces designated for the action were a sure indication that the operation would be large and difficult. We drove to Tel Nof and I even managed to eat dinner in the pilots' dining hall, a meal that I regretted the entire night I spent flying above the area of the operation. We entered the area the moment the shelling of the police station began, and it took only a few minutes before I saw the lights of a Jordanian reserve force en route from the direction of Nablus. I reported the information to Sharon, and after the vehicles turned off their headlights I continued to provide him with updated estimates of their location.

I could see from the plane that the battle being fought in and around the police station was a difficult one. My radio was linked into the brigade radio network, and I could hear all the reports and commands as they were transmitted. Less than an hour after the operation began I observed the Sayeret reconnaissance unit fire on the first vehicles of the Jordanian reinforcements. The Jordanian army had been established and trained by the British and was well prepared to contend with such situations. Infantry forces quickly leapt from the vehicles and began a flanking maneuver aimed at attacking the Sayeret. There was no direct channel of communication between the Sayeret and brigade command, and I functioned as a relay station for communications between the two.

After the battle I went straight to brigade headquarters and walked into Sharon's office. He was tired and contemplative after a difficult night with considerable casualties. He was concerned about the Sayeret after the tough battle in which their commanders had been wounded. "Go to the base at Sataf," he told me, "and see how we can help them." When I arrived at the Sayeret base at Sataf near Jerusalem I found a familiar scene: a unit with many wounded members after a difficult battle. The concept of combat trauma only started to be widely recognized many years later, especially after the Yom Kippur

War. I spoke with people and listened to them recount the stages of the battle as they experienced them. And in the course of that long day, I watched them become themselves again.

THE BIG LEAP WITH THE 88TH BATTALION'S B-COMPANY DURING OPERATION KADESH

I returned to brigade headquarters toward evening. Officially, I was on my way to being discharged, waiting for the final operation on my arm and the recovery period at Convalescent Home 3. Still, with the brigade licking its wounds after the difficult battle I found myself unable to just get up and leave. My visit to the Sayeret accentuated these feelings. "Arik, I'm not going to be discharged," I said when I walked back into Sharon's office after returning from the visit. "Do you have a position for me?"

Sharon lifted his head and looked at me with tired eyes. "You're staying?" he asked, just to be certain. "Arik," I said, "I can't be discharged now, and I'm not going back for any medical treatment."

Sharon did not hesitate. "A company commander from Motta's battalion was just killed," he told me, although I already knew. "Go to Motta. He'll turn the company over to you." It was only a short distance from Tel Nof to the Bilu military base, where the 88th battalion was located, and fifteen minutes later I was already meeting with Gur, who had been told that I would be assuming command of B Company. My arm was still in a cast from my shoulder to my palm, but neither Gur nor Sharon had any doubt about my abilities at this point. It was my decision, and as far as they were concerned I was fit for any mission. In the evening, I met with the company's officers, including my deputy Pinhas (Alush) Noy, who was awarded the Medal of Courage for his role in the battle at the Qalqiliya police station. The next day we began a training program near Nes Harim, and I quickly got to know the soldiers and officers. It was there that I first met Company Sergeant Major Zvi Vander, who was a never-ending source of energy and good spirits. Vander would remain with me for many years, during my reserve duty with the 98th Battalion and as master sergeant in the 71st Battalion, the first battalion under my command.

After one week of training at Nes Harim I felt well integrated into the company. There were incessant rumors about a war that was about to break out, and I decided to clarify the issue with the most reliable source possible — the brigade intelligence officer. Mahanaymi let me in on the carefully guarded secret of the French airlift that was then underway in the dead of night, carrying weapons such as non-recoil cannons, and the British and French pledge to provide us with air cover in the event of war in the Sinai Peninsula. I returned to the company tent encampment at Nes Harim feeling tense and anxious. All I told my officers was that the rumors regarding a major operation were well based and that we would undoubtedly receive orders soon. All I needed to do now was to get rid of the cast that was limiting my arm movement. I asked the company medic for my medical file and then made off with a pair of scissors while he was distracted. Within a few minutes, I cut off the cast and liberated my arm. The zipper-like stitches that ran the length of the scar on my arm remained in place and were only dealt with after the war, when I asked the battalion doctor to remove them.

For us, the war started with a long drive and a night encampment at Hatzeva in the Arava near the road to Eilat, a route that was meant to deceive the Egyptians into thinking that Jordan was the target of our operation. We left Hatzeva in a long convoy of trucks via the Faran (Jirafi) riverbed toward the Egyptian Kuntila police station near Eilat. On the way we had to get out and push because most of the trucks did not have front-wheel drive. But by the time we crossed the flat hard-surfaced desert towards the Egyptian police station at Kuntila it was as if we were driving on an asphalt road. We didn't have to wait long before the front force of the brigade reported that it had conquered the police station and that we could continue advancing along the road. On the way to the Mitla Pass in central western Sinai were the fortifications at Bir A-Temed, which our battalion was supposed to take, and the Egyptian army base at Nakhel in the center of the peninsular. When dawn started to break, we were driving quickly along the road between the fortifications of A-Temed.

I ordered my men to get out of the vehicles, and we spread out to the right and left of the road, entered the trenches of the Egyptian forts, and took them over. Immediately following our conquest of the fort, we were attacked by Egyptian MiG fighter planes, which shot rockets and bursts of automatic gunfire at us. We spent all afternoon feverishly digging pits. Shortly after the air attack came to an end, my men spotted three Egyptian soldiers approaching the fort and brought them to me. I told one of my officers to take the prisoners to one of the trenches and to kill them. "Uzi," said Benny Gefen, an older reservist who was in command of the communications squad. "I can't believe my ears! Did you just issue an order to have them executed?" I immediately understood the significance of what I had said, and I stopped the officer, instructing him to drive the prisoners to the paratroop force in the rear. The memory of this near mistake remained with me during all the wars in which I took part, and I owe my integrity as a soldier to Benny Gefen.

My company did not participate in the bloody battle of Mitla, and when the fighting at the Pass ended we were ordered to travel northward to prepare for an air-drop into the southern Sinai Peninsula. We sat in the planes waiting to take off, but we were stopped at the last moment. Avraham Yoffee, commander of the 9th Brigade, had reported via radio that he had conquered Sharm el Sheikh, and the General Staff now regarded the drop there as unnecessary.

After the war ended the debriefing within the brigade took three days and involved all officers above the level of company commander. There were accounts of the stages of fighting, of the parachute drop of the 890th Battalion near the Colonel Parker pillar, and of the brigade's advance into the Peninsula and the conquest of the Kuntila police station, the at-Tamad forts, and the Egyptian army base at Nakhel. The most controversial issue, which aroused significant debate and criticism, was the battle of Mitla. Sharon ordered the brigade to enter the area without paying sufficient attention to the Egyptian forces that were dug in there, and this resulted in a fierce battle in which dozens of paratroopers were killed. Only later did I learn that senior officers including Eitan, Rur, Davidi, and deputy brigade commander Yitzhak Hofi had had an extremely tense meeting with Sharon regarding his role in the battle at Mitla. The commanders who fought and suffered heavy losses at Mitla were unable to forgive him for not being involved in the difficult part of the fighting, after Hofi's and Gur's forces came under heavy enemy fire. The accusation that Sharon was not on site when the brigade was bleeding ultimately proved to be much more important than his urge to enter the Pass under the guise of an exploratory patrol. At the end of the Sinai War Sharon left his position as brigade commander and was assigned a position with the General Staff's Training Department that did not involve commanding combat forces.

A convoy of trucks transported our battalion along the south beaches of the Sinai Peninsula, dropping off every company at its designated location. One event that took place during this journey, related to the spoils of war, remains forever engraved in my memory. The convoy stopped in the town of Abu Rudeis, which had been abandoned both by its local inhabitants and its foreign citizens, most of whom were expert consultants for the manganese mining and oil drilling operations in the region. When we stopped outside the town for lunch, I immediately noticed that many soldiers skipped the meal and instead looted the villas of the foreign experts. I summoned my company runner to stand with me at the junction, and one by one, we stopped all the looters — soldiers and officers alike — who were on their way back, carrying radios, fans, and other looted items. No one escaped the booty checkpoint we set up, and a mountainous pile of goods soon formed. Using a jerry-can full of kerosene, we lit the pile on fire.

We reached the area which we were supposed to secure. It was vast — stretching from Dahab in the north, which after the Six Day War emerged as a great scuba diving and recreation site, to A-Tor, where Gur and two companies of our battalions had recently been dropped by parachute. During a thorough patrol of the area which lasted almost two weeks, a Bedouin shepherd helped us locate the temple of the Egyptian goddess Hathor on the peak of a rocky mountain known by the Bedouin as Serabit al-Khadim. The temple was accessible by only one narrow path. From below, the mountain looked like all the other mountains in the area, but when we reached the summit we were treated to a breathtaking sight: a row of giant tablets made of reddish Nubian sandstone bearing hieroglyphic script; a large altar that had been preserved in its entirety; and the foundations of pillars indicating the past existence of a large structure which the Egyptians had used to worship the goddess Hathor. A few weeks later, when we returned to patrol the area, we saw two of these hieroglyphic pillars being transported northward by Air Force helicopter to an unknown destination. Many years later, during a visit with a high-level visitor at the home of Defense Minister Moshe Dayan, who was serving as CGS during the 1956 Sinai Campaign, I recognized the pillars of the temple of the goddess Hathor standing among the looted antiquities that Dayan collected in his home. Only then did I understand where the helicopter had been headed.

Our next assignment was to serve along the armistice line separating the two halves of divided Jerusalem, and we spent a wintry and at times snowy two months manning positions along the winding border that cut through the city. It was during this stint along Jerusalem's city border that I reached the conclusion that I had given all I could to the 88th Battalion. Now, in the relative quiet that pervaded Israel after the Sinai War, I could allow myself to return to civilian life and to complete my engineering degree at the Technion.

The stormy but unique period during which I took part in Israel's reprisal operations, which culminated with Operation Kadesh, had a lasting impression on the IDF. Looking back in retrospect, we can perhaps better assess not only the positive aspects of this activity, but its darker side as well.

Years later, when he was prime minister, Arik Sharon said that:

> *History must assess the reprisal operations not in light of their military achievements alone, but also in light of what we have succeeded in building here over the past 50 years. During the reprisal operations, our trustworthy, professional hand grasped the sword, securing moral values with great cunning, in order to enable our other hand to absorb Jewish immigration; build industry, agriculture, and institutions of education and science; and tirelessly seek the path to peace. It was only because we were then able to find suitable solutions for our security problems that we were later able to achieve periods of relative calm, which allowed us to reach the present and look toward to the future with hopes of a thriving democratic Jewish state living in security and peace. The road was not an easy one, and I know that more challenges lay ahead. But when I look back on the glorious Zionist undertaking we have created here — that is the true payoff for the reprisal operations of those days.*

I agree with Sharon that we were young men imbued with exceptional conviction and courage. We also possessed a kind of naïveté that no longer exists in Israel. Still, I have serious doubts that the reprisal operations provided Israel with the deterrence and security Sharon claimed they did. Historical data from the period of the reprisal operations suggest that they were not overly effective in curbing infiltration and attacks. I also disagree with Moshe Dayan's assertion, which Sharon also quoted, that "we do not initiate battles in peacetime." In many cases we actually provoked the enemy on the other side of the border and incited war under the orders of Sharon himself. A truthful analysis of 'who started it' throughout the history of the IDF reprisal attacks reveals that we were not always as pure as snow.

At the same time, the contribution of the reprisal operations of the 1950s, in which Israeli forces dared to attack military bases beyond its borders, must be considered in broad historical perspective as a torch leading the Israeli military. Without this contribution the low morale that pervaded the IDF during the first few years following the War of Independence might have continued. The reprisal operations of the 1950s maintained and further developed the principle of 'venturing outside the fence' first initiated by Charles Orde Wingate and the Haganah-based Special Night Squads in the 1930s, and were the stimulus that helped the IDF as a whole embrace a new concept based on offensive initiative.

4

A Civilian Break

A DISABLED IDF VETERAN

I returned to the kibbutz after being discharged. My left arm, still half paralyzed despite the best efforts of the orthopedists, still needed one more operation. On arrival at Tel Hashomer hospital to set a date for the operation it quickly became apparent that I was neither a soldier nor yet a disabled IDF veteran. This meant that I had no choice but to be examined by a special panel to receive the status of a disabled IDF veteran with the rights that went along with it.

The summer began, but being a semi-invalid meant that I was unfit for physical work and so I was assigned the job of kibbutz night watchman. My time as night watchman was relaxing and enjoyable, and gave me ample quality time to quietly contemplate my future. As the summer drew to a close, Rivka Weinstein, who was known as 'the mother of the Nahal (the Hebrew acronym for 'fighting pioneer youth') and the Gadna', asked me to help organize the convention of our kibbutz movement — the Union of Kvutzot and Kibbutzim — which was scheduled to take place at Kibbutz Tel Yosef during the Sukkot holiday. Her request could not be refused.

The political and movement oriented aspects of the event was the responsibility of Weinstein and Zvi Brenner, a short, jumpy and energetic man from Kibbutz Afikim. Brenner was not hindered by his visible limp, the remains of an injury from a pre-state operation of the Palmach. He was one of the few Palmach members who had a personal relationship with Ben-Gurion, partly because at heart he was a true member of Ben-Gurion's Mapai party. The meticulous preparation and ability to cope quickly with the problems that arose during the event made it a highly-praised organizational success. But this would have no bearing on the kibbutz's traditional position towards academic studies, and I decided to resume my studies at the Technion without seeking kibbutz authorization.

My subject was initially electronic engineering, but after three years of soldiering, mechanical engineering seemed to me to be more practical. Before the beginning of the academic year I told the kibbutz secretary about my decision to continue studying at the Technion. Not asking for any assistance, financial or otherwise, my status became one of a kibbutz member on extended leave. As a disabled IDF veteran I was eligible to receive a tuition scholarship, as well as a small loan to cover living expenses (which would be paid back when I began working as an engineer). Tutoring noncommissioned naval officers in preparation for their matriculation exams in mathematics, physics and chemistry provided me with a small income as did working in a chapter of the scouts with the oldest age group: the eleventh and twelfth graders.

The high academic level of the students of the IDF Academic Reserves who began studying at the Technion immediately after high school was impressive and I was jealous of the ease with which they learned. My studying relied more on logic and experience than on memory.

I began to undertake more public activities, at first as the chair of the committee of my program's students and later, during my third year, as the elected chair of the Technion's Student Union. During the academic year my weekends were divided between visiting my mother at Tel Yosef and seeing my girlfriend Naomi, who was now studying medicine in Jerusalem.

THE ESTABLISHMENT OF SAYERET MATKAL

One day during my second year at the Technion, Arik Sharon asked me to go to the General Staff base at the Kiriya campus in Tel Aviv for a meeting. By that time Sharon was serving as a department director within the Training Department, an administrative position to which he had been exiled after the Sinai war. This stormy and creative man was mired in controversy all his life, controversy that from time to time brought him low when he was overcome by his adversaries. His time in the Training Department was one of these low points, but he never stopped being active and certainly never stopped thinking creatively. In Colonel Sharon's office was none other than Meir Har-Zion, who in the meantime had established a cattle farm in the Lower Galilee which he named after his sister, Shoshana. He had also been summoned to the meeting.

Sharon got straight to the point: the General Staff had decided to set up a special elite unit under its direct supervision to carry out special missions in accordance with its needs. We spent two days thinking about the principles and the concept on which the unit should be based. Har-Zion dealt with the missions concept and I dealt with the organizational structure of the new unit. Sharon was grateful for our recommendations and exempted us from any further involvement in the undertaking. Avraham Arnan, who actually established Sayeret Matkal, consulted with Har-Zion extensively during the first few years of building the unit.

During my third year at the Technion, amongst other things, I chaired the Student Union, directing a major student strike against the new Technion bylaws, giving press conferences and radio interviews and conducting negotiations with the Technion administration. The weakness of Technion President Yaakov Dori, a legendary figure in the IDF who had served as CGS during the War of Independence, was surprising. Chairing the Student Union taught me some important lessons, including insight into the weaknesses of managers when facing a well-organized campaign. The strike ended a few months later in a compromise that could have also been reached without the strike.

Despite my already intensive extra-curricular activity, there was also time to take a weekly French class at the Technion. Years later, living in Paris during a year-long sabbatical at the Foundation for Strategic Research (FRS) (a French think-tank engaged in the research of strategic and technological issues, and subsequently as the head of the defense ministry delegation in Paris), the basics of the language acquired from my teacher Enoch at the Technion came flooding back to me. Every time my French surprised me, a voice inside said: 'Thank you, Enoch.'

MARRIAGE AND LEAVING THE KIBBUTZ

Naomi and I decided to get married during the summer at the end of my third year at the Technion and I met with kibbutz secretary Meir Shachar, who had been involved in all my struggles to study at the Technion, to tell him that I was leaving the kibbutz. It felt as though I was standing on the threshold of a new yet familiar world, with complete independence and without any fear, knowing that I could rely only on myself. I recognized firmly that from now on I had to trust my abilities.

It seemed unreasonable to keep the money saved from my regular monthly salary during my service in the paratroops because it had been earned while I was still a kibbutz member and felt as though it didn't belong to me, so I transferred it all to the kibbutz (in those days kibbutz members who left their kibbutzim were not paid compensation). The only things I took with me were an iron bed, a cotton blanket, used since I had lived in the kibbutz children's house, and three pieces of furniture.

Naomi and I moved to Kibbutz Usha, where her parents were members. We were given a small room in a cottage at the edge of the kibbutz. During the summer vacation we worked in the Haifa oil refineries. We took a two-day vacation to get married in a small family ceremony in Tel Aviv. Although our honeymoon was put off indefinitely, we would later be fortunate enough to take many trips together, each of which would feel like a honeymoon.

One day, Amos Berkowitz, the outgoing chair of the Technion Student Union, dragged me to a meeting with members of the young guard of the Mapai party, including Moshe Dayan, Gad Yaakobi and other figures who in 1959 were still quite young. I listened attentively to their enthusiastic and convincing arguments and they gave the impression that they truly intended to create an alternative to the old-guard Mapai party regime. However, politics held no interest for me at the time: I just wanted to begin my career as an engineer and considered going into politics at a later time.

However, I continued as the Student Union Committee member responsible for foreign relations. This position brought me to the Far East for the first time, and provided me with knowledge and insight that increased over the years, thanks to my contacts with friends and colleagues from Asian countries and the diverse defense work that became my career. My friend Reuven Merhav, who was also the secretary of the Israeli National Student Union, told me that a five-week seminar for Asian student leaders was scheduled to be held in Kuala Lumpur, the capital of Malaya (today Malaysia). The national students union were allowed to send two representatives to the seminar, and it had been decided that one should come from the Technion. The idea of spending five weeks in Malaya and Kuala Lumpur, which sounded so exotic and far away, enthralled me and although such a long absence so late in the academic year was a great risk, it was too good an opportunity to miss.

The seminar was held on the campus of the University of Kuala Lumpur and was attended by students from Sri Lanka, India, Indonesia, Singapore, Malaya, Japan, Vietnam and Israel. I joined the editorial board of the seminar newspaper that was published on a weekly basis and my English continued to improve during the program.

The seminar gave me a new appreciation and understanding of people from Asian countries and their cultures. It also taught me a great deal about the politics and the smaller social groupings within the minority and majority populations of those Asian countries. At that time, Malayan concern was growing that a merger with Singapore, with its two million Chinese inhabitants, would result in a Chinese majority and the ruling regime, which until that point had been Muslim, being overturned. I admired the complex sophistication of the students from India and the straightforwardness and courage of the students from Sri Lanka, in addition to their ability to eat food that was so spicy that the smell alone was enough to make most people's eyes water. I also learned to recognize the gentleness of the Vietnamese and the scholarliness and precision of the students from Singapore.

The experience was deeply enriching and I submitted a complete report of the seminar to the Foreign Ministry on my return.

PROFESSOR KAHAN

The class on industrial engineering and management, titled Production Engineering, was taught by Professor Yoel Kahan, an intelligent and experienced engineer who had worked for the Dutch railroads prior to World War II. During the war Kahan hid in Holland and somehow managed to make it through in one piece. During those difficult years he relied primarily on his intelligence and his sense of humor, which his students thoroughly enjoyed. During the last lecture of the course he shared this with us: "You are about to enter a world of young engineers. You have one year — two at the most — to ask all the stupid questions you'll never dare to ask later. Don't miss the opportunity."

Professor Kahan had a small industrial engineering consulting firm named Kheshet. The company offered consulting services in a variety of areas, including industrial-organizational consulting and consulting for non-industrial entities such as the Municipality of Tel Aviv. My friend Zivan Zimhoni, who had already been working for Kahan for three years, recommended that I should be hired as one of the firm's seven engineers.

The firm acquired a new client, a Jerusalem factory called Friedman and Sons, and working with them enabled me to join Naomi in Jerusalem for her last two years of medical school. It was prudent for me to pursue a supplementary engineering degree that required a project in a practical field and the subject of my project was the distribution of home refrigerators, one of Friedman's three main products. Professor Kahan agreed to be my supervisor.

My work at Kheshet set me on a path that took me further than I could ever have imagined. Dr. Teddy Weinshel was an engineer and worked with Kahan in the early days to establish the firm. Weinshel had studied for his PhD in business administration at Harvard University and, when he returned to Israel, he accepted a position at the Faculty of Business Administration at the Hebrew University in Jerusalem. He was looking for an assistant and Kheshet provided the link between us. Weinshel was teaching the foundations of production management based on case studies and, as his assistant, I was responsible for the discussion section with the students, a curious, inquisitive and talented group of young men and women.

At the beginning of the academic year Dr. Weinshel disappeared. Professor Dan Haft, chair of the Department of Business Administration, explained that at the last moment Weinshel and the department failed to reach an agreement on the terms of his employment and he would not be coming back to teach. I was asked to take the course's lectures as well as its discussion sections. It was a quantum leap, somewhat reminiscent of my jump from squad commander to company commander in the 890th Battalion. This marked the beginning of two years as a university lecturer, in addition to my job at the consulting firm. I also began studying for my MSc (Masters of Science) in operations research at the Technion. The academic work for my MSc was consolidated into one and a half days of classes on Thursdays and Fridays. I approached Professor Kahan and asked whether I could join the program, and if so how. Once again, Kahan came up trumps. "Go and join the program," he said. "As for the time — take half from the vacation days you have coming to you, and the firm will provide the rest."

During my third year teaching at the university in Jerusalem, when we were expecting the birth of our daughter, the young Eilam family moved to Haifa, where Naomi was to begin her internship at Rambam hospital and I was to begin studying for my Masters degree. After another period of reserve duty as a deputy battalion commander, I rushed to the hospital in Haifa to see Naomi and baby Osnat. Soon after the birth Naomi went back to work at Rambam to complete her internship, and I divided my time between my clients at Kheshet, who were located all over the country, teaching business administration in Jerusalem and studying for my Masters degree at the Technion.

Professor Haft told me that Professor Ezra Solomon from Stanford University was visiting Israel, and that he wanted us to have lunch with him. We met in one of Jerusalem's restaurants, which in those days were quite simple. Professor Solomon was a short man with glasses, dark skin and a sharp eye. Our conversation over lunch was pleasant and covered a wide variety of subjects. Two weeks later, to my surprise, Haft called me with some exciting news: "You were accepted to Stanford University's special training program for business administration instructors." The international program, attended by lecturers from India to Brazil, was supported by the US government, which provided complete funding and generous tuition scholarships that also covered the travel costs of participants' families to California. By the time we would have to leave Naomi would have already completed her internship and received her medical degree and we decided it would be foolish to pass up such a challenging, promising and generous offer. I told Professor Haft that my answer was yes and then spoke with my Masters advisor at the Technion, Dr. Adi Ben-Israel, who had guided me through a meticulous exploration of the theory of linear programming. Every month I had anxiously scoured the professional literature to make sure that nobody had published anything on my research subject. By the end of the year my work was submitted and defended before a group of professors, and even earned a high grade.

America in the 1960s was heaven on earth. Our time in California was an important period for the family and a productive time of study for both me and Naomi, who received a grant to take part in a medical study at the Stanford University Hospital. The year away also provided us with the rare opportunity to get to know Winnie and Dave Silver, a delightful Jewish couple who adopted us during our time in the US and with whom we are still in touch today. Also enlightening was the diverse human mosaic of participants in the course at Stanford, which gave me a better understanding of the many countries from which they came. The course was attended by people from countries all over Asia, including the Philippines, Thailand and Taiwan, and a large group from India. The Middle East was also represented, with two Egyptians, an Israeli and an Iranian.

DAVIDI OFFERS ME THE 71ST BATTALION

I returned to Israel in January and immediately began looking for work and a place to live. Brigadier General Aharon Davidi, who was by then the IDF's chief infantry and paratroop officer, summoned me to a meeting. We had stayed in touch since my first days as an officer in the 890th Battalion and later in the Paratroop Brigade, and it was good to see him again. Davidi was Chief Infantry and Paratroop Officer but had a very modest office. His straight reddish hair was cut short and he wore the same beard as always, which now had scattered patches of gray. Most important, however, was the familiar look of wisdom and kindness in his eyes. Davidi welcomed me with a smile, calling me by the nickname he had always used for me: 'Zil Zil! Welcome back! The time has come for you to take command of a reserves battalion,' he said. At any other time, I would have agreed immediately but, with my thoughts still in California, I needed to think it over.

Returning to Davidi's office two weeks later, I was able to tell him without hesitation that I would be happy to assume command of a battalion. After two years as deputy battalion commander under Elisha Shalem in the reserves, I knew what was in store. It meant a serious increase in responsibility, as well as isolation at the top of the chain of command. During my last tour of reserve duty I had commanded a battalion during a major brigade-wide exercise but it was only when I actually received the new 71st Battalion that I truly understood what a privilege it was to build and shape a new battalion from the ground up.

GETTING FAMILIAR WITH WEAPONS DEVELOPMENT

My search for employment continued. I contacted the Weapons Development Department of the IDF Operations Branch and asked for a meeting with the Department Director Colonel Yitzhak Yaakov. Dr. Adi Ben-Israel, my Masters' thesis advisor and a weapons development reservist, also passed on my name to the department and recommended that they get in touch with me. The General Staff base was in a building that had been standing since the days of Templar settlement and the German Colony of Sarona; it now housed the Weapons Development Department. Colonel Yaakov, a sturdy man with short curly hair and penetrating blue eyes, received me in his office. In a deep voice and businesslike tone, Yaakov told me about the department. But after thinking it over, I decided not to join his team.

PIONEERING AT BEIT SHEMESH

The civilian sector was more appealing and I accepted an offer to take over production management of the Amnur factory in the town of Beit Shemesh. Amnur was a subsidiary of the Israeli company Amcor that manufactured kerosene home heaters, washing machines and large refrigerators for kitchens and businesses. Its production lines were somewhat similar to those of the Friedman factory in Jerusalem.

The job of production manager is demanding and extremely time consuming in any factory, but in the tiny Amnur facility in Beit Shemesh, which struggled from month to month just to stay afloat, the demanding nature of the job was extreme. Indeed, when it was time for Naomi to give birth to our son Nimrod, I dropped her at the Tel Hashomer hospital and dashed to work, only returning later in the afternoon — but Nimrod had already been born.

Just when everything appeared to be going well at Amnur, a problem arose relating to my reserve duty. Every since my appointment as battalion commander, Davidi had been pushing me to attend a reserves company commanders' course, which would last 'only six weeks'. The factory manager was horrified when he heard my request for six weeks' leave. Motta Gur, my brigade commander, even came to the factory in uniform — with his red beret and rank of colonel — to meet Ergad Yaakobi, the factory manager. Gur pleaded with Yaakobi to do without me for six weeks, but his efforts were unsuccessful.

Finally, a compromise was reached whereby I would participate in only half the training course. I went to Sharon, who was already a general and was now serving as the director of the Training Department, and explained the problem. Sharon called the commander of the training base near Netanya and instructed him to meet me half way. In the end, I attended the first week of the course, one week in the middle and the final week, during which I commanded a challenging final exercise involving landing a company by helicopter and a live fire exercise with a target known only by maps and aerial photos. When the course was over I was summoned to the office of Uzi Narkis, then OC Central Command, who awarded me the rank of major.

My compromise, however, did not solve all my problems at Amnur. Yaakobi left on a trip to Europe to visit a number of industries for more than a month, and during his absence I functioned as both factory manager and production manager. During this period I brokered a resolution to a dispute with the workers and achieved a new monthly production peak. Yaakobi felt undermined by this and when he returned from Europe our relations took a turn for the worse. My position became untenable and I decided to embark on a new path. Colonel Yitzhak Hofi, who had been Sharon's deputy when the Paratroop Brigade was established, was now serving as director of the Operations Department of the IDF General Staff.

Hofi heard from Gur about my difficulties and offered me a job in the defense ministry. A tender had just been issued for an experienced engineer for the Purchasing and Production Administration and I decided to apply for the position. The men on the tender committee were all unknown to me, including the chairman, who was a director of one of Israel's defense industries. The chairman, who had short gray hair and glasses with thin gold-plated frames which gave him the appearance of a Prussian military officer, seemed older and more experienced because of the questions he asked. The interview went well and I was extremely disappointed to be told, two days later, that I had been the committee's second choice. The following day I received a call from the chairman himself, who introduced himself as the director of some company or another, and he asked me if was interested in coming to work for him. Quickly putting two and two together, I politely told him that I would consider his offer. But I knew I would not take the job.

Colonel Yitzhak Yaakov, who was still serving as the director of the General Staff 's Weapons Development Department, never stopped trying to recruit me. He offered me the opportunity to manage the Department's Branch 2. After consulting with Brigadier

General Davidi and Colonel Hofi, who were very encouraging, I decided to take the job. Then it was back to the Induction Base to put on a uniform again, receive the military gear issued to all soldiers and make my way to the General Staff base. The unknown world of military research and development awaited me, and with this, my 10-year civilian hiatus came to an end.

5

The 71st Battalion and The Six Day War

SETTING UP THE BATTALION

Setting up a new organization of any kind is always a unique experience. It comes with expectations, hopes, uncertainties and tensions about its character, the people involved, the possibilities of success or failure, and what the future holds in store.

The initial training program of a new reserves battalion is a formative event with immense importance for the battalion's direction and the way it will function in the future. There is no way to predict the capabilities of the soldiers and officers and the types of relationships they will form with each other. There is also no way to know whether the battalion officers and the platoon and company commanders will be positive, authoritative and charismatic leaders, or, alternatively, too soft-hearted to effectively fill the positions they were assigned.

Still burdened by issues surrounding management of the Amnur factory in Beit Shemesh, I had no choice but to arrive to my battalion's initial training program two days late. It was pouring rain at the height of winter in early 1967 as I drove south towards Arad where the battalion encampment had been set up. This was rare for southern Israel, and I could already see water flowing in the usually dry riverbeds. When I reached the encampment I was greeted by deputy battalion commander Dan Ziv and a battalion-wide inspection was held. During the inspection I spoke about the challenges we faced, the fact that everything we were doing was new and the training program that would crystallize us all into a strong unified force. Forty years later Knesset Member Zevulun Orlev, who was a soldier in the battalion at the time, told me that he could still remember the reverence with which they viewed their first battalion commander.

Aside from Dan Ziv whom I knew from the 890th battalion, I knew almost no one in the 71st battalion. Ziv, a short, sturdy, and muscular man with light hair and a prickly mustache, grew up on Kibbutz Ayelet Hashachar. He had been a platoon commander during Operation Kadesh and was awarded the Medal of Courage for his role in the battle at Mitla. He already had experience commanding a company in the reserves, and the position of deputy battalion commander was a promotion for him. I also knew I would find master sergeant Zvika Vander in the battalion. Vander was my company sergeant in the 88th battalions B Company, and after I moved into the reserves and assumed command of A Company in the 98th Battalion, I took him on as my company sergeant major.

The rain poured down for an entire week. However, that did not stop us from carrying out the training program as planned, and I could feel the battalion beginning to take shape. The final component of the battalions' initial training program was a live-fire battalion exercise. Its aim was to employ all the companies to conquer a number of fortified targets using the mortars and heavy machine guns of the supporting company and the brigade artillery forces. I knew that brigade commander Motta Gur and his command staff would be coming to observe the exercise, and this was an another factor that motivated me to strive to plan and implement it flawlessly. I issued the orders to the company commanders calmly and effectively, while trying to control my own anxiety. I was particularly concerned by the fact that it was a live-fire exercise. I knew we needed to maintain safety distances for the artillery and mortars and to pay special attention to the direction of fire of the heavy machine guns to prevent accidents and a night-time disaster. The exercise commenced, and Gur was by my side the entire time. There was a tense moment when the two forward companies reached the line from which they were supposed to charge the main target, and I realized that the artillery shells used to soften up the target before the charge were falling farther and farther away from the target and increasingly close to our forces. I immediately ordered the two companies to hold their positions and the artillery to hold their fire, and out of the corner of my eye I could see the color returning to Gur's face. Fortunately, I was unable to see my own.

The reserve battalion's final exercise involved a complicated and difficult night-time amphibious landing and an attack on a fortified target. The plans called for a landing on the breach near Atlit south of Haifa and a march carrying all of our equipment — including mortars, heavy machine guns, and ammunition — along the mountain ridge north of Zichron Yaakov, where there was a target for a live-fire exercise. After a few hours of bucking around on naval landing crafts, neither easy nor particularly pleasant, we landed on the beach south of Atlit and began to make our way eastward among the banana groves toward the mountains. Leading the battalion I worried that the route I had chosen might not bring the battalion to the target in time which would lead to rushed preparations for the live-fire exercise, thus endangering my soldiers. As we walked through the night I suddenly felt the weight of my position bearing down on me, forcing me to make the most of all my senses and to remain as clear-headed as possible.

We reached the point at which the forces were supposed to split up for the attack, and I was concerned that the men were too tired by the long night march and that this could distract them and endanger adjacent forces. The heavy mortars we had carried up the mountain broke the night-time silence with their barks, quickly followed by the sound of machine guns, rifles, and sub-machine guns. The exercise ended, but I could only breathe easy after every company reported that it had completed its mission and that no one had been hurt.

Although it was nearly dawn it was still completely dark outside when I assembled the entire battalion in the main fort we had attacked. The air was filled with the bitter smell of explosives and gunpowder that is familiar to anyone who has ever been to war. I declared the exercise a success and praised its clean and precise execution. "With a battalion like this," I concluded as the soldiers listened attentively despite their exhaustion, "I would be willing to embark upon any mission assigned to us, in any war." I was unaware that the Six Day War and the difficult battles in Jerusalem were just around the corner.

PRE-WAR READINESS AND TRAINING

It was just a few months later that Egypt's expulsion of UN observers from the Sinai Peninsula and its blockade of the Straits of Tiran at Sharm El-Sheikh sparked a general mobilization of IDF reserves. Eventually, after most of the reserves had been mobilized, the paratroop units were also called up, and the two weeks that followed were dedicated to training and getting better acquainted with the soldiers and commanders. We were designated to be dropped at El-Arish, across Egyptian enemy lines, and to help Major General Israel Tal's division (at the time the 84th Division, but today the 162nd) move along the Sinai coast.

We wanted to train the battalion in dense, multi-story urban warfare without giving the men an explanation of exactly why we were doing so. In retrospect, it turned out to be the most suitable preparation for the war in Jerusalem, into which we were thrown with no advanced warning or preparation. The Ben Shemen Youth Village had three-story buildings, some of which had been built close enough to simulate urban densities. I asked the Youth Village director to let us use the buildings for training, but he refused saying it was "not educational."

"But the training is critical for us to prepare for the war that may soon break out," I insisted. In the end, the director agreed, and for an entire day company after company received training in urban warfare on the grounds of the Youth Village. When the battalion was discharged after the Six Day War I returned to Ben Shemen to thank the director.

On Saturday, June 3, two days before the outbreak of the war, Brigade Commander Gur and his staff set out on a tour of Jerusalem. Did he know something we did not know? In any event, he chose not to bother us battalion commanders with the tour and instead sent us home to rest. At the time, while the orders to parachute into El-Arish were still standing, the brigade commander's decision to give us a break before the beginning of the war was certainly understandable. However, with the wisdom of hindsight, Gur would have been wise to take us to Jerusalem as well.

At home in the Yehud neighborhood of Givat Avia, I spent a quiet Saturday with Naomi and the two children. Jupiter, our vigilant German shepherd puppy, was also happy to welcome me home. During my short leave, I worked on finishing the ditch that all homeowners were obliged to dig since citizens were required to improvise air-raid shelters. On Sunday we travelled to the Tel Nof air base with the rest of the brigade to equip ourselves with the necessary equipment for the drop and to deliver the equipment that was supposed to be dropped later after we completed the conquest of El-Arish.

We set up camp in the fruit groves of Kibbutz Givat Brenner. At dawn on Monday June 5, the Israeli Air Force began its operation, and our ears were filled with the roar of aircrafts taking off and landing at the nearby Tel Nof base. We followed the radio reports tensely and were encouraged by their optimistic tone. During our final briefing just before noon I said my final words to my battalion and briefly went over the mission of parachuting into enemy territory south of El-Arish, attacking the city, and conquering it from the south. My men looked particularly nervous as I tried to imbue them with confidence. I stressed two other directives as well, both lessons from past wars: property was not to be looted and prisoners were not to be harmed after they raised their hands and surrendered their weapons. I was convinced — and I remain convinced today — that these two imperatives are not only crucial from a moral perspective, but that if not respected they can pose a serious threat to our ability to fight.

But after that final briefing the mission was suddenly aborted and were sent with the rest of the brigade to Jerusalem for what we thought would be just a routine manning the armistice border that ran through the city. My company commanders and I set out for Jerusalem, while deputy battalion commander Dan Ziv, battalion Headquarters Company Commander Zvi Bash and Master Sergeant Vander were charged with transporting the entire battalion to the Jerusalem neighborhood of Beit Hakerem by bus. It was only when we got close to Jerusalem that we heard bursts of heavy machine-gun fire whizzing over our heads and understood that the war had begun in Jerusalem as well.

The 71st Battalion was assigned the task of breaking through enemy lines at Wadi Joz and the tomb of Simon just north of the Old City. I took my company commanders to tour the area and make plans. The city had already been shelled, and from time to time the sound of automatic weapons could be heard along the border. Almost instinctively I walked towards the interconnecting trenches north of Shmuel Hanavi Street. As night fell we saw the positions from which the Jordanians were firing and the barbed-wire fences and minefield between them, and marked the location as a possible point to break through the lines. Another possibility was to break through via Mandelbaum Gate, and from there to approach Wadi Joz and the neighborhood of Sheikh Jarah. Gur approved the plan, and I continued planning the details of the operation under the pressure of time.

One major difficulty was the fact that we only had one aerial photo of the city. Central Command Intelligence, which was headed by Lieutenant Colonel Gideon Mahanaymi, my friend from the paratroops, had well-organized, detailed files of all the Jordanian positions along the city's border. Command headquarters also had detailed and updated aerial photos of the entire area in which we would be fighting. Unfortunately, however, we were never provided with any of this material. Some 59 years later, during the second Lebanon war, history repeated itself, and field intelligence files for southern Lebanon, which were full of information about Hezbollah's fortifications system, remained in the safes of the Intelligence Branch, and never reached the fighting forces that needed them most.

We needed a place with some light to plan the attack, and I looked for local residents who would be willing to open their door to us. The couple that emerged from their bomb shelter to help us opened not only their home but their hearts as well. They made generous sandwiches, and the strong smell of hot sweet coffee soon filled the apartment. Only later, after the battle for Jerusalem, did we learn that they had given Yoram Zamush, the commander of A Company, an Israeli flag — the flag that was hung on the lattice at the edge of the Temple Mount complex above the Western Wail on the day Israel conquered the Old City.

The final plan for the Battalion's push into Sheikh Jarah and Wadi Joz is described in full, albeit in a brief and somewhat monotonous manner, in a document entitled "Details of Battalion Operations — the Campaign for Jerusalem," which was written on June 15, 1967, when everything was still fresh in our memory.

THE WAR IN JERUSALEM...ERSONAL PERSPECTIVE

During the first stages of the battalion's operations in the neighborhood of Sheikh Jarah following the breach, I had to function as a combat soldier, and at most a squad commander. This was the situation when I led my operations officer, my intelligence officer, my headquarters company commander, and my runner in taking over a

Jordanian position on the border that was pouring fire on the opening we had made in the fence and preventing the entry of our forces. It was the same story when my small staff and I were dragged into battle with Jordanian forces near the American Colony Hotel. When being fired upon, the immediate soldierly response is to charge the origin of fire, and that is exactly what we did. A few years ago during the battalion's annual Jerusalem Day gathering, my radio operator during the war told me that during that skirmish, when the Jordanians lobbed a hand grenade at us, I quickly pounced on him, knocking him to the ground and lay on top of him. "That's how you saved my life," he told me. I did not remember that part of the battle, but I clearly remembered feeling physically detached from the battalion. This troubled me, even though it was only temporary and I was in constant radio contact with my company commanders.

After my staff's battle in the American Colony, deputy battalion commander Ziv managed to broaden the breach in the fence to allow jeeps with recoilless guns through. I climbed onto the engine mount-

Uzi Eilam leading the 71st battalion of reserve paratroops in the Six Day War from Augusta Victoria towards the conquest of the Old City Jerusalem

ing of one of the jeeps and was able to see all the places where the battalion's companies were still engaged in fighting. During the early hours of the morning I reached the house where the battalion staff had established a temporary headquarters. It was a large house belonging to a wealthy family, and I instructed my men to use only one or two rooms and to let the family members go about their business.

By afternoon almost all the gunfire had ceased and Gur summoned me and the commander of the 66th Battalion to a commanders meeting in the yard of the Rockefeller Museum during which he presented new orders. Yossi Fredkin, commander of the 28th Battalion, was still stuck near the Rivoli hotel with most of his battalion, contending with Jordanian forces who were engaging them from the walls of the Old City. Gur presented plans for a night-time conquest of Augusta Victoria and the Mount of Olives. The plans placed most of the burden on the 71st Battalion, which had sustained fewer casualties than the others. After he finished issuing the orders I told Gur that Yoram Zamosh, commander of A Company, had requested to be the first to enter the Old City, if and when we were to do so. Gur's response to my request was simply "OK," and to this day I am still not certain whether he gave it ample consideration or simply answered without thinking, distracted by the imminent assault on Augusta Victoria and the Mount of Olives. The Old City was not even mentioned in the course of the order issued at the Rockefeller Museum. Shlomo Goren, Chief Rabbi of the IDF, also made no reference to the Old City when he joined us at the museum after the issuing of the order. Instead, he spoke of his mother's grave on the Mount of Olives. I promised to personally escort him to the grave once we were in control of the Mount of Olives. At that point, I never imagined that just one day later I would be standing by his side moments after our entry into the Old City, and that I would actually end up escorting him to the Western Wall.

The attack that began that night was initially halted due to an error of the supporting tank forces, which turned toward the bridge near Gethsemane instead of turning left and advancing to the saddle between the Augusta ridge and the Mount of Olives. We were joined by the reconnaissance unit of the 80th Brigade under the command of Micha Kapusta, who tried to turn the tanks around and send them in the right direction. They paid for their efforts with the death of five soldiers, killed by Jordanian fire from the city walls. As we waited to begin the attack we received word from Central Command that the 60th Armored Brigade of the Jordanian army had started mounting a counter-attack in Jerusalem. Gur scrapped the planned assault on the Augusta ridge and the Mount of Olives, and we spent the entire night deploying teams to stop the Jordanian armored forces. Our teams were armed with bazookas and rifle grenades, and we also integrated a platoon of French manufactured SS10 anti-tank missiles into our defensive formation. As morning approached I returned to our temporary command headquarters exhausted after two sleepless nights, and I was surprised when operations sergeant Eliezer Lavi told me that the woman of the house had sent me a plate of chicken fricassee and some fresh aromatic hot coffee. At that moment it was just what I needed, and the taste of the food and smell of the coffee are still as fresh in my memory today as they were early that morning.

At dawn I was again summoned by Gur, who had not assembled a command group but rather sought to refresh our memories regarding the night-time attack on Augusta Victoria and the Mount of Olives. "This time," Gur explained, "we will have the support of the Air Force and the support of the 155th Artillery Battalion." The brigade was still recovering from the difficult battle at Ammunition Hill, and the Augusta Victoria ridge was defended by a dug-in and well defended company fort. I was aware of the dangers posed by another battle like Ammunition Hill, but I trusted the ability of my men and I knew that the attack plans had taken the risks into consideration.

It was a cool and quiet morning at battalion headquarters. The window overlooking the valley that lay between us and the Augusta ridge and the Mount of Olives was wide open, and the sun began to rise in the sky...eep and calming blue. A soothing quiet pervaded the entire sector, and a festive feeling of sorts was in the air. We were not overly concerned by the threat posed by the Jordanian company position on the Augusta ridge, and we had not yet started to think about the Old City as part of the day's plans. Yoram Zamosh, commander of A Company, stayed back to command the reserve force consisting of two half-tracks vehicles we had used to evacuate the wounded of the previous day. Zamosh knew that he was supposed to wait in a gorge in the Valley of Olives near the Palace Hotel until receiving further orders. Our assessment was that we would not need him during the battle for Augusta Victoria, and this turned out to be accurate. The battle up the ridge to the Jordanian army position was easier than we expected, and it was there at the peak that we received Gur's order via radio to enter the Old City through the Lions' Gate. There were no preliminary orders, and no planning or coordination. Clearly, the historic significance of the reconquest of the Old City had overshadowed all standard combat procedures.

Zamosh's force was closer to the Lions' Gate that all other units of the brigade, and I immediately ordered him to enter the Old City. I could clearly picture the image of the city and the wall's gates, and I remember thinking that it seemed wrong to have the entire battalion enter the through the same gate. Acting on this assessment I ordered deputy battalion commander Ziv to enter the city with D Company and the supporting company via the Dung Gate. I quickly descended the road leading to Gethsemane and the Lions' Gate with my staff, and C Company, under the command of Ze'ev Barkai, followed us down to the Lions' Gate. I do not recall our route to the road that led to the Lions' Gate. I was floating, as if in a dream.

A Company was there led by its two half-tracks, and it was not moving. I jumped into Zamosh's half-track and, over the rumble of its engine, yelled, "Why aren't you going in?" He said that our tanks were shelling the gate, and explained that he was waiting for them to stop shooting. Before he finished speaking we were overtaken by the half-track and command car of brigade commander Gur himself, who had decided that history required that he personally be the first to enter the Old City. In my opinion, this flew in the face of all relevant military considerations. I sent A Company after him and followed with my staff. The positions along the City walls and on both sides of the gate were manned by Jordanian soldiers, and we exchanged fire a number of times on our way to the Temple Mount.

Before long we reached the Temple Mount plaza and I was astounded by its whiteness, its largeness, and the quiet that pervaded it. Gur was there, and I asked for his authorization to look for the Western Wall. By that point the flag that had been hung by Zamosh and Moshe Stempel on the lattice on the edge of the Temple Mount was waving high above the Wall. I do not recall how I found the stairs that led to the Wall, but within minutes I was standing with the small staff of the 71st Battalion in the small yard that had stood adjacent to the Wall for centuries. The small yard was empty and silent. I gazed at the giant stones and the small plants poking out from between them. And, although I neither cried nor prayed, it was clear to me that we were experiencing an historic moment of exceptional importance.

Benny Ron, my weapons development officer, had a camera and can be credited with immortalizing the first pictures by the Wall after its conquest. I was informed by radio that Rabbi Goren had arrived at the Temple Mount plaza along with his assistant and right-hand man Rabbi Menachem Hacohen, and that the two rabbis were with the Battalion's B Company. I sent a soldier to bring the rabbi to the Wall, where I met him. Goren was in a highly elevated spiritual state. He was grasping a shofar (a Jewish ceremonial ram's horn) which he had brought with him. He tried to blow it, but the excitement of the occasion stopped him from making a sound. "Rabbi," I said to Goren, "Give me the shofar. I play the trumpet, and I know how to blow a shofar." I succeeded in issuing a number of clear, loud blasts from the shofar, and Benny got the historic moment on film, adding it to the collection of pictures that captured the Israeli army's first moments by the Western Wall. We sang "Hatikva" and Naomi Shemer's new song "Jerusalem of Gold," and then went back up to the Temple Mount plaza to make preparations to continue searching and mopping up the Old City.

The war in Jerusalem had not yet ended, and the battalion had a number of wounded men who had been hit by the fire of Jordanian legionnaires who had spread out in the alleyways of the Old City. The 71st Battalion suffered another casualty during our last skirmish in Jerusalem, which took place adjacent to the New Gate, close to the Jewish Jerusalem. I joined C Company, which was fighting a Jordanian force that had dug in at the small Knights Hotel. One of our soldiers had been killed and more were wounded. The force inside was an effective Jordanian squad made up of soldiers who were determined to fight. My sense was that, after two days of fighting and the experience at the Western Wall, the war had come to an end for my men. I took a red-headed platoon commander named Bar-On, a machine-gunner, and two other soldiers, and climbed up the sewage pipes that ran down the wall of the hotel. We scaled the wall to the second floor, where the Jordanians had been located. After a quick mopping up of the hallway and the rooms on the floor we reached a staircase, and it appeared that the Jordanians had already ascended to the roof of the hotel. From there, they continued to shoot downward and managed to hit my deputy Dan Ziv, injuring him in the arm. We charged the open roof, and, in the short gun battle that ensued, during which I was also injured by shrapnel, we killed the courageous Jordanian soldiers. I placed D Company commander Musa Gilboa in command of the battalion and promised to return from the hospital as soon as possible. I called over battalion physician Yigal Ginat and asked him to ride with Ziv and me to Hadassah Hospital "to make sure they don't dare force us to stay," which they of course attempted to do. After our wounds were tended to, Dr. Ginat assumed responsibility for the remainder of our treatment and we returned to the battalion.

The battalion had a quiet night in the Kishla, the old Jerusalem prison dating back to the days of Ottoman rule near Jaffa Gate. The following day the entire battalion left Jerusalem to Abu-Dis and al-Azariyya east of Jerusalem.

UP TO THE GOLAN HEIGHTS

The war was still not over, and we all knew that Israel still had a score to settle with the Syrians. I understood from Gur that he had no intention of operating his force as a brigade, and, although we were able to rely on the brigade framework for logistical support, no brigade-wide orders were issued. On Friday June 9, I told Ziv and Headquarters Company Commander Bash to arrange transportation to the Golan Heights for the battalion to take part in the fighting there, if and when it began. I headed north with part of the battalion staff earlier, and went directly to the command headquarters of OC Northern Command David Elazar. That afternoon, while the Golani Brigade was waging a heroic battle at Tel-Fakher and the 8th armored brigade was engaging the Syrian forts, Elazar found the time to meet with me. "I am here with a paratroop battalion from Jerusalem," I told him, even though the battalion was still on its way. "Can we play a role here?"

I was astounded by the gentleness of Elazar's voice. It had a pleasant ring that I recognized years later, when he was CGS during the Yom Kippur War. "Go to (Major General, Res.) Elad Peled, commander of the division that will attack the central Golan Heights tomorrow. Join his forces."

Early the next morning I was already sitting with Elad Peled in a position overlooking the Golan Heights. I was charged with leading a force in across the Syrian lines by helicopter that afternoon, conquering Tel Fares, and holding Rafid Junction in the southern Golan Heights. By that point my battalion was operating like a well-oiled machine. I issued the orders to the company commanders with ease, and it felt good to know that the battalion's entire logistical rear was in the experienced hands of Headquarters Company Commander Bash and Master Sergeant Vander. On Saturday afternoon we assembled in the flatlands north of Sarona in the Lower Galilee and waited for the helicopters to arrive. Flying over the Syrian forces we could see the movement of tanks and other vehicles below, most of which were retreating eastward. We landed on the slopes of Tel Fares and there was no significant resistance on the part of the Syrians. During the night we were already able to leave the Golan Heights and go back to Jerusalem.

AN HISTORIC CEREMONY ON THE TEMPLE MOUNT

With his sense for immortalizing history, Gur decided to hold a celebratory review of the entire brigade on the Temple Mount plaza. Battalion flags appeared out of nowhere and the whole brigade — including the wounded who could make it there from the hospital — took part in an impressive inspection near the al-Omar Mosque. I felt the need to conclude the war with a different, more intimate event just for the 71st Battalion.

After the brigade-wide ceremony I assembled the battalion on the southern steps of the Temple Mount plaza, which formed a theatre of sorts. There, I stood before the battalion and, in a few words, summed up what we had accomplished during the war. I told them that a time would come in the future when we would be able to better assess the historical significance of our role in the war. I also reminded the soldiers that "at the end of the last battalion-wide exercise, after the landing and the live-fire exercise, I told you that with a battalion like this, I would be willing to embark upon any mission. This still stands. I am proud to be the commander of this battalion, and I salute you." There I stood wearing my steel helmet and my spotted uniform, which had seen many battles and much blood, and saluted the battalion. Saluting is rare among Israeli combat troops and even

Blowing the Shofar with Rabbi Goren at the Western Wall during the Six Day War

rarer in reserves. Without a word, the entire battalion rose to its feet and saluted. It was a long, moving moment of sharing the unique powerful bond that is experienced only by comrades in arms after a difficult war.

I only began the difficult duty of visiting the bereaved families after the war was over and once the soldiers of the battalion had all been discharged. After inquiries we carried out within the battalion, I was able to tell the members of each family how their loved one had died. Many bereaved parents asked to tour the route of the battalion's battles, and I promised to fulfill this request. A few weeks later the battalion command and company commanders undertook a tour with the parents and loved ones of those we had lost. The most difficult point along the route came when we reached the houses where five soldiers from the battalion had been killed. They were soldiers of C Company, which had been fighting at the location without their company commander, who had been injured at the beginning of the skirmish, and without a deputy company commander, who had remained in the rear. In both houses the Jordanians had shown fierce resistance. We referred to one of the houses as "the house with the burnt roof," and the other as "the house of death." Along with the parents we climbed the external stairs of the "house of death" until we reached the second floor. Pools of congealed blood of the fallen soldiers had remained on the steps, and I still get chills when thinking back on that moment with the parents, as we all stood there silently in sorrow, staring at the blood.

6

Weapons Development — The Technological Edge

The transition from war in Jerusalem back to Branch 2 of the Weapons Development Department was abrupt. My branch was responsible for the development of weapons systems for virtually the entire army. The branch's small staff was like a hand: each individual finger was not strong enough on its own, but together we were an exceptionally powerful fist. The branch's work focused on shooting mechanisms, gunnery and the armored forces, electronics and the initial development of optronics and night vision. Branch personnel included Major Leon Dostes from the armored forces, who had immigrated to Israel from Greece after a stint in the Greek army. Gunnery was the responsibility of a soft-spoken, blue-eyed captain named Elizur Peled. Our explosives man, Major Alex Alhanani, amassed a massive stock of explosives and explosive devices in the basement of the old Templar building at Sharona. The building housed the entire Weapons Development Department, and I would hate to think what might have happened if one of Alex's toys had accidentally detonated. Dov Adelbaum-Eden was a civilian IDF employee and an electronics expert who had been educated in the United States. Danny Avivi, responsible for optronics, was a civilian who had immigrated to Israel from the US. His past included a shady episode in which he had contributed to Israeli security in some way and, as a result was unable to return to America. The seventh member of our team was Benny Ron, a creative and energetic first lieutenant who worked on a variety of issues.

On July 26, 1967, Operations Branch Chief Major General Ezer Weizman promoted me to the rank of lieutenant colonel. As a result of the war the minimum period of time necessary for promotion was shortened, and after only eight months as a major I suddenly became a lieutenant colonel. Shortly thereafter I received an official letter, signed by CGS Yitzhak Rabin, approving my secondary appointment as commander of the reserves 71st Battalion, in addition to my appointment as director of Branch 2. My multiple positions helped more than it hurt, as I did not want to part with the battalion and couldn't just sit in my office in Tel Aviv without taking part in the War of Attrition that followed the Six Day War. My involvement in military operations provided my weapons development work with important insight and depth. In this way, serving as an active battalion commander in the paratroops proved to be an advantage.

The Weapons Development Department's main trophy from the war was a collection of data and statistics about the damage sustained by tanks on both sides during the war. This information — especially regarding our battles with Soviet-made tanks — was of immense interest to Western armies in general and the US in particular. The Western armies had not had a major confrontation with Soviet weapons systems since the Korean War of 1950–1953, and many found the data we compiled from the Six Day War intriguing. Information on Soviet weapons systems and Soviet military doctrine was also important for West Germany and provided a sturdy foundation for long-term cooperation between the Israeli and West German defense establishments.

MR. BÖLKOW AND DR. HELD

One of the assets we accumulated after the Six Day War was a special relationship between the Weapons Development Department and Messerschmitt-Bölkow-Blohm (MBB), a German aerospace company owned by Ludwig Bölkow. MBB was a private company, a remnant of the aeronautics industry established by Germany during Word War II. One evening, just a few days after the end of the war, Colonel Yitzhak Yaakov asked me to take two visitors on a tour in the Sinai Peninsula. It was a Saturday morning, and I picked the guests up at the Tel Aviv Dan Hotel in my Susita, the Israeli fiberglass-bodied car driven by lieutenant colonels in the IDF in those days. I was unaware of the important status of Mr. Bölkow, the senior of the two men, and of the unique character of Dr. Held, the director of Bölkow's research laboratory. The two men had had flown to Israel in Bölkow's private plane, and there I was picking him up in my tiny, noisy car. I drove straight down to the Sinai, with the two visitors suffering from the lack of any reasonable leg-room in the cramped back seat. First, we drove along the northern road in the Sinai and then moved over to the central road. A raging sandstorm limited our visibility to dozens of meters, and it was hard to keep the car from sinking in the hills of sand that formed in the middle of the road.

We finally reached an area containing dozens of Soviet tanks and armored vehicles that had been disabled by Israeli tanks and the Israeli Air Force. Each time the two guests got out of the car and inspected the bombed-out vehicles like two children in a toy store. They examined the damage that our tanks had inflicted on the Egyptian tanks, and were excited to find Russian RPG anti-tank grenades lying on the ground beside the bombed-out convoys. It took all my persuasive capacity to prevent Dr. Held from blowing himself up with a warhead with a fuse that was still active. Late that night, after a long day in the field, I brought them back to their hotel.

Without a doubt, this day was the beginning of a marvelous

cooperative endeavor with Bölkow's company in general and Dr. Held's development laboratorities in particular. We set up a testing area near a military base located south of Netanya to which we dragged a few bombed-out Russian tanks. Dr. Held was then in the early stages of an effort to develop anti-tank missile warheads, and the opportunity to carry out tests in Israel was an invaluable gift. Held was a long-armed, long-legged man with glasses who spoke English well (albeit with a heavy German accent), and insisted on working from early in the morning to late in the evening. Put simply, he liked his work. It was chilling for me to think that, during World War II, many other well educated and gifted German professionals were also enthusiastic about developing means of killing and extermination.

For us in Israel it was a perfect opportunity to position ourselves on the technological forefront of developing advanced shaped and capped charges for the warheads of the future. Our relationship with Dr. Held continued, and many of our accomplishments were based on his wisdom.

METHODS OF BORDER DEFENSE

For us it was clear that, contrary to the biblical expression, the land would not "have peace for forty years" (Judges 3:8) and that Israel's borders would continue to play a central role in our lives. Branch 2 was given a free hand to initiate development over the issue of defense, and First Lieutenant Benny Ron quickly proposed the idea of erecting an electronic warning fence.

The principle underlying Ron's proposed apparatus was based on integrating springs into the barbed wire fence and on micro-switches that were responsive to the movement of the fence. The commander of a military base located on the Mediterranean Coast agreed to have his base serve as a test case for the concept, which proved the apparatus's warning capability. After the system had been functioning for a few weeks, we discovered a problem that stemmed from geological movements which caused the angles of the fence posts to change over time. This, in turn, resulted in a change in the tension of the barbed wire fence and set off a false alarm. Ron's innovative, ingenious, and ultimately successful solution was to use "bouncing putty," a flexible, putty like modeling substance, to stabilize the fence's sensors.

Before the Six Day War the challenge of securing Israel's borders had also occupied the Americans. The US wanted to assist Israel in preventing the penetration of our border without recourse to military operations, such as the reprisal operations of the 1950s. The signing of an American–Israeli cooperation agreement provided us with devices for observing the border day and night and the joint discussion of ideas for warning systems.

GENERALS VERSUS GENERALS

The major advantage of the Weapons Development Department and Branch 2 (which was linked to all the corps and services of the IDF) in particular was the fact that it fell under the direct supervision of the Operations Branch chief, the source of operational and budgetary authority within the IDF. However, our close relationship with Operations Branch Chief Weizman and his deputy, Rehavam Ze'evi, also came at a cost.

When I returned from my first tour of reserve duty with the battalion in the Jordan Valley, Ze'evi summoned me for a meeting to hear my insights and recommendations. While I was still presenting my detailed account of what I had seen and my thoughts on the possible solution to one problem or another, Ze'evi led me into Ezer Weizman's office. "I want the Operations Branch chief to hear what you have to say," he explained, and I repeated my account. Weizman asked me a long list of questions, and finally dropped a bombshell: "Why don't you drive up to the northern border and carry out a survey on how they handle the problems of border defense?" he suggested. I knew I would have no problem gaining access to OC Elazar, and

I returned to the Weapons Development Department with a great sense of pride. However, when I explained my assignment to Colonel Yaakov, who was a seasoned expert when it came to the backroom politics of the IDF, he looked at me with his blue penetrating eyes and slowly gave me the following advice: "Never, ever come between two generals," he warned, "because in the end, you're the one who's likely to get burned." I never made the trip up to the Northern Command, and I made careful note of this lesson on how to survive in the General Staff.

A NEW ASSAULT RIFLE FOR THE IDF

Another unique member of the team of professionals that worked with Branch 2 was Lieutenant Colonel Uzi Gal, developer of the ingenious Uzi sub-machinegun, which won praise for both him and Israel the world over. Gal was not only a talented and creative; he was also meticulous and pedantic like only a native of Germany could be. He had been assigned to the most appropriate place for inventing and developing light weapons, and it soon became clear that his current dream was to develop a new rifle for the IDF. The term assault rifle was still new to us, but we were aware that many different countries were working on the challenging task of developing a lightweight rifle with a rapid and reliable rate of fire. Together, we embarked upon the adventure of developing a new assault rifle without knowing exactly where it would lead.

Despite his strength as a brilliant technician it was difficult for Gal to find his place on the team. His was the generation of 1948, and he was older than us all. Nonetheless, we were obliged to provide him with a place to work and a team to help him fulfill his dream. The logical framework was Israel Military Industries (IMI): the primary Israeli source of light weapons and light ammunition, and manufacturer of the Uzi submachine gun. On the face of things the endeavor looked promising enough, and IMI accepted the idea and allocated Gal work space and a team. But IMI's own technical experts in the field of light weaponry, led by gifted technician Israel Blashnikov, were unwilling to play second fiddle. This meant that two development projects were now simultaneously underway within IMI, working in ever-increasing competition with one another. IMI management preferred its own team, but the fact that Lieutenant Colonel Gal had made progress and had emerged as a competitor of Blashnikov was indicative of his skills and extraordinary talent. At this early stage in my defense R&D career, watching the projects unfold taught me an important lesson about the power of personal ambition and the role of politics in all competitive projects.

A few months later, when I was second in command of the Jordan Valley Brigade, I saw OC Central Command Ze'evi carrying a model of Blashnikov's assault rifle slung over his shoulder. Rafael Eitan, who was serving as the chief paratroop officer at the time, was also armed with the rifle. I was amazed, because at that point, the tests and the competition were still underway. I now understood that the rules of the game had changed, and that it was now personal and political. Ultimately, Gal's rifle had significant advantages over Blashnikov's. However, as a result of Eitan's unwavering support for Blashnikov's rifle — which was known as the "Galil" — Operations Branch Chief David Elazar decided in its favor.

The Galil was actually a Kalashnikov adapted to fire 5.56 caliber bullets. Although it won the competition, much time passed before it was put into use within the IDF. During the Yom Kippur War soldiers had no assault rifle whatsoever — neither Israeli-made nor the American-made M-16. At the end of the war a number of Israeli units began using Kalashnikov rifles captured during the fighting.

As an infantryman, light weapons development was a personal priority. I have never forgotten something said to me during the first ceasefire of the Yom Kippur War by Uzi Eilat, commander of my battalion's B Company during the Six Day War. Eilat, who by 1973 was serving as the battalion's deputy commander, was back for the funeral of his brother, who had been killed in the war. When he stopped in to see me at the R&D Unit on his way back down to the Sinai Peninsula, he hit me with the following stinging criticism: "You took care to develop air weaponry and naval weaponry," he said, "but you left us — you left the infantry — with no advanced weapons whatsoever." During all my years in the field of defense research and development, these are words I have been unable to forget, even if I had wanted to.

AN EMERGENCY TEAM

During the summer of 1968 I was summoned to meet with Operations Branch Chief Weizman. "We have to deal with the problems that have arisen along the Suez Canal after this week's heavy shelling and the casualties we've sustained," he told me. "We decided to establish an emergency team to examine the issue and to propose new concepts for defenses and deployment. Brigadier General Avraham Adan (Bren) of the Armored Corps has been selected to head the team, and you will be a member representing the infantry, as well as the issue of technology and weaponry. You've been assigned a Dakota airplane and two helicopters, and you will have access to anything else you need. The issue is a high priority, and you're going down to the Sinai on Sunday."

We were familiar with the situation along the Canal from our first tour of reserve duty, and we knew the extent of our soldiers' exposure to shelling along the Canal. The government's policy, which was spelled out clearly by Prime Minister Golda Meir in her typically decisive, non-compromising manner, was "not to move even one inch from the water line." Although ditches had been dug in the ramparts above the banks of the canal, the high number of casualties caused by the most recent exchanges of fire proved that the protection they provided was insufficient. On the Sunday we were flown to the Sinai in the Air Force Dakota. Adan's team included communications expert Lieutenant Colonel Shlomo Inbar, an intelligence expert who was one of the most senior lieutenant colonels in the corps, Lieutenant Colonel Uri Ga'ash, who was later appointed as commander of the Armored Corps, and, as bureau chief, Major Yaakov Lapidot, who would later serve as OC Home Front Command.

Adan was congenial and soft spoken. These qualities, in addition to his short stature and the blonde lock of hair that hung across his forehead, were misleading, as the man himself was decisive and determined. He was a good choice to lead the project. We immediately began a series of tours along the Canal to learn the terrain and prepare ourselves for the task of generating a new defensive concept. The instructions of CGS prescribed an Israeli presence right up to the water line within a string of forts, and the close proximity to the Egyptian enemy dictated massive defenses for the soldiers. At the same time we needed to provide for safe observation and firing capabilities from the high rampart running the length of the Canal. These requirements resulted in the idea of a fort resembling a well-protected hedgehog with a protrusion at the front for observation and firing capability. We worked night and day, using architects, engineers, and contractors who won tenders for the jobs, and started their work along the canal building what came to be known as the Bar-Lev Line.

After the team completed its task of generating a new concept for defending the water line and as the work along the canal drew to a close, Adan was appointed commander of the Sinai Division. In late December 1968 he informed the team members that all of our recommendations had been adopted by the General Staff.

OPPOSITION AND THOUGHTS ON THE CONCEPTION

However, not all members of the General Staff were supportive of our stationary approach to defending the Canal. Two of the most outspoken opponents were Arik Sharon and Israel Tal, who spoke at a special meeting I attended. Sharon had been designated for the post of OC Southern Command and Tal was about to finish his term as commander of the Armored Corps. Tal supported the use of mobile forces alone, and opposed the permanent fixed presence of Israeli forces on the ground along the Canal. This approach came as no surprise coming from an Armored Corps commander, as motion was an integral element of the defensibility of tanks and their ability to surprise the enemy. For his part, Sharon called for adding an element of depth to the thin line of fortifications along the canal, and when he was appointed OC in 1969 he initiated the construction of a second line of rear Israeli posts 10–15 kilometers to the east of the Canal line.

On the southern front all senior defense establishment figures subscribed to a concept that took into account the possibility of an Egyptian surprise attack, but underestimated the Egyptians' ability to achieve their goals through such an action.

Despite budgetary difficulties the Engineering Corps continued to try to devise a means of crossing wide water obstacles such as the Suez Canal. Gillois landing rafts provided a realistic means of achieving this capability. A single raft could be placed in the water and serve as an independent means for transporting vehicles, and could also be linked to a chain of other rafts to form a bridge. Despite President de Gaulle's embargo policy, the French were willing to provide us with such rafts.

However, the efforts of our Engineering Corps were overshadowed by "the roller bridge"...anal-crossing project that became the pet project of Operations Branch Chief Major General Israel Tal. Tal's faith in the project was unlimited, and he provided it with a wealth of funding and human resources.

In the debates on purchasing policy that took place within the General Staff, I and others argued that the roller bridge was still in preliminary stages of development and we needed to equip ourselves with alternative solutions, such as the Gillois landing rafts until the roller bridge could prove its effectiveness. The opponents of purchasing the rafts, mainly Armored Corps officers led by Tal, emphasized that the rafts were not armored. Despite the opposition, it was ultimately decided to purchase a small quantity of Gillois rafts from NATO surplus. Within the IDF these rafts were known by the name "Timsakh." Not long had passed before the Yom Kippur War broke out, and when the roller bridge was brought to the Canal it turned out to be a complete failure. Instead, the Gillois rafts we had acquired allowed us to move forces to the other side of the Canal.

Although not completely justified, much of the blame for the failure of the early stages of the Yom Kippur War has been placed on the Bar-Lev Line. Many years later I toured a few points along the Maginot Line, the long and highly invested defensive line that France built along its border with Germany prior to World War II. To France's chagrin, the Germans waged a brilliant war of movement and flanking to bypass the impressive line that hitherto had been the pride of France, transforming it into a silent memorial to a failed strategic and tactical conception. After my visit to the Maginot Line I began to ask myself what we had been thinking. Why we had failed to learn from the experience of the French? What had possessed us to reinvent the concept of static lines of defense after its miserable failure just a few decades earlier?

WITH THE BATTALION ON THE CANAL DURING THE WAR OF ATTRITION

Notwithstanding my comments above, the Bar-Lev Line nevertheless provided an adequate solution for the physical security of the troops during the shelling of the forts themselves. I had a stormy tour of duty with the 71st Battalion in the Sinai Peninsula during the winter of early 1969. We manned forts from the northern Sinai across from Port Said to the south, across from the city of Suez. The Egyptians were active and carried out a variety of attacks on Israeli positions and their access roads. I knew the border and its weak points well. I came to appreciate the security provided by the fortifications during my time at battalion headquarters, which was located in one of the positions in the middle of the sector.

CREATIVE SNIPERS' WAR

The roads leading to the positions along the Suez Canal were the Achilles' heel of the Bar-Lev Line because they were near the rampart, and whoever travelled on them was exposed to shelling and ambushes. The Egyptians wisely placed soldiers in high trees and towers built especially for this purpose, and these observers were able to shoot at vehicles approaching the forts and monitor our troops within the forts themselves. It was a special challenge for our snipers to take them out, as they were typically well camouflaged. We were extremely pleased each time we saw someone fall out of a tree after we shot at them. We also made efforts to achieve effective observation capabilities, but in a more mechanical and sophisticated manner, by means of a hydraulic fire fighting crane. We brought in a hydraulic fire-fighting ladder from the US that could reach a height of 30 meters. It even passed the meticulous inspection of Operations Branch Chief Tal and was also approved for use by the Ordnance Corps.

MOSHE DAYAN VISITS THE FRONT LINES

One day while we were still stationed on the Canal, we were informed that Defense Minister Moshe Dayan would be coming for a visit. Sinai Division headquarters provided two M-113 armored vehicles, which were known by the troops as Zeldas and were extremely rare at the time, to transport the defense minister to the northern sector of the front. I reported to the Baluza military base to welcome Dayan and bring him to the battalion's sector. We drove along the Canal in the two Zeldas, with Dayan in the lead. Suddenly, Dayan stood up in the moving vehicle. 'Moshe,' I said to him, 'there are snipers on the other side. It would be best if you sat down.' I was concerned that the Egyptians would recognize his well-known black eye patch and injure him. What could I do?

"No, no," Dayan responded, in a quiet authoritative voice, defiantly belittling the danger. "I want to see the other side of the Canal." This time we were fortunate that the Egyptians did not shoot at us and that we reached the large position that held battalion headquarters safely. The Egyptians routinely monitored the convoys and would begin shelling the forts into which supply convoys entered minutes after their arrival. Our procedure was to immediately send those arriving with the convoy into the bunkers and to wait and see whether or not the Egyptians would start shelling. When we entered the position, I asked Dayan to accompany me down to the fort's large bunker. "Most of the soldiers in the fort are assembled in the there," I told him. "That's the place to talk to them." But Dayan insisted on staying above ground, and he asked me to assemble the soldiers to meet with him in the open area within the position. I was unable to convince the defense minister that this posed a danger, and we were forced to hold the meeting in the open area of the position outside the bunker. This time there was no shelling and I was relieved when the visit ended and we were on our way back to Baluza. On the return trip Dayan did not insist on standing and exposing his black eye patch to the Egyptian snipers across the Canal, and the visit ended without incident. His actions during the day bore testament to the man's exceptional courage, which bordered on suicidal. The problem with Dayan's behavior was that in demonstrating his own personal bravery — in a manner for which for there was no justification — he forced all the soldiers of the post to expose themselves to the same unnecessary danger. This three-week tour of duty along the Canal with my reserve battalion was especially turbulent, and the battalion and the units serving with us during the tour lost six soldiers and saw more than 10 wounded. Despite the effective protection with which the bunkers provided the soldiers, the War of Attrition claimed casualties not just from the Air Force, in its campaign against Egypt's SA-2 and SA-3 missile batteries, but from the ground forces along the Canal as well.

7

The Jordan Valley

MY FIRST TOUR OF ACTIVE RESERVE DUTY

Just a few months after the end of the Six Day War my battalion was called up for reserve duty in the Jordan Valley. It was the early days of border infiltrations and cross-border attacks, and there had still been no significant hostile activity in the region.

Immediately after the Six Day War Palestinians from Jordan began to cross the Jordan River back into the territory we now held. Initially, these were people who had fled during the war and were trying to return home. Later, however, infiltrator groups began working to send armed fighters across the border in an effort to build resistance cells in the West Bank. IDF policy was to prevent these border crossings and to attempt to seal the border as hermetically as possible. Implementation of this policy was assigned to IDF Central Command and its Jordan Valley Brigade.

In the spring of 1968 Colonel Rafael Eitan became the first commander of the Valley Brigade, and I came to visit him at brigade headquarters at the military base at El-Jiftlik. I asked Eitan where the Palestinians tended to cross the Jordan River, and his immediate response was that they crossed over everywhere. I continued on to the Jericho police station, where the headquarters of the battalion holding the southern part of the Jordan Valley was located. Elisha Shalem, my friend from the 890th battalion and the reprisal operations of the 1950s, was the sector's battalion commander on reserve duty. I asked Shalem the same questions I had asked Eitan, who directed my attention to a map of the region hanging on the wall in his office. Along the Jordan River, which now also served as the border, were a few clusters of colored pins. "What are those?" I asked.

"We've been here for three weeks," Shalem explained, pointing at the colored clusters, "and these are all the crossings we've identified during that time." He then did a quick statistical analysis for the short period and concluded that there were in fact a few preferred points of crossing along the river. The paratroops from the reserve battalion marked seven crossing points, which remained ingrained in my memory. The precision and accuracy of the information with which Shalem gave me became abundantly clear when the Valley Brigade confronted the problem during my service as its deputy commander and commander. When searching for traces of border crossings, we focused most of our attention on the crossing points identified by Shalem after just three weeks of duty in the sector. These points were also the primary focus of night ambushes. I had no doubt about the importance of thoroughly and systematically collecting intelligence information and assimilating it through operations.

MY SECOND TOUR OF ACTIVE RESERVE DUTY

At the beginning of March 1968 my battalion was again called up for reserve duty in the Jordan Valley. By this time the sector was already hot, and PLO infiltration into Israel had become a routine occurrence. The positions along the length of the Valley along the Jordan River were already built with fortifications to protect soldiers from direct fire and shelling. The Jordanian army provided the PLO with significant support by hosting them in their positions on the eastern side of the river and enabling them to observe the area before embarking on their missions. The Jordanian army also provided supportive artillery fire for infiltrating Palestinian cells that encountered Israeli interference.

During my second tour of duty in the Jordan Valley, Operations Branch Chief Weizman came to the Valley for a quick visit. He landed his light French-made Alouette helicopter at a landing pad near the Jericho police station, where I met him and took him by jeep to battalion headquarters for a short briefing. Weizman, an open and lively man, asked a few questions and then invited me to join him in his helicopter to take a look at the Valley from above.

After we landed half an hour later, Weizman finally let me into the secret: in two days time the IDF would launch a wide-scale operation in the Jordanian town of Karameh, the point of origin of most PLO operations in the region and the residence of Yasser Arafat. I drove to brigade headquarters to meet with brigade commander Eitan, who immediately agreed to integrate the 71st Battalion into the planning. For the operation itself we could use two companies from the battalion. A third company would be provided by the regular paratroop brigade, and we were also supposed to receive a company

Reporting to Rafael Eitan during the Karameh operation

of Sherman tanks from the armored battalion of the reserve brigade that was attached to the Valley Brigade. The following day we were joined at the Jericho police station by Colonel Shmuel Gorodish (who later changed his name to the Hebrew Gonen), commander of the 7th Armored Brigade, along with his company commanders and his brigade staff, to perform reconnaissance on the Jordanian territory where the 7th Brigade was supposed to operate. We ascended to the position that controlled the Allenby Bridge, and I told them everything I knew about the Jordanian positions along the border itself and deeper inside Jordan.

The day before the operation I was called to brigade headquarters at the Jiftlik military base, where brigade commander Eitan presented us with a short briefing that outlined, among other things, the task of the 71st Battalion: to conquer the Jordanian fort at the Damiya Bridge, and to hold it while controlling the road to the north with fire power in order to cut off access to the town of Karameh. The regular paratroop brigade and Sayeret Matkal were charged with the operation within the town itself and sealing off of all escape routes.

I assembled the Operations Branch officer and his men and the commander of the 155 mm gunnery battalion to plan the artillery support for the brigade's operation. Eitan's plan called for the tank battalion to cross the Jordan River over the bridge, to advance south of the Adam Bridge position, and to climb up to the flatland in order to achieve control of the road to Karameh with tank fire. My battalion consisted of three paratroop companies, including a regular company under the command of Nachum Alon, a tank company under the command of Tuvia Leshem, deputy commander of the tank battalion, a unit of SS-11 anti-tank missiles, and an additional platoon-size force under the command of Captain Gadi Manela. When we finished working, we were all relieved to have a coordinated brigade-wide plan.

According to Brigadier General Menachem Aviram, commander of the armored reserves brigade, our plan was "an insane plan that succeeded." It called for crossing the Adam Bridge under the cover of darkness just before dawn. Support would be provided by the entire 155 mm artillery battalion, which would carry out heavy shelling of the Jordanian position, and the anti-tank missile section, which would target the Jordanian tanks inside. The plan then called for following the main road that passed through the position. From there, we would attack the position from the rear, mop up the trenches, and destroy the tanks inside, in an east to west movement.

The operation as a whole began before dawn and the Sherman tanks sunk in the mud of the wet Jordanian agricultural fields. As a result, the burden fell on us. We advanced under the cover of heavy shelling, aided by our intimate familiarity with the plan for covering artillery fire we had devised before the operation. This wild, courageous, and dangerous maneuver was successful and quickly brought us to the other side of the position without injury.

However, in the heat of battle Deputy Battalion Commander Tuvia Leshem failed to stop as planned when we reached the position in order to turn around and mop it up. Instead, the tank company continued to race ahead toward the flatland. In the meantime the sun rose and the Sherman tanks were easy prey for the Jordanian M-48 Patton tanks. One after another five of our tanks were hit and went up in flames. I sent Gadi Manela and his men in their half-tracks to extract the soldiers from their burning tanks, as Jordanian tank shells flew overheard. Manela worked calmly and with great determination under fire, pulling the men out of harm's way and transporting them to the medical evacuation station. For this action, Manela was awarded the Medal of Courage.

In the meantime we took over the position, losing Yitzhak Penso, who was killed, and company commander Asa Kadmoni who was wounded. The position was quiet, but Jordanian mortar and cannon artillery fire continued to rain down upon us during the day. Through-out the morning, I travelled in my two half-tracks, one for my staff and the other for communications and artillery support. In some cases, a deafening "Long Tom" shell would fall at a location just after we left.

We also had to supervise the Engineering Corps' construction of the "cage bridge," which was meant to facilitate the crossing of our Centurion tanks, for which the Adam Bridge was too narrow. The Jordanians had a well camouflaged artillery observation officer, and each time the engineering soldiers tried to continue building the bridge they were pushed back by another barrage of artillery fire.

Another task was handling evacuation of the wounded. For this purpose we chose a relatively protected area east of the Jordan River, where the brigade's medical pick up point was located, and where helicopters could land to evacuate the wounded. I was relieved when all the wounded were evacuated, but, as far as I was concerned, the long day of fighting ended only after we managed to use the Centurion tanks of the 7th Armored Brigade to drag our burned-out Sherman tanks back into Israeli territory, and after the last soldier had returned to Israeli soil.

ERETZ HAMIRDAFIM ("MANHUNT LAND")

A considerable mystique developed in Israel at the time around Eretz Hemirdafim, the fight against infiltrators from Jordan in the dry gullies and wadis along the Jordan Valley in the years after the Six Day War. Two explanations come to mind. The most important one seems to be the failure of the initial phase of manhunts and the high price we paid for this failure with the lives of senior commanders. Another reason appears to have been the ability of Rehavam Ze'evi, OC Central Command, to orchestrate an effective PR campaign that kept the manhunts, the Jordan Valley, the Central Command, and its OC in the headlines.

Valley Brigade Commander Colonel Arik Regev, who had replaced Colonel Rafael Eitan, was killed during "the Jiftlik Manhunt" on July 26, 1968 during a battle with infiltrators who had taken cover in the caves of Wadi Milha, not far from Valley Brigade headquarters.

Captain Gadi Manela, Regev's operations officer, was killed by his brigade commander's side while charging their position. After the deaths of Regev and Manela, Israeli tanks were ordered to fire on the caves, killing the infiltrators hiding inside. At the time the lessons of the Jiftlik manhunt were not properly internalized, and we continued to pay a high price in the loss of senior commanders.

Lieutenant Colonel Moshe Stempel, Colonel Motta Gur's deputy in the 55th Paratroop Brigade that fought in Jerusalem during the Six Day War, was killed during a manhunt in Wadi Shubash on September 19, 1968. Reconnaissance battalion commander Lieutenant Colonel Zvi Ofer was killed during a manhunt in Wadi Kelt in December 1968. The March 11, 1969 "cave manhunt" near the village of Majdal Bani Fadil took the lives of Major Hanan Samson of Kibbutz Mizra, company commander in the 28th Paratroop Reserve Battalion, Major Yossi Kaplan, the Valley Brigade's Operations Branch officer, and Sergeant Boaz Sasson. Eventually, the Central Command and the Valley Brigade learned their lesson, and manhunts gradually assumed the form of an orderly, well planned, and well-coordinated systematic procedure. Colonel Yehuda Reshef was assigned to replace Arik Regev as commander of the Valley Brigade.

After the heavy losses sustained during those early efforts, Colonel Yehuda Reshef and his deputy Lt. Colonel Moshe Levi brought order and precision to the Valley Brigade's manhunt procedures. By the time I joined the Valley Brigade as deputy commander under Levi, who was promoted to command the brigade, manhunt procedures were organized, efficient, and quite impressive. Levi, known in the army as Moshe-and-a-half because he was so tall, went on to become the army's CGS. He understood that such a complex operation had to be orderly and systematic.

The first stage of a manhunt always involved the discovery of infiltrators' tracks on the border fence. The fence was lined by a dirt road that was cleared every evening by a command-car dragging a roll of barbed wire to make it easy to find footprints in the pale dusty surface. It was patrolled each morning to see whether someone had crossed the border. The Bedouin trackers that took part in the morning patrols identified signs of incursions and footprints of infiltrators, and used them to accurately track the route they were taking toward their targets in the West Bank. The Bedouin trackers were the spearhead of the tracking effort, and the forces of the Haruv Battalion, the reconnaissance battalion in the Valley, made extensive use of them whenever necessary.

The most interesting and challenging task of the Valley Brigade commander was undoubtedly the job of directing manhunts. It was the brigade commander who coordinated all the various forces involved of the effort. He knew where each force was at all times and decided when to transfer forces from one search area to another while receiving reports about the precise status and location of the tracking effort. Close knowledge of the topography of the region was extremely important, as many decisions were based on it almost instinctively, as well as on past experience with infiltrations and integration of this knowledge with the updated information provided by the searching forces.

BACK TO THE JORDAN VALLEY AS DEPUTY COMMANDER OF THE VALLEY BRIGADE

At the request of OC Central Command Ze'evi, supported by Operations Branch Chief Weizman, I decided to leave Branch 2 of the Weapons Development Department to accept an assignment as deputy commander of the Jordan Valley Brigade. Ze'evi promised me that I would be the next brigade commander, replacing Moshe Levi who had already held the position for close to a year. The prospect of promotion certainly played a role in my decision to accept the offer, as did my sense of duty, in light of the increasing challenges posed by the War of Attrition and my feeling that my service with the battalion was simply not enough.

When I arrived to the Valley in early November 1969, the brigade was engaged in a diverse range of activities, including the defense of positions against shelling by the Jordanian army, which made no effort to hide their support for the infiltrators. Another aspect was in the Dead Sea when it became clear that one route of infiltration was across the salt lake by means of rubber rafts.

Under the management of Ori Even-Tov, Israel Aerospace Industries' Factory B (later known as Mabat) assumed responsibility for developing a series of routine security measures. An ingenious technician by the name of Pini Dagan developed a turret of sorts that was mounted on a command car. The device, which integrated an infrared floodlight and a Belgian machine gun, was officially known as the "Marbel," but everyone referred to it as "Dagan," after the man who developed it. The Haruv Battalion specialized in using this weapon.

The war of the positions was an issue in itself. It involved an ongoing process of building and fortifying positions under the direction of the Valley Brigade. The brigade construction officer worked with contractors to plan and improve the defenses and the quality of life of the soldiers in the forts. Battalions, mostly of reservists, passed through the Valley like trains through a station, and this placed a heavy burden on the brigade commander. At times the region was assigned regular service battalions which were a pleasure to work with, as opposed to the reserve battalions, which were not always cohesive and quite often suffered from a high rate of turnover. Briefing and cultivating reserve battalions required especial intensive efforts. The positions themselves were under direct fire from across the river and also from the Jordanian artillery. Light weapons attacks were also carried out by Palestinian cells who would cross the river and take up positions from which it was comfortable to fire on our positions in the middle of the night. The Valley Brigade had to come up with some way to counter this threat, and the ensuing game of cat and mouse with the infiltrators was a permanent aspect of our work.

When I came to the Jordan Valley I was already a paratroop battalion commander with two tours of active reserve duty along the front lines in the Valley under my belt. I also had other strengths, including my ideas about the integration of technology, my connections to the world of research and development, and my contacts in the Israeli defense industry and the General Staff 's Weapons Development Department. I embarked upon the assignment determined to maximize the use of technology on the unique battlefield presented by the Valley. I knew which defense companies would lend us weapons that were still being developed so we could test them in the field. As a result we were able to arm ourselves with a variety of lethal devices, such as explosive rods, mortar shells for being booby-trapping, electronic activation systems, Claymore anti-personnel landmines that were developed in the United States for the Vietnam War, and many other weapons. In essence, it was a strategy based on a loose collection of countermeasures against the infiltrators' methods, which were in the constant process of changing, expanding, and growing increasingly technologically advanced. The brigade's engineering staff and, to some extent, its munitions personnel, were responsible for work in this area.

I dived into my work as deputy brigade commander with intense energy, not limiting myself to the organizational and logistical aspects of the brigade, as I knew I had been designated to replace Moshe Levi as its commander within a few months. It was concrete preparation for my imminent move into the position of commander.

The Dead Sea sector was unique and differed in many ways from the rest of the Jordan Valley. Our analysis of the infiltrators' mode of operation in the Dead Sea focused on three basic elements: the point of origin of each cell, the intended target, and the route linking the two locations. In the Dead Sea area the infiltrators' targets were concentrations of Bedouin in the Judean Desert and their points of origin were the water-filled and vegetation rich riverbeds on the eastern side of the Sea, which gave them enough cover to hide for a few days while they got organized. To stop them from making the crossings, we started sending teams to these staging areas, either at night in rubber rafts or during the day in helicopters.

I never lost sight of the fact that I would soon assume command of the brigade, and my most important task from this perspective was finding a suitable candidate to serve as my deputy and operations branch officer. For operations I set my sites on Uzi Eilat of Kibbutz Beit Hashita, who was pleased by the offer and who took a leave of absence from the kibbutz to take the job.

Every aspect of operations in the Valley involved contending with the infiltrators, who often displayed creativity and resourcefulness. Concern for the security of the soldiers in positions along the front lines was reflected in fortifications against attacks from flat-trajectory weapons and from Jordanian artillery shelling. We also needed to gauge the exact distances of the Jordanian positions on the eastern bank of the Jordan River. I managed to borrow one of the two Dutch-made laser devices owned by the Weapons Development Department, and I used it to convince the Armored Corps, including Israel Tal, its commander at the time, that when it came to measuring distance, lasers were better than gunners. The laboratory's laser device, which quickly came to be in high demand, was passed from position to position and ultimately provided us with a precise map of distances reflecting the vital needs of each position. To reinforce our efforts to protect the positions and their surrounding areas, we assembled all the weapons that the defense establishment was developing at the time, as well as knowledge on modern booby-trapping tactics and remote activation systems.

It was clear to me by this point that the war we were engaged in was a war of minds, and I knew that, in this sense, the main burden in the campaign was shouldered by our extremely capable brigade Engineering Officer Captain Tzvika Mor. One night we heard a blast from one of the fort's booby-trap mechanisms. The next afternoon a team led by Engineering Officer Mor and the southern deputy battalion commander made preparations to go into the field. Fortunately, they began checking the system from east to west, which enabled them to discover a trap. This time, the idea was truly diabolical: our own stake mines had been booby trapped and connected to an activation mechanism located on the eastern side of the Jordan River. Beside our explosive devices, which appeared to be in proper working order, lay a dummy that looked like an infiltrator who had been killed in action, with some rolled up wire and a loose explosive shell by his side. The dummy and the ground beside it had been splattered with red paint to increase the verisimilitude. Gideon, the deputy battalion commander, found the soap dish that served as the switch, and Mor clipped the copper wires leading across the river. The charges were later detonated.

One of the difficulties consistently faced by the IDF was the constant turnover of reserve units without the necessary skills and knowledge in an arena where even the morning patrols required training and experience. This turnover meant that by the time a battalion learned operating procedures and principles along the front line, it was rotated out and replaced with another battalion. In some cases, usually in the aftermath of particularly troubling incidents, we were allocated light aircraft that flew over the patrol road before the patrol reached the area. We also tried to counter the remote radio-transmitted detonation of booby traps from across the Jordan River by using light aircraft flying overhead to make our own transmissions early in the morning, prior to the ground patrol.

During my efforts to prepare the brigade for the day I would assume command and to find a suitable deputy, I started eyeing Lieutenant Colonel Ofer Ben-David for the position. At that time, Ben-David, a native of Kibbutz Kfar Giladi, who was a few years older than me, was serving as the Hebron district commander. To me, the short, sturdy, intelligent man with a Hashomer-style mustache seemed like a quick learner and right for the position. Something about him was reminiscent of the rugged Galilee — rough and irritating at times, but loyal and down to earth. I knew we would work well together.

MOSHE-AND-A-HALF 'S LAST MANHUNT

As deputy brigade commander I was permitted to join the commander on manhunts only after ensuring the necessary logistical support. This included preparing additional forces and dispatching them on search missions, acquiring more helicopters if necessary and making sure that water, cold juice, and sandwiches were prepared and delivered to the forces engaged in the search, to prevent them from dehydrating in the extreme heat and scorching sun of the Jordan Valley.

We studied every manhunt carefully and learned all we could from them. Still, there was no way to guarantee that neither mishap nor injury would occur since no two manhunts were identical. A good example began on a Friday morning with discovery of indications of border penetration, just like most others. The search was run in a routine manner but by the end of the day we had not found the infiltrators. The trackers insisted that trails led close to the populated Palestinian area on the mountain ridge, and in accordance with standard procedure we placed ambushes in the locations where tracks had last been identified. The mission was assigned to regular forces from the Paratroop Brigade. The Jewish Sabbath was about to begin, and Brigade Commander Moshe Levi was scheduled to go home on leave to Kibbutz Beit Alfa. I was left to recall all the forces that had taken part in the search, make sure that everything was returned safely to its proper place, and assume the post of commander for the duration of the Sabbath.

It was a quiet night in the Jordan Valley, but not far from the mountain ridge a paratroop ambush force engaged a cell of infiltrators in a firefight in which two soldiers were killed. The next morning at first light I surveyed the area from above in a helicopter with the commander of the trackers unit in the Valley. When we reached the site of the incident it was clear that the skirmish had been with the cell we were looking for. The infiltrators had backtracked, and their path now led eastward. I immediately issued an order by radio resuming the manhunt, and within no time the brigade's well-oiled manhunt mechanism was back in operation. When I informed the brigade commander that the pursuit was back in motion, he told me that he would return to the base later, and requested that I should not wait for him and that I run the manhunt myself. At 1:30 p.m. Levi arrived and joined our forces (the OC Central Command had been with us for a few hours). More than an hour later, when I was convinced that Levi had been sufficiently brought up to speed on the manhunt, I turned command over to him and reverted to the position of deputy. We had been walking along the upper bank of a gorge for a short time when we spotted the cell moving quickly along the floor of the deep riverbed. After opening fire on the cell below us, we suddenly came under automatic light-weapon fire from the opposite side of the gorge. Bullets from the two long bursts of gunfire hit Levi in the thigh; they also struck the arm of the Haruv Battalion's operations officer, who was with us as well as our radio man. I bandaged the radio man and took his radio in order to continue running the manhunt.

All of a sudden, I heard Ze'evi calling my name: "Uzi!" he screamed, "Come quick! Moshe's sliding down!" I ran over to where the tall heavy wounded man was slipping down to the gorge, and it took all our strength to drag him to a goat trail where we could lay him down. I ran the rest of the manhunt until its conclusion while tending to the wounded, issuing orders to the forward Haruv team, and fearing that additional bursts could be fired at us at any moment. The cell had been a small but resourceful fighting unit. Levi and the two other wounded men were carried up the hill on stretchers, and the members of the cell at the bottom of the gorge were killed. We had not, however, managed to capture whoever it was that had fired on us from across the gorge.

I assembled the troops, who were dispersed throughout the area, and ordered that a network of ambushes be set up to capture the shooter. I walked up to the flat area where the helicopters had landed and was about to fly back to brigade headquarters when OC Ze'evi stopped me. "Uzi," he said, "from now on, you are the brigade commander." At the moment, I was too busy tying up the loose ends of the manhunt to appreciate what had just happened. It was only when I got back to brigade headquarters that it hit me that I was now alone at the top.

As a commander Moshe Levi symbolized, more than anything else, order and a systematic, methodical approach. His behavior and leadership style reflected a concern for the major and minor details of brigade operations, as well as caution and concern for preserving human life. Ironically, it was Levi's lot to be wounded during a manhunt and to finish his tenure as brigade commander being evacuated by stretcher on a helicopter. During my tenure as brigade commander the border crossings continued, as did the manhunts. As luck had it, and as a result of the experience and insight we acquired, we suffered no more casualties. Based on the lessons we learned from the treacherous manhunts in the Jordan Valley, the brigade commander was no longer part of the forward force. This rule applied to senior members of the brigade staff as well.

During one of the manhunts I was accompanied by OC Ze'evi and his deputy chief Yona Efrat. "Why don't you move ahead a bit?" they nudged. "That way you can get closer to the forward team and the trackers."

My response was clear and decisive and issued with the authority of a commander in the field: "I am exactly where I need to be," I told them, "and you're not to move even an inch ahead of me." This time, I was pleased to see, my commanders were more disciplined.

During the manhunts we learned an interesting lesson about the work of the trackers. During most of a manhunt it was the trackers who led us on the search for the trail. However, at a certain point they would slow down and allow the Haruv Battalion's forward team to move ahead of them. This was a sign that we were getting close to the infiltrators' hiding place. The instincts of our Bedouin trackers during manhunts were almost never wrong, and this enabled us to cautiously prepare for their final and decisive stages.

KING OF THE VALLEY

After the drama of the manhunt during which Brigade Commander Levi was wounded and I was appointed brigade commander, there was no time to celebrate my appointment. It took a number of weeks for my deputy-designate Ofer Ben-David to tie up all the loose ends as military governor of Hebron and to join me in the Valley. For me, the move from deputy commander to commander felt natural. Nonetheless, I was still struck by the heavy burden of overall responsibility and the sense of isolation that came with the job. Infiltrations continued, forts were fired upon, and our ambushes continued to result in firefights with penetrating infiltrator cells. Our operations across the border in the Jordanian section of the Jordan Valley and the Dead Sea also continued, as did the manhunts.

The reserve soldiers passed through the battalion like passengers through a train station; maintaining a relationship with them was both challenging and important. Every month I had to get to know the new men who had just started their reserve duty in the Valley. I found that being able to call them by name and to demonstrate that I knew something about their civilian life resulted in a special connection and generated exceptional motivation.

I will never forget the experience of going down to the brigade's war room on nights when offensive infiltrator operations were taking place along the border, which was virtually a routine occurrence. The ring of a telephone in the middle of the night, and the sound of the voice on the other end reporting that "the position is under fire" or "the ambush near such and such location has been engaged and is exchanging fire," was as startling as a snake bite and made my heart skip a beat. After a frantic race down the stairs to the war room, the picture would start to become clearer with the help of a battery of telephones and military radios. The tension was broken with an endless stream of coffee and thick cheese sandwiches. Because of those late night meals I weighed 100 kg (220 lb) by the time I completed my tenure as commander of the Jordan Valley Brigade. I have fond memories of the special operations carried out by Sayeret Matkal or special teams of the Haruv Battalion that involved crossing the Jordanian border. These operations were carried out at night and were meticulously planned down to the smallest detail. They were closely monitored by brigade command from the moment they began until the soldiers' safe return, and an emergency plan was always ready in case we needed to extract the force.

The never-ending battle of minds between us and the enemy, in which we emphasized the integration of technology in all possible situations, was a central component of Valley Brigade operations. An important principle was recognition of the operational and technical capabilities of our enemy. It was almost impossible to break routine during our operations along the front line — with its permanent positions, its roads on which our vehicles drove each day, and the regular work required for maintaining a coordinated system. It was clear to us that the enemy we faced was a combination of infiltrators... learly irregular force with a propensity to improvise — and the professional, well-trained standing army of the Kingdom of Jordan.

Our insights on the enemy's modes of operation against our positions meant we often had a better grasp on potential threats than Central Command. This was well illustrated by a visit paid by OC Ze'evi to the Hadas position. Ze'evi arrived for a quick visit to the position, which was located in brigade's central sector, with his deputy Yonah Efrat the day after a major night-time skirmish that had taken place nearby. I joined Ze'evi and Efrat in their Alouette helicopter, flown by Danny Hamitzer. I attempted to convince the OC to land far from the position and to drive the remaining distance, but to no avail. Instead, the pilot set the helicopter down next to the position in terrain that was visible to the Jordanians across the border.

We entered the position and heard a briefing on the events of the previous night. Ten minutes later, we left the fort and walked toward the helicopter. Just after Hamitzer had taken his seat by the controls, we heard a shell fall nearby, followed by others. We made a dash for the helicopter and scrambled into our seats, but despite Hamitzer's efforts to start the Alouette, the engine did little more than sputter. In the meantime the Jordanians continued their artillery range-finding and the shells began to fall increasingly closer to our location. It took an effort to convince my commanders and the pilot to abandon the helicopter and take cover while we still had the chance. We ran about 30 meters and took cover in a dip in the ground that was not deep but that nonetheless did the job. The moment we got to cover, out of breath and panting, a shell scored a direct hit on the helicopter, which burst into flames. I restrained myself from telling Ze'evi "I told you so." More than anything, I was angry with myself for not being sufficiently insistent and for failing to convince him of the logic of landing beyond the range of the Jordanian artillery.

The IDF had two fronts during the War of Attrition, one in Southern Command along the Suez Canal and the other in Central Command along the Jordan River and the Dead Sea. The Jordan Valley front was not only the interest of the Central Command and its OC but of the General Staff as well. CGS Haim Bar-Lev made sure to personally congratulate Valley Brigade commanders by phone after a successful manhunt, and sometimes even dragged the General Staff with him to visit the Jordan Valley.

OC Ze'evi made effective use of the General Staff 's visits to convince it of his need for additional funds and resources, and I once had a heated discussion with Ze'evi on this very point. It began when I proposed dismantling three positions along the border and giving up the tank company that was permanently stationed in the Valley, as well as the 155 mm gunnery battalion. My recommendation was based on data regarding operational activity and the frequency with which we actually made use of tanks and artillery, and on the fact that our coverage of the sector would remain sufficient even with fewer positions. Ze'evi opposed my recommendation, and justified his position by saying: "What will they say about us at the General Staff?" I was convinced that we could make the cuts, and I told Ze'evi that as the commander in the field I would assume responsibility for them. After many weeks of deliberations and discussions, the OC finally acquiesced and we made the cuts. As I expected they had no negative ramifications.

There was an enormous discrepancy between the realities on Israel's borders along the Suez Canal in the south and in the Jordan Valley in the center of the country on the one hand, and the relaxed atmosphere on the home front on the other hand. Some people today still look back longingly to a time when wars were fought only on the front lines, leaving civilian populations intact.

Ever since our return from the US, Naomi and I dreamed of owning a detached house. On the eve of the Six Day War construction was finished of our house in Savyon, but we did not move in until after the war. During the post-war period I served in the Jordan Valley. Receiving leave every second weekend was a valuable gift for the family, but it also presented a profound fortnightly culture shock. On Friday afternoons the Savyon country club was full of people, and the sound of tennis balls bouncing off of racquets echoed throughout the neighborhood. The pool was full of swimmers of all ages, and the green lawns, so different from the stark dry and grey terrain of the Jordan Valley, were covered with relaxed people sitting in comfortable reclining chairs engaged in pleasant conversation. The sound of background music piped in through speakers concealed within shady trees was a weird counterpoint to the explosions of the Valley and the short spurts of harsh metallic voices on army radios. The tranquil mood seemed foreign and surreal. It forced me to get used to the fact that life was very different outside the pressurized atmosphere of the Jordan Valley. I was both drawn to the peace and quiet of the relaxing background music and at the same time repulsed by it. And yet if it were possible, I would still rather return to things as they were then: when wars were fought along the borders, far from the calm and tranquility of the civilian home-front.

BLACK SEPTEMBER — THE CALM AFTER THE STORM

Then things suddenly went quiet in the Valley. The reason was the war that King Hussein waged against Yasser Arafat and the PLO in September 1970, which has gone down in history as "Black September". This name was also later adopted by a radical terrorist wing of the PLO responsible, among other things, for the murder of eleven Israeli athletes at the 1972 Munich Olympics.

A few weeks after the Jordanian offensive against the PLO we noticed a decline in the scope of infiltrator operations in the Valley. We knew nothing about the failed September 1 attempt to assassinate King Hussein, which marked an important turning point in the King's approach toward the Palestinian groups. Like the rest of the world, we looked on as three passenger planes were hijacked and forced to land in Jordan by members of the Popular Front for the Liberation of Palestine and their passengers taken hostage. The violence continued on September 18, 1970, when hundreds of tanks of the Syrian armored forces crossed the border with Jordan in support of the Palestinians in their war against the Jordanian army, posing a significant threat to the Jordanian regime. From the Jordan Valley we looked on as large IDF forces were moved up to northern Israel at the request of the US, in an effort to deter the Syrians from conquering the whole of Jordan.

The more pressure the Jordanians put on the Palestinian groups, the more it eased our burden in the Valley. The major reason for the decrease in infiltrations was that the Jordanian army no longer assisted the infiltrator groups who were now being pursued by the Jordanians. When springtime arrived and the water-level in the Jordan River subsided, we witnessed surreal scenes of PLO members crossing the Jordan with their hands in the air, surrendering to Israeli forces. I regarded it as my responsibility to issue a special order to all units in the Valley to refrain from opening fire, to take the Palestinians into custody (albeit with great caution), and to transfer them to IDF intelligence for processing. None of these developments caused us to reduce our readiness or our alert level, or to ease up on drills relevant to our war against the infiltrators, which had been developed over the past few years at the cost of the lives of so many soldiers and commanders. But somewhere deep in my heart, I began to ask myself whether there was anything left for me to do in the Valley.

8

From the Weapons Development Department to the R&D Unit

A CALL FROM BAR-LEV TO RETURN TO THE WEAPONS DEVELOPMENT DEPARTMENT

On Thursday June 10, 1970, exactly three years after the end of the Six Day War, my secretary informed me that CGS Chaim Bar-Lev wanted to speak with me. My curiosity piqued during the few seconds it took her to put the call through, as there had been no infiltration across the border or across Jordan River for weeks now. He got straight to the point in his typically soft and quiet tone and said that I was being recalled by the General Staff to take over the Weapons Development Department of the Operations Branch.

The news was surprising and created a quandary. On the one hand, I had done much to improve the brigade that was the spearhead of the Central Command. On the other hand, I understood that it was appropriate for me now to direct the Weapons Development Department, where I had previously served as a branch director. The new calm on the Jordanian border made this decision easier.

Nonetheless, it was no easy matter to leave the Valley so suddenly and to get used to the idea that the dust, the heat, the manhunts, and the operations were things of the past. As I made the move, I felt the need to understand what had taken place in the Weapons Development Department and why the CGS needed me to take on the job so urgently. I quickly learned that the reason was a crisis in confidence between Weapons Development Department Director Colonel Ben Bar-On and Operations Branch Chief David Elazar.

THE IDF'S ASSAULT RIFLE

The unbridgeable difference of opinion between Bar-On and Elazar surrounded the decision to prefer the assault rifle developed by Israel Blashnikov of IMI over the rifle developed by Uzi Gal as the standard weapon for IDF infantry. This decision went against the recommendations of the Munitions Corps and the Operations Branch's Weapons Development Department. With great integrity and courage, Weapons Development Department Director Ben Bar-On fought for his position, which was based on the performance of the two models during the competition. Unfortunately, his struggle was in vain. I was sorry about the command decision and about the injustice suffered by Bar-On, my former commander, who was forced to end his service in the IDF on such an unpleasant note. During his struggle over the issue, Bar-On set a standard of behavior that has guided many officers in research and development administration over the years. His struggle taught us to fight for what you believe in if you are convinced that you are right, and not to fear those higher up in the chain of command.

I had barely managed to remove my dusty red paratrooper boots and clear my nose of the distinctive smell of the vegetation that grew along the winding, slow Jordan River, when I returned to a pile of papers, a steady flow of meetings and discussions, and a world of technology and long-term decision making.

Returning to the General Staff as a former combat brigade commander with a first-hand understanding of the meaning of war boosted both my confidence and my authority in the weapons development arena. There were no 100 days of grace, or even a week for that matter. My experience as director of Branch 2 masked the suddenness with which I took over the department. The list of issues that needed attention forced me to hit the ground running. It was imperative to begin dealing with the major issues as soon as possible, and one of these issues was the fire-control systems for tanks. Major General Israel Tal had already stepped down from command of the Armored Corps to make way for Major General Avraham Adan. Tal established the Tank Program Administration, which would later start work on the development of a new Israeli tank known as the Merkava.

"OUT OF THE NORTH EVIL WILL COME" (JEREMIAH 1:14)

The events of September 1970 in Jordan and Yasser Arafat's relocation to Lebanon with his associates refocused our attention on Israel's northern border. Armed with almost two years of experience as deputy commander and commander of the Valley Brigade, I was able to see things from both a technological and operational perspective. Major General Yitzhak Hofi was OC Northern Command, and I recommended that we set up a team of regular army officers and reserve officers with a variety of skills to carry out a survey and to propose a comprehensive defense system for the northern border. Hofi gladly agreed and even assigned liaisons from the Northern Command to assist with coordination and the necessary data. After a few months of intense work we formulated a concept and made a plan based on a technologically advanced warning fence supported by larger and smaller radars at various locations. The plan also called for the integration of day and night optical systems, which were meant to ensure full coverage of the entire border. The team calculated the costs, came up with an estimated time frame for building and installation, and submitted the entire recommendation to the Northern Command for debate and authorization. We were bitterly disappointed when Hofi announced that the plan was rejected because of its expense. Unfortunately, subsequent incidents like the 1974 hostage situation at Ma'alot and a large number of border crossings and terrorist attacks proved that Hofi had been too short-sighted to recognize what we at the Weapons Development Department saw so clearly. After learning lessons the hard and painful way, the Northern Command began investing much larger sums than what our team had initially proposed. The operational concept underlying the team's recommendations is still applicable today.

FIRE CONTROL FOR TANKS

The issue of fire-control systems for tanks had been under discussion ever since the laser distance-measuring devices of a Dutch company outperformed the best gunners of the Armored Corps. With some justification, Major General Tal was convinced that logical training and discipline of soldiers were the keys to victory. In Armored Corps training programs Tal stressed that tank gunners should learn to hit a target with the first shell during tank-to-tank battles. A competition between man and machine, some of the Armored Corps best-trained gunners versus the Dutch distance measuring-devices, took place at the Munitions Corps' testing area south of Bat Yam, with Colonel Yitzhak Yaakov and Major General Tal leading the two competing groups. Time after time the laser demonstrated its superiority over the best Armored Corps gunners, and even Tal became a believer in the laser technology. Nonetheless, this technology was still in its early phases of development and had a long way to go before it could be integrated as part of a fire-control system for a modern-day tank.

WHERE TO DEVELOP? — THE IDF VERSUS THE DEFENSE MINISTRY

Under the command of Lieutenant Colonel Simcha Maoz, the Weapons Development Department's System Analysis Branch completed a comprehensive study of the feasibility fire-control systems in tanks. Although a laser distance measuring device would certainly be an important component of such a system, even back then, in 1971, the system was also meant to use a computer for processing data and transmitting commands to the tank cannon. Simcha Maoz, Dr. Adam Shefi, and the personnel of Branch 2 proved that the fire-control system would significantly improve the chances of hitting a target with the first shell. The Weapons Development Department concluded that the quality of Israel's tank fleet should be upgraded for both military and financial reasons, and decision makers within the IDF decided to buy fire-control systems for the IDF's tanks. We knew that the Americans had been working on developing such systems for a number of years, and the professional journals were full of publications regarding the development efforts of the Hughes Corporation and the six system prototypes that were already being tested by the American ground forces. We in the Weapons Development Department recommended that the IDF buy a few models from the Hughes Corporation and begin the process of assessment and preparation for armament.

This state of affairs revealed a major difference between IDF and defense ministry policies. The ministry's policy, which I understood and wholeheartedly accepted only later while serving as director of the R&D Unit, was to cultivate the technological and industrial capacities of the local defense industry. During my years as director of the R&D Unit, and later as Director of the Administration for the Development of Weapons and Technological Infrastructure (MAFAT), I came to the understanding that the best and safest way to develop the local defense industry was to entrust the development of advanced weapons systems to Israeli entities. However, during this early struggle between the IDF and the defense ministry I led the push for purchasing weapons from the Americans, while my former superior, Brigadier General Yitzhak Yaakov, now deputy chief scientist of the defense ministry, insisted that the tank fire-control system be developed by the Israeli defense industry, with the idea of assigning the primary role in the project to the Israel Aerospace Industries (IAI).

Operations Branch Chief Elazar and CGS Bar-Lev threw their full support behind our position to buy American. In the defense ministry Director-General Yeshayahu Lavi, former commander of the Communications Corps, and Tzvi Tzur, advisor to the defense minister, sided with Brigadier General Yaakov. Late June and July 1971 were filled with feverish meetings and discussions regarding whether to purchase the system from the US or to develop it in Israel. During our campaign to convince influential figures within the defense establishment we met with Major General Tal, Brigadier General Avraham Tamir, the Operations Branch assistant director for planning, and the director-general of the defense ministry. Finally, a meeting was scheduled to discuss the issue with Defense Minister Moshe Dayan on Friday July 30, 1971.

Operations Branch Chief Elazar told me that he could not attend the meeting in the minister's office, and that the CGS and I would be the IDF's only representatives. I decided to meet with the CGS on Thursday, the day before the meeting, for a relaxed discussion of the issue. I learned from his office that he was about to leave for the Tel Hashomer army base, and I waited for him outside his car. The moment it started to move, I opened the door and sat down next to him, my heart beating furiously. Bar-Lev looked at me coolly with an amused expression but did not appear to be particularly astonished. My audacity provided me with a valuable one-on-one meeting with the CGS. I spent the entire trip to and from Tel-Hashomer delivering a detailed briefing in preparation for the upcoming decisive meeting with the defense minister.

MOSHE DAYAN'S RULING

The next morning I made my way to the defense minister's office as if I was going into battle, my stomach hard and my heart racing. I knew I had done all I could to prepare for the high-level discussion, and I had no doubts about my ability to present the arguments in a persuasive manner. The meeting was attended by Defense Minister Dayan and Tzur, his advisor, Director-General Lavi, Deputy Chief Scientist Yaakov, CGS Bar-Lev, and myself. Yaakov began by presenting the defense ministry's opening arguments, and I presented the arguments of the IDF. After I finished my presentation, the CGS also backed the IDF's position, and announced that he would agree to limit the number of tanks deployed and to use the funds he saved to purchase and install the systems.

Lieutenant General Tzvi Tzur, who was typically calm and composed, was infuriated by my arguments, and I could see his face growing red with anger. Perhaps, he thought, I might convince Dayan, who might decide against the defense ministry's position. After everything was said and clarified, the defense minister began to sum up the meeting in his characteristically direct manner. With his one eye Dayan looked at Bar-Lev and me and said: I was convinced by your arguments, and I should be concluding this discussion in accordance with the position of the army. "However," he continued, "if I do that, I will have to fire these gentlemen," he said, pointing to Tzur, Yaakov, and Lavi, "and that is something I have no intention of doing..."

That was the end of the discussion, and it was clear to Bar-Lev and me that Dayan had thrown his support behind the defense ministry. Later, I learned that this was how Dayan handled situations where he had to deal with issues that did not interest him. What he really meant to say to us was: "You're all big boys — solve the problem on your own."

On the Sunday I was summoned urgently to the office of Operations Branch Chief Elazar, who told me that he and Tzur had met and were considering merging the Chief Scientist's Office with the Weapons Development Department. In such a case, he asked, would I agree to serve in the joint unit as Brigadier General Yaakov's deputy director? I told them that I saw no problem with the idea in principle, but that I would like to discuss the matter with Yaakov himself. The next day a lunch with Yitzhak Yaakov at the Harel restaurant near the Kiriya suddenly appeared on my schedule.

I then had another private meeting with Elazar to convey my affirmative response. Elazar already knew that he was about to be appointed as the IDF's next CGS, and he was pleased at the increased chances of harmonious relations between the IDF and the defense ministry. The fruit of the merger was a new entity that was to be called the R&D Unit. In hindsight there are several questions that are still hard to answer in the never ending interactions between personalities and policy. Without the understanding between Tzur and Elazar after the impasse in the meeting with the minister, would the merger between the Chief Scientist's Office and the Weapons Development Department ever have taken place? Was the understanding reached between Yaakov and me an important factor in the process? Both sides were in a problematic situation: the IDF because the defense minister ruled against it, and the defense ministry leadership because Dayan explicitly said they had erred on a professional level. These factors certainly forced Tzur and Elazar to accept that they had to find a way to prevent such confrontations in the future. By clearly indicating that he had no intention of dealing with these issues, Dayan pushed these two intelligent men towards a solution — the creation of the R&D Unit. Since then the body has changed somewhat, expanding into the Administration for the Development of Weapons and Technological Infrastructure, which is known by its Hebrew acronym, MAFAT. But the principle of soldiers and civilians working side by side, providing a bridge between IDF development projects and the defense ministry's responsibility for creating technological infrastructure and overseeing development, is still in place today.

BUILDING THE R&D UNIT — BOLDNESS AND CREATIVITY

This was the beginning of an intense period of planning and action during which we worked to quickly develop the organizational concept of the new entity while preserving the civilian–military ratio between the personnel incorporated into various sub-units. We also needed to decide on the structure of the new unit and the way it would operate. Would it consist of autonomous units with specific technological disciplines, or would it be a matrix structure organization, in which many disciplines work together to address multidisciplinary issues? We also needed to consider the way the General Staff was structured and the fact that the General Staff would in practice serve as ground forces headquarters.

The Weapons Development Department was responsible for delineating development projects, based on an understanding of the needs of the different corps of the ground forces. It was somewhat different for the Air Force, the Navy, and the Intelligence Corps, and the R&D Unit needed to make preparations to provide them with technological support and the necessary assistance in handling contractual agreements for development projects. Purchasing and development — two clearly linked areas of activity — were then in early stages of development, and we needed to create the policies and organizational structures necessary for smooth operations in both areas. Foreign relations was another area we needed to start developing, not only in order to represent the narrow interests of the Weapons Development Department, but also to extend technological cooperation for the entire defense establishment. We also began paying more attention to issues of technological infrastructure, both in terms of its relative prioritization compared to other issues and in terms of recruiting people to work on infrastructures.

Yitzhak Yaakov and I worked well together as a tightly-knit team. He was responsible for providing the experience, vision, and broad views that he had in such abundance. We needed to be sensitive about the delicate balance between the army and the defense ministry in all areas. We were open minded, and paid close attention to the positions of both sides in order to launch the vessel of the new R&D Unit on the stormy seas of the Israeli defense establishment. We also needed to address more detailed issues, such as standards and ranks, bringing in personnel from the military and civilian sectors, and external recruitment. Addressing all of these issues required the working space necessary to consolidate the Unit's offices and facilities at the same location, or as close together as possible.

The Golden Mean — Between the General Staff and the Defense Ministry The Unit was up and running in record time. Within a few weeks it was already possible to discern emerging working styles, the Unit's influence on administrative work, and its role in the decision making process.

The R&D Unit was established because of the dichotomy between the General Staff and defense ministry in the realm of research and development and was meant to prevent tensions like those that surrounded the tank fire-control system. However, even as the Unit was taking its first steps it was clear to us that, although the senior officials of the defense ministry were no longer part of the struggle, the IDF/defense ministry dichotomy had penetrated into the Unit and we often found ourselves mediating between the opposing views of the IDF and the ministry. In many cases we had to adopt a position on whether to purchase a specific weapons system or to develop it in Israel. We made such decisions with the help of a staff which was in some respects new to the world of R&D and wholly inexperienced when it came to relations between the army and the defense ministry.

David Elazar, the new CGS, chose Major General Tal as his second in command, transforming him into a key figure on the General Staff from January 1, 1972 onward. For Tal it was a return to the center of power within the IDF in comparison to his position within the defense ministry's Tank Program Administration. After concluding his tenure as commander of the Armored Corps, Tal had dedicated all of his time towards developing the Israeli Merkava tank and was naturally appointed the first director of the Tank Program Administration. The establishment of the Merkava Tank Program Administration was an important stage in the program's establishment as a permanent body within the defense ministry.

Confrontations regarding the desired traits of the new tank continued to plague the defense ministry, and Dayan was forced to hold a debate that was unprecedented in scope to decide between the differing approaches. The two-day meeting was attended by all Armored Corps commanders of the rank of lieutenant colonel and above, the generals of the General Staff, and senior commanders within the Ordnance Corps and the Quartermaster's Branch. Moshe Dayan was accompanied by his advisor Tzvi Tzur, the director-general of the Defense Ministry, and his economic advisor Professor Pinhas Zusman. The minister had the patience to listen to the long technical presentations and the heated arguments. Of all the Armored Corps officers in attendance, only one — Avraham Rotem — had the courage to oppose Tal and to support the position of corps commander Avraham Adan.

Tal, who always regarded himself as the senior authority on tanks in the IDF, succeeded in retaining his dominant position and persuaded both Bar-Lev and Elazar, who were also past commanders of the Armored Corps, to adopt his concept. I was sorry to see Adan, who was extremely honest but decidedly uncharismatic, receive such a stinging defeat. Even Amos Horev's experience, insight, and professional authority failed to withstand Tal's persuasive attack. Dayan was left with no other choice but to sum up the two days of discussions by concluding that the Merkava project would go ahead unchanged.

Major General Tal established himself quickly and effectively in his new position of Operations Branch chief. However, it soon became clear, both to him and to others, that the IDF was more complicated and less controllable than he would have liked. One example was the Air Force where Tal couldn't assert his authority. Benny Peled, who replaced Motti Hod as the commander of the Air Force, turned out to be a tough nut to crack. My relationship with Benny Peled and the rest of the Air Force command was pleasant and businesslike. I first met Peled when he was still a colonel serving as director of the

Air Force's Air Department and I was a lieutenant colonel serving as director of Branch 2. One day, we were both invited to a meeting with Operations Branch Chief Ezer Weizman on a sensitive matter that was in dispute between the Weapons Development Department and the Air Force. Peled presented the the Air Force's position in his typically fluent and confident manner. When Peled finished speaking, Weizman turned to me and asked to hear what I had to say. Calmly and quietly, I presented the arguments I had prepared, one after the other, but I was not sure if they were convincing. Weizman, himself a former Air Force commander, turned to Peled after a few moments and said: "Binyamin, the boy's right!" To his credit, Peled not only accepted Weizman's decision but also complimented me on the way I presented my arguments. It was the beginning of a long relationship based on mutual respect and admiration, which lasted until Peled's death in 2002.

It was difficult for Tal to accept us...trange new and active entity connected to the General Staff and the IDF on the one hand and the defense ministry and the defense industries on the other hand. What was difficult for Tal created difficulties for the Unit. Within the Unit we still needed to continue building sub-units while creating harmonious relations between the civilians and military personnel. We also needed to instill confidence in the professional departments, to support them, and to make sure we had selected the right people to direct them.

COOPERATION IN THE REALM OF MILITARY TECHNOLOGY

The IDF and the Israeli defense establishment were technologically much weaker than technological superpowers such as the US, France, Britain, and Germany. One way Yaakov thought up to help create programmatic responses to future technologies was to establish the Center for Technology Analysis and Forecasting. It was a brilliant move, but took a long time to bear fruit. Dr. Shmuel Bar-Zakai, who had just returned to Israel with a doctorate from the United States, managed to captivate Yaakov, who chose him to head the new center.

Tel Aviv University provided a home for the new center and Bar-Zakai was awarded the rank of Adjunct Professor. As deputy director of the R&D Unit I participated in Yaakov's working meetings with Bar-Zakai, and I was uncomfortable with the discrepancy between the topics that Yaakov wisely selected for future work and the hollow words of Bar-Zakai. Only when I replaced Yaakov as director of R&D was I able to work toward replacing Bar-Zakai. Tel Aviv University President Yuval Ne'eman and I agreed to send Baruch Raz, a young scientist from the university's teaching staff, to Boston for two years of advanced training in technological forecasting at MIT. Two years later Raz returned, replaced Bar-Zakai, and focused the center, which still exists today, on a new path.

We needed to find new ways to close the technological gaps between Israel and the superpowers. In our favor we had the cumulative experience of two wars against Soviet weapons systems: The Kadesh Operation of 1956 and the Six Day War of 1967. This experience and the weapons systems that we captured attracted the Western countries with which we enjoyed good relations and served as a foundation for defense cooperation. The Western countries' defense industries also went to great lengths to learn as much as they could about Soviet technology.

After the Six Day War the IDF was perceived as an impressive and victorious army, a factor that helped create increasingly close relationships between Israel's military establishment and some Western countries. However, the Six Day War also had the opposite effect of alienating the IDF and distancing it from some of the Western powers, primarily for political reasons. This was why the British halted cooperation with us on development of their Chieftain tank, forcing Israel to embark upon independent development of our own Merkava tank. The British development project had benefited from use of the desert terrain of the Negev as one giant testing area, as well as the extraordinary assistance of IDF Armored Corps and Ordnance Corps personnel under the leadership of Israel Tal, then commander of the Armored Corps, who regarded it as a project of the utmost importance. The Israeli role in the project was based on a British–Israeli contract for the provision of Chieftain Tanks, which were scheduled to enter service in Britain in 1967. The contract with Israel was annulled in 1969, and the British marketed the tank, which was resistant to dust and sand as a result of its development in the Negev, to Iran, Kuwait, Oman, and Jordan.

For us, the stinging British decision to sever ties military technological ties with Israel was a slap in the face. It taught us that we could not always count on continuity in military relations, especially when political considerations had the potential to suddenly halt processes that were already under way.

After the Six Day War, France under President Charles de Gaulle also made a 180-degree about-face in its relations with Israel, putting an end to the golden age of French–Israeli defense cooperation. The severance of defense ties with Britain and France — the two major industrial powers in Europe — created a situation in which we found ourselves pushed toward the United States. As a result Israeli—American cooperation in defense related R&D continued to intensify. Here too the curiosity and interest of the armies in question were important, as were political considerations and decisions.

We had much to learn from the Americans, and in the early 1970s we could base our long-term plans for the future according to what we saw the Americans doing in the present. During my first days as director of the R&D Unit we commissioned the services of a small consulting firm staffed by former employees of Israel Aerospace Industries (IAI). It was headed by Professor Moshe Arens, and the task we assigned it was to formulate a concrete program for Israeli research and development. Arens's work resulted in a well organized two-volume technological engineering program based primarily on what we could learn from the Americans in openly published sources. This was the beginning of Israel's independent technological path, which bore fruit only after years of work and investment in Israel's national laboratories and defense companies.

Our relationship with the Americans continued to grow closer, and we were convinced that the R&D Unit should have a representative in Washington. Lieutenant Colonel Yaakov Granot, an Ordnance Corps officer who was assigned to my branch of the Weapons Development Department back when I was director of Branch 2, was chosen for the position.

Before the Six Day War we had a formal framework for cooperation with the Pentagon in the area of defenses against border infiltration. We decided not to establish a new cooperative framework but rather to add appendices to the existing agreement. In this way, stage after stage, areas that we regarded as important for maintaining a military technological dialogue were added to the agreement. Every new sub-framework was assigned American and Israeli representatives from the relevant corps of the military — the Air Force, the Navy, and the ground forces. We encouraged direct contacts between the American and Israeli officers responsible for the various issues, and we quickly realized that these frameworks were extremely strong. The privilege of travelling abroad to meet interesting counterparts, to gain new insights, and to acquire assistance in weapons development, emerged as an attractive perk that the R&D Unit could offer military officers.

Although we scaled back our contacts with Britain and France as a result of political decisions our relationship with Germany took a different course. Over the years we had developed a working routine of meetings, military dialogues, and visits to German defense industries. A warm and open relationship continued to develop with the MBB Company thanks to Mr. Bölkow, its owner, and Dr. Held, the director of its development laboratories. As mentioned, this relationship dated back to the visit of these two men to the Sinai Peninsula after the Six Day War. These international relationships opened before us a world of warheads and shaped and capped charges. The IDF's Operations

Branch chief frequently headed our delegation to the German–Israeli dialogue meetings, and the Germans also made sure to send senior generals to participate in the dialogue. When the Merkava tank went from the stage of drafting and analysis of the many different design possibilities to the purchase of critical sub-systems like the motor, the ignition and caterpillar track system, hydraulics, etc., the Germans were open and supportive.

Over the years I developed a warm personal relationship with Peter Runge, the pivotal German Defense Ministry official in charge of technology and purchasing. Peter, with his booming voice and huge thirst for beer, instilled fear among both Israelis and Germans, but I found my way into his good graces and was frequently sent by our people to set the record straight with him.

YITZHAK YAAKOV'S PERMANENT REPLACEMENT

After the R&D Unit had been in operation for one year, we felt that the new entity had effectively established itself within the IDF and the ministry. It was unclear how long Yaakov would want to retain his position as director, and it was important for me at that point to be promoted. I explored the possibility of being promoted to the rank of brigadier general as chief engineering officer, chief ordnance officer, or deputy chief of the Quartermaster's Branch.

I met with the CGS, who knew about my efforts to be promoted. I should stop worrying, he told me, as Yaakov would step down as director of R&D at the end of the year and I had been designated as his successor. Shortly after that meeting Yitzhak Yaakov went abroad for a planned six-week trip to the Far East and Australia. It was decided that I would function as Acting Director of R&D during his absence, and I received two letters of appointment to the post: one from the IDF and the other from the defense ministry.

No sooner had the wheels of Yaakov's plane to the Far East left the ground than I initiated a meeting with Benny Peled, the new commander of the Air Force, to discuss the possibility of selecting a deputy director of R&D from the Air Force. Peled liked the idea and promised to think it over and to propose a number of candidates. My assessment was that selecting an Air Force man as my deputy would be an important first step in better integrating all the services of the IDF into the operations of the R&D Unit.

I attended my first General Staff meeting on May 13, 1972, one week before my 38th birthday. It was a situation assessment attended by Defense Minister Dayan and his advisor Tzvi Tzur. Intelligence Branch Chief Eli Zeira presented intelligence data and threat assessments, and Tal, the Operations Branch chief, presented the main principles of the concept of his branch. Tal's comments were aimed at moving in the direction of grand policy and the definition of national goals, which to me seemed appropriate. When Dayan spoke right after the Intelligence Branch and Operations Branch briefings, he expressed his opinions with clarity and sarcasm. Zeira, Dayan asserted, should represent the Intelligence Branch and not the Arabs. He also emphasized that while Tal had the right to express his opinions, even if they were unconventional, he, Dayan, disagreed with some of them.

Dayan's concept was consistent with his character. He maintained that we needed to take advantage of all opportunities and, if forced to fight, to use them to achieve relatively small territorial conquests, which he referred to as "corrections." He did not, however, regard the conquest of large territories and capital cities as worthwhile. He maintained that Israel had neither the reason nor the ability to launch a preventative war, but he did not rule out striking a first blow. Dayan's comments were consistent with those made by CGS Elazar and there was a distinct impression that they had coordinated their comments. After Zeira, Tal, and Dayan, all the other speakers, including Air Force Commander Peled, were entirely unimpressive.

The routine work dictated by the multiple roles played by the director of the R&D Unit was staggering, and my demanding scheduled took me from issue to issue and from meeting to meeting. I found myself dealing with efforts to retain Yedidia Shamir, the civilian deputy director of the R&D Unit who was now considering resigning. Shamir's modesty and integrity, and his experience in the development of electronic systems, made him a calm and dependable authority. When I learned that there was a good chance that I would be the next director of R&D I knew I wanted him by my side, and I made every possible effort to convince him to stay. I asked Yaakov and Itzhak Ironi to assist me, and Shamir ultimately agreed.

The position of acting director introduced me to new issues. A meeting with Tzur and Air Force Colonel Yosef Ma'ayan, who was subsequently appointed to the post of commander of the Air Force Equipment Squadron, focused on secret and sensitive cooperation with the Germans. It also provided me with an opportunity to observe the working methods of Tzvi Tzur, who took effective advantage of his status as advisor to the defense minister and a former CGS to summon military officials to his office for meetings and consultations.

Tzur's power as advisor to the defense minister also stemmed from Dayan's unique working style, and his preference for focusing only on specific issues. Dayan entrusted Tzur with responsibility for the defense budget, for working with the defense industry, and for all aspects of coordination with the IDF. Tzur's control of a large part of the ministry's R&D budget, as well as the initial procurement of advanced weapons systems, meant that he occupied a position of pivotal importance within the ministry. However, it was only when I began functioning as acting director of R&D that I learned how he operated. One day I was summoned to Tzur's office for a consultation on an air-to-surface missile with electro-optic homing which Rafael was developing at the time. While I was in the reception area, Benny Peled walked out of Tzur's office. Tzur told me that he had been trying to convince the Air Force commander to reduce the Air Force's request for missiles to ensure its approval by the IDF and defense ministry. Tzur rightly felt that if the requested budget was too high and threatened other IDF priorities, the CGS might ask the defense minister to kill the project. I was suddenly let in on this secret and highly charged issue, and was asked to prepare an analysis and comprehensive proposal to justify the missile's continued development.

Development of the missile, later named the Popeye, was eventually completed successfully, and the Air Force armed itself with a substantial stock. Even the American company Martin Marietta, in partnership with Rafael, opened an assembly line to build missiles for the US Strategic Air Command.

At the time missile and rocket development was a source of contention between IMI and Rafael. Many years later IAI also embarked upon work in this area. Tzur asked us to prepare a document recommending a division of responsibility between the two government-owned defense laboratories, IMI and Rafael, in the realm of rocket propulsion. This was my first experience in shaping policy on technological infrastructure. At the end of the meeting we saw no option but to lay out a compromise between the two companies, who were in the midst of a fierce battle for preferred status within the defense ministry, and to make sure that each entities' rocket propulsion infrastructure would match the weapons systems they were supposed to develop.

During its first year in existence, the R&D Unit underwent a process of acclimatization. The military department directors needed to internalize the fact that both the defense ministry and the defense industries had policies and concerns that transcended military considerations. It was essential that the civilian department directors, including my scientific deputy Yedidia Shamir, be aware of the desires of the various corps of the IDF, but also remain strong and confident, despite their heavy work load, and not give in to the whims and demands of their colleagues from the military. This principle remained relevant during all the years of my work in defense R&D, and I applied it myself during my tenure as director of MAFAT. Tzur and Elazar's decision to establish the R&D Unit branded the new entity with the tensions and conflicts of interest between the defense ministry and the IDF. The golden mean between these interests required, and will always require, that senior officials overseeing R&D administration within the defense establishment possess a thorough understanding of these conflicting interests and a wise sensitivity of how to go about navigating them.

AN IMPORTANT VISITOR — ANOTHER TEST

As if the burden of serving simultaneously as the deputy director and acting director of the R&D Unit was not enough, I now had another challenge: a secret visit to Israel by the defense minister of an African country. As the guest of Defense Minister Moshe Dayan, the official arrived for his first visit in Israel accompanied by his Intelligence Branch chief, his wife, and a personal assistant. I was assigned to serve as his official escort during his visit, and preparations began approximately two weeks before he arrived.

We met our guests at the airport and brought them to the secure and isolated special hosting facilities laid on for such confidential high-level guests. Assistant Defense Minister Tzvi Tzur and I met at the secret hosting facility to finalize all the details of the visit, which was to include a tour of the Jordan Valley and Jerusalem. Major General Rehavam Ze'evi would host the visitors during this part of the visit, and he accepted the plans we made for him with virtually no objections. The weather was hot as it usually in the Jordan Valley and we could only talk comfortably inside in the airconditioning. At the end of a long day touring Jerusalem we decided to forego any other activities and allowed to guests enjoy a quiet dinner, without any ceremony. The minister told me that he was extremely pleased with his visit, and that he knew that to a large extent I was responsible for its success. It felt good to receive a compliment from such an impressive man and to know that the great efforts I made were appreciated.

On the last evening of the visit, Moshe Dayan hosted a farewell

dinner in the garden of his home in Tzahala, and Naomi was invited
to join me for this special event, along with Tzvi and Rachel Tzur,
Shimon and Sonia Peres, David and Thelma Elazar, and Eli and Esther Zeira. Before we took our seats at the tables, Dayan gave us a
tour of his personal antiquities garden and provided us with fascinating explanations based on his love of archeology and his extensive
knowledge of the field. His words during dinner were warm and full
of hope for future cooperation. Naomi and I were proud and honored
to be in such company. The gifts presented to the visitors that evening were also extraordinary. The African defense minister received
a specially bound bible decorated with gold ornamentation, a gift
that was typically bestowed upon only the most distinguished guests.
Dayan gave the defense minister's wife an ancient necklace that was
more than two thousand years old. The necklace enchanted everyone
and from the moment Dayan placed it on her neck, she refused the
other women's requests to take it off to allow them a closer look.

As far as Tzvi was concerned, the task of preparing the visit and
escorting the guest was yet another test. A few days after the visit,
Yitzhak (Brigadier General Yitzhak Yaakov) and his wife Shula returned from the long trip they had been on. According to my journal,
I drove to Ben-Gurion airport to meet them early Friday morning at
the ungodly hour of 3:40 a.m. "Yitzhak and Shula returned from their
trip chubby and relaxed......rote at the time. Tzvi told me to deliver a
message to Yitzhak, telling him that he was needed for a meeting
that very same morning at 11:30 a.m. I updated Yitzhak during the
hour before his meeting with Tzvi but there was no time to go into
details. Yitzhak wanted to hear "how I had gotten on with Tzvi and if
things at R&D were fine overall." During his first meeting with Tzvi
after his return, Yitzhak heard a flattering report of my work during
the period of his absence, which contained terms such as "balanced,"
"good judgment," "quick response," and "diligence." Although I was
happy to hear these compliments from Yitzhak, deep down I wondered whether he had somewhat embellished Tzvi's assessment to

encourage me and ease his retirement as Director of R&D.

A few days later I went to see Tzvi's loyal and trustworthy assistant Avraham Ben-Yosef , who had asked to speak with me personally. Ben-Yosef confirmed that the trial period of Yitzhak's absence had gone well, and that the successful visit of the African minister and my careful management of all the details had strengthened Tzvi's opinion about the success. However, Ben-Yosef 's most important news was that the CGS had formally recommended to the defense minister that I be promoted and appointed to the position of Director of the R&D Unit at the end of the Jewish year. As the position answered to both the IDF and the Israeli defense ministry, Tzvi had done his part and had recommended me on behalf of the defense ministry.

I knew that the transition would take place sometime in September or October 1973, and I could clearly see that Yitzhak was having trouble finding the will to resume control of the R&D Unit. It was extremely clear why Yitzhak was distancing himself from all contacts with the General Staff, and particularly from Operations Branch Chief, Major General Israel Tal. I was also not particularly comfortable with Tal either, and didn't like the way he often postponed our meetings at the last minute. This was why it was interesting years later for me to find an entry in my journal about a meeting with Tal (to which Yedidia Shamir accompanied me), which described him as having been in a great mood. Upon reading the entry, I wondered whether this anomaly was because he had just been selected to receive the Israel Defense Prize for his role in promoting and developing the rollerbridge. I shall return in a later chapters to the odyssey of the development of the roller-bridge, which had been planned to serve as a way of crossing the Suez Canal.

During my service as Acting Director of R&D we became deeply involved in the drafting of R&D policy, and Simcha Maoz, who was gifted with thorough economic thinking and a broad systemic outlook, was recruited to assume a central role in the effort. It was necessary, however, to find ways to encourage Simcha to work. After arguments with R&D personnel and people at the General Staff, or when something did not work out as he planned, he would often withdraw and move to the sidelines. Yitzhak abandoned his role in shaping R&D policy and Simcha took part in a working meeting with Tzvi to discuss how to best present the new policy. We worked together on a presentation for the Council for Production and Development, the senior defense ministry forum that Tzvi headed and that included the branch directors of the defense ministry, the directors of the defense industries and the government owned defense laboratories. We suggested to Tzvi Zur that we present the Council with a survey of the budgetary framework and prepare discussion points only on the main issue of specialization centers. Tzvi was wisely hesitant about conducting a discussion on the matter without General Staff approval. I took it upon myself to brief Tal on the work we had done, but I first wanted to meet with Brigadier General Avraham Tamir, assistant director for planning of the Operations Branch, to enlist his help in convincing Tal. I had been dreaming of a joint symposium of the General Staff and the senior officials of the defense ministry where we could present all aspects of Israeli policy on defense research and development. I thought the term "symposium" would seem less intimidating and less binding in the eyes of the branch chiefs of the General Staff. Yitzhak chose to remain uninvolved in many aspects of work, and this resulted in a heavy load and an uneasy feeling.

During a meeting with me, Yitzhak and Yedidia, Tzvi Zur announced that the change in R&D leadership would take place on October 1. The speed of the transition came as a surprise for Yedidia, who had still not decided whether to resign or to agree to our request to stay on. The lack of clarity surrounding the selection of the military deputy continued. During the meeting, Tzvi raised the possibility of having just a civilian deputy, who would in any case serve as the number two official at R&D. I knew that after my conversation with him that air force commander Benny Peled had also spoken with Tzvi. I also knew that the CGS wanted there to be a deputy director from the army. Tal, however, vehemently opposed the very idea of a deputy director of R&D from the air force. "I won't have it!" he insisted. "It's against the founding principles!" For me, it was clear that Tal, as chief of the Operations Branch, saw the R&D Unit in overly narrow terms as belonging to him and as a body meant primarily to serve the interests of the ground forces of the IDF. Within the rectangle between Tzvi Zur, CGS David Elazar, Tal, and Peled, I found myself in a mediating position which enabled me to continue promoting the idea of a deputy from the air force, based on my belief in joint inter-arm efforts in research and development.

At the end of the process the air force accepted my approach and proposed Lieutenant Colonel Nahum Dayagi for the position of deputy director of R&D. On the civilian side we upgraded the status of the civilian deputy and made Yedidia second in command of the R&D Unit. This created a balance that pacified the civilian element of R&D and the defense ministry, and at the same time assured we would get the significant technical contribution of an officer of the air force's Equipment Squadron. The development plans included many important issues that were meant specifically to serve the air force, and Nahum's contribution to the Unit was important.

The development plans for the ground corps were not in an ideal state. One day Tal summoned us on short notice to his meeting with the corps commander. Ground Department Director Yehoshua Rozen and I went up to his office, where we observed some of the less pleasant interpersonal sides of Israel Tal. I summed up the meeting in my journal as follows:

The discussion revolved around the tank assault kits. Previously, we had drafted a document, reviewed it with Tal, and, at his request, revised it approximately one and a half months ago. However, since then no progress has been made whatsoever. The whole time, [Major General Avraham] Adan was constantly pressuring us to authorize the expense of development work for bulldozer and plow kits, which

Tal wanted to hear nothing about. Tal's opposition was based on principle and had to do with the concept, not with the lack of utility or excessive budget. We had never sent the last document to the corps because Tal had not authorized it to be sent before we discussed it with him, and he never found the time do to so. In the meeting, Tal found himself pushed to the wall by Adan (justifiably in my opinion), with no way to justify the time it was taking him to address the issue. He then asked us a few questions about the document, which he had not read, and blew up, telling us that the work was worthless and that he had no R&D justification for the request of the corps. Later, he regained his composure somewhat and said that the equipment would be finalized as we made progress toward approving the model.

At one point during the meeting I got angry and spoke to Tal in a harsh tone, telling him that I refused to be rebuked simply in order to cover up problems with his working style, his failure to delegate authority, and his priorities regarding the issues that interested him (such as the Merkava, the roller-bridge, etc.). I decided that if he continues on as Operations Branch chief, I would stop being so nice.

This episode with Tal, who had just been appointed deputy CGS, was enough to show me what was waiting just around the corner, with my imminent appointment as director of R&D.

SUMMING UP MY TENURE AS DEPUTY DIRECTOR — SELF EXAMINATION

That year, the eve of Rosh Hashana, the Jewish New Year, was particularly special for me, as it was preceded by a public announcement of my imminent appointment as director of R&D. At home things were tense in light of the many expectations. In a journal entry from the period I describe how "Osnat jumped up and down in excitement and was overcome with joy when they showed my picture (smiling, but somewhat contemplative) on the television screen and announced the news." I had already had three personal meetings with the main people in the defense establishment with whom I was supposed to work closely — deputy CGS Tal, CGS Elazar and Itzhak Ironi, director-general of the defense ministry. At the beginning of the new year I was filled with positive energy and ready to begin a new chapter in my career.

One of the most important issues I managed to conclude was a meeting with Yedidia in which he agreed to carry on in his current position for another year. I also told Tzvi about how important it was that Yedidia remain in his position as civilian deputy director, especially since there was no better candidate for the position. During my meeting with Yedidia, I found that he understood the situation and knew there was no serious candidate to replace him. The meeting was easy for me, because the relatively straightforward situation meant both that I would plead with him and that he would agree. I was very pleased that this is in fact what happened. I suggested to Yedidia that Tzvi call him and personally ask him to stay on, so that that the request would be coming from the most senior authority within the ministry, and he liked the idea. I also spoke with Yedidia about Nahum Dayagi. Yedidia was concerned that Nahum's appointment could harm his standing as the deputy director of R&D because he was an outsider and was not sufficiently charismatic and assertive, and that this in turn would make it hard to work with the department directors. I acknowledged that there was some truth to what he was saying, and that meant we would have to organize things in the office a bit differently. We ended our discussion by agreeing that we would dedicate the month ahead before the transition to planning our roles and the division of responsibilities. We also agreed that Yedidia would be second in command while that Nahum would be third in line. At the same time, I considered the possibility of asking Benny Ron to replace Ronny Katzin as assistant to the director of R&D. Ronny had told me long ago that he had wanted to leave R&D

and that he had only stayed on because of me.

On Sunday afternoon, Tal called me from his home. He had been working on drafting his remarks for the upcoming General Staff meeting on the strategic situation, and he asked me to meet with him at his home. I cancelled all my meetings and appointments and drove to Tal's house in Rehovot. When I arrived, he was wearing only shorts and not even a t-shirt (although he later put one on), and was informal, although still characteristically decisive and resolute. I began by saying that I believed things would change in the defense ministry once Tzvi left as planned and all the issues he had been handling were transferred to director-general Ironi. Tal maintained that the defense minister would not give any more power to the General Staff, and that there were three possible scenarios: (1) that the minister himself would assume Tzvi Zur's responsibilities and get into the thick of things; (2) that the minister would appoint a new deputy minister to take on the work; and (3) that the minister would delegate the responsibilities in question to the chief scientist of the defense ministry.

On the subject of work in research and development, Tal was critical of the concept underlying the organization of the Unit and blamed CGS David Elazar for setting the unit's current dependence. In any event, he explained that he regarded R&D as an independent unit that was subordinate to the Operations Branch only administratively. R&D needed to work directly with the services of the IDF and with the CGS, Tal continued, and it was his role to serve as the head of the ground arm of the IDF with regard to issues related to R&D. In all other areas, Tal promised to work with the R&D Unit like he did with the Adjutant General's Branch and the Quartermaster's Branch. Tal's assessment sounded realistic and wise to me, and I agreed without hesitation. With surprising generosity, Tal said that we could even appeal decisions on ground-related issues to the CGS. With a lighter heart and a greater sense of responsibility, I drove from Tal's house directly to a meeting with the CGS.

At the very beginning of the meeting Elazar asked me to give him my assessment of the current state of affairs of the R&D Unit. I told him that the Unit functioned as a separate body that had not been integrated into the Operations Branch or the services of the IDF. This surprised the CGS, who immediately asked if this was the fault of R&D, the services of the IDF, or the deputy CGS. I told him that, to the best of my knowledge, it was not the fault of R&D, and that if the blame lay anywhere, it must be divided up between the deputy CGS and the services of the IDF. I quoted what Tal had to say about the R&D Unit's status and told him that if this was an accurate reflection of things, it meant not only a great deal of responsibility for me, which I was willing to accept, but also a greater burden on him as CGS in terms of work and the need to take notice of certain issues. Elazar agreed that the fact that Tzvi Zur would be out of the picture this year changed many things, and the impression I got was that he was not sorry about the change. Elazar said that he had not yet let Tal off the hook with regard to his role in directing the administrative work at R&D and in various parts of the IDF. But Tal was a man of extremes, Elazar explained. For him, it was either all or nothing. "If it doesn't work," the CGS said, "then we'll work like this." With a pat on my back and a shake of my hand, he walked me into the lounge in his office. I left with mixed feelings: certain that I had Elazar's support, which pleased me, but acutely aware of the great responsibility I was assuming and the complexity of my new position.

My meeting with Itzhak Ironi, director general of the Defense Ministry, was different. Ironi told me that the minister had informed him that he would assume responsibility for all the issues with which Tzvi had been dealing. Ironi knew that he needed to prepare himself, and he wanted to make use of the R&D Unit for all the ministry's activities. He appeared stable and trusting but lacked Tzvi's charisma and charm. We agreed that we would begin by meeting on a weekly basis and then decide how to continue. I left the meeting deep in thought, concerned about the director general's weakness in the face of the demands from the army. I also feared the traditional approach of the military industries which he had directed before he was appointed director-general, according to which Israel Military Industries (IMI) enthusiastically endorsed every request from the IDF. I believed that the Unit could in fact help Ironi carve out more authority for the defense ministry in its interactions with the IDF and the General Staff. I also regarded this as a difficult challenge, as well as a way to fortify the status and authority of the R&D Unit.

The general atmosphere 10 days before the beginning of the Yom Kippur War was complacent. No one dreamed that such a grueling war would soon engulf the country, claiming so many casualties and transforming so many parts of Israeli society. The eve of Rosh Hashana, the Jewish New Year, is typically a time for self-examination, and this was even more true for me in light of the job I was about to begin after the holiday. I briefly summed up in my journal my tenure as Deputy Director of R&D as follows:

By briefly reviewing my tenure as deputy director, it is possible to sum up the work that has been done by the R&D Unit until this point, and perhaps also what needs to be done in the future.

We set up the R&D unit and Yitzhak, for the most part, instituted the structure and working methods of its sub-units.

We established initial procedures, and we now need to establish more detailed procedures.

We began the proper signing of contractual agreements and now must address the entire subject of contracts, with bodies within the defense establishment as well.

We recruited the maximum authorized number of employees, and we now must replace a number of key people.

Although we achieved integration between the development plans of the services of the IDF and effective work with the air force and the navy, the internal administrative work within the services of the IDF is still insufficient.

We put the R&D Unit on the map within the IDF and the defense ministry, but we have not yet taken full advantage of our exclusive ability to dictate procedures, policy, and oversight, and of the new teeth that were added to our budget.

Although we produced a number of good reports, there is still much room for improvement in terms of the subjects that have not yet been covered and the quality of the work. There is also room for improvement in the presentation of the subjects we did address.

We established project-focused agencies, and there is now a possibility of establishing a joint front with the Defense Ministry Acquisition Administration. This, however, is only a beginning, and it remains to be seen how it will actually be implemented.

We institutionalized our connections abroad, particularly with re-gard to the "Mighty Waters" project. However, we have not yet effec-tively addressed our other connections and the issue of technological information collection.

As director of R&D, I would still need to address these and many other undertakings, which all together were very challenging.

The Jewish year 5734 (September 1973–September 1974) had begun. As part of my process of self-examination, three days before I was supposed to be appointed as director of R&D, I wrote a journal entry spelling out what I hoped to achieve during my first year on the job. On a personal level, I resolved to develop a working style that would give my deputy directors and department directors a large degree of independence and encourage initiative and high quality work, but that at the same time would also enable me to retain effective control. I thought it was important to establish working procedures that would provide me with time for quiet thought and reflection, reading, and level-headed decisions regarding concrete issues, R&D organization and personnel, and long-term policy. My plan was to establish a position of authority and influence by ensuring proper working procedures and relations with the CGS, the deputy CGS, and the heads of the different services of the IDF on the one hand, and senior defense ministry officials on the other hand. In the office I planned out a division of responsibility that would truly make Yedidia my second in command and delegate to him a suitable portion of the work. I also believed it was important to upgrade the role of Nahum, my military deputy, to that of an autonomous deputy providing substantial assistance and taking on a share of the burden. I outlined detailed plans for the different departments of the R&D Unit. In particular I outlined ideas for Yehoshua Rozen's Ground Force Department, which addressed not only the addition of new people but new responsibilities within the defense ministry, instead of simply leaving it as a Weapons Development Department of the ground forces. I paid a great deal of attention to supporting the Planning, Economy, and Systems Analysis Department, which would provide the framework for discussion and approval of the multi-year R&D plan and for creating a framework for annual updates. Another important task for the Planning, Economy, and Systems Analysis Department was to facilitate the discussion and approval of R&D policy within the General Staff and the defense ministry. Yet another important goal I identified at the time was to stabilize our budgetary resources in accordance with the multi-year plan and policy, and to ensure that neither the IDF, various services in the IDF, the financial advisor to the CGS, or anyone could tamper with these resources because of the constantly changing pressures under which they operated. I also gave high priority to the task of completing the work on specialization centers, and the attempt to generate a clear course of action on assigning new development projects. It was still necessary to provide content and to convince the defense establishment of the need for the new Economic Branch, as well as to establish the role of the Systems Analysis Branch as of the source of advice and assistance to the whole system on inter-arm issues and other central issues within the defense establishment.

I never doubted for a moment Yitzhak's role in developing the R&D Unit's innovative, revolutionary concept and principles of operation. I was grateful for his ability to see things in proper broad, long-term context, which he effectively incorporated into the process of establishing the unit. After retiring from the IDF, Yitzhak was appointed by Chaim Bar-Lev as chief scientist of the Commerce and Industry Ministry, where he also left a clear imprint of his originality and creativity. We stayed in touch after he left for New York to try his luck as a civilian technological entrepreneur. As my work in Paris was winding down in 2001, I was saddened to hear about Yitzhak's arrest and the charges that had been filed against him for compromising Israeli security. At the request of his lawyers, I met with Yitzhak in the hotel in which he was being detained during his trial in order to understand what he had done and how, if possible, I could help him. Based on these meetings it became clear to me that Yitzhak had in fact committed some serious security offenses. After reading the draft of the book he had planned to publish and which was the source of the charges, I told him that the book could have easily been "cleaned up" to prevent him from getting into trouble, and that it was a shame that he had not done so. The fact that I was unable to speak on behalf of his innocence left me deeply saddened.

9

The Research and Development Unit During the Yom Kippur War

DIRECTOR OF RESEARCH AND DEVELOPMENT

On Monday October 1, Yitzhak and I went in to see Tzvi Zur, the assistant defense minister, who announced the conclusion of Yitzhak's term as director of the defense ministry's R&D Unit and officially appointed me to the position. The ceremony with the CGS took place in the evening, and was attended by Naomi and our children Osnat and Nimrod. It also marked Nahum's appointment as deputy director of Research and Development, and his promotion to the rank of colonel. I was promoted to the rank of brigadier general by Tal and Elazar, the CGS himself. Tal was extremely friendly, and even added a congratulatory note to the bouquet of flowers he sent me, which he signed using his nickname, "Talik." During my last conversation with Yitzhak before we went up to the Chief of Staff's office, I told him I was concerned that I might not have the long-term perspective and the broad understanding of the issues that the job required. Although he told me that these things would come with time as I did my job, I was not sure if he really meant it or if he said it just to reassure me. Despite how happy I was to reach this long awaited day and to finally receive the appointment, I was concerned about the many complex issues that lay ahead.

I spent my first day as director of R&D in meetings with my deputies to define precisely each of our realms of responsibility, and in a meeting with the R&D department directors, which included an update on working procedures for the department directors and for the unit as a whole. I also had two meetings with Tzvi. One was related to our relations with Asia, and the other was a routine working meeting between Tzvi and the director of Rafael (the Hebrew acronym for the Authority for Development Arms Systems). The minister's hall was directly connected to the office of the CGS, and I decided to try to barge in on Elazar in order to enlist his support in my efforts to institutionalize my membership in the General Staff Working Group, as well as Nahum's membership in Tal's Operations Branch Working Group. Tal had previously opposed the appointment of an air-force officer like Nahum as deputy director of R&D, because he saw the Operations Branch Working Group as the supreme forum of the ground forces. I was concerned that he would work against us in the Working Group by not providing Nahum with the status and authority required to fulfill his position both inside and outside the R&D Unit. I managed to get ten minutes alone with the CGS. After explaining the problem and receiving his authorization and his advice how to proceed, I left with an extremely positive feeling toward Elazar as a person. Before I left his office he told me that we still needed to sit together for a long, serious meeting. At the time neither Elazar nor I had any idea that this was a meeting that would never take place, and that the war that was about to break out would shift our focus so rapidly.

The day I was appointed as the director of R&D, Yonah Efrat replaced Rehavam Zeevi as OC Central Command. In the evening, I drove to the Binyanei Ha-Umah convention center in Jerusalem for the farewell ceremony held in Zeevi's honor. Jordan Valley veterans were well represented by the outgoing OC and I felt a deep identification with the sentiments expressed on stage that evening. Just a few days later, when we were in the midst of the first days of the defensive battle of the Yom Kippur War, I recalled how relaxed and carefree we all were, and how we all failed to notice the dark storm ahead of us.

AND THE WAR BEGINS...

On Friday morning, the day before Yom Kippur, Tal's bureau chief informed me that we were on alert-level B. Later that morning during an impromptu meeting of the General Staff I learned that we were actually closer to alert level C. In my journal I wrote that during the meeting, Intelligence Branch Chief Eli Zeira spoke of clear indications that preparations for a joint Egyptian–Syrian attack were underway and informed us that the families of the Soviet advisors in Cairo and Damascus were being evacuated by airlift. Nonetheless, his assessment was that there was no real chance of a war breaking out, and that the worst that would happen was that the Syrians would try to snatch part of the Golan Heights and perhaps one of the settlements. Zeira also estimated that the Egyptians would limit themselves to massive shelling and perhaps a cross-border incursion. Although Moshe Dayan was present at the meeting, he allowed the CGS to lead it and did not interfere. It was decided to leave the alert level unchanged and to suspend leave for all on-duty regular forces and reserve forces, but not to mobilize the reserves on the day leading up to Yom Kippur, the holiest day in the Jewish calendar. This was not my first General Staff meeting, but now that I had officially assumed my new position I took my role much more seriously and kept detailed notes on the main issues that were discussed. My notes, which reflect everything said at the General Staff meetings throughout the entire war, were saved under the title assigned by the R&D administrative secretariat: "The War Journal."

Friday October 5, 1973

Briefing at General Staff Headquarters (concluded at 12:00 noon)
Intelligence Branch

Syria – is in an emergency layout and has carried out an exercise for conquering the Golan Heights. Two squadrons of Sukhoi-7s were moved up to Damascus from the more remote T-4 airfield.

Egypt – An armored exercise combined with a state of alert regarding a possible IDF incursion during the exercise (day and night). The Canal Zone has been reinforced...

There is considerable anxiety and serious concerns about a possible Israeli attack against Syria and Egypt.

This has stemmed from a number of actions of the IDF: A paratroop exercise in the Sinai Peninsula.

During the Yom Kippur War 99

The air battle in Syria, which has been understood as a planned component of a series of provocations aimed at heating things up.

Our many aerial photo flights.

The print media in both countries are feeding the general mood and their hostile intentions. The Russians sent 11 Russian cargo planes (6 to Egypt and 5 to Syria), possibly to extract Russian personnel from the two countries. There is no explanation for this.

Most Soviet shipping vessels left Alexandria this morning.

The Intelligence Branch Assessment: The probability of a war initiated by either Egypt or Syria is low, and their actions are the result of their fear. There is a possibility, albeit an extremely unlikely possibility, of a limited Syrian or Egyptian attack in the form of a quick grab and subsequent advantageous use by Syria, or a raid or a shelling attack by Egypt.

Things may begin to evolve and then spin out of the Arabs' control. The General Staff

The CGS accepts the Intelligence Branch assessment as reasonable. Alert-level C has been declared throughout the IDF. The regional commanders have the authority to make exceptions in applying alert-level C (sleeping arrangements, etc...). The state of alert applies to all command personnel of the reserve units. The CGS estimates that if there is a plan to attack from Syria and Egypt simultaneously,

we will receive prior warning. If we do, we will
mobilize the reserves. Mobilization will be carried
out via [the Israeli military radio station] Galei
Tzahal.

At 5:45 a.m. on the morning of Saturday October 6, I was awakened by a phone call from Tzvi Zur, who was already in the office. He asked me about the state of various Rafael facilities. The R&D Unit already had representatives at the General Staff Command Center (which in Hebrew is typically referred to as ha-bor, or "the pit"), and I was able to answer his question within just a few minutes. At 8:30 a.m. I was again awakened by a phone call, this time by Colonel Avi Har-Even, who was on duty in the Command Center. Har-Even told me that they were starting to implement a silent mobilization of the reserves. By 10:00 a.m. the CGS Preparatory Working Group had already met. It turned out there was now general certainty that a war would break out on two fronts and that it would begin at 6:00 p.m. that evening. I asked Nahum, Colonel Yehoshua Rozen, and Colonel Yaakov Livni to join the Deputy CGS Preparatory Working Group meeting which Tal led at noon. The meeting addressed the overall effort to build an order of battle for both fronts, as well as a number of other issues. At 2:00 p.m., when I was on my way back to the General Staff Command Center from a meeting with the R&D department directors, the air-raid sirens began to wail. Intelligence Branch Chief Zeira, who was walking toward me at just that moment, went pale, and muttered, "So, it's starting in spite of it all... They're getting the planes in the air." I could hear a sense of surprise and disappointment in his voice and I felt my heart sink.

I headed down to the Command Center for three hours of confusion and lack of clarity. I noted that the General Staff war room looked like a brigade war room and was so noisy that it was impossible to think straight. The radio transmitters that lined all the walls, each monitoring a different frequency, sputtered out broken bursts of conversations of our military units in various theatres. For me, the metallic sound of the voices over the radio conjured up the familiar feeling of being under fire in battle, when you hear the whiz of every burst fired in your direction and the sound of every shell falling near you. At a certain point Tal talked with Colonel Dan Shomron, the commander of the 14th tank brigade, the front brigade in the Sinai Peninsula. Shomron reported that the 7th Egyptian division had not yet entirely crossed the Canal and was not yet moving eastward on the Gidi Road, as the rumors circulating in the Command Center had it.

By afternoon, the entire staff and all the department directors were in the office, tense and anxious to hear a rundown of the situation. Simcha Maoz received my permission to join a logistics team serving with the division commanded by Arik Sharon. The following day a few other R&D staff members who wanted to and could join the war on the front were also released from their responsibilities within the unit. My heart told me that my place was also at the front with the soldiers, but my head knew that this was neither right nor possible. In the evening the R&D department directors received instructions regarding the issues on the agenda and the major tasks required of us. They included:

- Assisting in quick weapons acquisition, if required.
- Planning and establishing teams to collect data for subsequent lesson generation.
- At this stage, there would be no mobilization of our reserve forces.
- Maintaining the NBC (nuclear, biological, chemical) Defense Department in full operation.
- Maintaining a core staff in the Ground Department and mobilizing its people into the war effort.
- Providing assistance in weapons acquisition by the professional departments of the R&D Unit (Electronics, Planning and Economics; Missiles and Rockets; and Infrastructure).

We then set procedures for updating and pinpointing with an emphasis on information security, and scheduled a meeting for 8:00 a.m. the next morning. This gave us the feeling that the R&D Unit was beginning to organize itself and to play a supporting role in the war, although we still lacked a true understanding of how difficult the war would actually turn out.

When I got home Nimrod was asleep, under the influence of the sedative that Naomi had given him. Without it the worried child had been unable to relax. Naomi and Osnat were relatively calm, and the neighbors came over for an update and to hear words of encouragement. I did the best I could to radiate optimism although I too was unable to hide my anxiety.

Despite my concern I waited until 6:00 a.m. the next morning, Sunday, October 7, to go down to the Command Center to learn about the events of the previous night. Nothing significant had been received from the Suez Canal front, and to me this seemed to be the result of unclear and incomplete reporting. The Syrians had taken advantage of the night to penetrate deep into the southern Golan Heights. They still held our Mt. Hermon post, which was now color-coded red and prominently displayed on our maps to indicate an enemy position. I briefed the department directors at 8:00 a.m., and immediately afterward I met with former R&D Department Director Ben Bar-On and my assistant Ronny Katzin to discuss the various ways of going about generating lessons. We discussed a draft agenda for discussion with the department directors as soon as possible. We also talked about the need to begin operating on the fronts with the fighting forces. At 9:00 a.m. I went down to the Command Center for a meeting of the Operations Department Director's Preparatory Working Group, in which the Intelligence Branch and the Operations Department provided a more exact update regarding the situation. My journal contains the following description of the meeting: "It was attended by almost all the despondent officers of the Command Center – the primary corps commanders, generals in the reserves, and others." I must admit that I was also drawn to the Command Center by the urge to know what was happening on the front lines. Nonetheless, the R&D Unit had plenty to do, and participating in the preparatory working group meetings in the Command Center played an important role by facilitating smoother operation of the unit. I held a meeting with the department directors on preparations for gathering data for subsequent lesson generation, and I took clear notice that this was well received by all participants, who now felt that they were playing a role in the war effort. However, it was also clear that they were extremely tense and that it was difficult for them to relax. That Sunday, the second day of the war, they hardly worked; every time I returned to the office from the Command Center, everybody was desperate to hear about ongoing military developments.

The situation on the front lines went from hope to despair, as the air force swung from mission to mission and from theatre to theatre like a pendulum. In the morning our planes carried out successful attacks against the anti-aircraft defenses and airports in Egypt. In the midst of an attack on the Egyptian missile batteries, however, the mission was suddenly changed, and the air effort was now refocused on the Golan Heights. There, the initial task of providing emergency support for our ground forces was replaced by an attack on the Syrian missile batteries in order to establish freedom of air action in the air over the Golan Heights. In the afternoon we had a relatively good Deputy CGS Preparatory Working Group meeting, which was supposed to be immediately followed by a CGS Preparatory Working Group meeting. This was the turning point. The CGS Preparatory Working Group was repeatedly delayed until eventually the CGS himself announced that Tal would be flying up to the northern command post, that he himself would be heading down south, and that Ze'evi had been appointed as acting Operations Branch chief.

The sense of discouragement that overcame all of us was compounded by the fact that Colonel Itzik Ben-Shoham, commander of the 188th armored brigade who until that point had been holding off the 3rd Syrian armored division, had been either seriously wounded or killed. His deputy and their operations officer had also been either seriously wounded or killed, and now there was no one to take matters into hand within the brigade. Ben-Shoham, with his black hair and laughing eyes, had been a highly skilled and extremely professional commander. The same day, Sunday, October 7, I had been scheduled to visit his brigade as part of Moshe Dayan's order to plan a new obstacle against a Syrian attack in the Golan Heights. But the war broke out and we never made it to the Golan Heights. Instead of meeting Ben-Shoham up north as planned, we listened as the military radio transmissions testified to the almost impossible battle he had commanded.

From the south we received persistent reports that Egyptian tanks were rolling through the 10-kilometer area located to the east of the Canal, and that communication with some of our strongholds had been lost. Dayan returned from the south and infected us all with his despondency. Rumors holding that Dayan himself had described the unfolding events as "the destruction of the Third Temple" (a way of referring to Israel) spread like wildfire through the General Staff Command Center. At the end of the day, Haim Bar-Lev flew north to work with OC Northern Command Major General Yitzhak Hofi, Elazar flew south to determine what actions needed to be taken there, and Tal remained at the Command Center. Again, interpretations abounded. The preparatory working group meetings in the Command Center were conducted through the fog of cigarette smoke, as a bluish cloud floated above the group. The pungent smell of sweat mingled with smoke that stung their eyes, but stronger than anything else was the smell of fear. The ventilation system in the Command Center was not designed to accommodate such a large number of people, and it appears that fear was not the only thing bothering the officers. They were suffering from a lack of oxygen as well.

On the third day of the war I was charged with the task of updating the branch heads of the defense ministry. The meeting was run by director-general Itzhak Ironi, and it was also attended by the directors of the defense industries. The director-general requested that the working group be provided with a daily summary of the events on the front lines. During the first meeting, the group sat mesmerized for 40 minutes, listening to an overview that was designed to be balanced, realistic, and optimistic, to the extent that this was possible under the circumstances. Ironi asked that a summary be presented at 5:00 p.m. each day, and my participation in all the meetings of the working groups and preparatory working groups in the Command Center provided a solid foundation for those presentations. In the long term, these meetings also helped boost the status of the R&D department.

HARD TIMES

On Monday, October 8, I was exhausted when I finally got around to the task of writing in my journal to sum up the day's events at the end of the day. At 6:00 a.m. that morning there had been an air of optimism in the Command Center. The Northern Command had drawn up plans to use Brigadier General Rafael Eitan's division to push the Syrians eastward and to use Brigadier General Moshe Peled's division to push back enemy tanks from south to north. Divisions here are referred to by the name of their commanders and are justifiably attributed the same characteristics. There was a positive feeling regarding people like Eitan and Peled, who were leading the battles against the Syrians. In the course of the day both Syrian infantry divisions were almost completely routed and the southern Syrian armored division was halted. However, later in the morning, when Rozen and I listened to radio communications from the northern and southern fronts and when we heard the details of the battles, it became clear that things were not so simple. Air force pilots were engaged in non-stop efforts to provide support for the ground forces, and I thought to myself how wonderful our pilots were. The Golani Brigade launched a failed attack on Mt. Hermon in which 30 of our soldiers were killed and 70 wounded, and it was not at all clear that these numbers were final. Thus far, Mt. Hermon had cost us 100 lives.

In the south it was decided to proceed step-by-step. First, Major General Avraham Adan was supposed to move southward from Quneitra and to clean the entire area between Artillery Road and the Canal. Then, Sharon's division was supposed to attack from south to north. In the meantime, Albert Mendler's 252nd division needed time to recover from the battles of the previous day. Arik's division had no noticeable impact on the fighting during the day, and we did not know why. Adan's division worked hard and, through intense efforts, managed to advance toward the Firdan Bridge. In the afternoon Albert was ordered to operate in the southern sector to stop the advance of the masses of Egyptian tanks that had entered Israeli territory via the Gidi Road. All in all there were now 600 Egyptian tanks on Israeli soil, which almost equaled the number of remaining tanks in our three depleted divisions. Between the morning and the end of the day our great optimism was gradually but rapidly being transformed into a terrifying realism.

Nahum and I went to pay a visit to the Control Post, the command center of the Israeli air force. There, I had the privilege of sitting next to Brigadier General David Ivry and behind Major General Benny Peled during a large air battle in the south. Dozens of our planes were in flight, in the midst of an attack on the missile batteries, and tension filled the air. During their radio transmissions it was interesting to observe how the pilots spoke so differently than the soldiers on the ground. Everything was short and succinct; there was no time for anything else. Benny Peled's neck and broad shoulders tensed up whenever he received a report of a difficult battle or a pilot in distress. I sensed a connection with Benny Peled, David Ivry, and Rafi Harlev as they conducted the major air campaign. For a moment I felt as if I was one of them. After the war and during all the subsequent years that I engaged in defense research and development, that air battle remains branded on my memory.

During a Deputy CGS Preparatory Working Group meeting held later that evening, R&D was assigned a mission: facilitating a quick learning process for operating Soviet T-62 tanks and understanding their weak points. We were already aware of more than 100 abandoned shot-up T-62 tanks near Quneitra, and we had actually started the process that morning.

We first encountered Soviet tanks during the 1956 Sinai campaign, when the Egyptians were using T-34 tanks. These tanks had been developed during World War II and were no more capable than the American Sherman tanks, also made during the war. During the Six Day War the Egyptians and the Syrians were already using T-55 tanks, which were far superior to the T-34s in armor, cannon, and fire-control system. We knew a bit about the T-62 tank from publications and intelligence reports, but the West had not yet deciphered all of its secrets. The Soviets tended not to supply their most advances weapons systems to other countries, and when the decision was made to sell T-62s to Syria and Egypt, they already had models of their next tank, the T-72, which we would only encounter in the first Lebanon war, during armored battles with the Syrians in the Beqaa Valley in northeastern Lebanon.

Ultimately, the efforts to retrieve the Syrian T-62 tanks from the Golan Heights proved successful, and the Ordnance Corps began immediate work on them at Tel Hashomer.

October 8 was a day almost too difficult to bear, and at day's end I thought that it might be a good thing that the general public was not privy to the real, concrete wartime worries, but was rather receiving its information via the radio and the press. I retired for a few hours of sleep with the hope that it would be a quiet night and that the next morning would open a decisive day in the Golan Heights.

But it was neither a quiet night nor a quiet day in the Golan Heights. Gloom pervaded the Command Center, and Operations

Department Director Yankeleh Stern and Brigadier General David Hagoel, Assistant Operations Branch Chief and Aryeh Levi's replacement in time of need, surveyed the difficult situation in the Golan Heights. During the night the government had decided to use all force possible against Syria, and Major General Menachem Meron was charged with establishing the rear line in the Sinai Peninsula, which would serve to contain the advance of the Egyptian divisions.

With a heavy heart I went up to my office to present the morning briefing to the R&D Staff Working Group, and I made their lives even more difficult by vividly describing the state of affairs. The mood in the Command Center improved at 10 a.m. as a result of the report that Colonel Avigdor Ben-Gal and his 7th brigade had succeeded in holding off the 3rd Syrian Armored Division. Our air force did excellent work, attacking all its desired targets in the Golan Heights with relative freedom. Later in the day, during an afternoon meeting of the CGS Preparatory Working Group, we suddenly received reports of a successful attack against targets in Damascus (the Syrian General Staff compound, air force headquarters, the Defense Ministry, and a number of power stations) and Homs, and against a large Syrian radar facility in Lebanon. Joy again returned to faces in the Command Center, which was typical of the regular mood swings within the country's military nerve center during wartime.

During the morning we also worked on ordering TOW anti-tank missiles from the United States. The arrangements and records with which we were dealing were aimed at ordering equipment according to Tzvi Zur's instructions, in coordination with Assistant Operations Branch Chief Aryeh Levi and Director-General Ironi. Due to the overwhelming sense of distress, we ordered 120 launchers at a price of approximately $10 million in great haste. The Americans had not even agreed to supply us with the systems yet. A few months before to the outbreak of the war we raised the possibility of purchasing a few models of American TOW anti-tank missiles for evaluation purposes, but Tal had vehemently objected. "The IDF is saturated with anti-tank systems," the Operations Branch chief roared in a thundering voice. "There's no need for any more!" Everyone knew that he was referring to tanks, and that according to his approach, tanks and tanks alone were supposed to deal with enemy tanks. Tal enjoyed complete sovereignty over all things related to Israeli's ground forces, and all we could was to clench our teeth and remain silent. Now that we were coming to appreciate the power of the Russian Sagger missiles that were being used with menacing success by Egyptian infantry forces and costing us so many disabled tanks with concomitant loss of life, everyone understood just how essential anti-tank missiles were to the integrated battlefield.

The first days of the war were difficult for us all. It was not easy for me to disconnect myself from the Command Center, even when there were no preparatory working group meetings or meetings of any other kind. Under the circumstances Yedidia had assumed practical direction of the Unit and all routine business. On the fourth day of the fighting, almost everyone who had requested to take on a combat role or a combat-support role in the war was released from the Unit and sent to the front. To fill the gap we called up some of our best reserve officers to build ad-hoc frameworks for thinking through and consolidating data collection for the immediate generation of lessons of the fighting. We wanted to achieve the capability to immediately generate technological solutions and to collect data for the subsequent generation of lessons. The daily briefing that was prepared for the expanded defense ministry Working Group had become an extremely popular event and was now in high demand.

At 3:00 a.m. on Friday, October 12, after the Deputy CGS Preparatory Working Group meeting, we met with the Operations Department director, the Intelligence Department director, and the Air department director about the Soviet SA-6 anti-aircraft missiles. The mood in the Command Center was completely different that morning, mainly due to the success of our armored forces in Syria. Eitan's division launched an offensive at 11:00 a.m. and stopped the

Syrian advance some 10–15 km from the border (the "purple line," or the 1967 ceasefire line) just before dark. In contrast, the air force lost seven attack planes in the course of the day...erious bloodletting. By that point, 80 of our planes had been shot down. People had a bad feeling about the seemingly never-ending duel between our planes and the missiles, and there was a great sense of frustration with the fact that we still had not been able to acquire even one SA-6 missile system, which had taken us and the West as a whole completely by surprise. We asked Sayeret Matkal (the elite General Staff commando unit) to make acquisition of such a missile, or of essential pieces of its warhead, a top priority, to help us to develop counter-measures for our planes, even if only partial ones.

At R&D, things started to move and to take shape: Rozen sent the combat weapons system survey teams to the southern and northern fronts, and appointed Lieutenant Colonel (Res.) Itzik Yaakobi, former director of Branch 2 of the Weapons Development Department, to supervise them. Shalom Eitan, director of the Electronics Department, played an active and decisive role both in organizing the TOW training material and consolidating data for the generation of post-combat lessons and the lessons necessary for quick response. The Americans finally authorized the provision of TOW anti-tank missiles, and we sent a team to the US to learn how to instruct troops to use the missiles. In the Command Center I came across Yitzhak listening to the radio transmissions of the 7th brigade as it advanced. He looked old, tired, and sad. I dragged him over to help NBC Defense Department Director Yaakov Livneh write procedures. We also mobilized a large number of R&D reservists who started to take part in the work, and the general feeling was that things were beginning to move in a positive direction.

I continued briefing the top defense ministry officials with sessions entitled "What's New on the Front," which prompted the director-general of Israel Aerospace Industries to request a special briefing for their senior working group. The meeting was a unique encounter with some of the people undertaking the practical work who both wanted to know what was happening on the front and were pleased to hear about technological aspects and future directions for work. The endless questions that followed the briefing were extremely relevant and provided me with important ideas to think about for thought for the future.

One day before the briefing of the Defense Ministry Working Group, Chaim Carmon, assistant to the director general of the defense ministry, asked me to come meet a friend of his. His friend, it turned out, was Chaim Israeli, a former aide to David Ben-Gurion who was now serving as a special aide to Defense Minister Dayan. During our very first meeting Israeli impressed me as an exceptionally wise and friendly man. He asked me many questions, about the situation, the T-62 tanks, the structure of the IDF, the role of tanks during war and the proper approach toward continuing the war with the Egyptians. I got the sense that although the voice belonged to Chaim Israeli, the questions actually revolved around issues that were troubling Defense Minister Dayan and that perhaps it was Dayan himself who was actually asking the questions. The following day Chaim Carmon asked me if I would accept an appointment as the spokesperson for the Defense Ministry. I refused, feeling that the large network of people in the R&D Unit needed leadership and that it would be wrong to abandon the reins of the Unit in the middle of the war.

At 6:00 a.m. on Saturday, October 13th I heard that Ben-Gal's 7th brigade had encountered an array of anti-tank missiles, and Yossi Ben-Hanan, one of Ben-Gal's battalion commanders (and the husband of Anat, my driver from the Weapons Development Department), had been wounded. An Iraqi division that entered the fighting had pinned down our 210th division, under the command of Brigadier General Dan Laner, and was preventing it from coming to the aid of Moshe Peled's 146th division located to the south. The morning began with a feeling of strangulation. An early meeting with Tzvi at 7:00 a.m. and a CGS Preparatory Working Group meeting at 7:30 a.m. relieved the sense of unease somewhat, but not the troubling feeling that we were now fighting with all our forces without leaving anything in reserve. Some consolation was provided by the realization that our air force controlled the skies and was dictating the pace and the direction of the war in the air. By the end of the day things were clearer than they had been at the beginning of the day: the Iraqi division had unwittingly entered the open jaws of three Israeli brigades, and at least 80 Iraqi tanks had been destroyed. The obstruction in the northern Golan Heights that had been blocking the advance of the 7th battalion where Yossi Ben-Hanan was injured had not yet been breached, and the Golani Brigade commanded by Amir Drori and a reserve paratroop brigade led by Haim Nadel were sent to assist Eitan and Dan Laner's divisions. The IDF finally appeared to have recognized the value of infantry in the war. In the fighting by the Canal we had already seen that Egyptian infantry forces with Sagger missiles constituted a serious threat to our tanks. Major General Albert Mendler, commander of the southern division (the 252nd) in the Sinai Peninsula, was hit by an Egyptian anti-tank missile and died of his injuries, and Kalman Magen took over his command. Haim Bar-Lev went down to the Sinai Peninsula to assume command of the front as a whole and to prepare the forces there to hold off the major attack that the Egyptians had been observed preparing over the past few days. Elazar returned encouraged from a visit with the troops by the Canal, and that had a positive impact on all of us. There was also a successful operation of the paratroops in the depths of Iraq, aimed at disrupting the flow of Iraqi forces to the southern Golan Heights. The paratroops' accomplishments included, among other things, the demolition of a large bridge and the destruction of tanks while still on their transporters. Our success in stopping the convoys on this route generated a sense of confidence and an overall positive feeling within General Staff headquarters.

As a result of the relatively significant lull in the fighting we now began to notice the talk in the defense ministry corridors and to hear the general criticism and accusations that were emerging regarding a variety of issues, including:

- The errors of the Intelligence Branch and the Intelligence Branch chief in particular.
- Our underestimation of the importance of infantry forces, which had now been proven to be mistaken.
- Our underestimation of the importance of anti-tank weapons and the assessment that "the IDF is saturated with anti-tank systems," a view originally voiced by partisans of the tank corps.
- The air force's inability to provide close-range support for the fighting forces on the ground.
- And even criticism of the Israeli navy.

This time, however, there seemed to be a good chance that we would remember these issues and address them after the war, in contrast to the aftermath of the Six Day War, when the sweeping victory caused us to grow complacent. Nonetheless, when sitting down to begin learning the lessons of a war it is always crucial to remember that no war is similar to the one that preceded it.

A TURNING POINT IN THE WAR – THE EFFORTS TO CROSS THE SUEZ CANAL

At the end of the tenth day of the war I wrote in my journal that although the war had only been going on for 10 days, it felt much longer. "In the evening, everything calms down and everyone goes to rest up for the next day of battles in accordance with the rules of this curious game of death." We also felt as if a decisive movement in the Sinai was finally within reach. We knew it would not happen quickly, but it was clear that the process had begun.

It started with hundreds of Egyptian attack sorties and attempts by Egyptian infantry and tank forces to improve their positions.

Intelligence Branch officials informed us that the Egyptians had moved additional tanks eastward across the Canal during the night, bringing the number of operating tanks to 1,100, and had launched a major offensive in the direction of the Mitla and Gidi Passes. That evening during the CGS Preparatory Working Group meeting Elazar sounded unusually optimistic, arousing more positive feelings in us all. Amir Drori and the Golani Brigade, and Haim Nadel and the 317th Paratrooper Brigade, had breached the obstructions in the north in support of the divisions of Eitan and Laner, and we could now direct our full attention to events in the south.

During the tenth day of the war, 200 Egyptians tanks were reported destroyed. However, only in the afternoon were we able to begin staging the appearance that one of our divisions was breaking out in order to draw the Egyptian forces into a trap we were setting for them and to crush them. In the war room we heard frightening radio transmissions from the Israeli 162nd division. The operations officers calmed us down and told us that it was all part of an Israeli deception plan, which was ultimately successful. The Egyptians advanced in pursuit of the retreating 162nd division and the pounding of the Egyptian tank brigade began, making it possible to initiate a substantial offensive action at the Canal. An official announcement of the total number of casualties of the war until that point placed the number at 656. The same day the authorities announced the death of Major General Albert Mendler, the commander of the Sinai Division.

The US Defense Department finally authorized the shipment to Israel of military equipment in American military planes. Huge A5-Cs (Galaxy) and C-141s (Hercules) were already on their way to Israel carrying hundreds of tons of ammunition. In a few days, 70 TOW missile launchers were also scheduled to arrive in Israel, accompanied by the team we had sent to the US expressly for that purpose. I was at Ben-Gurion airport when the first Galaxy landed. It pulled up close to where we were standing and opened its gigantic rear doors, and a shiny polished American tank rolled out, with light exhaust puffing out of its engine. This boosted our morale tremendously, as the knowledge that we had the support of the most important superpower was of the utmost importance. After unloading its cargo the Galaxy just stood there with its enormous wings sloping downwards. To us, it was the most beautiful plane in the world. Tzvi told us that the Americans had agreed to fly Phantoms at the quicker pace of four planes per day, and this was an important source of encouragement for our severely degraded air force.

Within the R&D Unit we had the feeling that things had finally balanced out and that a great deal of important work was now underway. Those who had joined the troops on the front lines and those who had joined in the efforts were doing good work, while the rest, including 50 R&D reservists who had been mobilized during the first days of the war, were engaged in gathering information for generating lessons and were in the initial stages of the analysis process. The R&D Security Advisory Committee was assembled in order to brief its members on the situation and to consider how they might be integrated into the effort. During a discussion we had after the briefing, I realized the extent to which they had been craving meaningful involvement of some kind. What I wanted to do more than anything else was to visit the front. Tzvi authorized me to do so in principle, and I was now waiting for a window of opportunity to join the CGS on one of his trips to the front.

After the meeting with the Advisory Committee, we began to consider the changes we would need to make in our annual plan and our more longterm plans. We still had no way of knowing if there would be changes in substance, but by now it was clear that there would have to be changes in priorities. Our general feeling was that despite the American aid we would actually have to rely more on ourselves in the future. The same day Defense Minister Dayan stopped me and asked: "Can't we produce an anti-tank missile here in Israel?" I said it all depended on the time-table. Dayan continued to press me with his well-known directness: "Yes or no?"

"Yes!" I told him. "Of course we can. But it needs to be clear that the preparations for production are likely to take about a year."

"What if the Americans provide us with the knowledge and the authorization to produce them?" the minister persisted.

"In that case, the time-table would be shorter," I answered, seeing no reason to burden him with any further details.

"You need to get ready to begin production," Dayan declared. I was pleased because he supported our belief that there were some areas in which we would need to rely only on ourselves in the future. It was also good to see that Dayan had managed to pull himself out of the great despondency that had engulfed him during the first few days of the war. I told him that we would begin working on it, and that the production of anti-tank missiles would undoubtedly constitute only one of many issues that would require such attention.

On the morning of Tuesday, October 16, after a sleepless night in the Command Center, I wrote in my journal that Arik Sharon's division "attempted to accomplish the impossible tonight, but has yet to succeed." I was referring to their attempt to break through the 21st Egyptian division, to land the 55th brigade under the command of Danny Matt as a bridgehead on the west bank of the Canal, and to position the roller-bridge there. The crossing operation which Arik had insisted on implementing since the beginning of the war was good (apparently, he insisted on implementing that plan, and only that plan). The Egyptian army had thin forces at Deversoir on the west bank of the Canal, and with the help of mobile forces we could push back the anti-aircraft missile batteries far from the area or destroy them altogether. This, in turn, would enable our air force to operate freely and to support our forces more substantially than they previously had been doing.

Proudly, but with a sense of concern, I followed the 55th brigade's crossing operation. I knew that the 71st battalion, now under the command of Dan Ziv, my deputy in Jerusalem during the Six Day War, was the first to cross the Canal in rubber boats and to establish the bridgehead. I was with them in spirit. But when the light of day broke it became clear that an Egyptian force had taken control of a junction en route to the Canal and that the 600th brigade of Arik Sharon's division had not yet not reached the Egyptian bridges that were still standing. To make matters worse, our crossing equipment — including the roller-bridge, the mobile "Timsakh" landing crafts (French made Gillois rafts), and the Engineering Corps' rafts — were delayed en route due to technical problems and difficulties on the battlefield. In the Command Center there was great concern regarding the bridgehead's fragile situation. We were worried about the impact of the Egyptian artillery, which could take out the entire bridgehead. Another major concern was that the Egyptian air force, still enjoying the defenses of its anti-aircraft missile batteries, could also focus massive attacks on the bridgehead. "The paratroops are doing it!" said voices in the Command Center excitedly, over and over again. At one point I drove home to rest a bit, but I only managed to worry Naomi more. I could not tell her about the crossing operation that had not yet succeeded and that was still underway, but I was also unable to hide my concern.

The Command Center continued to draw me in with terrifying strength, and I could not help but spend a great deal of time there. At the entrance I found Ezer Weizman in conversation with Mordechai Bar-On, brother of Ben Bar-On and the composer Yechezkel Braun, who had served as adjutant to Moshe Dayan during the Sinai Campaign. Weizman was talking about the Israelis' trauma, about cracks in the image of leaders including that of Dayan, about how necessary it was for people to mobilize themselves psychologically and to increase morale, and about the need to reorganize the IDF. Although he had no doubt that we would win the war, he emphasized that serious failures had taken place: in building the IDF's order of battle, in Israeli intelligence and intelligence assessments, and in the policy realm. The war broke out during a break in Weizman's military career, while he was working as a private businessman, and he was called up to serve as an advisor to the CGS. We accompanied him down into the Command Center, where we learned that Danny Matt's 55th brigade had been reinforced by nine or twelve tanks that had been transported to the west bank of the Canal by the self-propelled French Timsakh (Gillois) rafts. The resulting sense of celebration was justified, as the bridgehead was now reinforced by tanks, which increased our chances of stabilizing and expanding it. People were also pleased with the success of the Gillois landing crafts, which I, among others, had fought to purchase when we realized that we had no other battle-ready crossing mechanism. The rafts, which were meant to be linked together and fashioned into a long bridge by the Engineering Corps, also got stuck in the sand, as the weight of the tanks they bore made them almost useless. The roller-bridge, which had offered so much promise and which was even awarded the Israel Defense Prize before its development was even complete, was now left far behind.

On Wednesday, October 17th, Hoshana Raba, or the last day of the Sukkot holiday, we all hoped for good tidings. According to the briefing delivered during the morning visit of the defense minister and the CGS to the Command Center, Arik Sharon had had a relatively quiet night. Still, the obstruction that was blocking his forces' advance toward the Canal had not yet been breached. Uzi Yairi and the 35th paratroop brigade were brought in as reinforcements from the southern sector. During the morning we also heard that difficult battles were being fought at the Chinese Farm. The two Egyptian brigades, which we knew had been ordered to move southward to disrupt our efforts to cross the Canal, simply did not move. In the course of the day Arik's division managed to transport forty armored vehicles across the Canal by means of the Gillois rafts. At the same time, in an operation commanded by Dov Tamari, Adan's deputy, Adan's division succeeded in transporting twelve rafts to the edge of the Canal, and the Engineering Corps had already started to build the first bridge.

The roller-bridge had still not been used. One reason was that its cumbersome structure required more than the four tanks that were originally planned for it to be dragged through the sand. More critically, the threat of the enemy on the ground prevented the kind of quiet work needed to deal with such a complicated apparatus. The plan proposed by the CGS and approved by a nod of Dayan's head envisioned Sharon remaining with his division on the east bank of the Canal in order to get organized, while Adan would cross the Canal with his two brigades and make a push southward in order to block the retreat path of the 4th Egyptian division. This would leave the entire third Egyptian army surrounded on the east bank of the Canal. For the first 36 hours, the Egyptians appeared to have incorrectly assessed the significance of our crossing operation. Now, they were attempting to hold us off and were paying a heavy price in the process.

Despite the pressure of working group meetings, briefings on the battles, sessions of monitoring military radio transmissions, and consultations in the Command Center and the defense ministry, primarily with Tzvi Zur but also with director-general Ironi, I could not completely forget about the R&D Unit. The morning that Adan's division started to cross over to the west bank of the Canal the R&D Unit's main office was in disarray. The announcement of a staff meeting which I had planned had not been relayed properly, and the offices were still littered with the young female soldiers' bedding. "This place should not look like a tavern!" I bellowed as I entered the office. The anger was necessary. I could understand the girls' state of mind. They had been acting a bit crazy due to worry and lack of information, and imposing an element of order was a necessity. In the end, we had a good staff meeting. I began with a briefing regarding the situation on the front, followed by a session in which each department director explained what he was working on. This provided a good opportunity to issue clear instructions for each director's realm of activity. Everyone understood that in addition to addressing the issues directly related to the war itself we also needed to prepare ourselves for an ongoing state of warfare that could continue for weeks or even months. The fact that everything was clear and well understood was reflected in the energetic response from staff.

At the height of the frantic situation that the war dictated, Tzvi requested an update regarding the integration of the TOW missile system. He also wanted to begin generating lessons regarding the weapons systems developed in Israel that had been used during the war. We talked about the need to take measures within the research and development institutions in order to effectively adapt to the current state of ongoing war. Although we needed to prepare quick response capability (QRC) on the institutional level, I thought it was also important to simultaneously maintain infrastructure and continue the major development projects. Tzvi asked us to prepare an outline for an in-depth discussion on the subject, and we started to work on it at R&D.

During the afternoon of that same long day, which, like other days during the war, felt like it had neither beginning nor end, a situation evaluation was conducted in Tal's office. The meeting was attended by Meir Amit, former CGS Yigal Yadin, Intelligence Branch Chief Eli Zeira, former Intelligence Branch Chief Aharon Yariv, former Logistics Branch Chief Amos Horev, Professor Yuval Neeman, and History Department Director Colonel Avraham Lenz. It was an interesting and informative discussion during which I thought to myself how that forum was the national security council of the people of Israel in every sense of the term. Tal did a good job of chairing the meeting, and much of its content was recorded in my "War Journal".

On Thursday, October 18, the day after the Sukkot holiday, a special atmosphere prevailed in the Command Center. When I had been there the night before, Adan had only managed to move one battalion over the Canal to the west bank, and it was reported that the bridge was damaged. The area surrounding the bridge had sustained heavy artillery fire, and the tanks had damaged one of the connectors as they sped across the raft-bridge. "It's not serious," they reported from the field, "but it will take some time to repair." At the end of the nighttime meeting of the CGS Preparatory Working Group, we were told that the bridge had been restored through improvisation by simply placing the bridging apparatus of a bridging tank across the broken portion.

I met with Operations Department Director Yankeleh Stern in order to incorporate plans to get hold of the SA-6 anti-aircraft missile batteries into the orders for our forces that had crossed the Canal. On Thursday morning there was another dip in morale when an Egyptian tank brigade reached the crossing area and managed to disrupt our effort. The war room maps now bore red arrows representing an Egyptian paratroop brigade en route to Adan's 217th brigade, which had already crossed the Canal. The faces of the officers in the Command Center who were following the developments via the radio transmissions reflected the severity of the situation. But in the afternoon Stern told me that the blockage had been opened, our forces had been ordered to attack the missile batteries, and the process of crossing the Canal had resumed, reviving our chances of getting our hands on the troubling SA-6 missiles.

In the R&D Unit I felt as if I was bearing the burden of pushing things forward all on my own. I was the person who was kept up to date on developments and who asked for and received instructions from senior officials, and this meant that only I could take the initiative and indeed was obliged to do so. Still, it often seemed to me as if everyone else was paralyzed, whether by the fear felt by all Israelis during the war, or by the lack of confidence resulting from the breakdown of routine. The main office was also paralyzed, and the young women soldiers were frightened. I sat down with my deputies Yedidia and Nahum and my assistant Ronny to plan a discussion on how R&D institutions should function during periods of ongoing warfare. During the meeting I was forced to repeatedly reiterate my different lines of thought to create a common denominator of understanding and agreement. The issue that seemed most important at the time was the right balance between quick responses to the challenges of the war and ongoing projects that had continue. It was also important to continue tending to the technological infrastructure although on a limited basis. It was a difficult period for everyone. In such times, people either display an ability to work well under pressure or succumb to their personal limitations. The director of the Missiles Department was an industrious engineer with a rigid and limited way of thinking. The director of the Electronics Department, in contrast, had a broad outlook, a sense of optimism, and the ability to make things happen. The director of the Ground Department appeared to be as hard working, sensible, and efficient as he had been during peacetime.

Twenty-four hours after the construction of the first bridge over the Canal, the TOW team we had sent to the US — Gabi Nagel, Michael Nagel, and Benny Ron — landed in Israel on an American plane. The three reported to the R&D offices in spotted uniforms, pale and tired, but content. We immediately drove to the Bat Yam firing range to observe the first TOW missile firing in the country and to meet the team they would join which would train troops in using the missiles. The test was attended by many senior officers including IDF Training Department Director Major General Meir Zorea, his deputy, Chief of Infantry and Paratroopers Colonel Emanuel Shaked, and others. The battalion commander designated to head the new TOW battalion was told to fire the missile at a tank target 1,200 meters away and scored a hit. Encouraged, I returned to the Command Center and jokingly told people there that a TOW missile had already taken out one tank. Only after hearing their enthusiastic cries of joy did I tell them that it had not actually happened in battle, but at a target range.

It was impossible to follow the progress of the battles without considering the personal aspects involving people I knew intimately. In the Golan Heights, Elisha Shalem and his battalion of paratroop reservists managed to conquer a Syrian position manned by an infantry battalion while destroying 10 Syrian tanks. The position had been a menacing obstacle that had halted the advance of Eitan's division in the northern Golan Heights. I had previously served in the same battalion as Elisha's deputy, and I knew many of its soldiers and officers. I was overjoyed and filled with pride when I heard the news.

A less cheerful personal element involved former R&D Department Director Colonel (Res.) Ben Bar-On. Ben had set out for the southern front with the teams charged with collecting data for subsequent lesson generation. After a few days he learned that his son had been killed when his tank was hit while fighting with a tank brigade. Ben managed to reach the burned-out tank from which he removed his son's body. When he returned to the General Staff base he came into my office and told me the story. He actually managed to find the tail of the RPG that appears to have struck one of the weak points of his son's tank, setting it ablaze. Ben gave me the tail, which remained on my desk as a painful but encouraging reminder throughout all the subsequent years during which I worked serving the country.

I wanted to travel down to the Canal with Elazar. The groundwork for the trip had long been ready, authorized in principle by Tzvi and coordinated with Assistant Operations Branch Chief Brigadier General Aryeh Levi. However, when everything was ready I was suddenly ambushed by a meeting in Tal's office. The meeting was neither beneficial nor detrimental to any significant extent, but it caused me to miss my flight. There was another flight to the southern front the next day, but Elazar was in a foul mood due to the state of affairs, which again looked bleak, and he only brought Aharon Yariv along with him. In the meantime we made progress in integrating the TOW missiles, and Elazar ordered that they be put into operation on the northern front as soon as possible in order to reinforce our tenuous line of defense in the southern Golan Heights along the purple line, which at the time was held solely by outmoded Sherman tanks.

As the war raged on the first delegation of American military experts arrived in Israel, circling high above the battlefield like eagles in wait. We had to prepare their reception with almost no advance notice. We knew what we wanted from them: advice and training for the American weapons systems we had purchased for our air force and our ground forces. We also had a clear understanding of what they wanted from us: data to generate lessons regarding the confrontation between western and Soviet weaponry, as well as the intelligence which we were gathering during the war. Nahum, my deputy, was charged with coordinating our contact with the American advisors, but I knew that as the director I would have to be involved. I took advantage of the preparatory meeting on hosting the American delegation to coordinate the generation of lessons within the air force, with a focus on air-to-ground issues, with Colonel Yosef Maayan of the air force Equipment Squadron and Colonel Yossi Hankin of the Air Force Weapons Division. Because Nahum was an air force man himself, his presence was a great help in forging a good relationship.

I finally found an opportunity to leave the General Staff Command Center, but only in order to enter a different command center – that of the Southern Command in the Sinai Peninsula in Um Hashiba. I approached the CGS as he was about to leave for a flight and he agreed to have me join him. I hoped we would go into the field to observe our combat forces, but most of our time was dedicated to a meeting between Moshe Dayan, Haim Bar-Lev, and Major General Shmuel Gonen. I assumed that the meeting had to do with the insubordinate Major General Arik Sharon, whom some already wanted to remove from his post three days earlier. Sharon, who had served as OC Southern Command until he was replaced by Gonen in July 1973, was convinced that he understood what was happening on the southern front better than Gonen. Sharon thought that some of Gonen's decisions were mistaken, including several critical decisions of fundamental importance, and for this reason he refused to accept the authority of the new OC from the moment the war began. Sharon's independent decision making continued even after Bar-Lev arrived to command the southern front; and indeed Bar-Lev also had difficulties with Sharon's own personal agenda. But anyone who really thought that Dayan would agree to relieve Sharon of his command in the middle of the war was sorely mistaken. Dayan's special relationship with Sharon had a long history, beginning in the early 1950s, when he appointed Sharon to set up the legendary Unit 101. During the entire period of Israel's reprisal operations, Dayan, then serving as CGS, recognized Sharon's abilities and the contribution he made to the fighting spirit of the IDF. Even after the Sinai Campaign, in the wake of the difficult battle fought by the Paratroop Brigade at the Mitla Pass, Dayan dismissed criticism of Sharon, who had entered the Mitla Pass without receiving an explicit order to do so. "It's better to ride on the backs of noble steeds," insisted Dayan, "than to beat lazy oxen with a shepherd's staff."

I kept my eyes and ears open with regard to everything and began to gain a clear picture of the interesting and extremely unusual situation that had evolved in the southern front. Bar-Lev was serving as an authoritative, supreme advisor, but was unable to issue direct orders. At the same time, OC Southern Command Gonen, though somewhat deferent and despondent, nonetheless continued to play the role of OC. Uri Ben-Ari, who was promoted to the rank of brigadier general during the war, served as the Southern Command's combat bureau chief. Ben-Ari functioned quietly and methodologically while Asher Levy, a senior and highly experienced Brigadier General, functioned efficiently as the Command's administrative bureau chief. Elazar recognized the unusual state of affairs in the Southern Command's command structure but was powerless to change it. Instead, he supervised developments from a distance and relied on Haim Bar-Lev to handle the situation on the ground.

Throughout the day we followed the battles from closer proximity than we could have from Tel Aviv, and realized that Adan was in true form, conducting a stubborn and impressive day of fighting and even asking the Southern Command to allow him to continue his push the following day. Kalman Magen, now in command of the division of Albert Mendler who had been killed in battle, was holding off the advance of the enemy in the southern sector and had refortified his force. Sharon was occupied with the conquest of the Missouri stronghold, the menacing Egyptian position on the east bank of the Canal that had broken all the attacks of the 600th Brigade until that time. At the same time, two Israeli paratroop battalions were already operating along the west bank of the Canal against Egyptian commando units that had been sent to disrupt the crossing. These battalions had achieved substantial successes and were already highly valued by the Southern Command. Top level infantry forces again proved their value on the battlefield, and every time the tank brigades encountered an obstruction that looked like trouble, they requested the support of a paratroop battalion. By this stage of the war we had already concluded that we would need to invest a great deal of work in developing weapons systems for our excellent infantry forces. The ineffectiveness of the armored infantry brigades compared to the paratroops was a clear indication that we needed to reconsider how to address this issue in the future. It was clear we would have to develop different means for mobilizing and arming the armored infantry to allow them to fight alongside tanks. We flew back on an aircraft known as an Arava, which had been developed as a military–civilian aircraft by Israel Aerospace Industries with Ezer Weizman and Aharon Yariv, the reliable behind-the-scenes figures of the CGS. The plane travelled fast, but the roar of the engines was deafening. Elazar boarded the plane, sprawled out on his bench, and immediately fell asleep, despite the sound of the engines.

"The Security Council Decides on a Ceasefire within Twelve Hours," screamed the newspaper headlines the next morning. The Israeli government had agreed, the papers reported, but Cairo and Damascus had not yet issued responses. Toward evening, the Egyptians agreed, and it was actually Damascus that remained silent for the time being. We thought that the Syrians were still preparing a

counter-attack against Mt. Hermon, after we had finally re-con-
quered the summit at the steep price of another 60 casualties from
the Golani Brigade.

The R&D Unit now had to organize itself and to adopt a regular working schedule to begin addressing routine working problems.
During a staff meeting just before what we regarded as a rather ques-
tionable cease-fire we decided to begin a regular working regimen.
Our return to work "as usual" was also reflected by limiting ourselves
to two informational meetings per week and the resumption of regular working meetings.

As the hostilities began to wind down, debates regarding the
lessons to be learned intensified. They dealt with a variety of issues,
including:

- The organizational structure of the IDF.
- The role of the armored forces.
- The importance of the infantry.
- The anti-missile capabilities of the air force.
- Independent military production in Israel, as opposed to reliance
  on weapons acquisition abroad.

The delegation of American military experts started giving us trouble when they realized that our people wanted only their help and
were not interested in providing them with anything in return. We
got in touch with Mordechai Gur, the Israeli military attaché in
Washington, who immediately scheduled a meeting with U.S. Defense Secretary James Schlesigner. While still at the Pentagon, Gur
called Yaakov Granot, our representative in Washington, and told
him that our work with the American delegation would be "half and
half," meaning that we would have to give them something to satisfy
their curiosity to a certain degree. I spoke with Intelligence Branch
Chief Eli Zeira, and coordinated the change in plans for the visit of
the American experts. We decided we would start with an intense

series of tours in the areas where battles had been fought.

On the morning of Thursday, October 25 after the US issued us a stern warning the Israeli government was forced to completely abide by the ceasefire. This was neither the first nor last time we would try to achieve an additional, last-minute military success before a ceasefire to give us an advantage in future negotiations. It was also not the only time we did so for other reasons — such as pride, maintaining image, and deterrence. The hasty authorization of the IDF's entry into East Jerusalem and the rushed, borderline incompetent combat procedure implemented for this purpose during the Six Day War may have stemmed from a desire to avoid finding ourselves in the midst of a ceasefire that would have prevented us from taking advantage of an historic opportunity. During the first Lebanon war (1982), fighting also continued despite international decisions. With the wisdom of hindsight, it is clear that we did not benefit from this extended fighting in any way. During the second Lebanon war (2006), the operations mounted during the last two days were also consistent with this pattern of behavior. This historical pattern obliges us to consider new ways to improve our ability to conduct the final phases of future wars in a different, more logical manner.

A few hours before we accepted all the terms of the ceasefire, Israeli forces made operational use of the TOW missile on the northern front, destroying one Syrian tank that burst into flames and hitting five others tanks, the tops of which had been exposed but which were not completely destroyed. All in all, thirteen missiles were fired during the incident, and although it did not change the course of the war, it nonetheless gave us a good feeling: the new system had already proven itself.

We decided to take advantage of the ceasefire to begin collecting data to be used for generating lessons from the war. During a meeting with Yedidia, Nahum, and Ronny, I presented what I regarded as the main points, which included broad reference to the structure and equipment of the IDF. It was still quite early to be discussing lessons,

182 | Eilam's Arc

since the war wasn't really over yet. We lacked complete information regarding the issues we discussed, and the data collected by the R&D teams on the front was also still in a crude state. Nevertheless, I believed that the time was right to construct a foundation and to fill it with content later, with the understanding that we would be able to make additions, changes, and improvements as we proceeded. For the enemy, we hypothesized a scenario of good air forces, a surprise air offensive aimed at paralyzing our air fields, and a strong ability to strike at our strategic depth during an initial attack. We assumed that the enemy navy had already learned from its defeat, particularly with regard to electronic warfare. For the sake of discussion we assumed that the enemy's ground forces still possessed the same strength they had at the beginning of the war, but had not undergone significant qualitative improvement.

As for Israel, our assumption was that we would be forced to make do with human resources limited by the number of new draftees into the regular army, and by the number of soldiers being added to the reserve forces, a function of the first number. We assumed that the quality of the cross-section of our soldiers would remain high, and that it would therefore be worthwhile to make efforts to use the human resources of the IDF. Our assumption about the air force was that we would need to build substantial anti-aircraft defenses both in our rear and in close proximity to our fighting formations to contend with enemy air power and to free up our air force to carry out counter-attacks. To cope with the enemy's armored forces and to free up our armored forces for surprise offensive actions, we regarded it as necessary to equip the army with modern antitank missiles like the TOW and artillery with advanced shells. The problem presented by the large number of enemy infantry forces appeared to be solvable by means of artillery, anti-personnel tank weapons ("Flechette" warheads), and shrapnel shells.

I regarded the issue of command and control on the level of the combat divisions and the General Staff as critical. Other important aims included secured and impenetrable communications, particularly in light of our success in listening to the enemy during the war, and improvements in the area of electronic warfare. I was quite aware that we had not yet studied the tank battles, which were the largest in history in terms of the numbers of tanks involved. We had not yet considered the characteristics of the Sagger anti-tank missiles or the significance of the Egyptian anti-tank ambushes. We had also had not yet acquired a full SA-6 missile system to help us find its weak points and develop defense mechanisms and tactics for the air force. At that point we still did not understand the significance of our inability to see what was happening on the other side of the hill on the battlefield. This lesson emerged only later, and eventually motivated us to begin developing UAVs — unmanned aerial vehicles.

10

War Lessons and the Treasure Hunt

INITIAL LESSONS OF THE 1973 WAR

When the fighting died down after the ceasefire the personnel from the R&D Unit who had joined the combat troops or the logistical support units returned to the Kirya government campus in Tel Aviv. The teams charged with collecting combat data for analysis returned too, bringing with them important information and impressions. The air force also held a combat analysis conference that focused on air battles and the challenge of the Egyptian and Syrian surface-to-air missiles. Air Force Commander Major General Benny Peled invited me to a meeting of all the squadron commanders and unit commanders above the rank of lieutenant colonel. I was the only one wearing the green uniform of the ground forces in this highly focused, five-hour discussion. I was impressed by the freedom of speech that Peled afforded his officers. These men were not merely letting off steam after a difficult and often frustrating war; they were also voicing exceedingly meaningful criticism.

Teams from the Israeli Navy, headed by Colonel Herut Zemach, also joined us, providing encouraging data about the missile boat battles. Much of their success stemmed from the electronic warfare systems that were installed on all missile boats. During an early 1973 meeting on working plans held in the office of the Operations Branch chief, Major General Tal vehemently objected to the Navy's development plans, declaring that "The navy doesn't need more electronic warfare devices" because "the ships anyway look like Christmas trees." The war clearly proved that the Navy was right. In a more recent painful naval event that took place during the Second Lebanon War 33 years later, a successful enemy attack on the INS Hanit was clearly the result of weaknesses in Israeli naval command and intelligence.

When Simcha Maoz, director of the R&D Planning and Economics Department, returned from the logistical position he had been filling in Sharon's division, he was harshly critical of the confusion and helplessness he had found in the Southern Command, saying that much of the needed equipment was either inoperative or did not arrive at all.

The time dedicated to preliminary working group meetings and other consultations was now freed up for a wide range of issues including meetings with defense industry executives, preparations to reorganize our work plans, consolidating the vast amount of data collected by the R&D teams and other IDF units, and the beginning of work with the American analysis delegation. I consulted with Brigadier General Yitzhak Yaakov about our work with the Americans, and he wisely advised me to fit the work into the already existing framework of the R&D department's cooperation with the Americans. This, he said, would ensure that each area remained under our control, thereby displaying the political astuteness of a past master.

On Thursday, November 1, less than a month after the beginning of the war, the defense minister and all IDF division commanders attended a special meeting of the CGS working group. Dayan presented the thesis that we would soon need to attack and destroy the Third Egyptian Army and to do as much damage to the Second Army as possible. I thought Dayan was actually too delicate when he also asked the generals to stop besmirching each other in the newspapers. Elazar echoed this point when he summed up the conversation, passionately calling for an end to the war between the generals. "We have excellent soldiers and a wonderful army," he said. "Don't destroy them."

On Friday, November 2, the Command Center was on high alert in light of explicit reports that the Egyptians were planning to launch an attack aimed at creating a corridor for the Third Army, which they had not managed to achieve through diplomacy. The next morning I went to the Command Center with a great sense of concern only to find it relatively empty. I was chatting with Chief Infantry and Paratroop Officer Emmanuel Shaked about the importance of the lessons learned in the fighting when Colonel Avigdor Ben-Gal walked in. Ben-Gal, the hero of the Golan Heights battles, was lanky, unattractive and enchanting all at once. We greeted him enthusiastically and listened with great interest as he described his experiences during the war. Ben-Gal said that the Syrians were crazy, that they attacked and shot a great deal, and that we were lucky that they were not as skilled we were. Although he lost three battalion commanders during the war, he assured us that he still had excellent company commanders. I thought to myself how the war had been fought primarily by officers of the rank of brigade commander and below. The General Staff was responsible for facilitating air support and providing ammunition and reinforcements. But the primary war effort and credit for the achievements belonged first and foremost to the fighting forces themselves.

REHAVAM ZE'EVI AS OPERATIONS BRANCH CHIEF

One immediate outcome of the war was changes in the General Staff. A phone call from the office of the deputy CGS informed me that Rehavam Ze'evi had been appointed chief of the Operations Branch and that Avraham Tamir had been appointed chief of the Planning Branch and would be promoted to the rank of Major General. I wondered what Ze'evi's role would be – would he work alongside Deputy CGS Tal or under his authority? I also wondered how all this would affect the R&D Unit. I went upstairs to ask Tzur what he thought about the changes, but he just told me that he had not yet spoken with Elazar about them. Later, Tzur called and said that as far as he understood I would be answering to the CGS and working in coordination with the chief of the Planning Branch, and that he viewed this as a good arrangement.

That evening I stopped in to see Ze'evi, who fleshed out the picture with a more details about the re-delegation of authority. Ze'evi proposed moving R&D's Planning and Economics Department over to the new branch. It wasn't clear to me where he got the idea so I quietly and patiently began to explain the structure of the R&D Unit and the logic behind its Planning and Economics Department. At one point, when Ze'evi sounded as if he didn't get the point, I got irritated and raised my voice, and told him that he could dismantle R&D Unit as far as I was concerned. My anger apparently took him off guard, and he stopped badgering me about the issue. I understood that we were now in a complicated period of instability and uncertainty and that a great deal of effort, patience, and diplomacy would be needed to protect the R&D Unit from the surrounding madness. Within the R&D Unit itself Yedidia began working full time on working plans, and Nahum focused his attention on the unit's work with captured enemy weaponry which involved consolidating data for lesson generation, and contact with delegations from abroad.

An urgent meeting of the General Staff was called. Prime Minister Golda Meir was about to fly to Washington for meetings with President Nixon, and the General Staff was asked to advise her on whether she should agree to a corridor for the encircled Egyptian Third Army. Most members of the General Staff decisively opposed allowing such a corridor, and the meeting focused on the different ways of dealing with the Third Army. Sharon proposed focusing the effort to the north and cutting off the Second Army as well. Tal radiated extreme pessimism, arguing that attacking the Second Army would be "suicide" and that it was essential to achieve a separation of forces in order to rebuild our strength. Elazar summed up by saying that the General Staff opposed the provision of a corridor for the Third Army. He also supported an effort to destroy the encircled Third Army, but not completely and not at a high price. Furthermore, he did not rule out Sharon's proposal to cut off the Second Army. I knew Sharon's way of thinking during my time as his intelligence officer in the Paratroop Brigade in the 1950s. He had the ability to effectively combine knowledge of the field and a thorough understanding of the location of enemy forces and exceptionally accurate assessments of the enemy's capabilities and intentions. To me, Sharon's plan sounded ingenious and could have helped us attain a better bargaining position.

Within the R&D Unit we now got into a fresh momentum of orderly work, still working under the shadow of a possible collapse of the ceasefire. We made progress towards an agreement for cooperation with the American Department of Defense's Department of Research and Engineering. An entry in my journal describes the work as follows:

A draft agreement regarding cooperation with DDR&E on lessons... was ready, and I went upstairs for a meeting with Tzur. The assistant defense minister looked exhausted, but he offered insightful comments, as he tends to do, and approved it in principle. He also asked me who at the General Staff had seen it and agreed to it, and I told him that Benny (Peled, commander of the Air Force), Binyamin (Telem, commander of the Navy), and Eli (Zeira, Intelligence Branch Chief) had seen and agreed to it and that I approved the final text. He said that it was fine, and that although Tal might make some noise about it afterwards, no one complains these days about someone who takes the initiative. We talked a bit about the unstable General Staff and about the fact that appointing an Operations Branch chief and a Planning Branch chief was a good idea, but not enough to clean up the situation. Tzur told me that Elazar was now going through the most difficult period in the history of Israel's chiefs of the General Staff, with a divided General Staff, a slew of people saying "I told you so," and no one he can talk to and consult with

freely (except for Tzvi). He talked to me about Tal, who continues to
constitute a bottleneck in the decision-making process. I almost said:
'Why not remove him from his position?' Even more serious was
Tzur's description of the embarrassment, helplessness, indecision
and hostility within the government. Abba Eban is in Romania,
Sapir is raising money, Moshe is in his office, Golda is somewhere in
between... and nobody knows what needs to be done!

We were most worried about the global political situation. Also
disconcerting was Henry Kissinger's feverish scuttling from one
Arab capital to another. And on top of all that was the Soviet threat
of calling for a discussion in the UN Security Council if Israel did not
return to its borders by November 22.

Saturday, November 10 was a quiet day that gave me a chance
to work in peace. Tal, who had just been appointed OC Southern
Command, had been selected for complicated reasons. I remembered
what Tzur had said about Tal, and I thought that Elazar certainly
knew things that we didn't know and that perhaps this was his way
of distancing Tal's negative impact from the faltering General Staff.
With the temporary appointment of Ze'evi, who was experienced
and had served as assistant Operations Branch chief, Elazar would
have someone he could depend upon. For two hours on that quiet
Saturday morning, with no threat of a General Staff meeting or other
meetings on the horizon, I was able to present to Tzvi the main points
of my new working plan for 1973–1974, the data on human resources
within Rafael, and the main points of the agreement for cooperation
with the Americans regarding the lessons of the war.

Motta (Mordechai) Gur, our military attaché in Washington,
arrived in Israel for consultations. A major portion of our conversations
on the encrypted telephone had to do with how to respond to the
American requests for data on the performance of the Maverick and
Walleye air-to-surface missiles.

After a friendly handshake, Gur asked me about "his" brigade (the

55th) during the war, and I gave him a brief report. Tzur explained to him the details of the agreement we had drafted for cooperation with the Americans regarding the generation of war lessons. I was impressed by Tzur's command of the details, and pleased by the persuasive manner in which he presented the issue and his conviction about what needed to be done. Later, I met with Gur again, gave him a copy of the complete draft agreement, and provided him with additional explanations.

Once it became clear that the ceasefire was holding we were able to revert to the regular routine of General Staff meetings. The meeting on Monday, November 12 was attended by the defense minister. During the meeting, Dayan presented his view of the three phases of activity that he believed should follow the signing of the ceasefire agreement. Throughout the entire war, and even before it began, Dayan tended to remove himself from the chain of command, sending Elazar to Prime Minister Meir to make critical decisions and then acting as an advisor, not as the commander in chief of the army. He did not hesitate to fly to the front, and, in a few instances, we were surprised to learn that he had actually placed himself in the line of fire. A typical example was his visit to Sharon's forces at the "hatzer," the bridgehead east of the Suez Canal which at the time was being shelled day and night. But none of these limitations impaired Dayan's sharp and lucid analysis, which was as usual extremely convincing.

Dayan made a case for the following three phases: (1) Clarification of the terms of the agreement, which was expected to take a few days. (2) Stabilization of the lines by withdrawing from the western side of the Suez Canal. (3) The beginning of peace talks. The negotiations could blow up and fighting could resume during any one of the phases, Dayan explained. The General Staff meeting was supposed to focus on the inquiry about the war that the CGS had announced to the media and the process of lesson generation but quickly turned into a more general discussion on policy and orientation, combining talk about morale and faith in commanders. Yitzhak Elron chose to attack the defense ministry establishment, which he argued was damaging the IDF by prioritizing the development and production of weapons in Israel over buying weapons from abroad. I interrupted with a few comments while noting to myself how far I had strayed from the traditional IDF opinions I held in the past. Tzur did not get involved in the debate but rather addressed the topic of development and production in Israel, in his characteristic broad, intelligent, and elegant manner. During his summing up of the meeting, Elazar also addressed the point made by Elron, but rejected his arguments and endorsed the position of the defense ministry.

Gur visited our offices for a two-hour meeting that began with a discussion of the actions that needed to be taken with the American lesson-generating delegation. We agreed that Gur would meet with the American deputy defense secretary as soon as he returned to Washington and work towards signing an agreement. Gur was about to ask our defense minister to agree on his early return to Israel in order to assume a post on the General Staff, and he spoke frankly and openly about his intentions. We talked about the lesson-generation agreement with the Americans and about the best way to start working with them. There was absolutely no reason for concern when it came to our handling of the American delegations, as the issue was being handled skillfully by my deputy, Nahum Dayagi. The task of adapting our work plans to the situation that emerged after the war was also progressing well under the direction of my other deputy, Yedidia Shamir.

The most troublesome subject at the time was long-term planning, for which we needed systems analysis, the area that Simcha Maoz was supposed to direct. I regarded Simcha as a diamond with great potential among other jewels in the R&D Unit. Unfortunately, Simcha was really like a diamond, not only brilliant but hard. He was hard on himself and he made it hard for those around him, making it difficult to incorporate him into the Unit. I agreed to the request of Major General Tamir, chief of the newly established Planning Branch, that both Simcha and Dr. Adam Shefi, who also seemed ill at ease since returning from the war in the north, would move to the new branch in order to build a systems analysis department. As time passed this department evolved into an integral component of the IDF planning system, and I was pleased that by giving up these two unique people R&D was able to make a significant contribution to the structure of the IDF Planning Branch and to the overall work of the General Staff.

Saturday, November 17 was another quiet day. It was six weeks after the war had begun, and I went up to meet with Ze'evi on my own initiative. I really wanted to talk about the changes within the General Staff. Ze'evi had submitted his resignation a few days earlier, ostensibly as a result of his failure to convince the General Staff to adopt his proposals about handling the lessons of the war. However, it seemed to me that this was just the tip of the iceberg, and I came to hear what he had to say. Before I went in to see Ze'evi, Tal's bureau chief Yigal stopped me and told me that Tal had asked him to inform me unequivocally that both R&D and the new Planning Branch would be coordinated by him directly, and that this arrangement had been endorsed by the CGS. I assumed that Tal had pressured Elazar to agree to the arrangement, which to me seemed rushed and wrong. Tal was not only deputy CGS and responsible for coordinating all the branches of the General Staff, he was also the commander of the southern front. How did he intend to find the time to coordinate the General Staff?

Ze'evi talked about a number of things: about Elazar and the instability within the army's senior command; and about Tal, who was in exile in the south and was trying his hardest to return and about his resignation, adding that Elazar had begged him to stay. Ze'evi shared with me his feeling that the CGS was not keeping him — his own Operations Branch chief — in the loop, and was not providing him with guidance and instructions regarding policy. It saddened me to hear what Ze'evi had to say. It wasn't new, but it added more dark colors to the picture that was emerging. With surprising candor he also said that he would advise Elazar either to resign immediately or to fire whoever necessary in order to impose order and discipline. It was clear that Elazar did not have the authority for such bold action and would need the full support of Dayan and Meir for a clean sweep. According to Ze'evi, the people who needed to go were Gonen, Sharon, and perhaps Tal as well, "just to ensure that he won't disrupt things and give everyone the run around." He was less clear about who should stay. Indeed, this was a complicated and difficult question, partly because it's never a good idea to switch horses mid-race, especially since we were still only in the midst of a ceasefire. I did not completely agree with Ze'evi's claim that Elazar had still not returned to his old self and that this was the root of the problem. I didn't know about Dayan's role but I was sure that he was trying to save his own skin. My understanding of the situation reminded me of the proverb from Ecclesiastes, "he who increases knowledge, increases sorrow," and I knew that the near future would be filled with explosive political developments.

A large delegation from the US Congress arrived in Israel to get firsthand impressions about the situation in Israel after the war. This important visit received considerable attention and we all worked hard to arrange tours in the north and the south and organize briefings on the war experience. The plans included a visit to the display of captured enemy weapons at the Beit Lid army base, and the R&D Unit was charged with overseeing this part of the program. As we drove to Moshe Dayan's house for a meeting with the entire delegation, Tzur and I discussed the situation in the General Staff. I told him about my conversation with Ze'evi, about Tamir's efforts to build up the new Planning Branch, and about my impression that the CGS needed to rest a bit and then to take matters into his own hands. Tzur agreed, and added that "if they keep running things as they have been, it will come back to haunt them." It was clear to me that he was referring primarily to Elazar, the CGS.

The defense minister hosted all the members of the American

congressional delegation in the garden of his home in Tzahala, and worked his magic with light conversation and a presentation of his antiquities. During the evening the group was briefed by Intelligence Branch Chief Eli Zeira, who gave a polished and brilliant presentation; by Elazar, who surveyed the stages of the war; and by Air Force Commander Benny Peled and Navy Commander Binyamin Telem. Overall, we made sure to radiate not only strength but more confidence than we really felt. At the same time we spared no effort in expressing our gratitude for the logistical and political support the US had provided Israel during the war.

The visit to the display of captured weaponry took place two days later and was impeccably organized. The Technical Intelligence Department was responsible for the collection of an impressive variety of all types of armored vehicles, tanks, cannon and missiles. It was a display that provided in a snapshot a clear picture of what we had been up against during the war. It also enabled us to go into detail about each weapons system, most of which were Soviet made. I began the visit with a talk comparing Soviet and Western technologies. The director of the Technical Intelligence Department provided delegation members with detailed explanations during the tour, after which we reassembled for my concluding remarks. The tour finished with a sense that we had clearly conveyed the message regarding Soviet weaponry and the assessment of the global Soviet threat. It was a brief moment of satisfaction in a sea of difficulties and worries.

On Tuesday, November 20, we had a special General Staff meeting attended by Prime Minister Golda Meir. Dayan, Elazar, and Tzur sat at the head of the table, and after the Intelligence Branch and the Adjutant General Branch presented information that was neither new nor especially interesting, the prime minister entered the room. The group immediately fell silent. Meir took her seat and immediately lit what must have been her umpteenth cigarette of the day, and then carefully studied the group. Silenced by fear of the prime minister, few were brave enough to request the floor. Benny Peled, who was the first to speak, spoke of the widespread feeling that the political goals were not clearly defined and that the combat soldiers did not understanding why they were risking their lives. Adan, Amos Horev, Sharon, and Gonen also spoke. Sharon stressed the readiness and the high morale of the forces. In the days that I worked closely with Sharon as his intelligence officer, I learned that it was always necessary to understand not only what he said but what he meant. During the meeting it seemed to me that his intention was not to please Dayan or Meir, and that perhaps he was trying to prepare the ground for the proposal he had raised during the previous General Staff meeting: cutting off and surrounding Egypt's Second Army, as we had done to its Third Army.

Gonen, who appeared to be trying to recover from the feeling of being cornered since the first days of the war when he failed to function as OC Southern Command, supported Sharon's proposal. Tal's remarks marked a clear turning point in the discussion. As commander of the southern front he presented the thesis that we were weak, much weaker than we had been before the war, and while doing so he cited the number of commanders that had been killed. He argued that what we needed was disengagement from the Egyptians at any cost in order to refocus our efforts during the next year on rebuilding our forces. In the heat of his speech, Tal quoted "someone" who at a difficult point during the beginning of the war had said that all was lost. This was a clear reference to Dayan and this infuriated the defense minister, Elazar, and others in the room. The other speakers were scathingly critical of Tal's defeatist attitude, particularly Sharon and Adan. People started to quibble about the veracity of Tal's insinuation. The atmosphere was electrifying, and some people interjected with comments reflecting the tension and the pressure which we were all under. Meir listened attentively and contemplatively, and did not interrupt the discussion.

Dayan stressed the balance between us and the enemy. In his opinion, we had grown stronger in terms of weaponry and ammunition, and our positions in both the north and the south were extremely uncomfortable for the enemy, both militarily and psychologically. Elazar spoke in favor of a defensive strategy in all sectors, but also emphasized our ability to mount an offensive in one of them, in the event that the Egyptians began military action. As far as he was concerned, it was preferable to attack the encircled Third Army to further weaken it.

Meir calmly praised the quality of steadfastness, which was not surprising. After all, she symbolized the refusal to be flexible, for better and worse. To illustrate her point she talked about the negotiations with Kissinger in Washington, which she had found particularly difficult. Although the American secretary of state had claimed that he was unable to get the Egyptians to agree to Israel's conditions for a ceasefire, she explained, we maintained our position and remained steadfast, and in the end we were successful. "At such a juncture," Meir concluded, "we cannot appear to be weak, because this could spell our end." We left the meeting with the feeling that Meir was in fact strong and was not giving up the reins of power, that Dayan had recovered, and that Elazar seemed fine as well. The defeatist approach found no support during the rest of this unusual meeting, and we all felt that Tal's days on the southern front were numbered.

A VISIT TO THE NORTH

A week had passed since the meeting with the prime minister, and we finally found the time and, more importantly, the resolve to make the trip up to the tense but calm northern front, where the entire reserve army was still mobilized. My deputy and the director of the R&D Ground Department were pleased when I invited them to join me. We began in the morning with a calm, frank, businesslike hour-long meeting with Yitzhak Hofi, OC Northern Command. I first met Hofi in 1956, when he became Sharon's deputy in the Paratroop Brigade which had just been established. During my service with him at brigade headquarters, I grew to appreciate his wisdom, his ability to listen to others, and the calm strength he radiated. These qualities served him well during the difficult first days of the war in the Golan Heights, and later as a successful director of the Mossad and an accomplished director-general of the Israeli Electric Corporation. During Hofi's tenure as director of the Mossad, I was pleased to be involved in giving advice on technology issues.

Four days before the beginning of the Yom Kippur War the defense minister visited the Northern Command and was convinced by Hofi's assessment that there was a real chance that the Syrians might soon launch an attack. Dayan returned to his office and ordered the preparation of a plan to contain attacks by the Syrian tank and infantry divisions. The R&D Unit was charged with dealing with this urgent task. In fact, we had been scheduled to conduct a tour of the Golan Heights to this end on the Sunday after Yom Kippur. We called up some reserve officers and drew up a draft plan that involved adding landmines in the most likely corridors for a Syrian attack. We also considered adding an array of remotely operated short-range artillery rockets capable of covering the corridors susceptible to a Syrian tank breach. We planned to reinforce the system with an optic radar-detecting array in selected zones along the border. By that Sunday we were all at war, and we were never able to implement our plans to construct the effective, technologically advanced defense system against the Syrian attack corridors.

During the meeting Hofi emphasized the need for early warning of enemy movement that was indicative of an imminent attack. The R&D Electronics Department Director was instructed to check the compatibility of the radar then being developed by Elta Systems. We also considered acquiring American-developed geophonic systems that could either be air dropped or dispersed by artillery.

Officers of the Northern Command took us for a long, exhaustive tour of the entire area. We were briefed on the battles and provided with a view of the battlefield on which the gigantic tank battle was fought, a view that inspired both awe and admiration of our men. I had a clear memory of the voices of commanders over the radio during the most difficult and decisive hours of the battles, and this memory was immediately and chillingly linked to the sight of burned out Israeli and Syrian tanks that now littered the landscape.

We were also treated to the unique experience of being able to look down from the Tel Shams fort on the suburbs of Damascus through 120x20 binoculars. Visibility was good, and Damascus seemed only a hop, skip and a jump away. It was a feeling of strength and of control of the balance of power between us and the Syrians, but it was important not to allow ourselves to become drunk with power. I was pleasantly surprised to run into Elisha Shalem, an old friend and former commander.

Toward evening, Elisha assembled the company commanders of his reserve paratroop battalion for a meeting, just as we used to do during reserve duty in peacetime. There, I met old friends and gladly chatted over steaming hot sweet black coffee, answering questions about enemy anti-tank weapons, the Israeli assault rifle then under development, the American M-16 (which we would purchase as soon as possible), and my views on the war. The conversation reflected the insight of the intelligent, concerned men and helped me develop new ways of thinking about things. It also strengthened my opinion that the infantry would remain a critical component of any future war. I left with a great sense of admiration for the courage and resourcefulness of those paratroopers.

IN QUEST OF THE TREASURE

Before the fighting really ended we had already begun the preparatory work of consolidating the requests for weapons systems from the US. Although the American airlift, which bought us primarily artillery shells and tank ammunition, was an impressive gesture in retrospect its major impact appears to have been as a morale booster. Post-war assessments indicated that there had not even been a shortage of artillery shells during the war. Rather, the problem was our inability to transport the munition to the fighting units. In some cases logistics officers themselves held on to considerable quantities of ammunition in the event it might be needed by their units. In other cases, fighting in the combat zones prevented ammunition from reaching the front-line units. This, however, is all wisdom after the fact, for as the war was being fought, the fighting units were crying out for ammunition, and the American airlift appeared to provide an essential lifeline.

I found myself involved in the work of organizing the IDF's suggestions for new weapons and weapons systems we wanted from the US. After the trauma of the outbreak of the war, and the subsequent long and hard campaign with so many casualties, we had the somewhat hysterical conviction that we needed to arm ourselves with everything we could get from the Americans. In this spirit, a fitting codeword was selected for the effort: "Treasure." At one point, the Israeli defense minister himself planned to fly to Washington to personally present the requests to the American secretary of defense. Tzur told us to consolidate the many wish lists of the different services of the IDF into one master list to be presented to the Pentagon. We also prepared a comparison of Soviet and American weapons systems to justify our request for advanced systems.

Fittingly, the air force's wish list reached for the sky. They included air-to-surface missiles with electro-optic homing devices and the most advanced radar systems available, including some that were still in development. The artillery corps requested Lance missiles, and also Multiple Launch Rocket Systems (MLRS), which were still being developed by Lockheed for the US military. The list also included advance night vision equipment, which at the time was available only in the US, and advanced voice encryption systems for communications systems (in order to save ourselves a long and expensive development process). The trauma of the tank attacks in the north and the south demonstrated the need for air dropped mines or mines distributed by artillery rockets, which were still in the final stages of development by the American military. At the top of the list, in what could be seen as the height of our audacity, were Pershing missiles. Pershing missiles could carry a nuclear warhead and had a range of more than 600 kilometers. The Pershing II missile, which completed development in 1974, was extremely precise due to its final homing capabilities. We, of course, asked to purchase missiles with conventional warheads, but we were unable to explain our request for the missile which, as far as we were concerned, was purely strategic.

In retrospect, it's more than clear that most of the items on the lists were a reflection of the trauma of the Yom Kippur War. We know now that it was because of this trauma that we wanted the arms to create new brigades and divisions, primarily in the tank corps. We also know that stress on quantity placed a tremendous burden on the economy and diverted our attention from the qualitative requirements of future weapons systems. The hunger for arms that prevailed throughout the IDF after the war was a huge encumbrance, to be paid for over the course of many years to come.

Tzur was scheduled to join Defense Minister Dayan on the trip to Washington to present the "Treasure" list and said that the CGS had suggested that I join them as well. It was also suggested that I stay for a few more days and accompany Dayan in his meetings, which sounded interesting and exciting. However, within a few days the excitement died down and the trip was postponed indefinitely, mainly because the Americans refused to receive such a high-level delegation for arms procurement so soon after the war. In the end Dayan flew to Washington with Tzur alone, who took all the material that we had prepared for him.

Dayan's visit didn't help the arms acquisition program very much. The Americans agreed to supply us with M-16 assault rifles, a small number of tanks and armored personnel carriers, and a small, carefully calculated number of planes. We also received authorization in principle to purchase increased range optically-guided air-to-surface Walleye bombs, as well as increased range optically guided HOBO bombs. However, Dayan was unable to convince the Americans to provide us with Redeye man-portable surface-to-air missiles, Lance missiles for the artillery, or laser-guided bombs. To us, the policies of the Pentagon seemed more rigid than ever, and without the easing we expected after such a difficult war.

The death of David Ben-Gurion on December 1, 1973 had great significance for us all. The "old man," as everybody called him, slipped away quietly while the army, imbued by his vision but by now with its own purpose and structure, was fully mobilized and ready for a possible collapse of the ceasefire. We can only guess what was going through Ben-Gurion's mind during the last seven weeks of his life. Hundreds of thousands of regular and reserve soldiers accompanied him in spirit on his final journey. I remembered him standing by my bed at Tel Hashomer Hospital after Operation Black Arrow, asking how I was feeling. I remembered him in the mid-1950s leaving Jerusalem every Friday to spend Saturday on Kibbutz Sde-Boker, as my comrades in Sayeret Tzanhanim (the elite paratroop reconnaissance unit) and I provided him with an armed escort between Beer Sheba and his hut at Kibbutz Sde-Boker. We remembered his long-range political vision after the Six Day War, as he warned of what was about to happen in the West Bank.

We did not give up on the "Treasure," but we had to wait until the war was truly over to pursue it further. In the south, this was accomplished by means of the Kilometer 101 talks led by General Aharon Yariv. In the north, it was accomplished by the ceasefire agreement with the Syrians and the redeployment of our forces to the line that had served as the border before the war.

A few months later Motta Gur was already CGS, Major General Herzl Shafir was appointed as Operations Branch chief, and the second "Treasure" delegation left for talks in Washington. Prof. Yuval

Ne'eman, the defense minister's scientific advisor, and I went through the lists again to clarify what exactly we were seeking. We could not leave the request for Pershing missiles off the list, even though we did not think the Americans would let us have them. The delegation was led by Herzl Shafir himself, and included the commanders of the Air Force and the Navy, the chiefs of the Quartermaster's Branch, the Intelligence Branch, and the Planning Branch, and the director of R&D. The meeting at the Pentagon was led by Herzl Shafir, who also gave the floor to the commanders of the different services of the IDF. I explained the technological and strategic issues, a task made much easier by the detailed knowledge I had acquired while compiling the lists.

At one point I found an opportunity to split off from the group for a separate meeting with the Assistant Secretary of Defense for R&D. During the meeting I brought up some of the items on the list that I regarded as more sensitive, such as thermal vision technology, voice encrypted communications, landmines, and warning devices dropped from the air. It did not take long for me to understand that there was no chance that the Americans would allow us to purchase these systems. The delegation as a whole enjoyed the talks with the Americans and left with the sense that we had told them what we wanted, that they had definitely understood, and that they would certainly agree to give us everything we asked for. This would not be the last time that we heard ourselves too well and failed to pay sufficient attention to the nuances of the American English spoken by our counterparts.

As soon as we returned from the "Treasure" trip we had to brief the new defense minister, Shimon Peres, and CGS Gur. We were still recovering from the tough war, and our feeling that the Americans simply had to approve our requests overshadowed more sober considerations. After Shafir summarized the visit and the meetings for Peres and Gur each of the generals added points that had to do with their respective areas of responsibility. I assumed the role of trouble maker, upsetting the comfortable picture by saying that the Americans would not approve the sale of systems that were technologically or politically sensitive. Peled, Tamir, and Shafir took me to task, and claimed that I did not know what I was talking about; they openly stated that the Americans would give us everything we asked for. It soon became clear, however, that they were overly optimistic. At that point I recreated my one-on-one conversation with the Assistant Secretary of Defense for R&D and all of a sudden clearly understood the rules of the game and the conditions under which the Americans would provide us with advanced technologies. My conclusion was that the US would give us advanced weapons systems only after we could prove that we were in the midst of developing similar advanced technologies. Their justification for releasing such technologies would be either that there was no reason to hide what we already knew, or that it would be in the best interests of the US to provide us with the systems to reduce the Israeli motivation to develop the technology. It seemed that the American consideration was to prevent Israel from rapidly developing home-grown technology with its own export potential. From the American perspective such a policy would also increase Israel's dependence on the US in the realm of advanced technology. This paradigm is still applicable today.

The "Treasure" episode left me with mixed feelings. On the one hand, there was a sense of satisfaction that I had been right and that everyone now realized it. On the other hand, I was also certain that my fellow generals did not share this insight on American policy and the question was how to make them understand and use this insight in the new strategic foundations necessary to put in place after the war.

We found time for a working visit to the senior R&D officials at Elta Systems. Our group was impressed by the performance of the Dagon marine radar, which had been impressively adapted for the purpose of detecting vehicles from dozens of kilometers away. In the 1960s, when the company was managed by its founder and first CEO Paltiel Maklef, Elta appeared to be an unorganized and wasteful factory that lost money. However, that impression changed over the years when we understood the wise, long-term strategy with which Maklef built his company's human resources. Elta's carefully selected teams, trained to work in all areas of technology from electronic warfare to advanced radar technology, became the basis of the company's success in the years to come. Elta's technological capabilities in electronic warfare made it a successful exporter not only to developing nations but also to industrially developed Western countries. In later years the capabilities that Maklef cultivated in radar technologies were used in the Lavi combat aircraft's radar system and the Green Pine radar that was built for the Homa missile defense system.

THE AMERICANS VISIT TO LEARN LESSONS

Unlike other fronts, the war at sea had really ended, and we were not surprised when the Americans began asking for information on our achievements in the naval campaign. The R&D Unit was the point agency for all these lesson-related visits, and we were therefore deeply involved in hosting the delegations and meeting the delegation heads. Admiral Lake of the US Navy led the process on the part of the Americans, and the two of us developed a warm personal relationship. However, we also learned the hard way that personal relationships are no guarantee of policy change. We were disappointed to learn that US Navy officers had been forbidden to discuss the Harpoon missile, which Israel wanted to buy. This created a situation in which we had to talk about our missile boat battles, the achievements of our naval electronic warfare system, and the Israeli Gabriel missile, while our American partners in the talks had only tidbits of information to share with us.

This was the first time that such senior officers of the US Navy had visited Israel after years in which US policy was to keep a distance from us. We wanted to make the most out of the American's curiosity to open a new chapter in our relations with the US Navy, but there was a larger problem and not just in naval affairs. We were summoned to an urgent meeting with the CGS about cooperation with foreign countries and Elazar said the aim was to sign agreements regarding all areas of cooperation, and that the Operations Branch, under the direction of Major General Ze'evi, would be responsible for coordinating the administrative work in these areas, including intelligence-related issues. Strengthened by this decision of the General Staff we continued our supervised contacts with the American naval delegation, and were surprised to find that Admiral Lake had been authorized by the Pentagon to provide us with assessments of their hovercrafts (based on their use in the Vietnam War) and the Harpoon missile. It was a dramatic change in policy, which led to the commander of the US Navy arriving from London carrying the secret documents we wanted to see so badly.

An advance team of the American lesson-generation and data-collection delegation arrived in Israel and was led by John Blesse, who had been appointed to oversee the entire mission. When the Americans were planning to begin working on processing the data we believed that we would receive all of their results. It turned out that we were too naïve. Blesse, a Major General and a pilot, was an alert and endearing conversationalist with combat experience from the war in Vietnam. Like many other high-ranking American officers, Blesse had both academic and military training. I liked this red-headed general with his combination of combat experience and engineering skills from the moment I met him. The first thing we did was to fly to the south and take a look at the battlefields along the Canal. The sight of hundreds of mostly burnt out destroyed tanks and vehicles was stunning. We saw how close the Israeli and Egyptian tanks had been to each other and felt as if we ourselves were fighting the battles. The air was still saturated with the strong smell of explosives and propellants, burnt-out vehicles, burnt oil, burnt rubber and plastic, and, worst of all, the unbearable smell of the corpses that had been left in the field and inside the armored vehicles.

We crossed the Suez Canal and reached the area where the Egyptian anti-aircraft missile batteries were laid out. There were SA-2 and SA-3 missile systems in their bunkers with the missiles inside. It was all left as if the aircraft detection and tracking radar had just been activated. The general was overcome with excitement and ran from one place to another like a kid in a candy store.

Not far from the underground headquarters complex was an air-field, which caught General Blesse's attention immediately. He was particularly interested in the underground airplane hangars built according to Soviet doctrine. We began to discuss possible ways of making immediate use of the information about the systems scattered in the field, such as the structure of the missile batteries, the headquarters' bunkers and to the defense concepts behind them. We all knew that the cease-fire negotiations would eventually reach a permanent agreement and that our forces would return to the east side of the Suez Canal, leaving us in a situation where we could no longer without access the area to glean battlefield information. During the flight back north we began devising a program of tests that would give us an idea of the durability and weak points of the Soviet fortifications. At the same time we spoke with Blesse and his men about the agreement about the findings of his mission, which still contained elements of contention.

At the end of the visit I understood that it would be necessary to go to the US and we received the authorization of the CGS to do so. The countdown for withdrawal from the western bank of the Canal was a significant consideration, and this made the issue urgent.

We had our own interest in collecting data regarding tanks that were hit (ours and the enemy's), especially the precise measurement of armor penetration. Our teams were at work on all the battlefields and at the Repair and Maintenance Center at Tel Hashomer, accurately and meticulously collecting data. Although we gave a copy of all the data we collected to the Americans, it was only many months later that we saw an interesting but extremely short summary of their findings.

The Israeli Air Force under the command of Major General Benny Peled had a particularly open relationship with the R&D Unit. This openness was based partly on Peled's and my mutual respect, and also because my deputy Nahum was an air force man. I had Nahum and Simcha Maoz join me for the general discussion on lessons for the air force, and they were grateful for this rare opportunity. We talked about how guided surface-to-surface missiles that home in on anti-aircraft missile system radar could help in our war against enemy surface-to-air missiles. Israel Aerospace Industries had developed a version of the magnetically-guided Shrike missile, which seemed promising to air force officials at the time.

I asked Chaim Israeli, assistant to the minister of defense, to schedule a meeting with Dayan. I told him that I did not think that the defense minister knew me well and that I wanted to speak with him about some aspects of the lessons and the impact on future research and development and production of weapon systems. Chaim Israeli got back to me the same morning and told me that "Moshe said that he knows you well and that you are a superb fellow. He said that he would be happy to receive you without any formalities and that you should drop in some time when you can." With a deep sense of trepidation I eventually got up the courage and dropped in on the defense minister for a short conversation. Although Dayan was preoccupied with diplomatic and political events in Israel at the time, he nonetheless offered encouragement for bold, original research and development programs and the creation of a broader production infrastructure for the defense industries.

One issue that seemed particularly urgent to us as the battles raged was to find a way to arm the air force with laser-guided bombs. Tzur had asked us to check the possibility of buying laser-guided weapons as soon as possible, and the task was assigned to a team of the R&D Missiles and Rockets Department, the R&D Electronics (and optronics) Department and the Air Force Equipment Department. Colonel Nahum Dayagi's input was an understanding of the laser-guided bombs based on his long service in the air force, and Yedidia, my wise and experienced second in command, also joined the effort. Within three days we had prepared a short document outlining the ways to equip ourselves with laser bombs. In the best case scenario the Pentagon would provide us with laser-guided bombs from the stock of the US Air Force or the US Navy. In the event that we were unable to acquire the systems in this manner, the document listed three alternate possibilities:

A. The Americans would authorize us to produce the bombs ourselves, and provide us with the technology to do so.
B. We would be permitted to purchase the sensor installed on the warhead, but we would have to adapt and produce the remaining parts of the system on our own.
C. We would receive no assistance from the Americans and must develop and produce the systems on our own.

Based on this analysis of our options, the document recommended Israel Military Industries as the producer in the case of option A; that the MBT department of Israel Aerospace Industries (which developed and produced the sea-skimming anti-ship Gabriel missile) as the developer and producer in the case of option B; and Rafael as the developer and producer in the case of option C. The document was focused and succinct, and only five pages long. Tzur praised the clarity of its recommendations and the swiftness with which it was prepared.

The Americans did not authorize the purchase of the smart bombs we wanted. We therefore assembled the senior officials of the five relevant defense industries for a politically charged and difficult discussion that was supposedly technical. We decided to establish a team headed by Missiles and Rockets Department Director Dr. Arieh Lavi in order to draft a recommended plan of action within two months. Eventually, after a few years had passed, it was the MBT department of Israel Aerospace Industries — the second option in our initial document — that assumed leadership of the project. In accordance with the American paradigm regarding the release of advanced technologies, we were permitted to acquire the advanced systems from the Americans only after we produced laser-guided weapons systems on our own.

A TRANSITION PERIOD

We entered a difficult period of tense calm in the Golan Heights along with the ceasefire talks at Kilometer 101 and in Geneva. We were plagued by interpersonal tension throughout the senior leadership made more difficult by embarrassment and a sense that Israeli political and military leadership had lost its way. Frequent changes in senior IDF appointments radiated a sense of instability from the top down. During a General Staff meeting held on Tuesday, December 18, the defense minister reviewed the talks that had been held with Henry Kissinger. Dayan did not say much that was new, and his words were received with marked silence. One response that had nothing to do with Kissinger came from OC Southern Command Shmuel Gonen, who was now under the direct command of Deputy CGS Tal. In an emotional tone, Gonen explained that the General Staff was the only forum in which he could speak out and assert his innocence. He then made accusations against Sharon, some implied and some directly, and proceeded to get into an argument with Moshe Dayan, who tried to refocus the discussion on its original subject. Gonen was upset and insisted on continuing his statement, and Dayan needed of all the sternness he could muster to put him in his place.

Tal was extremely concerned about the threat of the Sagger missiles which he himself had not completely understood before the war. During the years of the War of Attrition along the Canal, our observation posts had observed closed train cars arriving at the front lines. Each time such a train car reached the position of an Egyptian military unit, a long line of soldiers would form near the door, and the soldiers would enter the car one at a time. At first we made jokes about the train cars, referring to them as mobile sexual service units similar to the kind operated by the Syrian army before the Six Day War. However, we quickly realized that the train cars contained training simulators for Sagger missile operators. At R&D, we thought about different ways of addressing the threat with the American developed MK-19 40-millimeter grenade machine gun. This machine gun was vehicle-mounted, and had a firing rate of 350 grenades per minute and a range of 1,500 meters. We conducted a test firing of the weapon, and the entire General Staff Working Group came out to observe the wonder. However, the proposal to add the system to our armored vehicles was decisively rejected by Operations Branch Chief Tal. According to his dogma what he called "foreign elements" could not be introduced into tank battles. Although we started searching for a technological solution to the Sagger missile threat about 10 days after the outbreak of the war the moment the first missiles fell into our hands, we were unable to find a shortcut or a quick solution. As commander of the southern front, Tal now invoked his authority as deputy CGS, and, with the assistance of Colonel Rozen director of the R&D Unit's Ground Department and Colonel Shmuel Keinan of the Ordnance Corps, he put all his energy into finding a solution to the problem. The solution he selected involved positioning net fences and coiled barbed wire around tank encampments in order to cause early detonation of fired Sagger missiles before they hit the tanks themselves.

TALKS IN WASHINGTON AND A QUICK TRIP TO SCANDINAVIA

By early January 1974 the time had come to make a trip to the US to conclude and sign the agreement regarding the joint generation of lessons from the war. We finished drawing up a draft agreement at the last moment and brought it with us under "diplomatic escort" (a locked courier case containing an envelope sealed with red wax).

The visit was planned to begin with a weekend in New York for meetings with Israeli Defense Ministry Delegation Head Shmuel Dror and his people in order to prepare for the talks in Washington. The schedule included a full week of meetings in the capital, followed by a two-day visit to a Scandinavian country for high-level meetings aimed at opening a channel of technological cooperation between Israel and the country in question.

During the five consecutive days of talks in the US we experienced high points in which we felt we were very persuasive and low points in which we were simply unable to convince our counterparts. In the course of the week I met three times with Parker, chief deputy of the Defense Department's Director of Defense and Research Engineering (DDR&E), and these meetings reinforced the initial impression he had made on me. He was an intelligent, fair, hard-working, straightforward, with much influence. Parker reviewed copies of every document we prepared during the process of reaching an agreement on the role of R&D in the overall agreement. I also met with Admiral Lake, the navy man who became a friend of Israel, as well as with a number of generals from the US Air Force. The height of the visit, as I describe it in my journal, was an extremely positive one-and-a-half hour meeting with four star General Creighton Abrams, Chief of Staff of the American ground forces. During the meeting I openly and candidly answered the dozens of questions posed by Abrams and his colleagues. Creighton William Abrams was a courageous and creative armored battalion commander during World War II whom the mythological General Patton described as the best tank commander in the United States army. Such a compliment coming from Patton, who justifiably regarded himself as the best armored commander in the US Army, is indicative of Abrams' unique military skills. In 1972 Abrams was appointed to the post of chief of staff of the United States Army.

The anxiety I felt leading up to my meeting with this legendary

19 February 1974

Dear General Elazar:

General Talbott has briefed me in some depth on his visit to
Israel and to your Defence Forces. He was most pleased with
the complete sense of cooperation and openness with which you
and your officers treated him.

General Talbott also tells me that he was particularly impressed
with the very high degree of military professionalism he found
everywhere he went. His statement is borne out by the substance
and character of the information he brought back. It provides
clear evidence that thoughtful professionals have examined each
area in some depth. The fact that there were many differing
views serves as confirming evidence of the complete candor of
the individuals interviewed and of the variety of their combat
experiences in the October War.

I would like to express through you my appreciation to
General Uzi Eilam for originally suggesting that this visit
be made. It was a pleasure to talk with him during his
January visit to Washington.

Again, I would like to express sincere appreciation for all you
did to make General Talbott's visit a success.

Sincerely,

CREIGHTON W. ABRAMS
General, United States Army
Chief of Staff

figure dissipated as soon as the meeting began. Abrams was open and attentive, and he spoke in a calm and relaxed manner. It was obvious that the issues we were discussing interested him, and the experience he had accumulated during his many battles were clearly reflected in his comments. We talked about the lessons of the war, which were fresh in my mind. General Abrams not only asked questions but also analyzed situations and displayed a surprising degree of knowledge regarding our battles along the Suez Canal and in the Golan Heights. Abram's staff officers explained how William Scranton's Congressional Committee had been goading the Pentagon, and how not everyone in Congress was pleased by Israel's arms purchase requests, despite the fact that the requests enjoyed the support of the defense department and the military leadership, led by Abrams himself.

General Abrams died from lung cancer in September 1974, while on active duty as chief of staff of the American ground forces. After his death he was remembered in a fitting manner: the new battle tank of the United States army — central to the power of the country's ground forces — was called the M1 Abrams.

In 2007, thirty three years after that visit to Washington, Tel Aviv Stock Exchange Director Shaul Bronfeld approached me with an interesting story. While scouring the Library of Congress in search of sources for his MA thesis on US–Israeli relations during the 1970s he found a letter from General Abrams to General Elazar among the documents that had been released for public viewing. The letter is reproduced on the following page:

For me, the letter came as a complete surprise, albeit quite a pleasant one. In the midst of the upheavals then pervading the Israeli General Staff and Defense Ministry and the pressure on Elazar's assistants at the time, they appear to have simply filed the letter away and forgot to send me a copy.

Lt. Gen. Orwin Clark Talbott, with whom we cooperated closely and whom Abrams also mentioned in his letter, arrived in Israel at the head of a team of senior American officers when the battles were still raging, after the crossing of the Canal in the south and before we had reached a ceasefire in the north. General Talbott founded TRADOC, the United States Army Training and Doctrine Command, and served as its first commander. This tall, athletic man radiated serenity and authority and was a soldier through and through. Talbott served as an infantry division commander during the Vietnam War. During the early 1970s the US army decided to consolidate its doctrine and training activities under one command, and General Talbott, who had previously served as commander of the prestigious infantry base at Fort Benning, was appointed as deputy commander of the new command. The quick visit to Israel by Talbott and his men also included a courtesy call to the main offices of the R&D Unit, scheduled to last half an hour. After finishing my brief words of welcome and learning that the team had met only with administrative officers of the IDF, I offered the general my opinion of this arrangement. "We fought an exceptional war in the air, on the sea, and on the land," I told him. "On land, it was the largest armored battle ever fought, with thousands of tanks that pitted Soviet doctrines against Western doctrines. The infantry battles during the war also provided exceptional trials of confrontation between Eastern and Western conceptions and of dealing with Soviet weaponry on an extremely large scale. How do you intend to develop doctrines and build new training programs for the ground army without meeting the commanders of the combat units of the IDF?" For this reason, I explained, it was important for them to meet with commanders of the armored forces (Tal, Peled, and Ben-Gal), the infantry, and the paratroops.

Our guests immediately cancelled all their meetings for the rest of the day, and their half-hour courtesy call turned into a lively and thorough discussion that lasted four hours. We talked about the experience that the R&D teams had gained during the war and our initial data, and made assessments regarding the effectiveness of the weapons systems then in use by the enemy. At the end of the discussion I recommended that Talbott return for a longer visit with a suitable team to meet with the combat unit commanders. It was the beginning of a relationship between our ground forces and TRADOC that lasted many years. The relatively new Training and Doctrine Command needed to develop a fresh way of thinking and General Talbott decided to return with larger teams in order to learn the lessons of the Yom Kippur war. Our collection of data on the battles and the weapons systems used by both sides and the comparison we had undertaken between the two proved to be a temptation that the Americans were unable to resist. General Talbott was impressed by the candidness and directness of the Israelis with whom he met and the fact that he was provided with a spectrum of opinions on the lessons of the war. In his letter to Elazar, General Abrams emphasized his appreciation of the openness and honesty with which we presented the lessons of the war to TRADOC officers.

One notable trait of the Americans is their ability to make radical changes within both military and other government agencies. Every few years they would choose a certain area, shake it up, and reorganize it in ways that were often revolutionary. This not only enables them to periodically rethink issues with the help of people who are free to choose different courses of action, but actually requires them to do so. In some cases the Americans developed new concepts with catchy acronyms. The RMA, or the Revolution in Military Affairs, is a good example of a new concept that developed in the 1980s and was regarded as the basis for success during the wars in Iraq in 1991 and 2003. The new doctrine combined technological innovation including information technology, the concept of UAVs (unmanned aerial vehicles) and highly accurate remotely operated standoff weapons.

When military analysts praised the RMA after the second Gulf War they frequently mentioned Israel and the US in the same breath. Recently, nanotechnology, robotics, and biotechnology have been incorporated into RMA. There is also a plan to link all the combat forces on the battlefield within a framework of network-centric warfare. A sober assessment of the subject must, however, distinguish between marketing ideas and innovations that can truly improve capabilities. The momentum of the effort and the transformation of the acronym RMA into a buzz word pushed the issue into broader public consciousness.

The establishment of the Israeli R&D Unit can be regarded as a typical example of a structural change that helped generate new values and a consolidated approach that differed markedly from past approaches to defense development, research policy and R&D management. This new framework incorporated all the military issues with the issues that were under the responsibility of the civilian section of the defense ministry under one roof, and enabled us to address them as a whole. As a result of this integrative approach Israel's Administration for the Development of Weapons and Technological Infrastructure, known by its Hebrew acronym MAFAT, still oversees technological infrastructure, intermediate development issues, and large projects with the assistance of administrative bodies and project managements frameworks. With this experience we can conclude that structural change should not be a goal in itself, but rather should serve as a highly effective tool for bringing about substantive changes.

Our January 1974 visit to the United States concluded with a two-day visit to the capital of a Scandinavian country. Our ambassador to this country arranged a meeting in his home aimed at opening the door to defense related technological cooperation with Israel. The meetings were also attended by Brigadier General Hadar Kimchi, our military attaché in London. The central figure in the talks was the director of defense R&D of the host country, who had been heading its defense research in recent years.

We were welcomed to the capital city by the cold of the Scandinavian winter with thick snow falling around the clock. Despite the bitter cold outside, the atmosphere inside the ambassador's home was warm and cordial. A crackling fireplace created a serene, pleasant atmosphere, and we spent dinner getting to know one another and discussing the Yom Kippur War and current events in the country in question. The country's director of defense R&D turned out to be a wise and witty man and a wonderful conversationalist. We quickly found ourselves engrossed in a discussion on military, technological and political issues, and found ourselves agreeing on the importance of the human factor in all these fields. The meeting gave us the feeling that we had made a true friend. Without any ceremony we laid the foundation for defense-related technological cooperation that included electro-optics, an area in which the country in question excelled. Years later, Israel's defense industries, and primarily Rafael, forged a relationship with the research and development laboratories of the country in question, a relationship that was mutually beneficial to both countries.

Many things happened during my two-week absence from Israel. Elazar signed the separation of forces agreement drafted at the Kilometer 101 talks with Egyptian CGS General Mohamed Abdel Ghani al-Gamasy. Major General Avraham Adan was appointed to the post of OC Southern Command, Motta Gur resumed his post of OC Northern Command, and Yitzhak Hofi was appointed to head the Operations Branch.

Upon my return I tried to meet Tzur as soon as possible to update him on my meetings in Washington and my two days in Scandinavia. Tzvi Tzur always spoke in understatement, and in meetings it always seemed as if he was thinking out loud to illuminate complicated situations. When I would bring up my difficulties as director of R&D he never offered direct advice. During meetings he would let the other person analyze the problem and would use delicate, insightful questions to help them formulate for themselves whatever it was they wanted to hear from him. Tzur told me that General Tal, who had been removed from the Southern Command by Defense Minister Dayan, had returned to his position as deputy CGS for special tasks. He told me that Tal was still responsible for R&D and the Planning Branch, but it seemed there were more unknown than known elements about the army reorganization after the latest round of appointments. There was no logic in removing R&D from the Operations Branch, especially when it came to R&D's involvement with the army's forces. On a personal level I was not happy to be back under Tal's supervision, particularly in such a complex state of affairs.

Dayan wanted to breach the terms of the ceasefire agreement and launch an offensive aimed at encircling the Second Egyptian Army with a northward attack along the Suez Canal. This was the tactical maneuver suggested by Arik Sharon, but it had far-reaching strategic significance as well. What did the defense minister hope to achieve? Was it just an emotional decision aimed at erasing the disgrace of Israel's unpreparedness during the difficult days at the beginning of the war when he himself spoke of the destruction of the Third Temple, the euphemism commonly used to describe Israel's elimination? How did Dayan plan to deal with the American position, which Secretary of State Kissinger was orchestrating so skillfully?

In the situation that evolved toward the end of the Yom Kippur War, Dayan regarded Tal as an obstacle to the idea of encircling the Second Egyptian Army and made sure to distance him from the Southern Command. Avraham Tamir and I went up to see Tal in the office he had been assigned on the fourth floor of the General Staff building, far from the offices of the CGS and the Operations Branch chief. When we walked into his office we found an entirely different man, hunched over, depressed, speaking in low tones and in desperate need of encouragement. Tamir and I found out that Tal was spending most of his time preparing his testimony for the Agranat Commission, a judicial board of inquiry appointed to investigate the failings of the war. I was not happy to see Tal in such a despondent state but there was nothing I could do to ease his burden.

Elazar asked to meet with me a few days later, and when I entered his office I understood he wanted to discuss the Agranat Commission. I spent two hours with him between 11:00 p.m. and 1:00 a.m., and it quickly became clear to me that he too was tired and dejected. Elazar had to run the army, make decisions about alert levels and preparations for the possible continuation of hostilities on the Syrian front, work on appointments and try to settle the disputes between the generals. Only late at night could he find the time talk about his own predicament. His questions gave me an indication of the nature of the Agranat Commission's inquiry into his role in the war. The questions focused on whether he had effectively prepared the army for the war and what resources he had placed at the disposal of the army. My heart went out to Elazar, who suddenly seemed exhausted and helpless. In addition to the answers and explanations that I gave that night, I promised to prepare any written material I thought might be helpful. At that point, I never imagined that the Agranat Commission would identify the CGS, the Intelligence Branch chief, and the OC Southern Command as virtually the only ones responsible for the failures of the war. As I left Elazar bleary-eyed, struggling to continue running the army while preparing his testimony for the commission I reflected upon the outrageous injustice of it all. Tal had more than enough time to prepare himself for the commission, while Elazar was left without even the minimum amount of time necessary to pull together the required information and to develop a line of defense.

GIDEON MAHANAYMI VERSUS MOSHE DAYAN

A three-day conference of senior military commanders of the rank of colonel and higher began on February 12, 1974. The conference provided a framework in which to continue discussing the war as it had been done within the three regional commands, within the Air Force and the Navy, and within the Intelligence Branch. The conference was opened by the CGS who stated that discussion should focus on the war itself, and not its lessons. However, the tension in the air, and the many personal sensitivities and frustrations that were lurking below the surface of engagement of the issues, meant that

Elazar's request to focus on the war itself was ignored by virtually all the major participants. It was impossible to stop Shmuel Gonen from fighting to save his name and reputation from the conference podium. This was the opportunity of the ousted Southern commander to state his case before the forum that meant the most to him, and to argue that he had not failed in his duty. It was also impossible to stop Adan from launching a bitter attack against Arik Sharon. On October 7 and 8, Adan's division had been forced to launch its own attack against the Egyptian forces that had crossed the Canal. According to Adan (and Gonen), Sharon had only one agenda — crossing the canal — which prevented his division from taking part in the ultimately unsuccessful Operation Abirei Lev. We all remembered how terrible we felt when Adan's division sustained such heavy losses and failed to push the Egyptian forces back across the Canal. And we all remembered Dayan's remark about the destruction of the Third Temple after the second day of fighting.

Sharon responded to Gonen's accusations and Adan's stinging remarks with a combination of congenial language, humor, and brilliant ideas that bordered on demagoguery. Sharon was a true field officer, but also a master of manipulation who could use his sharp wit to identify opponents' Achilles' heels and take phenomenally accurate shots at them. When he took the podium to return fire he used a combination of serious arguments and stinging but humorous remarks aimed at his critics. It was a work of art that elicited outbursts of laughter from the audience. When Yitzhak Hofi, who had served as OC Northern Command during the war, took his turn to describe the war on the northern front, he simply could not refrain from directing a stinging remark southward: "The Northern Command," he said, "will be unable to demonstrate the brotherhood of arms demonstrated by the Southern Command from this podium... "

By the end of the first day it was clear that the conference was important, if only to bring all of us together and to give people the opportunity to express themselves, notwithstanding Elazar's prime objective of focusing on the war rather than on the person.

The prime minister attended the second day of the conference and stayed throughout the day until after nightfall to listen to the speeches and discussions. The open discussion that followed was opened by Haim Bar-Lev, who offered comments that clarified some of the maneuvers in the south. Slowly and calmly he staunchly defended the concept of outposts. As could be expected he also defended the Bar-Lev Line, the line of fortifications built by Israel along the eastern bank of the Suez Canal during his tenure as CGS. Bar-Lev, who had been dispatched to the south after the collapse of the command hierarchy on the front, refuted the criticism against Arik Sharon and argued that the battle in the south had certainly been subject to broad command supervision above the division level.

Up to this point there was nothing new in the discussion. However, as evening approached there was a bombshell. Colonel Gideon Mahanaymi rose to the podium with a "J'accuse" speech targeting the political leadership in general and Moshe Dayan in particular. Mahanaymi belonged to the 1948 generation and had served in the Palmah as a company commander in the 3rd battalion of the Yiftah Brigade. After 1950 he held various positions in the intelligence corps. A major in 1956, he joined the paratroops, replacing me as the intelligence officer of the brigade. During the Yom Kippur War Colonel Mahanaymi served as an IDF liaison staff officer to the UN, a position typically manned by officers from the intelligence corps. Gideon approached the podium looking pale. After expressing regret that Dayan was not present in the hall, he spoke to Prime Minister Meir and to all of us. He began by describing how Danny Matt had been removed from his position as a paratroop battalion commander because soldiers had been killed in a training accident during a live-fire exercise he had conducted. He then moved on to an account of the ousting of Intelligence Branch Chief Yehoshafat Harkabi and Operations Branch Chief Meir Zorea in 1959 when Israel Radio mistakenly broadcast the code words mobilizing the army's reservists, a débâcle that entered Israeli lore as the "night of the ducks." Before the crowd sitting in the conference hall, Mahanaymi called on Moshe Dayan to resign. Elazar allowed Mahanaymi to finish his remarks and did not attempt to silence him, but the next morning Mahanaymi was absent from the conference. When Dayan heard what Mahanaymi had said, he told Elazar "It's either Gideon or me at conference," and that was enough. For many years Mahanaymi, who had not been climbing the ranks rapidly in any event, was tainted by the Mark of Cain for rebelling against the defense minister. His promotion in the army was completely halted, and he was only promoted to the rank of brigadier general in 1976, as Yitzhak Rabin's anti-terrorism advisor.

After the drama of Mahanaymi's speech, the rest of the conference was anti-climactic. It was only later, after the demobilization of the Israeli reserves, that the reserve soldiers started a process of mass demonstrations expressing their pain and disillusionment about the way the government had conducted the war. These demonstrations ultimately led to the resignation of Meir, Dayan, and the entire government.

CONSOLIDATION AND STABILIZATION OF THE R&D UNIT

It was a time of high drama both in the IDF and the Israeli government, coupled with a tense military situation and a diplomatic process that would eventually lead to a permanent ceasefire agreement. But I was unable to take even a momentary break from directing the R&D Unit. The defense ministry was about to undergo substantial changes stemming from Dayan's announcement in February 1974 that he would not be a member of the next government. Tzur had long since said that he would soon step down from his position, a step that I was prepared for but not really happy about. Dayan had provided Tzur with authority and freedom of action that would be hard to find under another minister. Dayan would have nothing to do with budgetary issues and took no interest in the defense industries.

Issues related to R&D were also not a priority for him, and even international contacts and cooperation with foreign countries could not hold his attention. All these areas of responsibility were left to the skillful care of Tzvi Tzur. Yeshayahu Lavi, who had preceded Itzhak Ironi as director general of the defense ministry but had resigned prematurely, told me in a moment of candor that his resignation was due to the diminished powers of the director general in the Dayan-Tzur era. With Tzvi's departure, the R&D Unit stood to lose a solid source of support both within the ministry and the defense establishment as a whole. Tzvi informed me that a document he had prepared for Dayan recommended that R&D, the Production and Purchasing Administration, and the Budgets Branch be supervised by the director-general of the ministry. Director-General Ironi's door was always open to me and I felt confident of his backing.

The relationship between Rafael and the defense industries held great significance for the stabilization of the R&D Unit. While the war was being fought at high intensity most of our attention was focused on accelerating the production lines for the ammunition and weapons systems, and on efforts to carry out rapid response to the new threats. We passed on the data about the SA-6 anti-aircraft missile systems to Rafael in an effort to find a quick solution for defending our planes. Data about the Sagger anti-tank missiles, including missiles that were collected on the battlefield, were passed on to Rafael, the Israel Military Industries and the Laskov Unit of the Engineering Corps in an effort to develop immediate responses to the threat. Rafael had found an initial, albeit only partial response to the SA-6 missile towards the end of the war. Despite our best efforts it took more time to develop responses to the Sagger missile. Many ideas were tried at the Ordnance Corp's testing area on the Mediterranean shore, including the possibility of disrupting the missile command system in mid-flight, misdirecting the missile navigator, and physically obstructing the missile with a steel net in close proximity of the target. The simple Russian missile was not susceptible to our disruption efforts, and we only found a proper solution to the threat posed by the Sagger missile years later.

We began 1974 without the approved working plans we needed for reentry into normal life. The General Staff was still in a tumult, with continued tension in the Golan Heights and reshuffling of generals in senior posts. However, within the defense ministry Tzur was solid as a rock, and his influence enabled us to develop R&D working plans. The plans needed to accommodate both integration of the lessons of the war and the continued development of long-term projects. The Air Force, the Navy, and the Intelligence Branch had all generated lessons that were organized and well-developed in comparison to the ground forces, which were still occupied with maintaining their readiness and licking their military wounds. The defense industries were hungry for data, clear plans, instructions, and budgets from the IDF and the defense ministry.

We worked a great deal on arranging a meeting of representatives of all the defense industries, which was aimed at presenting the working plans for 1974. This gathering, which we referred to as the Developers Conference, was supposed to be the crowning achievement of our return to the routine work of defense research and development. There was a surprisingly high willingness within the different industries and the IDF to participate in the conference. Tzur, who agreed to speak at the conference, was enthusiastic, persuasive, and brilliantly organized.

With the tailwind of the successful Developers Conference I had a private meeting with Tzvi Alon, director of the defense ministry's Production and Purchasing Administration. During the meeting we agreed that contracts regarding development funded by the services of the IDF would be handled by the R&D Unit. Before the establishment of the Unit, the Production and Purchasing Administration was responsible for the defense establishment's contractual agreements. Now that there was a professional and increasingly stable agency within the ministry dealing with research and development, logic demanded that this aspect of the ministry's work be directed by us. These measures won the enthusiastic endorsement of the Production and Purchasing Administration. We started to feel that we were making progress and incorporating new areas of work beyond those outlined in the founding documents of the R&D Unit. The incorporation of meaningful changes into the administrative bodies of the R&D Unit remained an essential component of the Unit's mode of operation and development, and subsequently of the Administration for the Development of Weapons and Technological Infrastructure (MAFAT), which was established in 1980.

In late March it was officially announced that Tzur would be leaving the defense ministry. At a meeting of defense ministry branch directors, Director-General Ironi presented a diagram of the changes within the ministry's senior leadership. The interim report of the Agranat Commission recommended the removal of Eli Zeira, and Shimon Peres became defense minister after Dayan's resignation. After Ironi passed away suddenly, Peres appointed Professor Pinhas Zusman to replace him as director general of the ministry.

The defense ministry opened a new front in the battle for research and development with the appointment of General (Ret.) Amos Horev as the ministry's chief scientist, a position that had been vacant since the establishment of the R&D Unit. I knew Horev well and we shared both common language as well as mutual respect and understanding. I also knew that his gentle, cultured demeanor ensured that there would be no battles between us. Nonetheless, the appearance of such an experienced and authoritative figure on the defense R&D scene caused me some concern. Soon after he assumed the position of chief scientist he was chosen to serve as president of the Technion technological university and was only able to dedicate a small portion of his time to his job in the defense ministry. A few years later Defense Minister Shimon Peres appointed Manes Prath, the first director of the Dimona Nuclear Research Campus, to the position of chief scientist. Prath was an engineer and a charismatic director with the capacity and aspiration to build a bureau with vision, and he tried to start an enormous program of strategic research on current trends in defense technology. Although this may have been consistent with Peres's ambitions, it was not consistent with his ability to allocate resources. But it was the bureaucracy of the defense ministry that ultimately tied the hands of the new chief scientist, who eventually gave up trying to scale the slippery walls of the ministry. With the establishment of MAFAT, the office of chief scientist of the defense ministry evolved into its current incarnation. It was only natural to bestow the title of chief scientist upon the director of the new Administration, who was the civilian supervisor of the defense ministry's research and development hierarchy.

There were more upheavals ahead. With the publication of the interim report of the Agranat Commission on the first day of April it was clear that something was going on. Elazar announced that a special General Staff meeting had been scheduled for that evening. I expected the worst, and the meeting was repeatedly delayed. In the end my secretary said that the meeting had been rescheduled for 10:30 p.m., and that I should also listen to the ten o'clock news. Soon after I left home for the Kirya government campus, the radio broadcast the main conclusions of the Agranat Commission's interim report. The Commission placed the bulk of responsibility on CGS Elazar, Intelligence Branch Chief Eli Zeira, and Shmuel Gonen, who had served as OC Southern Command during the war. It also assigned blame to Intelligence Branch Research Department Director Arieh Shalev, director of the Egypt Branch of the Research Department, and the intelligence officer of the Southern Command. The Commission had so far left Meir and Dayan unscathed.

Surprised and shocked we all assembled in the General Staff meeting room. We were all well aware of the facts about the army's readiness on the eve of the war and the manner in which the war had been conducted. However, we had not been aware of how the Commission had interpreted its brief to investigate IDF's readiness for the war, the information the IDF had received during the days leading up to the war, and the actions that preceded the IDF's repelling of the enemy. According to the Commission, this meant limiting its investigation only to the events that took place until October 8, 1973, the date of the failed counter-attack in the south.

We all stood when the CGS entered the room. The tension was as high as it could be as we waited silently for Elazar to begin speaking. Elazar began his statement by saying that he had received the interim report that morning, and that he was appealing its findings. He then read us the letter he had written to Prime Minister Meir, in which he rejected most of the conclusions that incriminated him and divided responsibility between Eli Zeira and the defense minister.

Elazar then told us that, although he regretted having to say goodbye to us in such a way, he had informed Golda Meir that in light of the report he would be unable to remain the CGS and that Hofi would serve as acting CGS until further notice. With that, Elazar got up and left the room, leaving us sitting in silence, confused and not knowing what to do. The administrative secretary announced that the meeting was over, but everyone remained in their seats. It was impossible to leave the room that echoed with so many discussions that we remembered with such sharp and painful clarity. Among these were the situation assessment carried out two weeks before the outbreak of the war, when no one even imagined that war was approaching, and the meeting with Defense Minister Dayan on Friday afternoon, the day before the war, when Eli Zeira declared that war was extremely unlikely. During that meeting Elazar had adopted Zeira's assessment, while Dayan, who sat next to the CGS, did not explicitly disagree with the assessment, but nonetheless said things that suggested that he was not comfortable with it. The room also echoed with the General Staff meetings that followed the battles: the scathing criticism, the war between the generals, and Elazar's heroic efforts to reinstitute order within the army.

My heart went out to Elazar, who was battered and bruised by the

Commission report, and I thought back to the night he asked me for information on the R&D preparations to help his testimony before the Commission. I was troubled by the injustice that had been done to him – someone who had been the rock and the anchor of both the IDF and the Israeli population during the war, which began as such a surprise and ended with a decisive Israeli victory, despite the difficulties and losses along the way.

Despite these tumultuous events, work and daily life in the R&D Unit continued. One interesting event was the annual meeting of the Israel Physics Society, held at the Weizmann Institute two days before Passover in the spring of 1974. Prof. Israel Dostrovsky sponsored the conference, and I was invited to speak as a guest lecturer. I was familiar with the audience and worked hard on preparing my speech. The hundreds of physicists who filled the conference hall listened carefully to the main points of my assessment of the balance of power and balance of technology between us and the Arabs. My lecture focused on the contribution of research in general and physics research in particular to Israeli defense and security. There was no doubt in my mind about the importance of physics research for Israeli defense interests, and I said this to the scientists loudly and clearly. My talk was followed by 20 minutes of lively, intelligent questions and answers on a wide variety of issues. During the coffee break I was surrounded by people who continued asking questions and never left me alone. There were so many people who wanted to contribute but did not know how to go about it. This overwhelming expression of such a sincere desire to help stemmed from the shock of the war, which affected the scientific community like the rest of the country. At the time I was unable to provide detailed answers or to recommend defined paths of action. Nonetheless, I was convinced that in the future we would need to find a way to direct the scientists toward issues related to security research.

With Yitzhak Rabin

YITZHAK RABIN AS PRIME MINISTER

Unable to withstand the increasing public pressure following the war, Golda Meir resigned as prime minister on April 11, 1974. Yitzhak Rabin was chosen to replace her, mainly because, serving in Washington as Israel's ambassador, he was perceived as free from complicity in the errors made by the political leadership during the period leading up to the war. Rabin, who was popularly celebrated as the architect of Israel's success during the Six Day War, defeated Shimon Peres during internal Labor Party elections, but was nonetheless forced to appoint Peres as his defense minister.

Two months after the establishment of the new government, Rachel and Tzvi Tzur invited me and Naomi to their home for coffee one Saturday afternoon. Our friendship with the Tzur family had grown closer and continued to do so during the years that followed. Ernest Yefet, the powerful CEO of Bank Leumi, then the largest bank in the country was there, as was the president of the Australian Zionist organization. To our surprise, and with no fore-warning, the Rabins were there as well. The Rabins typically spent Saturday morning playing tennis and Yitzhak, who was a redhead from birth, would get sunburnt and looked as red as a beetroot. It was a unique experience to hear Tzvi, who had preceded Rabin as CGS, unhesitatingly ask Rabin a barrage of direct questions about his feel-ings as prime minister, about political battles, and about ministers in his government. Tzur was especially interested in hearing about Yehoshua Rabinovich, the new finance minister of whom Rabin had a positive assessment, supported by the financier Ernest Yefet. In this intimate forum, the shy, introverted Rabin felt more comfortable and was able to loosen up a bit. Little did I know that the prime minis-ter would soon ask me to become the director-general of the Israel Atomic Energy Commission (IAEC.)

This was the third time I had met Yitzhak Rabin. The first time was just after the Six Day War, when Yitzhak Yaakov had taken me around to show me off...aratrooper battalion commander who was also an engineer — as his new acquisition for the Weapons Development Department of the Operations Branch. I was extremely nervous when I went up the office of the CGS, having no idea what to expect. However, I quickly relaxed and answered his questions about my impressions from the Six Day War in Jerusalem, about what we could expect in the realm of military research and development, and mainly about the future war along the borders. During this first meeting I took note of Rabin's weak, soft, and hesitant handshake, and of the fact that he never looked you directly in the eye. My second meeting with Rabin took place during a visit to Washington before I was appointed director of R&D. Rabin, then the Israeli ambassador, invited me to give a talk about IDF research and development at the weekly embassy staff meeting. Ambassador Rabin was different from most Israeli career diplomats. He instituted a framework based on team work and information sharing among all the major officials at the embassy and I was impressed by the relaxed, businesslike atmosphere that pervaded the embassy. It was easy to recognize his special contribution to the sense of harmony and teamwork that characterized the embassy during his term as ambassador.

SHIMON PERES — THE NEW DEFENSE MINISTER

The beginning of a new era within the defense establishment encouraged me to quickly address the issues of defense R&D procedures and policy, which I regarded as critically important. It was important to institutionalize procedures, particularly when there was no longer an advisor (and deputy, for all intents and purposes) to the defense minister who could be compared to Tzur in character or authority. Moshe Dayan's resignation left an unclear situation in the upper echelons of the defense ministry leadership, with Pinhas Zusman, Motti Hod as senior advisor, and Amos Horev as chief scientist, but with no clear definition of their areas of responsibility. It was also important to institutionalize R&D procedures with the IDF, and the fact that the war had just ended provided us with the best possible timing for this undertaking. In the R&D Unit my deputies Nahum Dayagi and Yedidia Shamir, as well as Colonel Eli Levin, director of the new Planning and Economics Department, put a great deal of work into designing the procedures. We then distributed the resulting document, which caused a commotion. It incensed Amos Horev, who shot off an angry letter to the defense minister protesting the fact that the chief scientist had not been incorporated into the procedures. In a letter of his own, Defense Ministry Deputy Director-General Tzvi Tzafriri protested that the procedures we outlined were not coordinated with the Organization Branch of the defense ministry and demanded that they not go into effect until this was implemented. Yet again, I appreciated the great complexity of my position as director of R&D and the many disadvantages, as well as advantages, of an agency responsible to both the IDF and the defense ministry. The excitement did not bother me. In fact, I rather enjoyed it. After all, I knew that it would attract everyone's attention, and because I was convinced of the logic behind the procedures, I was not worried that they would be affected by bureaucratic opposition.

I asked Peres's office for a meeting to present the overall concept of research and development, and a meeting was scheduled relatively quickly. Peres looked exhausted, and I wondered what I could do to get him more alert and attentive. I started by introducing myself, but Peres quickly stopped me, declaring: "I know you from the (Jordan) Valley!"

"Ah, Ze'evi, Ze'evi," I thought to myself. "You did PR for me as well, with your endless stream of visitors to the Jordan Valley when you were OC Central Command." I then moved to an explanation of the unique structure of the R&D Unit, during which the minister bombarded me with questions regarding structure, authority and chain of command, relations with the chief scientist, and my opinion regarding the appropriate role of this position. I told him that the chief scientist of the defense ministry needed to be a bona-fide scientist capable both of holding the position on a full-time basis and of running the Defense Research and Development Advisory Committee. I praised the work of the Advisory Committee and said it was a wonderful body that could enable the chief scientist to effectively advise the minister and to help the director of R&D focus on the future of new technologies and engage in intelligent in long-term planning. I suggested to Peres that he regard the R&D Unit as the sole administrative body in the defense ministry and the IDF responsible for administrative work and preparing recommendations for development related decisions. By now, Peres was completely alert, and he asked questions about each of the major projects that were currently under development. I described developments in advanced air-to-air and air-to-surface missiles, as well as developments related to electronic warfare and communications systems. I also told him about the drive for naval-related technologies and the important lessons learned during the war at sea. In terms of ground warfare, I explained about the Merkava Tank project, which constituted the major thrust of development for Israel's ground forces and left too few resources available for development of all the remaining components of ground warfare. Peres asked specific questions that reflected not only interest and understanding, but concern on the strategic level. The approach he expressed during our meeting called for massive artillery and air support during a ground war. I promised to draft a document containing an analysis of different approaches to future development, the answers to a number of tank-related questions he had asked me, and a draft of the policy that was in the process of evolving within the R&D Unit. My hour with the defense minister flew by, and Peres asked me to return for another meeting in order to cover the subjects we had not had the time to discuss. I left his office with a positive feeling, certain that the defense minister's door would always be open to me. However, over the years it became clear that my meeting with Peres was a rare instance of benevolence on his part, and in our many subsequent meetings I never again saw him so eager to listen and to ask so many comprehensive and probing questions. Indeed, the Peres I met with later was concerned mainly with politics.

When Peres was appointed defense minister in Rabin's first government, he embarked on feverish initiatives to shore up relations and alliances with friendly countries. To this end I was dispatched to attend secret talks with the Swedish CGS and officers of his general staff. The aim was to fascinate them with stories about the Yom Kippur War, and the technological lessons we learned from fighting a difficult war using Western weapons against Soviet systems. Although in 1974 the Swedes maintained a policy of extreme neutrality, they nonetheless wanted to learn more about the Soviet threat. This is how the path to Swedish–Israeli cooperation was paved.

I also went to Paris on Peres' instructions. Here too Peres hoped to open the door to cooperation by enticing the senior commanders of the French army with the lessons of the Yom Kippur War. The most interesting lessons were tactical and technological, based on the confrontation between the Eastern bloc weapons and Western systems. Defense Minister Peres believed that the French were interested in the overall perspective offered by our experience. Peres – the architect of the very close special relationship between Israel and France between the mid-1950s up to the Six Day War — hoped to restore the former partnership. At the time the Israeli ambassador in Paris was Arthur Ben-Natan, a close friend and colleague of Peres from the days when they were both among David Ben-Gurion's closest advisors. Ben-Natan was sent to the French capital in the hope that his involvement in shaping the Israeli–French partnership before the Six Day War would bring about a renewed relationship. I made my way to the embassy on rue Rabelais directly from the airport carrying a bag containing accounts and conclusions of the lessons of the war in English. Most of the documents had been drawn up in jointly with the Americans, for their benefit. They covered the air, ground, and naval aspects of the war, and also dealt with a number of intelligence-related lessons.

In my introductory meeting and briefing with Ben-Natan in the embassy the ambassador listened to my accounts with mixed feelings, as he was still grieving the death of his son Amnon who had been killed during the war. However, Ben-Natan knew how to rise above his personal pain and took it upon himself to help prepare the meeting with the French CGS and his men. We reached the headquarters of the French General Staff which, like the offices of most leaders and government ministers in France, was located in an elegant mansion. The French officers understood English well but spoke little and asked only short questions. Ambassador Ben-Natan took part in the discussion, launching into explanations of the meaning of the lessons of the war in French, which to my untrained ear sounded beautiful. Ben-Natan was also able to provide extensive explanations on subjects in which the French officers expressed interest.

The Frenchmen did not open up immediately after the short visit, and Ambassador Ben-Natan had to work hard to thaw the political and military boycott that French President Charles de Gaulle had imposed on Israel after the Six Day War.

THE BUDGET WARS

While we worked on the comprehensive research and development policy document, we also had to guarantee our activity by ensuring a sufficient budget for the 1975 working year. Like the director of R&D, Yitzhak Elron, the CGS's financial advisor also wore two hats. His position in the defense ministry was called director of the Budgets Branch. Since Tzur's days in the office Elron had tried to thwart Tzur's budget policies but did not gain support from either the CGS or the defense minister. But the situation was different now. There was a new defense minister, a new CGS, and a new Operations Branch chief, and this presented the officials of the Budgets Branch with a prime opportunity to renew their opposition. Lacking Tzvi's strong support, I began to look for ways to safeguard the R&D budget. Past experience had taught me that every September the Budget Branch issued a document entitled "The Budgetary Framework for the Working Year." I noticed that once the document had been issued, discussions and appeals tended to yield only minor modifications. So I decided to produce an R&D budget before the Budgets Branch issued theirs. During the period leading up to September 1974, after advanced coordination with the director-general and after informing the CGS and the Operations Branch chief of my plan, R&D issued its own budget document. The financial advisor was furious: "How dare they?!" he roared. "Who authorized this framework? Only the Budget Branch is authorized to present budgets!"

During a meeting with the director-general of the defense ministry budget officials from the Budget Branch chose to minimize the areas of confrontation and to attack only the budget designated specifically for the R&D Unit. It was a transparent attempt to confuse the meeting participants — the director-general among them — by employing terms such as "budgetary program" and "financing program" and by completely ignoring the effects of inflation. Only later did I realize that these were the usual tricks used by the budget officials, and that similar tactics were employed in the struggles between the defense ministry and finance ministry which I participated in the years to come. In response, I chose to present the issue from a broader perspective, pointing out that the R&D Unit was responsible for handling all development projects, including those of the services of the IDF. In any event, the director-general was not taken in by the budgetary hocus-pocus. Itzhak Ironi may not have been a smooth talking charismatic leader, but he was a smart, experienced, and stable man. He understood that the right thing to do was to maintain his decision that the Budgets Branch mark the R&D budgets designated for the various different services of the IDF and transfer the administration of these budgets to the R&D Unit. Ironi also accepted the argument that the budgets of the services might be cut in 1975 and that it was therefore necessary to safeguard a larger primary budget for R&D. The discussion then turned from petty bickering but I knew that my success in the meeting was only one victory in what would be a very long campaign.

CRYSTALLIZATION OF DEFENSE R&D POLICY

One of the main components of the multi-year plan was the situation assessment regarding the overall state of military technology. Five years after the Six Day War, and after a significant increase in activity both in the development institutions and the defense industries, we were still lagging well behind the large superpowers, particularly the US. Prof. Moshe Arens, who would later serve as Israel's defense minister, resigned from his position as director of the Engineering Division of Israel Aerospace Industries and established a small consulting firm called Cybernetics. Arens proposed to us that he carry out a survey of military technologies and assess our ability to engage in each one. I trusted Arens and his small staff of Israel Aerospace Industries graduates whom I knew, and I was certain that their work would contribute to our efforts. The most important task was to assess the Americans' work in different areas of military technological development. The best way to acquire data on this issue was the relatively simple method of carefully reading the published professional literature and collecting relevant material. One impressive aspect of America's policy on public exposure of technological capabilities and weapons systems was the level of freedom they afforded themselves. Initially the way material was made public seemed almost outrageous but once we looked into the matter deeper, we started to understand the powerful logic underlying the way the Americans exposed their secrets. They simply knew how to carefully preserve the secrecy of areas that were truly sensitive and important. In addition to their capacity for distinguishing between sensitive information and information that could be exposed, the American system was also characterized by order, organization, and discipline. As a result, whatever needed to be classified remained classified, and declassified information did not have the potential to threaten security.

In contrast, our security restrictions were always very rigid, mainly because we were incapable of the same level of strict enforcement and did not possess the same culture of order and discipline. Our information security personnel, knowing Israelis all too well, also knew that the moment material regarding one area of a specific military technological subject was declassified full exposure was likely to follow. What followed was a regime of "all or nothing". We were subsequently forced to consider these limitations when we deliberated over authorizations for defense-related exports. In many cases it was difficult to authorize the export of a weapons system, even with reduced performance, in order to prevent foreigners from discovering the exact state of the technologies at our disposal. Even when we went to great lengths to downgrade the technology in sensitive areas exported systems would nonetheless provide the entire technological 'herd' with a window into technological developments that we wanted to keep secret. In contrast, the Americans had no problem providing advanced weapons systems such as fighter planes, which were technologically downgraded to a degree determined by the defense relationship between the US and the county in question. The highest country on the ladder as far as the Americans were concerned was Great Britain, and Israel was one rung down. And even when they did supply advanced systems like F-15 and F-16 fighter planes, they came with systems in locked boxes, which we were not allowed to open. Our problems adapting advanced air-to-air missiles to be launched from American planes (such missiles require electronic links into a plane's aviation system) intensified as the technological level of the weapons systems developed by the Israeli defense industries improved.

Prof. Moshe Arens and Cybernetics submitted a thick, black-bound, two-volume report on the state of military technology, which came to be known as the "black books". This assessment became an important part of the foundation for the research and development policy we were then developing. Arens still takes great pride in the contribution made by the pioneering work of Cybernetics to the strategic/technological thinking that developed in Israel in the mid-1970s.

During the process of developing our research and development policy, we had to undergo procedures that we would later come to regard as essential. These were processes of dialogue with the ground forces, particularly the armored corps, and the other services of the IDF, with an emphasis on the air force, the leading service. To this end I initiated a meeting with the new commander of the tank forces, Major General Moshe Peled. The meeting began with a long, private session between just the two of us, during which we agreed on the participation of R&D personnel in the armored corps brigade commanders' conference and the swapping of branch directors between R&D and the armored corps. We also spent a significant amount of time clarifying the main directions of development for the armored forces. After that, we invited the deputies and staff officers of the corps and the R&D Unit to join the meeting.

Overall, Peled displayed great interest in the Hughes fire-control systems and the distance gauge for tanks, an issue which a few years earlier had sparked a dispute between the IDF and the defense ministry and which was now the subject of intense interest in the armored corps. After fighting the largest tank battles in history during the Yom Kippur War, our need for advanced tank fire-control systems intensified. Such systems would mean a substantial technological leap and a significant future advantage on the battlefield. Moshe Dayan's refusal to settle the debate over whether to purchase American systems for the IDF or to have Israel's defense industries develop them had resulted in the creation of the R&D Unit back in August 1971.

However, it also left the issue of how the IDF would arm itself unresolved. I was pleased that the corps commander made his position so clear, and I saw no problem with making this issue a high priority for the R&D Unit. I could not, however, share with Peled my misgivings regarding the way we would actually acquire the fire-control systems for his tanks. My experience as the director of R&D had somewhat changed my perspective on the Israeli defense industries and enabled me to understand the importance of developing technologies in Israel. I told Peled that I thought we could evaluate two or three models produced by Hughes that were already at the end of the development process, but that we were also obliged to consider development and production in Israel. Overall, I regarded it as an important meeting in which we reached understandings with the major corps in the Israeli ground forces, which would prove important for our relationship and our future cooperation.

We now started to work on the big picture we had started to sketch out with the air force before the war with insights gained from the fighting both from the perspective of the Air Force Control Center and other air force related lessons from the war. Air Force commander Benny Peled made an important contribution to these additions, and our close personal connection encouraged him to be open and candid with me. I also came to appreciate another aspect of the issue while visiting Amos Lapidot, who had been the commander of the Hatzor Air Force base during the war. I first met Lieutenant Colonel Lapidot when he was director of the Weapons Development Department at the Air Force general staff between 1970 and 1972. We had had many discussions and quite a few arguments, but we developed a warm personal relationship which continues today. One of the most important and sensitive issues was the air force's battle against surface-to-air missiles during the War of Attrition along the Suez Canal. Despite the new acquisition of Phantom aircraft and the beginnings of new electronic warfare devices that came from the American lessons from the Vietnam War, the Israeli Air Force lost planes during this campaign. In the Operations Branch Weapons Development Department, we carried out a large study with the help of the sharp minds in our department and our reserve officers. The idea we came up with was a combined attack from the air with the innovative and smart use of long-range artillery.

The air force was not willing to discuss support from the ground, and, during a number of discussions we had on the subject Lapidot argued passionately that the air force was capable of handling the threats on its own. We never achieved the capacity to integrate artillery into the effort to defeat the Egyptian SA-2 and SA-3 missile batteries, and there is no way of knowing how many air force losses could have been prevented with such an integrated model.

Lapidot and I had a long candid discussion on the R&D Unit, Israel's ground forces, and the war's implications for the air force. One important insight was about the attitude of the air force towards air support for ground warfare. On the one hand, I knew Major General Benny Peled well, and I knew how he could be decisive and heavy handed. On the other hand, I saw that Lapidot or the squadron commanders I met in the conference after the war were not the sort of people who could be dissuaded from expressing their opinions when disagreements arose. Lapidot continued to climb the ranks of the air force and was later appointed as the tenth commander of the corps. He introduced me to Eitan Ben-Eliyahu, a young squadron commander who received command of his squadron during the war. Ben-Eliyahu, a 30-year-old Phantom pilot impressed me as an intelligent, energetic, affable, and charming young man. These characteristics remained a prominent part of his personality in every position he held in the air force until he himself assumed command of the corps. The meeting was also joined by two veteran navigators, who looked like grown-up children to me. I learned a great deal about the feelings of pilots and their sense of insecurity about the possibility of failed attacks against targets on the ground. I also gained a basic understanding of electronic warfare-based self-defense, and I learned that the pilots were not happy with this issue. The navigators lucidly explained how complicated it was to work with the precise American weapons systems during the war, calling it "in-flight office work". As a result of our discussion I came to truly understand the importance of developing standoff weapons, in which we invested immense efforts in subsequent years, even enjoying a degree of success.

The trauma of the war put the acquisition of long-range precise surface-to-surface missiles on the agenda. Such missiles were beyond the capabilities of the Lance missiles that the artillery corps wanted to buy. The Pershing missile were on top of our second "Treasure" list, although I understood that there was very little chance of us actually getting them under the American policy in place at the time. Nonetheless, the acquisition of precise surface-to-surface missiles remained on the agenda. In an effort to address the issue through an orderly process, I called a meeting to clarify the operational need for such a missile. The response was surprisingly high powered and the meeting was attended by Air Force Brigadier General David Ivry,

Brigadier General Yehoshua Sagi, the Intelligence Branch's deputy director for research; Weapons Development Department Director Yosef Maayan of the Air Force's Equipment Squadron; Colonel Simcha Maoz, representing General Avraham Tamir; and the entire senior staff of the R&D Unit. To me, the discussion seemed somewhat superficial. Nonetheless, the issue was dealt with fairly and logically, and everyone felt that we had clarified the somewhat unconvincing need for the missile and how important it was to start developing it. The R&D officials felt that the discussion had contributed not only to a better understanding of the issue, but to the positioning of the R&D Unit within the IDF and the defense ministry.

Another perspective we gained during the process of policy development had to do with scientific research. During the war, I entrusted responsibility for coordination with research institutions to Yedidia Shamir.

There was immense pressure from the researchers from the Hebrew University in Jerusalem and the Weizmann Institute to join the war effort. We were extremely sorry that we were ultimately unable to appropriately accommodate the scientists' desire to volunteer. At the time there was no workable framework for defense research within Israeli research institutions, and it was hard to get the scientists focused on issues of current and critical importance. It seemed to me that Yedidia's gentle personality, and his hesitance to address military issues with which he did not feel comfortable, were detrimental to the effort. Before the end of the war we visited the Weizmann Institute with the goal of finding ways to integrate the research community into defense-related R&D. The difficult war we had just gone through was still fresh in our minds, and all this motivated the researchers to join in the defense effort. Prof. Israel Dostrovsky became the President of the Weizmann Institute in 1971, after serving as the director-general of the Israel Atomic Energy Commission in the Prime Minister's Office for five years. The visit, planned as a three-hour discussion, evolved into a six-hour visit including a presentation of the Institute's defense-related research and development capacities. Prof. Shmuel Strickman was the Institute's star in the field of security. The professor...ormer Palmah fighter who always wore short pants – had long before won me over with his anecdotes and his naïve directness. Strickman was a genius in physical mathematics who also knew how to create things in the laboratory. He worked with us for many years after the Yom Kippur War and always received the budgets he requested, indicating how important his work was. We could not visit the Weizmann Institute without visiting the large computer known as the "Golem", the pride of the Institute. Today, a handheld computer can provide many times the computing output of the Golem, which then occupied an entire building. The visit concluded with lunch with the Institute's leading researchers at the home of the Institute's president, magnificent villa in a quiet green area. I was pleased to hear from Dostrovsky that the Institute had decided to encourage their scientists to take one-to three-year sabbaticals in order to work not only with the IDF but also with Israel's defense industries. This decision, made in the wake of the Yom Kippur War, gradually petered out.

One year after the outbreak of the war, during the Jewish holiday of Succot, we were scheduled to meet in the office of the CGS to discuss R&D policy. As I introduced the subject to the forum that had been assembled by the CGS, I held a copy of the most recently updated document on the subject. The defense minister's office had also received a copy, but I had not met with Peres on the subject because I first wanted to finish the meeting with the CGS. After I described the main points of the document to Gur, he took a quick glance at it, looked at me with his brown smiling eyes, and told me with great practical wisdom: "Uzi, as long as the document remains on the level of principle, you won't have a real argument with anyone. But, the moment you incorporate budgets and priorities, they'll be all over you."

Many years later, after I was already directing MAFAT after

three years of work on a broad policy paper including budgets and priorities for the different issues and needs, I realized just how right Gur had been.

The preparations for presenting the policy paper to the CGS included reviewing the material with my deputies one last time and giving a final polish to the issues that needed to be emphasized. Another aspect of the preparations which seemed important to me at the time involved mapping the officials attending the meeting and assessing the level of support or opposition of each participant to the proposed policy. I was concerned that Operations Branch Chief Herzl Shafir, whom we had not consulted while preparing the document, would be antagonistic even though I knew that he was not aggressive in nature. I assumed that Planning Branch Chief Major General Avraham Tamir would be positive and supportive, as the preparatory work had been based largely on premises taken from documents that he himself had written, and because he took part in the discussions that had been led by Major General (Ret.) Motti Hod, the advisor to the defense minister, in preparation for the meeting with the defense minister on the policy paper. Based on past experience I presumed that the director of the Budgets Branch would examine everything through the prism of money. It is a known truism that, from time immemorial, budget officials believe that they should be responsible for setting policy, instead of those actually responsible for carrying out the work itself. As for Air Force Commander Benny Peled, I was certain that he would come to the meeting prepared. However, with him it was difficult to predict whether he would support our platform or propose his own brilliant, but completely different thesis, and present it in a manner that was so persuasive that it would genuinely threaten the CGS's ability to approve my proposal. I spoke with Intelligence Branch Chief Shlomo Gazit the day before the meeting, and after a brief explanation he promised to look over the proposed discussion. I expected neither Michael Barkai, deputy commander of the Navy who was replacing Binyamin Telem while he was abroad, nor Quartermaster's Branch Chief Nehemiah Kain, who was about to be replaced, to express an opinion that could influence the outcome. I hoped that this would allow Gur to approve the proposal and allow us to continue incorporating content to serve as the basis for building the annual plans.

I began to present our proposal for the discussion on research and development policy, making sure to vary the music of my recitativo in the opera I was performing while noticing that the audience was interested and listening carefully. Suddenly, the CGS stopped me and asked: "Why do we need to approve policy? Isn't there already policy for research and development?" I was not certain if he was simply playing dumb, or trying to help us by providing me with a convenient opportunity to explain the policy. After all, I had met with him a few days earlier and he had given me the impression that he understood everything I said. I took a deep breath and broadened the scope of my comments on the military/technological situation assessment and the budgetary significance of the many actions required to implement the policy. I also provided examples of the main issues that needed to be included in the long-term working plans once the policy was approved.

As expected, Benny Peled was unexpected, and spoke against the principle of the R&D Unit functioning as a body with dual responsibilities. Indeed, Peled was the only general who understood the complicated status and problematic nature of a body answering to two masters within the defense establishment — the IDF and the defense ministry, and particularly the degree of freedom with which such a unique status endowed the Unit. As commander of the air force, he was concerned about the ability of the new unit to dictate R&D policy.

However, the air force commander opposed me in a positive tone: "What will you do if the entire budget is approved?" he asked "Will you be able to implement it?" As expected, the financial advisor to the CGS, Itzhak Elron, opposed setting such a large budgetary framework, as well as the long-term commitment that such a framework imposed on the system. Today (2011) — an entire generation and nine chiefs of general staff after the R&D policy discussion with CGS Motta Gur — we still have no multi-year budget plan for the entire Israeli defense establishment. Generations of finance ministry officials have refused and continue to refuse to surrender control over the annual budgets, and the respective committees that have recommended moving in the direction of multi-year planning regarding both content and budgets have thus far failed to rectify the situation. The country is run from year to year, sometimes in accordance with the political quagmire of inappropriate and exhausting haggling between the leadership of government ministries and officials of the finance ministry.

During the policy discussions the budgets branch argued that "the R&D budget has increased disproportionately." As we expected, General Tamir supported the proposal to develop long-term policies. While I was not surprised, I was happy to receive his well reasoned persuasive support. Herzl Shafir's support was also a pleasant surprise. With great wisdom and a strong grounding in reality, the Operations Branch chief declared that the first test of the policy would be the decisions regarding the 1975 working year. Arguing against the traditional narrow-minded army attitude towards R&D, Shafir said that the fact that our unit was not purely military made it the right kind of body to manage long-term development policy.

The CGS closed the discussion with remarks that I considered the best possible outcome we could hope for from the General Staff. The work presented at the meeting was solid and comprehensive, Gur said, and that the case for long-term research and development policy was both understandable and legitimate. Saying that he approved of the principles and the main points of the plan, Gur concluded by announcing that discussions regarding the major issues and the annual working plans would be held at the appropriate time.

While listening to Gur I was already thinking about the next challenge — the meeting with the defense minister and the message we would deliver based on the lessons of the General Staff discussion. It was crucial to ensure the minister's support for the budget, and most importantly not to give up on establishing the framework for the 1975 work plan. We felt the minister must understand the ongoing nature of R&D projects and the need to ensure a commitment to continuing them. Unlike the CGS, we felt the minister had to understand human resources issues in the context of building first-rate development teams within the defense industries. I knew that the general positive feedback we got in the General Staff meeting was not enough, and that we needed to strive for a concrete agreement with the minister. In those computer-generated projection days we made many changes to the transparencies we used during the presentation, incorporating lessons from the meeting with the CGS and additional elements that reflected the perspective of the entire defense establishment.

The day of the meeting with the defense minister finally arrived, and at 4 p.m. the entire leadership of the Israeli defense establishment met around a table loaded with fruit and soft drinks. The IDF contingent was led by the CGS and included the chiefs of the Operations Branch, the Quartermaster's Branch, the Planning Branch, the financial advisor, a group of three officers from the Air Force, and a representative of the Navy. Defense Ministry officials also arrived in full force, including Intelligence Advisor Yehoshafat Harkabi, Economic Advisor David Kochav, and Production and Purchasing Administration Director Zvi Alon. Peres also invited the directors of Israel's defense industries: Zeev Bonen of Rafael; Israel Aerospace Industries Director Al Schwimmer and his deputy Israel Roth; Avraham Makov of Israel Military Industries; and Israel Tal, who was now a civilian. As I stood before this huge audience, I thought to myself: "And a little child shall lead them" (Isaiah 11:6). I was rather nervous, but with the help of the transparencies that I usually used the presentation proceeded smoothly and clearly. Peres looked extremely tired, but that is how he always looked during those years. During my introductory speech he permitted himself to ask a few insightful questions. As soon as I was done, he focused the meeting by saying that there was no need to discuss definitions. We needed to talk about the issues themselves.

The discussion flowed smoothly, with the CGS repeating the conclusions of the meeting on policy principles that had taken place in his office. Gur argued that we were incapable of reaching a state of complete independence in obtaining weapons systems, and that each of the main R&D issues would have to be discussed separately in detail. Although Chief Scientist Amos Horev found it fairly difficult to be critical of a proposed with which he completely agreed, it was nonetheless prepared without him. In contrast, Motti Hod took pride in the committee he chaired with Avraham Tamir, Yehoshafat Harkabi, David Kochav, the financial advisor, and the director of R&D. They had conducted a preparatory meeting, he said, and were definitely in favor of our proposal. The discussion did not wake any sleeping bears and nobody got angry as I feared they might. Two and a half hours later, Peres closed the meeting with an excellent conclusion which left us with options for future action. We would have the freedom to plan and submit administrative papers on major development-related subjects, and the Unit would enjoy the support of the defense minister's office. The sun had come out in the dark jungle of the Israeli defense establishment and things were beginning to look good.

Late 1974 also marked the conclusion of another more personal project — the expansion of the Eilam family, which blessed Osnat and Nimrod with a baby sister named Noa. Naomi and I had been planning to have another child when the R&D Unit was still in its early days, but Noa only came into the world after things quieted down a bit after the wake of the bitter, difficult war. Noa's birth was also related in a roundabout way to the birth of another new creature within the defense ministry – the Department for the Security of Information, known in Israel by the Hebrew acronym Malmab, which stands for the Supervisor of Security in the Defense Ministry.

Issues of information security had been handled by a small team in one of the departments of the defense ministry, with the assistance of Israel's General Security Services. Defense Minister Peres and Director-General Ironi wanted a different of structure, and asked me to serve as a one-member committee to propose a structure for information security management in the future. Neither Peres nor Ironi had a problem with a military man investigating a matter that was security related but was also very much a civilian issue. They also did not know that that the family was now "plus one". During the three days when Naomi was in the hospital, I conducted a round of interviews and gathered material to write the report. When Naomi came home I left the house to her, little Noa, and her grandmother who came to help, and took Osnat and Nimrod with me to Jerusalem for the weekend. I wrote the report that Saturday in a quiet Jerusalem hotel and submitted to the minister and the director-general on Sunday morning. A few days later the Department for the Security of Information, of which Chaim Carmon was the first director, was born.

MY LAST DAYS AS THE DIRECTOR OF R&D

During my first working meeting with Gur just after he took on the position of CGS, he asked me how long I had been serving as the director of R&D. I told him that it had been a bit over a year. "Ah," he said, dismissing the issue, "then we don't need to worry." A few months later, however, I was surprised when Gur again raised the issue. It was during a private meeting with Gur about Yehoshua Rozen, director of the R&D Ground Forces Department. Tal had asked that Rozen be discharged in order to serve in the Armored Vehicle Administration which Tal had established within the defense ministry after his resignation from the IDF. Before the establishment of GOC Army Headquarters, the R&D Ground Department was the weapons development arm of Israel's ground forces. Its connection with the Operations Branch chief...ember of the General Staff who was also the senior officer responsible for all ground forces — was natural and understandable. Tal knew that I was not one of his biggest fans, and he preferred working with people whom he could subjugate without being talked back to. Rozen understood the unique status of the Ground Forces Department in comparison to the other departments within the R&D Unit, and at times made his colleagues feel that he was somewhat more important than them. Tal was trying to build a kingdom out of various projects related to armored vehicles and wanted to include the Israel Military Industries' project for artillery rockets in his realm. This led to harsh confrontations when I attempted to protect the R&D Unit. I was aware of Rozen's abilities and did not want to lose him. But when Tal came to me with the suggestion, Rozen himself asked me to let him go. So I went to talk to the CGS but was surprised by Gur's decisive opposition to Rozen's discharge. He completely ruled out the idea and didn't even allow me to make the case. "The IDF cannot give up an officer like Rozen now," he argued. I assumed that another reason for Gur's reaction was bitterness toward Tal, who had "just left the IDF and is already trying to steal good officers." I was happy and relieved by the outcome of the meeting.

However, I was also surprised when Gur told me: "I also want to talk to you about Uzi Eilam." I had no idea what he wanted to talk about, and neither did his bureau chief. It was clear to me that I would soon have another meeting with the CGS, and I left his office full of curiosity about the kind of positions Gur might offer.

The meeting with Gur about my future ended up taking place at Tel Hashomer Hospital. Like many paratroopers Gur suffered from back pains, and we talked while he was lying on a sort of Procrustean bed which stretched his body lengthwise. During the meeting Gur made me feel that the ball was actually in my court, and that I was the one who needed to tell him what I wanted to do after I finished my job at R&D. We both agreed that I would need to remain at R&D for another year. I told Gur about my past intentions to replace Nehemiah Kain at the helm of the Quartermaster's Branch, but quickly added that I did not regard this as a realistic possibility right now. Then Gur asked me the difficult question, whether I had completely ruled out the idea of military command positions. At the time, as a paratrooper, my promotion track would usually entail moving over to the armored corps and receiving command of a division. I wasn't enthusiastic about such a move. In light of the present situation in the IDF, Gur argued that I needed to stay in the army. He also said that one of his premises was that I could be a major general, and the question was whether I should take the command route or the General Staff route in which the time frame was shorter. Gur reminded me that the position of assistant Operations Branch chief was a way to reach the rank of major general, as Ze'evi had done. He mentioned the name of Chief Communications and Electronics Officer Brigadier General Shlomo Inbar as a possible next director of R&D. At that stage, Gur did not want to hear about awarding the rank of major general to the director of R&D, since he had enough troubles promoting the staff officers in the regional commands and did not have the energy left to fight for a major general at the head of the R&D Unit.

Questions regarding the future moved into the background for a few months, and the CGS did not raise these issues with me, for better or worse. Suddenly there was a storm in the skies of the R&D Unit, although not a very bad storm. Inbar, the Chief Communications and Electronics Officer, asked me if I intended to leave R&D, saying that the CGS had told him that the position was open and that he wanted to ask as a friend if this was indeed the case. I told him that I knew nothing about it.

A few days later, during the final preparations for a two-week trip to a country in Africa, I called Gur to say goodbye. Gur asked me to come up to his office, and told me with his somewhat naïve openness about the problems he had with Inbar. Gur felt that Inbar was an asset and should be kept in the IDF, and to this end he was willing to promote him to the rank of major general. The problem was that Inbar was not willing to stay in the army in any position, even as a major general, except as director of R&D. Then he told me that Inbar had already been offered the position of director-general of the Communications Ministry, and that he did not want to lose the officer whom he regarded as so important to the IDF.

Gur's proposal was that Inbar replace me and because I was what he called "young and assignable", I would be given a different position. I remembered the conversation we had a few months earlier, when I did warm to the idea of a promotion track based on a return to a military command position. But I still did not think that was the correct path for me.

I asked Gur if he really believed that I could do any job in the IDF. "Yes," he answered. "Look at me. I also made the move to the armored corps and commanded a division as part of a promotion track, although only for a short time." I agreed to discuss the matter again but set out with a heavy heart on my journey, which was supposed to be two relaxing weeks of interesting meetings in the African country in the company of Naomi, who was joining me for an extremely belated honeymoon.

In my efforts to prepare myself for a meeting with the CGS after my return, I jotted down an analysis of my situation and possible courses of action. Despite sincere belief in my capabilities and the knowledge that I had proven myself as head of R&D, Gur's sudden maneuver somewhat undermined my self-confidence. I wanted to continue moving on to other positions and to move up in the ranks, but I also felt that two years was too little for such a complex position, overseeing a unit that had only recently emerged from the Yom Kippur War.

I wanted to meet with Peres as soon as I returned so I went to his office to report on my meetings in the African country. Peres listened to my account of Gur's plans and gave me the impression that it was the first time he had heard it. Then he reassured me: "You don't want to leave R&D? Well, I don't want you to leave either, so you have nothing to worry about." After I left the his office, Peres's experienced military secretary Brigadier General Arieh Bar-On warned me that I should not be at ease, because when the CGS wants something badly enough, the defense minister can do nothing to stop him. I did not want to believe Bar-On at the time, but in the end he turned out to be right.

I decided to seek the advice of the wise and experienced Chaim Israeli, who was plugged into all the important sources of information in the defense ministry. "If Motta (Gur) really insists on it you have to leave," he told me. "It is best for you to assume the role of the underdog. This will ensure that you receive the maximum compensation you deserve for the ostensible injustices you suffered." Israeli's wisdom proved itself again, and only a few days had passed before a meeting between me, the defense minister, and the CGS was scheduled in order to settle the issue. Gur and I sat across from the minister, who did not know how to begin the discussion, which appeared to make him visibly uncomfortable.

Without further ado we got down to the matter at hand and acting on Chaim Israeli's advice I offered a vivid description of the problems of switching horses in mid-race, while the R&D Unit was still on its way up. Gur had already discussed the matter with Peres and had made his arguments, and I could clearly see where the discussion was leading. It was at this meeting that Peres informed me that Prime Minister Yitzhak Rabin wanted to meet with me about a future position which he did not specify. However, when Gur left the room, Peres asked me to stay and told me that Rabin was going to speak to me about heading the Israel Atomic Energy Commission, a position of great importance. "It's a position for the rest of your life," said the man whose name was associated more than anyone else with Dimona Nuclear Research Center and Israel's nuclear program. I understood that the matter had already been decided, and I resolved to consider what the prime minister had to offer. If it seemed like a good proposition, we could set a time-table for the transition.

11

The Israel Atomic Energy
Commission (IAEC)

RABIN MAKES AN OFFER

Brigadier General Ephraim Poran, the prime minister's military secretary, called me to schedule a meeting with Rabin at the Prime Minister's Office in Tel Aviv, early in September 1975. The Prime Minister's Office was in a building constructed by the Templars, who built the German Colony of Sarona, located at the heart of the General Staff military base in the Kiriya. I was extremely curious when I came to meet with Rabin. I entered the room where Ben-Gurion, Israel's first prime minister and defense minister, used to work when he was in Tel Aviv. Wasting no time, Rabin turned to me and in his deep, quiet voice said: "'Uzi. You were recommended as a candidate to direct the Atomic Energy Commission. Are you willing to take on the position?' Although I had already heard about it from Shimon Peres, I found myself momentarily speechless. I quickly regained my composure and told Rabin that in principle I agreed, but that I wanted to consult with a few people before giving him a final answer. I also told him that the position would require studying an enormous amount of physics and that if I took it, I would only be able to begin after a period of thorough study and theoretical preparation. Rabin was satisfied with my tentative answer and did not pressure me further.

I left the meeting in high spirits. After all, the prime minister had selected me for a position of great importance. But I was also worried how to prepare myself for this new challenge. I shared my misgivings with Poran, who reassured me by promising to help me in the task ahead and by telling me that, as far as the prime minister was concerned, the offer was final and still stood. Later, I learned that Shalhevet Freier, the director-general of the Atomic Energy Commission who had been appointed by Golda Meir, had developed strained relations with Rabin and with Peres in particular.

The prime minister held ministerial responsibility for the Atomic Energy Commission, and in this capacity he served as the Commission's chairman. In contrast to the prime minister, who served as the body's ultimate authority, the director-general was a professional in the field of atomic energy.

I made a list of people with whom I wanted to consult: Prof. Israel Dostrovsky, Major General (res.) Dan Tolkovsky, Prof. Saadia Amiel, and Prof. Yuval Ne'eman. Dostrovsky, with whom I had developed a personal relationship after the Yom Kippur War, had preceded Freier as director-general of the Atomic Energy Commission and was currently president of the Weizmann Institute. He was a brilliant physicist, well liked in the world nuclear research community, and had served as a member of the scientific advisory council of the director-general of the International Atomic Energy Agency (IAEA) in Vienna. I met with Dostrovsky in his office in Rehovot and told him about the prime minister's offer. He looked at me from behind the thick lenses of his massive, brown-framed glasses, with an expression that was wise, but at the same time somewhat critical and rather amused. He encouraged me by telling me that I was capable of doing the job well and that I had nothing to fear. "You'll learn what you need to learn," he said with confidence, "and there is nothing you need to learn about management."

Although Dan Tolkovsky, Ezer Weizman's predecessor as commander of the Air Force, was no longer working in the public sector,

I knew that he had once considered accepting the same position. I asked him to help me learn as much as possible about the job and how to do it well. Tolkovsky quickly got past his surprise at the prime minister's offer, and, like Dostrovsky, also offered level-headed advice that gave me the feeling that I could handle the position.

I chose Prof. Amiel as my tutor in the field of nuclear physics. Amiel was a department director at the Nahal Sorek Nuclear Research Center, and like other department directors, also held a teaching position at Tel Aviv University. He was a tall, pleasant man with combed-back hair that had already started to gray; attentive, intelligent eyes peered out from behind a pair of black framed glasses, and an elegant pipe that was always in his mouth. When he became defense minister, Shimon Peres chose Saadia Amiel as his scientific advisor, and I asked him to help me prepare to return to the world of physics.

I consulted with Yuval Ne'eman both because he had previously served as the director of the Nahal Sorek Nuclear Research Center and because of his expertise in the field of nuclear physics. I felt comfortable consulting with him because of our close, friendly relationship, which lasted until his death in 2006. Ne'eman, who assumed the position of director of the Nahal Sorek Nuclear Research Center in 1961 after being discharged from the IDF with the rank of colonel, was a nuclear physicist of international standing. Our relationship began when he was still serving as the president of Tel Aviv University, and it grew closer with his appointment as an advisor to Shimon Peres. Our harmonious working relationship began to develop as we labored together over "Treasure II", the revised list of procurement requests from the US after the Yom Kippur War. For Ne'eman, the fact that he had not won the Nobel Prize for his contribution to the discovery of the omega minus particle was a scar that refused to heal. Perhaps it was this humiliation that motivated him to again seek public recognition in the political arena.

At the time I also had a one-of-a-kind meeting with the Israeli newspaper Haaretz's senior defense correspondent journalist Ze'ev Schiff. Schiff had published an article on my appointment to the head of the R&D Unit in September 1973, and he now received permission to interview me as I was leaving. We struck up an immediate intimacy and in the course of the conversation we reached the conclusion that it would make sense to use the sabbatical to resume my academic activity.

I went back for another meeting with the prime minister to give him a final positive response to his offer and to discuss the necessary arrangements. During the meeting I proposed that I begin a mini-sabbatical on nuclear physics as soon as I left the R&D Unit, and Rabin agreed without hesitation. I told Rabin about my intention to begin teaching at Tel Aviv University, and he awarded me with another title that increased the burden I would soon carry: advisor to the prime minister on energy affairs. It was the days of the oil crisis. The oil-producing Arab countries had decided to decrease output by 5% a month in an attempt to force Israel to agree to withdraw from the territories it had occupied during the Six Day War. Saudi Arabia, the largest oil producer, went as far as to cut output by 10%. The price of oil, which rose from $2 to $3 per barrel between 1972 and the end of 1973, jumped to $10 in 1974 and to $36 by the end of the 1970s.

I quickly found myself in the midst of a completely different kind of environment. I had a spacious office in an old Templar structure at Sarona, a secretary, a car, and a driver to cushion my landing into civilian life. Before I began teaching at Tel Aviv University's School of Business Administration, I designed a program for studying the fundamentals of production management based on my experience at the Kheshet consulting firm and as a teaching assistant and lecturer at the Hebrew University of Jerusalem. I also taught a seminar on R&D project management, which the School of Business Administration designated for experienced managers in industry and other fields.

A MINI-SABBATICAL BEFORE DIRECTING THE ISRAEL ATOMIC ENERGY COMMISSION

Studying physics with Prof. Amiel was pure pleasure. The subject was my childhood love, and Prof. Amiel helped compensate for the fact that I had not engaged with it for so many years. I tackled nuclear physics with insatiable curiosity, particularly intrigued by particle theory. Part of my sabbatical program included trips to Europe and the US to meet with scientists at major energy research institutes. My business card, which bore the title "Advisor to the Prime Minister", opened many doors for me, and the oil crisis, then at its height, also served as an advantage during my meetings. I learned about the effort to encourage research and development in alternative energy sources and was impressed by the momentum created by the US government's announcement of a new energy policy with large government budgets for research and industrial facilities. Still, it was clear that these were long-term programs and that Israel and the West would remain dependent on oil and oil-producing countries for many years to come. I also visited geothermal energy projects and learned about the challenge of drilling deep enough beneath the earth's crust to make use of the intense heat beneath the crust.

In the US, the scientific advisor to the Israeli embassy in Washington coordinated a long series of visits and meetings for me, and I found my visit with Prof. Steven Weinberg, the 1979 Nobel Prize Winner in physics, particularly fascinating. Before the meeting I read everything I could on quantum theory and weak and strong forces.

Prof. Weinberg was a short, soft-spoken man, and somewhat of a dreamer. Although he was completely immersed in scientific research that would prove groundbreaking for future generations of physicists, he was also well versed in contemporary problems. We discussed the oil crisis and possible ways of finding alternative energy sources. Weinberg was certain that the US could lead the world effort in this direction, but it remained to be seen whether the issue would be a critical priority of US national policy as the need to develop nuclear weapons had been during World War II.

Prof. Abdus Salam, who was born in the small Punjabi town of Jhang which today is located in Pakistan, was Weinberg's co-recipient of the 1979 Nobel Prize for physics. At age 14 Salam finished high school with honors and was awarded a scholarship to the Punjab University. Four years later he won a scholarship to study mathematics and physics at Cambridge University's St. John's College, where he received a PhD in physics in 1951. Salam's dissertation was an innovative, fundamental study in quantum electrodynamics. As Yuval Ne'eman's teacher and supervisor he helped him develop his theory of particles, the basic constituent elements of atoms. In 1964 Ne'eman discovered the omega minus particle, while thousands of miles away Jewish American Professor Murray Gell-Mann was hard at work discovering and defining the elementary particles and fundamental constituents of matter he referred to as "quarks". Gell-Mann won the Nobel Prize for physics in 1969 and Prof. Salam won it in 1979. Only Ne'eman was left without a Nobel, a slight that always rankled.

Abdus Salam continued his scientific research in Britain. However, he never forgot his homeland Pakistan, serving as an influential member of Pakistan's Atomic Energy Commission and a scientific advisor to the President of Pakistan between 1961 and 1974. Pakistan cultivated a pool of scientists to work on issues of nuclear energy and built nuclear energy plants to produce electricity. During this period Pakistan also developed a nuclear weapon, but in that endeavor a different Pakistani scientist gained fame: Abdul Qadeer Khan, who studied in Europe and returned to Pakistan with the knowledge and detailed plans necessary to construct centrifuges for the enrichment of uranium. Khan quickly emerged as a major figure in the Pakistani nuclear weapons program and was also responsible for the establishment of a network for selling nuclear secrets which operated for many years, as the government of Pakistan turned a blind eye.

In contrast to Khan, Prof. Abdus Salam found a completely

different way to contribute to the community that went beyond his diverse research work. In 1964 Salam established the International Center for Theoretical Physics (ICTP) in Trieste, Italy. His aim in building this magnificent institution was to provide students from developing countries with the opportunities he had received as a boy due to his exceptional talents. I was intrigued by Salam and the ICTP alike, and at the end of an IAEA (International Atomic Energy Agency) conference in Vienna, I made plans to visit the professor. With no idea of what kind of tests I would encounter during the visit, I spent weeks reading books and articles that Salam had published. Salam did indeed test me, but not on the subject of particle physics. He had a dense, graying beard and thick black-rimmed glasses from behind which he peered out with an inquisitive expression that seemed to ask: "Who is this Israeli that has dared to visit my center?"

The high point of my marathon tour of energy-related people and institutions in the US was my visit to the Los Alamos national laboratory, preceded by a visit to the Oak Ridge laboratory where uranium was enriched during the Manhattan Project. With funding provided by the US Department of Energy, nuclear research laboratories in the US were in the process of converting their facilities to accommodate non-nuclear research, and issues related to alternative energy sources had begun to interest the nuclear research community. Alternative energy sources were also the focus of the presentations I heard during my visit to Los Alamos, where the emphasis was on geothermal energy and solar power. With a sense of reverence and awe, I ascended to the most secret and well-guarded laboratory in the United States. The way to Los Alamos climbs out of the desert flatlands of New Mexico through thick forests along a windy road. Almost three decades had passed since the conclusion of the Manhattan Project but the secretive culture was still in effect. I reached the site toward evening, and after a light dinner I met my scientist hosts for coffee and conversation by the fireplace.

As I sat in front of the fireplace in the lounge at Los Alamos I could imagine the arguments between J. Robert Oppenheimer and Edward Teller. The two men, both Jewish, were so different from one another: Oppenheimer with his fluent, soft, and musical way of speaking, and Teller, more abrasive and with his heavy Hungarian accent. Oppenheimer grew up in a well-to-do New York Jewish and was talented, broad-minded, and well-versed in a variety of subjects. He knew that the Manhattan Project had to focus on areas that were both scientifically and technologically feasible. The project team had many questions about the preferable type of fissionable material to use, uranium 235 or plutonium, and about the most suitable structure for the bomb. Teller, who fled from his home in Hungary in 1935, had ideas about a bomb that was even more powerful than the one developed under Oppenheimer's direction, and he fought for the right to develop it at the time. Oppenheimer's bomb was based on the fission of atomic nuclei into smaller, lighter nuclei. In contrast, the bomb that Teller envisioned was based on the opposite process — fusion of light hydrogen atoms into heavier nuclei. Both processes release tremendous amounts of energy, but Teller's assessment that the hydrogen bomb would be more powerful was accurate.

During my visit to the laboratories the following day, the security officers kept a close eye on me to make sure I did not stray into any restricted areas. It was there that I made the acquaintance of another Dr. Weinberg — Alvin Weinberg, the lab's long-time research director who retired from his position in 1973. At the time he was heading the Energy Analysis Institute at Oak Ridge and was among the first researchers to focus on the environmental effects of carbon dioxide emissions on the atmosphere. We talked about his role in developing electrical power plants and his experience, which he characterized as "hair-raising," working with the Jewish American navy admiral Hyman Rickover on developing nuclear reactors for submarines and for the production of electricity. "Working with the admiral," he explained, "was like being permanently strapped into a roller coaster at an amusement park." But despite the steep ascents and sudden drops of their joint nuclear development projects, Weinberg and Rickover had a good relationship that allowed both men to make an important contribution to the successful development of modern reactors for the production of electricity.

Weinberg's memories of the different programs he had directed prior to the war were an excellent introduction to the subject of the development of nuclear reactors for energy production. Weinberg also told me about the other development projects with which he had been involved, including the pressurized water reactor, which operated on the principle of boiling water and which was also developed by a research team under his leadership. The extreme, yet justified caution that guided the team that built Chicago Pile 1 at the University of Chicago remained a permanent feature of Weinberg's approach, which placed a great emphasis on safety. A few years later, leaders in the nuclear power plant industry and its lobby in Congress came to regard Dr. Alvin Weinberg as a threat to the financial viability of reactors and fought him tooth and nail until he was removed as director of the Oak Ridge laboratory.

I returned from my dizzying study odyssey abroad with reams of notes I had written down at the end of each day, which contained data, assumptions, equations, and forecasts. The material was diverse, and it would clearly take time for me to digest it all. However, I also had the feeling that the trip had added a new and critical depth to my understanding of the multiplicity of issues related to nuclear physics and nuclear energy. I returned to Israel with a greater sense of self-confidence and the ability to better tackle my new position, which still seemed far off on the horizon.

An important aspect of my preparations to begin functioning as director-general of the Israel Atomic Energy Commission was meetings with senior management officials of the IAEC and of the nuclear research centers at Nahal Sorek and Dimona. It just so happened that the key management officials had also helped build the two centers' nuclear reactors and research laboratories, and I dedicated a significant amount of time to speaking with them and carefully documenting what they said.

During the preparatory meetings I got to know the group of officials who were about to come under my direction: they were professionals, and most could already boast impressive accomplishments. They taught me a great deal about the closed nuclear research community which until that point I knew very little. For the first time I understood how their sense of isolation was intensified by the unique subject matter with which they dealt and about their inability to publish a large portion of their research in the academic literature. In the future...hought to myself...ould need to find a way to breech this heavy cloak of isolation.

SHALHEVET FREIER

I also met a number of times with outgoing IAEC Director Shalhevet Freier and his assistant David Peleg, who would later be appointed deputy director-general. Freier was bright and intelligent, and had a European cultural background. When I arrived in my office on the morning of my first day as director-general, I found a small, beautiful porcelain vase with a rose in it on my desk. Attached to it was a note that read: "Uzi, I wish you success!" I was pleased and heartened by his kindness and the warm welcome with which he received me. I could not have asked for a more pleasant first day on the job, which I had been so anxious about beginning.

Shalhevet Freier was born in Germany in 1920 to Rabbi Moshe Yissachar Freier and his wife Recha, the founder of the World War II Jewish rescue organization "Youth Aliyah". One year after he immigrated to pre-state Palestine with his family, Shalhevet was already serving as a soldier in the British army. He studied mathematics, and played a major role in the establishment of scientific ties between Israel and France as the scientific consultant of the Israeli embassy in Paris, where he served between 1956 and 1959.

Freier had an uncanny ability to assemble scientific teams to assist the IAEC in setting research and development policies and in adopting positions on concrete issues. During the meetings he conducted that I attended, it was abundantly clear that he made people feel like they could express themselves freely and at the same time maintained his ability to make the final decision. Freier was a quintessential bachelor who knew how to captivate the women around him. At times, he did so with a bouquet of flowers, and at other times he did so with a tasteful compliment. No matter how he did so, it was always with a touch of European style that brought the members of the fairer sex to their knees. His hair, which had already started to gray and which he always kept brushed across his forehead, gave him the appearance of a mischievous teenager. Indeed, he did in fact possess a playful sense of humor. I had no hesitations about asking Freier to stay on as an advisor. I trusted him to remain focused on the issues and the organization which he had just finished managing, and I knew he would provide me with loyal support. I felt that my knowledge of and experience with Israeli foreign relations and nuclear issues were insufficient, and Freier agreed to head the advisory team on policy and responses in the international realm.

NUCLEAR POWER PLANTS

A fascinating and extremely important subject in the field of nuclear research is the use of nuclear energy created for the production of energy. The technique for controlling the process of nuclear fission was developed by the Americans at the beginning of World War II under the leadership of Enrico Fermi and Leó Szilárd, two scientists who had immigrated to the US — the former from Italy and the latter from Hungary. The first reactor to control the fission process was built in Chicago, but the reactor and the team that built it were immediately integrated into the Manhattan Project for weapons development in order to use it produce plutonium. The scientists found that normal water could effectively control the movement of neutrons. Later, they discovered that heavy water serves the purpose as well; the Canadians built CANDU power reactors using heavy water as a moderator.

Within the framework of the Manhattan Project the Americans developed processes for producing the two fissionable elements for weapons. Plutonium 239 was produced by irradiating natural uranium (238) in a reactor and chemically separating the plutonium produced by the reaction. They attempted to produce uranium 235 through an electromagnetic process and through gaseous diffusion. Uranium 235, which is used in nuclear weapons, is enriched by centrifuges. This process, based on the slight but significant weight difference between uranium 238 and uranium 235, achieves separation through the use of the centrifugal force created by the rotation of the centrifuges.

After the war America's nuclear development program was divided into two primary directions: further weapons development (in a frenzied race between the US and the Soviet Union, and subsequently Britain, China, and France), and atomic development for civilian purposes. By 1957 the first commercial nuclear reactor had already started operating in Pennsylvania, and the Soviets had also learned how to use nuclear reactors to produce energy. During the same year the UN's International Atomic Energy Agency began to operate in Vienna. Oversight of these two types of nuclear development — development for the production of nuclear weapons on the one hand and development for civilian uses on the other hand — remains a high priority on the international agenda today.

By the time I entered the office of director-general, IAEC administration had made preparations for the construction of nuclear power plants for producing electricity, and the appropriate organizational measures had been taken within the IAEC administration and its research centers. Significant preparations for the era of nuclear electricity had also been made by the Israel Electric Corporation, which established a team of engineers and technicians to begin studying the issue in close cooperation with the IAEC.

Four years after the oil crisis of 1973 the push to develop alternatives to replace oil as the main source for the production of electricity began to wane. In the US, which had embarked upon a major drive to construct nuclear electricity plants, people started to question whether nuclear power was worthwhile in light of the high cost of plant construction. At the same time, however, two giant companies — Westinghouse and General Electric — continued work on the development and production of nuclear reactors and generators for electricity production, and competed with one another for the market in the US and around the world. Two countries that suffered from the oil crisis in particular were France and Japan, which decided to persevere in their efforts to build nuclear power plants. French and Japanese policy remained unchanged even after the relaxation of oil prices and today nuclear electricity provides for almost 80 percent of all electricity consumption in France and about 30 percent in Japan. Joint teams of the Israel Electric Corporation and the IAEC began examining various proposals for the construction of nuclear power plants, including those submitted by the American companies Westinghouse and General Electric, and those submitted by the French company Framatom.

No discussion of the beginning of the era of nuclear power plants would be complete without briefly mentioning the father of nuclear submarines, Admiral Hyman Rickover. Rickover, who came from a Jewish family that immigrated to the United States from Poland at the beginning of the 20th century, was talented and ambitious, and he had no hesitation about expressing criticism of mediocrity and stupidity. During World War II he was appointed to head the Electrical Section of the Bureau of Ships of the US Navy. He possessed operational experience on the high seas, both above and beneath the surface, technical knowledge and a sharp understanding of advanced technology.

In 1946 the United States decided to make use of the knowledge acquired during the Manhattan Project to develop systems that used nuclear energy to produce electricity. Rickover's work with Dr. Alvin Weinberg, the Oak Ridge laboratory's research director, yielded the pressurized water reactor, which generated power for submarines and aircraft carriers.

Two projects were based on the principle of the pressurized water reactor: the nuclear submarine and the electricity producing reactor, known as the Shippingport Power Station. Rickover managed both projects with an iron fist and was involved with all the details of their planning and operation. Five years later, in 1954, construction of the electricity production facility at Shippingport, Pennsylvania was completed, making it the first commercial electric power plant to operate on nuclear energy. The same period witnessed the launching of the first nuclear-powered submarine, known as the Nautilus, after which Hyman Rickover was awarded the rank of admiral.

In the early 1980s Rickover visited Israel as the guest of the IAEC We assembled the senior staff of the IAEC administration and of the research centers at the Nahal Sorek facility to meet the Admiral. At age 82, Rickover was completely lucid and full of energy. His personal escort was reprimanded because all the neon lights in the hallway leading to the meeting room were on. "Why do you allow yourselves to waste electricity like that," he asked. "Do you have a budget surplus?" His poor escort had no choice but to proceed down the hallway, switch by switch, fulfilling the wishes of the elderly energy conservation tyrant. In the meeting room the Admiral presented us with a brilliant lecture on the history of nuclear reactors.

The preparations for the construction of nuclear power plants in Israel included the selection of a site where it would be possible to safely operate a nuclear reactor. The danger which has been made so eminently clear with the early 2011 Japanese experience now is that posed by earthquakes. We considered a site near Nitzanim Beach, close to the Mediterranean waterline, in order to use sea water to cool the reactor systems. After much work we were forced to give up on the site at Nitzanim, and our surveys were refocused on the Western Negev desert. It was there, near Shivta, that we found a location that would fit the necessary safety requirements.

Preparations for the establishment of nuclear power reactors for the production of electricity could not be made without bringing the issue to the Israeli government for a critical discussion on the principle of the matter. Many questions needed to be answered such as budgeting, negotiations with the American companies and safety issues. Prime Minister Rabin agreed to bring the issue before the government for an initial discussion, and we worked hard with the Israel Electric Corporation preparing our presentation of the issue. At the time, Yigal Alon was Foreign Minister and Yehoshua Rabinovich was Finance Minister. Haim Bar-Lev was Minister of Commerce and Industry and in this capacity was also responsible for the Israel Electric Corporation.

Rather naïvely I thought that if we presented the issue in a clear and focused manner we would receive the broad support of the government. I was certain that the impact of the oil crisis had been great enough to convince the ministers of the project's importance. Rabin was willing to move forward to the second phase of preparing the project, and Bar-Lev also supported continuing the preliminary work toward purchasing the nuclear plants. We were surprised by the firm opposition of Foreign Minister Alon, which was based on diplomatic considerations. Israel was not a signatory to the Nuclear Non-Proliferation Treaty (NPT), he emphasized, and purchasing a nuclear power plant could potentially result in international pressure on Israel to sign the treaty.

As a loyal custodian of the public treasury, Finance Minister Rabinovich made a presentation that focused on the budgetary burden presented by the project and raised a number of points formulated in an intelligent and sophisticated manner. However, Rabinovich did not bother to inform his fellow ministers that, although the construction of a nuclear power plant required significantly greater investment than a plant fueled by oil or coal, the operating costs over its forty-year life were much lower than the operating costs of a plant operating on fossil fuels. Rabin concluded the meeting by leaving the issue open, but we knew that moving forward would involve a difficult struggle on our part. Primarily, it would require a concerted effort to change the positions of officials at the finance ministry.

We established contact with the US Nuclear Regulatory Commission (NRC), which was willing to share the vast knowledge it had acquired during its 20 years of operation. We drafted an agreement for Israeli–American cooperation, and I flew to Washington in 1979 with a group of Israeli nuclear safety officials for the signing ceremony. I tried to understand the great importance with which the US government viewed cooperation on safety issues, and all I could come up with was the possibility that they were hoping to use the issue to bring Israel into the Nuclear Non-Proliferation Treaty. Israel did not agree to sign the NPT, and still refrains from doing so today. Instead, it has opted to leave the status of its nuclear technological development intentionally vague.

While we were in America for the signing of the agreement, fate provided me with a startling once in a lifetime experience. The day of the signing ceremony, a mishap occurred in one of the reactors of the Three Mile Island power plant in Pennsylvania. The Americans informed us that they were dealing with the accident, and we were able to follow the events that followed in and around the site itself. At first it was all quite frightening. A helicopter bearing devices to measure the radiation levels transmitted data indicating higher than usual levels of radiation above the site. Although this reading later turned out to be mistaken, the data appeared extremely dangerous to the governor of Pennsylvania, who was following the developments from emergency headquarters in his office in the state capital of Harrisburg, along with advisors from the Nuclear Regulatory Commission (NRC). The governor ordered the evacuation of an eight-mile radius around the damaged reactor...opulation of 25,000. The media

With Prime Minister Menachem Begin while the author was director general of the Israel Atomic Energy Comission. At Begin's left is Shalhevet Freier, my predecessor at the IAEC

frenzy surrounding the event was immense, and even after it was announced that the initial radiation reading had been flawed and that radiation levels in the area were actually not high, no one believed it. The governor's evacuation order and the television images of the exodus of the population from the area surrounding the nuclear power plant were enough to firmly establish the general belief that a real nuclear disaster had taken place.

We were surprised when the directors of the NRC offered to take us on a tour of the site where the nuclear mishap had occurred. When we arrived at the site in a small convoy of vehicles, it was completely closed down. We took a relatively small tour next to the damaged reactor, and from outside we could see the structure of the reactor, the turbines, and the water cooling towers. We were not permitted to leave the vehicles, and we were taken to the site's administration building where we were briefed on each phase of the accident. It was still difficult at that early stage to ascertain all the details but we learned from briefings that at 4 a.m. the water pump supplying the

With Prime Minister Menachem Begin at the nuclear research center in Dimona

second cooling system had failed, which was unrelated to the first nuclear loop. The reactor technicians had not identified the problem as a loss of cooling water. Although the emergency pumps that were supposed to kick in automatically to return water to the reactor did in fact begin to operate, the water still could not reach the reactor core. During a drill carried out the previous day, the valves that allowed the emergency cooling water to reach the core had been closed, and someone had forgotten to open them again. Only a few hours after the core meltdown did the plant workers manage to get water flowing properly to cool the inside of the reactor. No radioactive material had been emitted from the sealing of the reactor structure, but the reactor itself was completely destroyed. On this basis our colleagues from the NRC concluded that the accident had been caused by a chain reaction of planning errors and some human errors. However, the American nuclear industry could be praised for the plant structure, which provided a safety backup that effectively prevented the leakage of radioactive material into the environment.

With president Chaim Herzog at the nuclear research center in Dimona

I recalled this explanation of the accident at Three Mile Island many years later, long after I had completed my tenure as director-general of the IAEC, when my wife Naomi and I were visiting the Ukraine and I insisted on visiting the museum at Chernobyl that documented the nuclear accident that had taken place there. Because the Russian nuclear reactors were not built according to the standard Western safety criteria, the temperature of the Chernobyl reactor was able to rise uncontrollably and resulted in an explosion. The explosion caused a huge fire, which contaminated the atmosphere by scattering radioactive material throughout an area of dozens of square kilometers.

Nonetheless, nuclear power plants remained on the Israeli agenda, and Prime Minister Menachem Begin was briefed on the preparatory work that had been completed while Yitzhak Rabin was in office. Our contacts with the American power plant production companies continued, as did our assessment of the designated site in the northern Negev. The fact that we had signed an American–Israeli agreement

With Shimon Peres at Dimona

for cooperation in the realm of nuclear reactor safety reinforced the good will and efforts of the American companies.

Our path toward the construction of nuclear power plants was overshadowed by one major obstacle: Israel's refusal to sign the Nuclear Non-Proliferation Treaty. We wrestled with the issue a great deal and regarded the idea of demilitarization as an intermediate means by which Israel could acquire a higher scientific standing. In 1974 the UN General Assembly called on all countries in the Middle East to sign the NPT, which envisioned the establishment of a nuclear weapons free zone throughout the region, and for the countries to pledge not to produce nuclear weapons. By that time an agreement had already been reached for the establishment of such a zone in South America, and most Latin American countries had already signed the Latin American Nuclear Free Zone Treaty in Tlatelolco, a section of Mexico City. Talks concerning similar treaties were held in the South Pacific and Southeast Asia.

With all of this in mind I asked Freier and the diplomatic team to prepare a draft Israeli declaration to be read before the United Nations stating that Israel supported the establishment of a region free of nuclear weapons in the Middle East. Of course, the declaration was to be conditional upon an end to the state of war in the region, in which Israel was threatened by its neighboring countries. The one-page draft declaration was formulated by Freier in an intelligent, sophisticated, and clear manner. We knew that Foreign Minister Yitzhak Shamir was about to leave for New York to take part in the UN General Assembly. With the help of David Kimchi, director-general of the Israeli Foreign Ministry, we managed to meet with Shamir and present him with the draft. The foreign minister was not, however, amenable to the idea, nor was he willing to listen to any explanations or efforts to persuade him otherwise. "What's been so bad about the situation so far?" asked Shamir. "Why introduce an element that can only result in pressure on us?"

We returned from the meeting disappointed with Shamir, but we did not give up the idea of a declaration in favor of a Middle East free of nuclear weapons. By the time I had my weekly meeting with the prime minister, Shamir had already flown to New York and was in the midst of discussions at the UN General Assembly. Understanding that we had nothing to lose, I decided to raise the issue with Begin. During our meetings Begin typically sat behind his desk while I sat across from him with his military secretary by my side. This time, however, our meeting took place in the sitting area of the prime minister's office, which meant that on that day Begin was more relaxed and open than usual. I had one hour with the prime minister, and I used it to discuss the subject of a nuclear-free zone in the Middle East. I began by first briefing him on the UN decision of 1974, the Treaty of Tlatelolco regarding a nuclear-free South America, and two additional agreements that were in the pipeline: one relating to the South Pacific and the other relating to Southeast Asia.

"What's the situation in Europe," asked the Prime Minister, "and what about our region?"

"In Europe," I explained, "all the countries have signed the NPT and are therefore not in need of another treaty. I have come to speak with you regarding the Middle East." The draft declaration I had proposed to the foreign minister was in front of Begin, and I explained the advantages we believed would result from making such a statement before the General Assembly. I also told him that I had failed to convince Shamir to present the declaration.

I could see the expression on Begin's face through his black-framed glasses, and I knew that he was convinced. I answered two more questions regarding the statement's emphasis on the new situation that would need to emerge in the region in order for Israel to sign the treaty. There was a long silence as I anxiously awaited the prime minister's response. "Froike," Begin finally said decisively to Brigadier General Poran, his military secretary, "have them put me through to the foreign minister at the UN." In no time Shamir was on the line, and without giving him an opportunity to explain his position, Begin told him to read the statement we had drafted at the IAEC regarding the establishment of a nuclear-free zone in the Middle East before the General Assembly. I never imagined that, 30 years later, this statement would still be serving to reduce pressure on Israel, which is the exact opposite of the outcome Shamir feared.

Menachem Begin recognized the importance of building nuclear power plants in Israel. He would periodically inquire into the work underway to select a site and the possibility of purchasing nuclear reactors for the production of electricity from the US or France. One day while I was in my office focused on work issues, Poran called from the PM's office. "The prime minister would like to speak with you," he said (he always made sure to refer to Begin as "the prime minister"), and without missing a beat Begin was on the line.

"Uzi," he said, in an enthusiastic and celebratory tone (he had already gotten used to calling me by my first name), "I just finished talking to Mr. Mitterand, the President of France, and we agreed that France would give us two nuclear reactors for electricity production.

I want you to fly to France tomorrow and to start taking care of it." I tried to explain that such a trip needed to be prepared and that we needed to coordinate with the relevant authorities in France, but Begin was unwilling to hear of a delay. "No," said the prime minister, "I spoke with President Mitterand, and we have no time to lose."

I promised Begin that we would begin working on the issue as an urgent priority, and we immediately established contact with the President's Office in Paris, the French Foreign Ministry, the CEA (the Commissariat à l'Énergie Atomique et aux Énergies Alternatives [the Atomic and Alternative Energies Commission]), and, perhaps most importantly, Framatom, the French nuclear reactor manufacturer itself, which could exert pressure on the various bodies of the French state administration. I flew to France as head of a joint-team of the IAEC and the Israel Electric Corporation, and Framatom assumed responsibility for hosting us. As a result of the advantageous combination of the green light from the Palais de l'Elysées and Framatom's financial interest in marketing its reactors, we were given red carpet treatment. Upon arrival we immediately began a marathon of technical briefings; visits to power plants built and operated by Électricité de France (EDF), the French national electric company; and an impressive visit to Creusot Loire, the giant steel factory that manufactured the huge tanks in which the nuclear reactor cores were installed. As a former engineer I walked mesmerized up and down the company's modern production lines, which worked safely and efficiently with steel sheets weighing thousands of pounds. The close attention paid to the quality of the steel processing and the welding that formed the parts of the tanks into one integrated complex was unparalleled. For me, the strong smell of the welding electrodes and the cutting of metal had an intoxicating effect.

Late in the day, when we finally concluded our visit to the metal factory, we were placed in the able hands of the officials of EDF. It was already dark, and we had a great distance to cover before reaching the nuclear electricity plant in the wine district of Bordeaux.

The centuries-old architecture that integrated so harmoniously into the beautiful city of Saint-Émilion served as a fascinating appetizer before our visit to the power plant site. The Blayais nuclear center east of the city of Bordeaux has been operating without incident for almost 30 years with four power reactors, each with a capacity of 900 megawatts. At the time of our visit one of the reactors had been shut down for maintenance, which enabled us to enter areas that were inaccessible during normal periods of operation. The French built their power reactors with the same style with which they built their cars, their electrical appliances, their houses, and even their military aircrafts and weapons systems. They were efficient and well-designed from an engineering standpoint, but they also possessed one more quality — elegance and a sophisticated appearance. With great pride the site managers showed us the plans for the reactors and their turbine systems. They placed particular emphasis on the safety control and oversight system, and claimed that French nuclear electricity plants were the safest in the world.

To answer our question about how they went about addressing the surrounding population's concerns regarding the risk of nuclear accident and the release of radiation into the area, they brought us to the visitors' center, which, even at midday on weekdays, was filled with adult visitors, families, and youth. The attractive visitors' center introduced guests to the processes taking place within the power plant and the reactor in language that could be understood by all. Blayais personnel emphasized that the center did not limit itself to on-site exhibits and media campaigns. Recognizing the importance of local opinion, Blayais had a program that included support for social, educational, and cultural activities for residents of the area. The managers of EDF and of the plant itself insisted that it was in their best interest to invest large sums of money in such activities in order to persuade local residents to support the continued operation of the reactors. It was true, they explained, that such activities could not completely prevent demonstrations and protests, and that violent

278 | Eilam's Arc

and destructive demonstrations had in fact taken place near a number of power reactors in France over the previous two decades. Still, they maintained, the majority of participants in the protests were members of various environmental groups and came from outside the local area.

With no intention of discrediting the environmental activist community as a whole, I can say that on many occasions I have seen people who opposed nuclear energy displaying varying levels of ignorance on the subject while making overwhelmingly superficial arguments against the construction of nuclear power plants. Some try to conceal their ignorance about the operation and safety measures of nuclear power plants with harsh words and the use of slogans. Nonetheless, France is an excellent example of a country that has adhered to a clear policy — in this case, the policy of becoming non-dependent on oil-based fuel — and successfully implemented it in both theory and practice.

But not even France, whose president and government enjoy significant political power and have the ability to make decisions and convince the public, could move forward in the face of massive public opposition. This was the fate of an innovative and interesting project by which France hoped to develop and begin operating a different type of power reactor than the ones already in existence: the fast breeder reactor. This kind of reactor was referred to as "fast" because the neutrons emitted from the fissionable material in its fuel moved more quickly than those in pressurized water reactors or boiling water reactors. The small development model of this type of reactor that was developed by the French Atomic and Alternative Energies Commission (CEA) was known as the Phoenix, while the large industrial reactor was known as the Super Phoenix. We were intrigued by the idea of fast breeder reactors.

The plutonium economy was based on the idea of using the considerable radiation emitted within the nuclear power reactor to make full use of the plutonium produced in the irradiated fuel. According to the calculations of French nuclear experts, this process creates more plutonium than necessary to fuel the reactor itself. In this way, the French scientists concluded, they could produce plutonium fuel for new reactors that would begin operating in the future.

I also visited the Creys-Malville facility, where the fast breeder reactor was built. There I learned about the achievements and technological breakthroughs of the project, as well as its failures and the concerns it raised. The heart of the power plant — the reactor — was as beautiful as a modern statue. The tank in which the nuclear process took place resembled an onion standing on its head, and the cooling pipes that brought water to and from the tank was also a breathtaking work of environmental sculpture. But cooling was also the Achilles' heel of the Super Phoenix, as the plans called for using liquid sodium, which had a corrosive effect on the piping.

Problems also existed outside the plant in the realm of public opposition. In July 1977, sixty thousand demonstrators marched toward the Creys-Malville reactor in protest. Ultimately, it was not the corrosion caused by the liquid sodium that shut down the world's largest fast breeder reactor but rather socialist Prime Minister Lionel Jospin's political obligation to the Green Party in his government. In 1996 the plant was closed for maintenance purposes, never again to resume operations.

Menachem Begin never saw the construction of a nuclear power plant in Israel, and Israeli supporters of nuclear energy also continue to wait. Shimon Peres, who in 1984 became prime minister in rotation with Likud party leader Yitzhak Shamir, also did not abandon the issue of nuclear power plants. It was François Mitterand's first term as president of France, and Peres hoped that their similar views regarding socialism and their memories of the golden age of French–Israeli relations would help facilitate French provision of nuclear power plant to Israel. However, although the technical background for the purchase of a power plant from France was already in place, political views proved to be a tough nut to crack.

Before leaving on an official visit to Paris, the city he loved so much, Peres asked me to join the small team that was travelling with him. The French, who knew so well how to honor their guests, housed us in a hospitality palace on Balzac Street not far from the Arc de Triomphe at the end of the Champs-Élysées. Battalions of security guards, waiters, and helpers of all kinds were assigned to the delegation.

French government ministers came to pay their respects to the Israeli prime minister, and we had a particularly friendly meeting with the leaders of the local Jewish community. Prime Minister Peres was in seventh heaven. The issue of the reactors was raised during the talks with Mitterand, and despite past differences over the bombing of the OSIRAK nuclear reactor in Iraq some three years earlier, we were given a green light — albeit a blinking one — to proceed. The French nuclear industry still had high manufacturing capabilities, even without enough buyers for their products, and the terms they offered were extremely worthwhile from a financial perspective. Ultimately, however, after months of waiting with the feeling that we were about to begin the process, Mitterand was forced to adopt the position of the French Foreign Ministry at Quai d'Orsay: that France would be unable to supply us with the nuclear power plants it produced.

When it comes to nuclear power plants in Israel, I still have the feeling that the country missed a great opportunity. The steep increases in oil prices and the global warming stemming from the greenhouse gas effect strengthen my view that Israel should again begin working toward the establishment of nuclear power plants. Today, the US, Britain, and of course Japan, China, and India have adopted a policy of accelerated construction of nuclear power plants for electricity production. There is no reason why the location selected in the northern Negev should not become the site of four power plants, which together would be capable of supplying 50 percent of Israel's electricity needs.

THE BOMBING OF THE OSIRAK NUCLEAR REACTOR — INFORMATION, ASSESSMENT, DECISION

By the early 1970s, after the Ba'ath party had established itself in power, Iraq had already started to acquire nuclear weapons in an institutional and systematic way. The Iraqis tied to purchase a graphite gas reactor for plutonium production from France, as well as a chemical facility for separating plutonium from uranium after its irradiation in the reactor. Even the most pro-Iraqi elements in France were unable to accede to such a direct and transparent request.

The moment I began working at the IAEC, I became privy to concerns regarding the possibility of Iraqi advancement toward the acquisition of nuclear weapons. The manner in which the Israeli establishment dealt with the situation was typical of a dynamic that is widespread in Israeli governance today, by which each involved agency strives to do the work itself. The IAEC was a good example. Its nuclear research centers possessed first-rate scientific and technological knowledge, and it seemed logical to make use of this knowledge to improve our understanding of Iraqi moves in the nuclear arena. The IDF's Intelligence Branch also monitored progress, with its units responsible for acquiring and analyzing intelligence data to formulate an intelligence assessment of the threats facing the country. An important aspect of Israel's efforts to chart the military build-up of Arab countries was an awareness of the possibility of an Arab country acquiring nuclear capabilities. Beginning in the mid-1970s, after India demonstrated its ability to operate a nuclear facility in 1974 and after Pakistan joined the race with its own substantial nuclear activity, Israel increasingly focused on gathering intelligence information and analyzing the threat posed by an Arab country's development of a nuclear weapon. I thought it only fitting that our scientists play their part in deciphering Iraqi advances toward the acquisition of nuclear capabilities.

We learned that Iraq's nuclear activity began in 1959. Its first step was to sign a nuclear cooperation agreement with the Soviet Union, followed by the construction of a Soviet research reactor in Iraq in 1963. By the late 1970s the Iraqi nuclear complex at al-Tawita near Baghdad already had two nuclear reactors: a Russian reactor with a capacity of two megawatts and a French reactor, known as Isis, with a one megawatt capacity. Both reactors were genuine research reactors that could not be used to develop military nuclear capabilities, although the work and the research carried out in both of them certainly provided scientists and engineers with significant knowledge and experience.

When Jacques Chirac became Prime Minister of France in 1974 the nuclear relationship between France and Iraq was upgraded. Chirac was responsible for an agreement by which France undertook to provide Iraq with two Osiris material test reactors for research purposes. Such reactors could help countries with advanced research capabilities test the effect of radiation on the materials being used to build nuclear power plants. The French called the reactors they had committed to build at the al-Tawita site near Baghdad Osirak 1 and Osirak 2, while the Iraqis preferred the name Tammuz, in reference to the Arabic month during which the Ba'th Party rose to power in the country. In 1979, when Saddam Hussein emerged as the sole ruler of Iraq, construction of Tammuz 1 was already in its advanced stages, as were the laboratories France had undertook to build near the reactor. The question of fuel for the reactor was particularly troubling, as Osiris reactors required the use of 93% enriched uranium, which is military grade. Another issue that raised concerns had to do with the number of Iraqi students that had been sent to American universities to study mathematics, physics, and the nuclear sciences.

According to Chirac's agreement with Iraq, France was supposed to supply Iraq with 80 kilograms of uranium 235 as fuel for the Osir-ak reactor. This quantity of fissionable material was sufficient for the production of two nuclear bombs per year. One possibility was that the French would undertake the development of 20% enriched fissionable fuel material known as Caramel and use it to start the reactor, but there was no evidence that the Iraqis had agreed to wait for this to take place. The scientists of the IAEC regarded the uranium track as the one that posed real danger. At the same time, work on the plutonium track also came to light, as the Iraqis set to the task of processing plutonium with the assistance of Italian experts. The Italians were working on planning and building the nuclear laboratories for the al-Tawita complex, including the processing of radioactive isotopes and materials that had been irradiated in an active nuclear reactor. Italian experts were engaged in planning and constructing a laboratory for the production of fuel with a production potential of twenty-five tons of nuclear fuel per year. The Italians also supplied the engineering knowledge needed to facilitate the separation of plutonium from fuel irradiated in the reactor, which could potentially yield approximately 10 kilograms of plutonium per year, assuming that the process were in fact used for producing plutonium from such a quantity of fuel.

This was the background for an important and fascinating experience that allowed us to see the power of cooperation among the agencies in Israel. We learned of the Iraqis' efforts to cultivate a cadre of scientists capable of continuing their nuclear research and development independently. Our understanding of Iraq's primary intention was based on their request, which had been refused, to buy a plutonium-producing graphite gas reactor and a facility for separating plutonium from irradiated fuel. We regarded French Prime Minister Jacques Chirac's authorization to supply the Osirak reactor as a window of opportunity for Iraq to join the ranks of the countries with nuclear capabilities through the back door. The combination of these elements indicated a clear intention on the part of the Iraqis to move forward on a path that would ultimately provide them with the ability to develop a nuclear weapon. Iran, which had been at war with Iraq since the latter initiated hostilities against it in September 1980, was also aware of this danger. Although Iran attempted to bomb the site of the nuclear reactors near Baghdad from the air on September 30, 1980, the operation caused only minor damage to the site. The primary damage caused by the Iranian bombing was the flight of the foreign French and Italian experts and delay of the work in progress.

To understand the significance of attacking the reactor, I was authorized by the prime minister to appoint an external committee headed by Aharon Yariv, an intelligent and experienced major general in the army reserves. The committee highlighted, among other things, the possibility that the international community would impose sanctions on Israel, as well as the possible disruption of the peace processes in the region. In addition, a separate report included technical information regarding the possibility of environmental contamination. In the diplomatic realm, it was important to emphasize that Iraq had signed and even ratified the NPT, and was under the active supervision of the IAEA.

I attended the meeting of the Israeli security cabinet that discussed ways of stopping Iraq's progress toward the acquisition of nuclear weapons, and I had no qualms about making my opinion known. One product of the brainstorming effort was a recommendation to submit a resolution to the UN for a nuclear-free Middle East. We recommended that Israel support such a treaty, which would be similar to the Treaty of Tlatelolco that had been signed by the countries of South America. Foreign Minister Yitzhak Shamir had already used the podium of the UN General Assembly to issue a call to all countries of the Middle East to begin negotiations toward a multilateral treaty for a region that was free of nuclear weapons.

I was fundamentally opposed to taking military action against the reactors at the time, and I continued to voice my opinion in the regular cabinet meetings. One day, Brigadier General Poran called to inform me, in an apologetic tone, that the prime minister had requested that I not participate in the upcoming cabinet meeting. Begin, Poran explained, felt that I had too great an influence on his government ministers. The request, however, did not prevent me from meeting personally with cabinet ministers. I made it my goal to convince Finance Minister Simha Ehrlich, who had impressed me with his intelligence, his wisdom, and his special relationship with Prime Minister Begin. Ehrlich's door was always open to me, and he listened to what I had to say. I also met a number of times with Interior and Police Minister Dr. Yosef Burg, who I thought understood the situation assessment I presented to him and would speak out against bombing the Iraqi nuclear facility at that particular time.

The third minister I approached was Prof. Yigal Yadin, deputy prime minister and the leader of the Dash party. Yadin was an extremely popular personality at the time: a well-known professor of archeology, he had served as CGS at the age 32 and as a member of the Agranat Commission in the aftermath of the Yom Kippur War. In the late 1970s and early 1980s he was a key figure in the Israeli political arena.

I knew that Begin regarded military action at the earliest possible date as a top national priority and had been working hard to persuade Yadin to withdraw his opposition. Other opponents to military action included Mossad Chief Yitzhak Hofi and the IDF Intelligence Branch chief, as opposed to Hofi's deputy Nahum Admoni and all the other military personnel involved in the discussions who were in favor of a pre-emptive attack on the reactor.

As part of our monitoring of the Iraqi efforts and the continuing high-level deliberations regarding Israel's response, we drafted another document in March 1981, entitled: "Bombing the Iraqi Osirak Reactor: Political Considerations." The document emphasized the fact that the Iraqis had initiated diplomatic activity — including contact with a number of UN countries on July 24, 1980 — to highlight the threat of an air attack against their nuclear center. The document pointed out that the air attack against the al-Tawita facility near Baghdad carried out by two Iranian Phantom jets had caused only minimal damage, but resulted in the flight of French and Italian experts. It also surveyed and analyzed international reactions to the

Iranian bombing and assessed that the US might ultimately be unwilling to join forces with Israel in an effort against the development
of the Iraqi nuclear program. The document also posited that an Israeli attack could provide Iraq with the legitimacy to withdraw from
the NPT regime, create pressure on Israel to join the treaty, and pose
a threat of sanctions and international isolation if it failed to do so.
The report concluded by emphasizing the danger of a possible military reprisal against Israel's nuclear center.

One day, at the end of my weekly working meeting with the prime
minister, Begin asked me to remain in his office. Calmly, and with a
deep sense of conviction, he tried to clarify his aim of "immediately
neutralizing the threat of nuclear weapons in Iraq." Begin argued
passionately that after the Holocaust it was unacceptable for Jewish
children to be in danger of extermination. "I need to do it now,"
Begin said at the end of the meeting, "'they won't dare to do it...'" This
comment was the only hint that the upcoming elections played a role
in the decision-making process, that Begin feared that he would be
defeated, and that, in his opinion, a different leadership would refrain
from bombing the Iraqi reactor. It is also important to remember
that, during the period in question, Israel was suffering from the
worst inflation in its history and that the polls were predicting that
the Likud would lose the elections.

I drove to Yigal Yadin's house. The Jewish Sabbath was about to
begin, and Yadin received me in khaki knee-length shorts and a
worn-out shirt. His wife Carmela served us coffee and cookies in his
office with its library of archeological books. The house was dimly lit,
and Yadin both looked and sounded despondent. He was tired and
no longer capable of fighting for his opinion. Yadin told me that he
had succumbed to Begin's pressure, particularly the PM's assurance
that if he did not vote in favor of the bombing, Begin would not make
the decision to carry it out. At that moment I understood that the lot
had been cast and that there was no way I could change the decision.

My final effort was to prepare a position paper entitled "The Political Significance of Attacking the Iraqi Reactor," which I sent to Foreign Minister Shamir on May 11, with a copy to the PM. In the paper we tried to impress upon the foreign minister that damaging the reactor would not eliminate the Iraqis' ability to develop nuclear weapons, as the reactor was only one link in the chain. We also emphasized that fissionable material could be acquired through alternative channels (such as from Pakistan), and that such acquisition may actually be encouraged by an open military assault.

The paper articulated clear opposition to rushing toward a military strike against the Iraqi reactor and reminded the foreign minister that we had already concluded that we had more time than it seemed — not a few months but a few years. This fact, we maintained, allowed us to be flexible in setting a suitable date for military action and an appropriate way of carrying it out.

The appendices to the document itself included chapters on Iraq's nuclear profile; on the Iranian air strike of September 30, 1980; on the position of the United States (including clarifications made by US Ambassador Sam Louis in a meeting with Begin, and by US Secretary of State General Alexander Haig); and on political developments in France, particularly the policy changes that had resulted from François Mitterand's election to the French presidency, and his declaration that France would stop supplying Iraq with nuclear materials. Other appendices focused on the possible political ramifications of an attack in the Iraqi context, the Arab-Muslim context, and the Israeli context, including the recommendations of the Yariv Committee discussed above.

On the evening of June 7, 1981, as Israeli Air Force jets were en route to Baghdad, I assembled the IAEC initial response team, which consisted of the deputy director-general, officials from the Foreign Relations Department, and former IAEC Director-General Shalhevet Freier. We understood that now that the decision had been made to carry out the air attack we needed to focus all our efforts on the difficult battle in the international arena. An initial draft response was drawn up that night, and the day after the attack the informational material was edited and expanded in conjunction with Israeli intelligence agencies and the Foreign Ministry. This initial material was sent out to Israeli consulates and embassies around the world the same day, and a few days later we had already generated additional information to contribute to the global information effort.

The morning after the bombing I went to Jerusalem to meet with the prime minister along with Mossad Director Hofi. Our aim was to try to persuade Begin to refrain from taking public responsibility for the attack. We argued that it would be better to leave things vague, as the Iranians, who had already tried to attack the reactor once, were also suspected of carrying out the attack. This was plausible at the time, as the Iran–Iraq war was still at its height. Begin, however, would hear nothing of it. "We have nothing to be ashamed of," he said. "On the contrary — let the world hear and judge for itself." After Hofi and I finished our meeting with Begin, I remained with the prime minister for our weekly working meeting during which I presented him with the materials that had been produced by the response team and the preparations we had made for the information campaign. At the end of the meeting Begin deviated from his normal practice of remaining seated behind his desk as I left, and instead got up and walked me to the door. "Uzi," he said, "placing a fatherly hand on my shoulder, "you'll see that it was all for the best."

"Mister Prime Minister," I answered, "the arguments of the past are behind us now. The task at hand is to fight an effective battle in the international arena, and that's what we'll do to the best of our ability." It pained me when, later that day, during a press conference at Beit Agron in Jerusalem, the prime minister repeated a mistaken justification someone had fed him for why the attack was carried out when it was, before the reactor went operational. In order to avoid risking the lives of the tens of thousands of civilians living in Baghdad, he explained, we needed to attack before the reactor began operating, because bombing it while it was operational would have caused the emission of nuclear fallout and a radioactive cloud above the entire Iraqi capital. Unfortunately, I was not at his side to intervene and provide an explanation that was more technically accurate, appropriate, and convincing.

The attack on the reactor was carried out four years after Begin's election as prime minister and after four years of working closely together on issues related to the IAEC, our weekly meetings, and visits to Israel's nuclear research centers. During this time I learned to appreciate Begin as a man of remarkable political acumen and as an honest, firm, and charismatic leader of his party, of the government, and of the country as a whole. Begin bore the burden of concern for the security of the people in a profound and concrete manner, and this was an important factor in his ultimately successful efforts to conclude a peace treaty with the Egyptians.

The threat of the Iraqi nuclear program filled Begin with a personal sense of duty and responsibility of the highest magnitude. However, at the same time he was also a Likud politician facing an election campaign in which the polls reflected an advantage for the Labor party, Likud's historic rival. Begin had what he regarded as decisive evidence that a Labor-led government would never decide to bomb the reactor. It was a personal letter which Shimon Peres had written to him, in which he urged him to refrain from taking military action. At the time it seemed to me that Begin's decision to announce Israel's responsibility immediately following the successful attack stemmed not only from his conviction that it had been a sacred mission of which there was no reason to be ashamed but from a political assessment of the advantage it would give the Likud in the elections. Even today, 30 years later, I still believe that these were his two primary considerations.

After the fact, however, I came to agree with Begin's decision, particularly the declarative and deterring dimension of the attack and the public statement that followed. Ten years later, after the first Gulf War, our assessment that Saddam Hussein would continue his efforts

to develop nuclear weapons in alternative, clandestine ways was prov-
en correct. From an historical perspective I believe that presenting
differing and opposing views during the deliberations regarding the
bombing was important and the right thing to do. Begin must also be
credited for the freedom with which he allowed differing opinions on
the subject to be raised during the cabinet meetings. I also think that
the prime minister was justified in deciding that it would be better
if I stop attending the cabinet meetings. Begin did not want me to
threaten the consensus he wanted to reach within the cabinet.

In late August 1981 we published a policy statement that provided
an extensive, detailed description of the Iraqi nuclear program and
the justifications for bombing Osirak. It was the beginning of a
period during which the IAEC assumed primary responsibility for
providing the Israeli Foreign Ministry and Israeli representatives in
world capitals and the UN with a regular source of rational, well-
based informational material. This included an effort to contend
with the report of the expert committee set up by IAEA, critical of
the Israeli operation.

THE INTERNATIONAL ATOMIC ENERGY AGENCY IN VIENNA

We were not pleased with the reactions to the Israeli bombing of the
Iraqi reactor, although we certainly were not surprised. The attack
was denounced by the spokespersons of a wide range of countries,
including the United States. In Resolution 487, the UN Security
Council unanimously condemned the Israeli attack, describing it
as being carried out "in clear violation of the Charter of the United
Nations and the norms of international conduct." At its regular June
meeting, the IAEA Board of Governors issued an unprecedentedly
stern condemnation, emphasizing that the strike had been carried
out on a member state's nuclear facility while under IAEA supervision
under the NPT. We knew we would face a difficult and complex
campaign during the IAEA General Assembly in September.

After four years as director-general of the IAEC before the Israeli attack on the Iraqi reactor, I had grown quite familiar with the IAEA, its director-general, and the political rules according to which it operated. Dr. Sigvard Eklund, who served as director-general of the IAEA for two decades, from 1961 to 1981, was a scientist and a friend of Israel. Membership in the IAEA was not conditional upon signing the NPT, and this is how Israel — along with India, Pakistan, and South Africa — found itself as a member of the organization without signing on to the treaty. In those days the agency was greatly influenced by Dr. Eklund's personality and outlook. Israel had a significant presence on the agency's Scientific Advisory Committee, of which Prof. Israel Dostrovsky was a member. Eklund greatly valued Dostrovsky's opinion and used to consult with him on a personal basis as well.

The IAEA holds its general conference every year in September. Most years it is held in Vienna, where the agency's administrative offices are located. However, once every four years the assembly is convened outside Vienna in one of the member countries. The first yea, the rest of the delegates and I made our way to Rio de Janeiro, where the Brazilians went to great lengths to put together a dignified and exceptionally well organized event. The Israeli delegation to the conference included our representative in Vienna and our foreign relations man, Ephraim Tarry. I was pleased that Eklund had also invited Prof. Dostrovsky to take part in the discussions of the Scientific Advisory Committee, as it gave me another opportunity to learn from Dostrovsky's vast experience with the IAEA.

The annual convention in Rio de Janeiro also provided me with firsthand experience with the internal politics of the IAEA, which to a certain extent mirrored the major blocs of countries in the international arena: the Western Bloc, led by the US; the Eastern Bloc, in which the Soviet Union set the tone; and the Third World, which consisted of countries in Asia, the Middle East, and Africa that referred to themselves as "nonaligned". At times, member countries within their respective blocs also worked within smaller sub-groups based on geographical proximity and ideological identification. In some cases, I observed, countries voted by bloc, resulting in a European vote, a Muslim vote, a South American vote, etc. As in the world as a whole and the UN in particular, here too Israel was almost completely isolated, and its primary loyal ally was the United States. At the Rio de Janeiro conference we observed the increasing isolation of South Africa that resulted from its policy of apartheid.

We forged a good relationship with the Germans through Hans Hilger Haunschild, director-general of the German Ministry of Research and Technology, who was responsible for the field of nuclear energy. Haunschild's high standing within the IAEA stemmed not only from Germany's influence within the agency, but also because of his captivating personality. The Germans were particularly active in the construction of nuclear power plants and even managed to think up new designs. The annual IAEA conferences were important events, and we spent a significant amount of time preparing for each one. Preparations were made in conjunction with our permanent envoy to the organization and the IAEC foreign relations team. I also consulted with Freier who consistently provided me with wise advice. I was to read the plenary speech we used each year to convey the messages we had decided were important. As a rule, the representatives of the Arab and Muslim countries would leave the room in protest each year as I made my way to the podium, which I found somewhat amusing.

The bombing of the Tammuz–Osirak reactor shocked Dr. Eklund. The usually friendly aging man, whose main priority had been to peacefully finish his two decades in office, unexpectedly found himself in stormy waters. He felt as if Israel had betrayed him and was deeply hurt. In addition, his agency, which he believed was responsibly and professionally carrying out its supervisory functions, was portrayed as incapable of supervising a country that was a signatory to the Nuclear Non-Proliferation Treaty. As far as Eklund was concerned, the Osirak reactor had been legitimately supplied by one member country (France) to another member country (Iraq) and was under the close supervision of his inspectors. For him, the Israeli attack was a blatant violation of the rules in which he had such great faith. Even before the annual conference he sent me a sharply worded letter to express his anger, and the troubling voices coming out of Vienna after the Board of Governors meeting immediately following the attack were also cause for concern. There was even talk of expelling Israel from the organization and stripping it of its rights to research funding and to engaging in cooperative efforts with member countries.

Before I left for Vienna we drafted a speech for the IAEA General Assembly, which I continued to polish after our arrival. I requested and was granted a meeting with Dr. Eklund. It was scheduled for early in the morning, and I arrived at the office wing of IAEA headquarters with time to sit down for a cup of coffee and quietly go over my speech yet another time. When I finally met with Eklund he was a different man, closed and reserved with a sad look on his face that seemed to ask: "Uzi, how could you do that to me?" Of course, I was unable to tell him that I had actually opposed the air strike. Instead, I passionately recited the main points outlined in our policy paper, with its details on the Iraqi nuclear program and the justifications for bombing the reactor.

Dr. Eklund told me that tempers were flaring within the UN in general and within the IAEA in particular, and that he could not promise that he would be able to help me in any way. Although I expected this reaction I left the meeting with a heavy heart. Early in the afternoon on the third day of the conference, the time came to deliver my speech. I knew that a resolution expressing stern condemnation was in the works behind the scenes, but I also knew that such a condemnation would not be a binding decision to expel Israel from the IAEA. I skipped lunch because of the tension, and my heart skipped a beat when the chairperson said: "And now the floor goes to the Israeli delegate." I made my way to the podium, trying my best to give my walk a relaxed bounce. As I approached the dais, the delegates of the Arab countries and the Muslim bloc filed passed me on their way out of the hall with expressionless faces. As usual, one representative remained in the proceedings to listen, and in some cases to interrupt my speech with loud responses known in parliamentary language as "points of order". This time, it was the Malaysian delegate who remained in the hall.

I have stood before many audiences in my life, but I cannot remember ever being in such a tense situation. I did not make the slightest deviation from my text, not out of fear of saying the wrong thing, but because the text was the only anchor I had to help me get through the ordeal. My voice trembled as I read the first sentences, and I mustered all my strength and courage in order to speak smoothly. Gradually, however, I was able to relax and began reading the text, paragraph after paragraph, in an increasingly stronger and more confident voice. My speech touched on the Iran–Iraq war and the fact that Iraq had initiated the hostilities. This crossed a line for the Malaysian delegate, who sprang to his feet and demanded to make a point of order. After receiving the chairman's permission, the Malaysian delegate launched into a short but passionate speech — which had undoubtedly been prepared ahead of time — that contained mostly contemptuous words and may have actually been an attempt to undermine my confidence. However, it had precisely the opposite effect. I suddenly felt calm and relaxed, and I answered the Malaysian delegate quickly and directly. I felt my words getting through to all the delegates who were sitting attentively and watching the exchange. I finished reading the final paragraph, which expressed both Israel's commitment to continue supporting nuclear energy for peaceful uses and its intention to remain a loyal member of the IAEA.

Full of adrenalin, I hopped off the stage in a daze which I snapped out of when my feet hit the ground. Delegates from friendly countries stood up and shook my hand as I walked down the central aisle on the way back to my seat. Only then, once I was seated with my colleagues and friends from the Israeli delegation, was I able to breathe easy and reflect upon what has taken place. My work, however, was not yet over, as the men and women of the media encircled our team requesting interviews. We had decided ahead of time that it would be worthwhile to make use of the opportunity to convey our message, and interviews were granted to the European and American media.

The difficult part of the conference was behind us. Indeed, the vote that took place the following day — coordinated and orchestrated through endless negotiations among the various groups — approved a resolution that froze Israel's research funding for an undefined period of time but did not call for Israel's expulsion from the IAEA. This clearly did not bring an end to the pressure or to the hatred that many countries felt toward us, and we knew that Israel's nuclear policy would remain in the spotlight for many years to come. Still, the massive initial backlash had passed, and we could now prepare more calmly for the future.

THE ISRAEL ATOMIC ENERGY COMMISSION DURING BEGIN'S TERM IN OFFICE

Menachem Begin's election in 1977 was a momentous event and marked the first time Israel had a prime minister who was not a member of the Labor Party in its various incarnations. Within the IAEC we were concerned about what this meant for us in the future and deliberated about how to prepare for the new political stage. We were most concerned by the prime minister-elect's lack of knowledge and experience, as well as the fact that most of the new ministers would be holding such positions for the first time. During the weeks between the elections and the formation of Begin's government we prepared a thick file with clear and detailed surveys of each of the areas for which the IAEC was responsible. We called it the "transfer of power file" and for those of us who mourned the Labor Party's electoral defeat, it was another painful milestone in the transition to new times. The file awaited the incoming prime minister in his office, but the transfer of the atomic baton took place during a meeting between Begin and outgoing Prime Minister Yitzhak Rabin, which was also attended by Ephraim Poran, the PM's military secretary. Rabin had been provided with a carefully prepared two-page summary to guide him through the meeting.

At my first meeting with Menachem Begin, I realized that I was dealing with a unique man who was different from all the other politicians I had ever met. His hair had already started to thin, and, when seen from close up, his body was thin and almost ascetic. The new prime minister examined me with wise, penetrating eyes from behind his thick, black horned rimmed-glasses. During conversations he never broke eye contact with his interlocutors, and this was a change I had to get used to. Rabin was introverted and closed, he avoided direct eye contact; Begin's direct gaze, in contrast, was almost hypnotic.

The new finance minister was Simha Ehrlich, a leader of the Likud's General Zionist wing and one of Begin's most faithful and devoted partners. I sensed that it would be wise to cultivate a closer relationship with him, which I did through instructive and informative meetings on nuclear-related issues. Ehrlich was a seasoned politician, and during our meetings he also proved to be a curious and intelligent man with Polish–European cultural traits and an exceptional sense of humor. I liked visiting his office, and I came to regard him as a reliable source of support and assistance.

Another minister from the General Zionist wing of the Likud party was Yitzhak Moda'i, for whom Begin established a new ministry: the Ministry of Energy and Infrastructure. The new ministry was charged with overseeing the Israel Electric Corporation, as well as the National Council for Research and Development, which was headed by Director-General Dr. Eliezer Tal.

Once again differences of opinion regarding nuclear power plants arose, and we had to meet with the prime minister to have him decide. Unwilling to leave the outcome to luck, I began prepping Begin during our weekly working meeting with an account of the problem and the positions of the two opposing sides. The meeting was scheduled to take place in the afternoon and was attended by Moda'i himself. My deputy David Peleg and I represented the IAEC. Moda'i looked calm enough, but his eyes betrayed a sense of tension. Aware that it was a charged issue, Begin decided to meet in the sitting area of his office in hopes that the more casual atmosphere would reduce the discord.

Moda'i began the meeting by presenting his arguments, and when my turn came I too presented my position to the PM. Peleg and I decided not only to present counter-arguments but to actively demonstrate that we were also willing to reach a compromise, more in the formal sense than in matters of substance. After listening to the discussion and asking questions, Begin told Moda'i that he thought that our proposal sounded reasonable and addressed the needs of the Ministry of Energy and Infrastructure. Although Moda'i was left with very little room to maneuver after Begin spoke, he nonetheless tried to do so. "But what will happen if these gentlemen fail to do what they just said they would?" he asked.

The prime minister's response was the well-crafted, carefully formulated answer of a seasoned leader: "Why Mr. Moda'i," said Begin politely, "you yourself said they are gentlemen. Can you imagine gentlemen not living up to an agreement?" Moda'i had been reprimanded, and we were elated but dared not crack a smile at the PM's response.

The creation of the Ministry of Science and Technology was another interesting chapter in the history of the struggles that the IAEC had to wage to maintain its standing and freedom of operation. In 1979, Likud breakaway Knesset Members Geula Cohen and Moshe Shamir established the Techiya party based on their resolute opposition to the Israeli–Egyptian peace treaty and the Israeli withdrawal from the Sinai Peninsula. Ne'eman ran as a candidate for Techiya in the Knesset elections of 1981, and on June 30 he was elected at the head of the party's new three-person Knesset faction. During his political career, Ne'eman joined members of Gush Emunim, and others from the Israeli political right wing, in taking up the cause of Greater Israel, although not for religious reasons. With the outbreak of the first Lebanon war, Ne'eman and Cohen joined Begin's government.

As a result of Techiya's entry into the governing coalition, Begin established the new Ministry of Science and Technology especially for Ne'eman. This new ministry would soon come to occupy a great deal of my time. During our first weekly meeting after the end of the fighting in the first Lebanon War, PM Begin asked me with his characteristic directness and honesty: "Uzi — the Techiya party is joining the coalition and I have decided to establish a Ministry of Science and Technology to be headed by Yuval Ne'eman. What can we give him?"

This was a development I had not anticipated, and I asked Begin for some time to check into it and to propose a suitable solution. My fear was that Ne'eman, who left the defense ministry in frustration in 1974 after not having been offered the job of deputy defense minister under Shimon Peres, would try to compensate himself by building a nuclear science empire.

I began a round of consultations, but one thing was clear: the direct connection between the prime minister and the IAEC must not be broken and the PM must remain the chairperson of the agency. It was also clear that the budgetary and administrative independence of the research centers had to be preserved and could not be transferred to a new ministry. We gradually succeeded in formulating a document that would provide Ne'eman with sufficient titles and respect without bringing the IAEC and its research centers under the authority his ministry. The two weeks allocated by the prime minister had passed, and I was still uneasy about the development. Begin raised the issue again at our weekly meeting: "When will I receive the document you promised me about the Ministry of Science?" he asked gently but forcefully. "It should already be on my desk, and the Ministry of Science was already supposed to be established." Squirming in my seat, I told him that the issue was complicated and too important to be rushed and asked for a week's extension. By the end of the week I had drafted a three-page paper that awarded Professor Ne'eman the title of Chairman of the Assembly of the Atomic Energy Council, a body that was convened by prime ministers once every year. It consisted of scientists, including many who had served in senior positions in the field of nuclear development. I explained to the PM that this did not supersede his responsibility for all our activities. For Ne'eman the title sounded sufficiently important, and he seemed not to understand that it was primarily honorary and gave him little real authority.

In the course of my work with Ne'eman I realized that he was still much more a physicist than a politician. Each time I raised a question related to particle physics, he seemed to forget everything else and would launch into a fascinating scientific lecture. I always prepared myself for my meetings with Ne'eman and made it a point to raise scientific issues. This ensured that, for the more than three years that we worked together until I concluded my term as director-general in 1986, I received a series of intriguing and instructive lectures on various aspects of physics. At the same time, of course, we were left with less time for weekly reports and updates, which did not trouble me a great deal.

ENERGY PRODUCING SYSTEMS — REALITY AND FANTASY

One of our efforts to find an alternative to oil dependency was the Riggatron project, which supposedly offered an effective means to produce power from nuclear fusion. The Riggatron project involved a star-studded cast of well-known personalities including: American physicist Dr. Robert Bussard; Dr. Yaakov Shani, an Israeli engineer who was living in the United States; Penthouse magazine founder and owner Bob Guccioni; businessman (and former military attaché to the Israeli delegation in Iran) Yaakov Nimrodi; former Israel Aeronautics Industries Director Al Schwimmer; Jacques Attali, advisor to French President François Mitterand; Shimon Peres Arik Sharo; Prof. Yuval Ne'eman; and even Prof. Edward Teller, the father of the hydrogen bomb.

Nuclear fusion processes take place naturally in stars, which generate energy through the fusion of nuclei of light elements into heavier elements. Carrying out fusion on earth requires a way to confine the extremely hot ionized plasma involved in the process. A method for doing so was discovered in 1950 by Russian physicist Andrei Sakharov, who developed a giant magnetic ring that could confine the plasma of the nuclear fusion substances within a magnetic field. Sakharov's apparatus was known as the "Tokamak," a Russian acronym standing for "toroidal chamber with magnetic coils."

A Tokamak — which resembles a giant bagel, or, in scientific terminology, a 'torus' — generates a powerful magnetic field capable of confining nuclear fusion processes. In 1982 Princeton University began operating an experimental Tokamak that facilitated energy production based on the fusion of deuterium nuclei into tritium, a hydrogen isotope whose nucleus contains two neutrons in addition to its proton, and whose weight is three times that of regular hydrogen. Over the years, similar facilities for the study of the magnetic confinement of nuclear fusion were built in Japan, China, the Soviet Union, Italy, Germany, France, Britain, Switzerland, and the US. As a guest of the nuclear research institutes in the United States, Japan, Italy, and Germany, I was able to visit these Tokamak facilities. I was surprised by the technological accomplishments they had achieved in order to magnetically confine fusion.

One day in the late summer of 1982, Yaakov Nimrodi and Al Schwimmer stopped by my office at the IAEC. Nimrodi was a wealthy businessman with a commercial network around the world.

Schwimmer, the former director of IAI who transformed the company from a few garages for aircraft maintenance into a full-fledged aerospace company, was looking for new challenges. Elkana Gali, a former member of IAI management, was the organizational engine of the project. Dr. Robert Bussard of the US and Dr. Yaakov Shani, an Israeli immigrant to the US, were working on developing a small Tokamak apparatus for one-time use. The basic idea of the project was to sidestep the major problems caused by the effect of intense heat on the substances that had to withstand it, and to find a way of working without investing a fortune in a facility designed to operate for many years. The Riggatron, or the poor man's Tokamak, argued Dr. Bussard persuasively, could bring us to the point of producing energy more quickly than larger facilities that were still in various stages of research and development. Bussard managed to convince Penthouse magazine's Bob Guccioni to invest in the project. Al Schwimmer was also fascinated by the idea, and became the moving force behind the engineering of the project.

Schwimmer had come equipped with printed literature and a few sketches of the facility that Dr. Bussard and Dr, Shani had developed. The material did not provide a clear picture of the concept, but I thought it would be wrong to reject the project out of hand. Schwimmer was excited and enthusiastic, and Nimrodi followed Schwimmer's lead, although he knew nothing about such technical and scientific issues. They wanted the IAEC to authorize the project and provide assistance in setting up a center for development in Israel. I promised to look into the idea and let them know. I called Professor Dostrovsky and asked him to head a committee to consider the idea of the 'disposable' Tokamak, being certain that Dostrovsky's wisdom and experience would help us understand the essence of the proposal. Dostrovsky and I put together an expert committee composed of scientists, engineers, and economists who were to be provided with the material that Schwimmer and Nimrodi left with me. Dostrovsky and the scientists on the committee possessed a clear understanding of the Tokamak and the experiments that had been done on it, but they had extremely limited material on the Riggatron project itself. Many weeks passed before they received additional material from Dr. Bussard, in response to questions posed by the committee.

In the meantime, an unprecedented drive was underway in Israel to have the project approved. Science Minister Ne'eman threw himself into the undertaking and discussed it with Prof. Teller during his visit to Israel. Arik Sharon, who was still serving as defense minister, responded to the pressures of his friend Nimrodi and told Brigadier General (Res.) Aharon Beth Halachmi, who was then director-general of the defense ministry, to get involved with the project and to try to help. Finance Minister Yoram Aridor was besieged by pressure to allocate $100 million to Israel's part in the project. Shimon Peres was in no need of persuasion by Al Schwimmer, whom he admired for his formative contribution to the establishment of IAI, to join the effort to start up the project. Peres was always mesmerized by grand ideas, and he quickly contacted his friend Jacques Attali, Mitterand's advisor, to convince the French president and, in his wake, the French Atomic Energy Commission to take part in the project. Schwimmer, Nimrodi, and Elkana Gali all maintained that France would become a partner in the project and would cover one-third of its costs. However, a quick check with my friends at the CEA revealed that this was completely untrue: actually, France had decided not to join the project because its scientists had identified no significant breakthrough in the material provided by Dr. Bussard.

In May 1983 Yuval Ne'eman received a letter from Prof. Teller, the father of the hydrogen bomb and a friend of Israel. Teller had met with Bussard and Schwimmer, who had explained the project to him. In his letter to Ne'eman, Teller encouraged Israel to consider taking part in the Riggatron project because it stood to make a contribution to the foundation of scientific knowledge and the prestige of the country. Out of a sincere interest for the good of Israel, Teller wisely refrained from asserting that Riggatron would provide an immediate solution to the world's energy problems. However, he also did not minimize the project's scientific value. As a result Ne'eman remained in support of the idea, but only in terms of scientific research. He maintained no overblown hopes of an immediate breakthrough in the construction of facilities for the production of hydrous energy. Finance Minister Aridor was under the unrelenting pressure of Nimrodi and Schwimmer, who were asking him to approve Israeli participation in the undertaking, including allocation of land for a factory and a project budget of $100 million. Aridor called on me first, to provide him with an explanation of the main idea of the project and to bring him up to speed on the assessment processes then underway. When he felt that he could no longer withstand the pressure and that he had to make a decision, he asked me to write him a paper that included a recommendation of how to proceed. I wrote up a three-page document that addressed the current status of the program, all the scientific opinions on the program, the French position, and the situation in the US, where, as we understood it, the relevant bodies had refrained from providing support. All in all, the document emphasized the scientific importance of researching the use of nuclear fusion. In the same breath, however, it concluded that the conditions were still not conducive to begin the manufacturing of industrial systems, and that the processes of development and establishing feasibility and economic profitability would still require a great deal of time. As expected, Aridor accepted the recommendations and Ne'eman did not appeal his decision. From their part, Nimrodi and Schwimmer disappeared just as suddenly as they had appeared.

FINISHING UP MY WORK AT THE IAEC

I had no intention of staying on as director-general of the IAEC forever. After more than seven years in the position, when Yitzhak Shamir became prime minister after the resignation of Menachem Begin, I felt the time had come for me to move on. I enjoyed working with

Shamir during his year in office. He was a down-to-earth and direct man, and — in comparison to the widespread corruption Israeli governance has witnessed in recent years–was decisively non-corrupt. My sources had also informed me that Shamir had been pressured by people within his party to appoint one of their own in my stead, but Shamir neither mentioned this to me nor even hinted that I might be replaced. For me, these reports actually motivated me to take my time in concluding my work at the IAEC, just to make a point.

After the 1984 elections, when the Likud and Labor parties established a national unity government with a rotating prime ministry, Shimon Peres moved into the prime minister's office. I felt it would not be right to resign at the beginning of his term, so I resolved to remain in my position a bit longer. One year after he came into office, I asked Peres for his blessing to move on. "Let me go," I said. "Nine years is a long time, and we need to make room for a new director to take over." Peres did not oppose my request, but he did ask that I recommend candidates to replace me.

A few weeks later I provided him with three names: Professor Yehoshua Jortner, Professor Haim Harari, and Dr. Yona Ettinger. Yehoshua Jortner was a professor at Tel Aviv University and an old friend, and Peres knew him from his days as minister of communication, when Jortner served as his chief scientist. Haim Harari of the Weizmann Institute was already a well-known personality in Israel and abroad. And Yona Ettinger had directed the Nahal Sorek Nuclear Research Center and had just returned from a two-year sabbatical in the US. Each of the candidates told me that if the prime minister offered him the job, he would take it.

Peres summoned Professor Jortner for a non-committal interview during which he was not asked to take the position. Instead, in 1986, he was appointed president of the Israeli Academy of Sciences, and during his 10 years serving in this capacity he made an important contribution to the sciences in Israel. Haim Harari was also not offered the position, and instead was selected to serve as the president of the Weizmann Institute, which he led to impressive research accomplishments in accordance with the highest international standards. Yona Ettinger was the sole remaining candidate, and he was appointed director-general of the IAEC only after Yitzhak Shamir began his term as prime minister.

12

The Administration for the Development of Weapons and Technological Infrastructure — MAFAT

THE EARLY DAYS OF MAFAT

I began thinking about my next career move while waiting for the prime minister to formally approve the appointment of the deputy director of the commission as my replacement. A political career did not seem appealing at the time so I began to consider business, feeling that my experience could be useful in the private sector.

I was then unexpectedly summoned for a personal meeting by Menachem Meron, director general of the defense ministry. Speaking in the name of Defense Minister Rabin, Meron asked me to accept the position of director of the Administration for the Development of Weapons and Technological Infrastructure, commonly known in Israel by its Hebrew acronym, MAFAT.

Meron told me what I already knew, that Dr. Ben-Tzion Naveh, the first director of MAFAT, had resigned, taking an offer to become CEO of Scitex, a graphics imaging company founded by Efi Arazi, who gave up fascinating and lucrative positions in the American defense industry to create one of the very first Israeli civilian start-ups.

I greatly appreciated Arazi's talents, creativity and captivating optimism. After giving up quarreling with the defense bureaucracy, Arazi directed all his efforts to developing advanced imaging systems for the civilian market. A serial entrepreneur at heart, Arazi knew that Scitex needed a manager to stabilize the company and oversee operations, budgets and finances, which never interested him. The Scitex board chose Ben-Tzion Naveh to fill the slot.

"The minister is asking you to take the position," emphasized Director-General Meron. I hesitated because the job seemed too similar to the one I had already held in the R&D Unit despite the change in title, and asked to discuss the matter with Rabin personally. In a friendly and relaxed meeting Rabin emphasized the difference between the new position and my old job of director of R&D. MAFAT was established by Arik Sharon during his term as defense minister. The original idea was to amalgamate the defense ministry's Production and Purchasing Administration and the IDF's R&D Unit into one agency that would handle the whole range of weapons procurement from R&D through the acquisition of systems off the assembly lines. Another of Sharon's innovations as minister was establishing a planning body within the defense ministry to serve as a counterbalance to the IDF's planning branch. This body was known as the National Security Unit and was headed by Avraham Tamir, the first chief of the IDF planning branch and an admirer and close associate of Arik Sharon. The merger of the R&D Unit and the Production and Purchasing Administration was ultimately unsuccessful due to the determined opposition of the defense ministry's workers union, which gave its full backing to the director of the Production and Purchasing Administration who feared the merger would cost him his job. Sharon still did not understand that in the defense ministry, with one of the strongest unions in the country, he could not act with the decisive bravado of the 1950s border raids.

Eventually a framework that incorporated a virtually unchanged R&D Unit and an expanded Technological Infrastructure Unit that had been extracted from the R&D Unit was established, incorporating a Foreign Relations Unit and foundations to accommodate new large program administrations. Rabin updated me on the current situation, and emphasized that I would work with him directly in the capacity of Chief Scientist and general defense advisor. He also proposed that I be on loan from the prime minister's office to the defense ministry, and promised to have the government approve a resolution ensuring that my personal rank of director general be carried over to the new position in the defense ministry. I knew I would be unable to refuse Yitzhak Rabin, and by the end of the meeting I accepted the position.

I was pleased by the opportunity to have private meetings with Rabin. Based on my familiarity with his working style, I knew that his door and his heart would always be open to me. Deep down I also wanted to complete my term as director of R&D, which had been cut short by my early departure.

More than a decade had passed since I left the R&D Unit, but I met no problems when I took over at the helm of MAFAT. Many people, particularly from the civilian side of the R&D Unit, were still there and were happy to have me back. Despite the changed name and expanded function I was familiar with the principles of answering to two masters — the defense ministry and the IDF. My renewed membership in the General Staff Working Group was also old hat. The only new thing was that many of my former colleagues had aged 10 years, which reminded me that I was also that much older.

During my years at the Atomic Energy Commission I had not been privy to the difficulties and complex challenges stemming from the IDF's longterm presence in Lebanon. The IDF had been in Lebanon since the first Lebanon war (1982), which Prime Minister Begin adamantly referred to as "Operation Peace in the Galilee." I insisted on visiting southern Lebanon to acquire a first-hand understanding of how the IDF and the SLA (the Christian South Lebanon Army that was allied with Israel) were addressing the threats to their positions and mobile forces in the area just across the border, which we referred to as the "buffer zone" between Israel and Lebanon.

My visits to southern Lebanon started at the Fatima Gate, the main passage through the border fence that Israel referred to as the "Good Fence" (in reference to the freedom with which some inhabitants of southern Lebanon were permitted to cross into Israel to work in the Jewish settlements of the Galilee). The dangers were made clear by the requirement to wear body armor vests and we travelled in civilian high-powered Mercedes limousines to conceal the presence senior Israeli officers who were such an attractive target for snipers and anti-tank missiles.

I recalled the terrifying sensation of driving fast along the narrow roads of southern Lebanon from the days when I headed the lesson-generation team during the Lebanon war. We darted from one defended location to another as quickly as possible as our officer escort reported each leg of the journey in code over his radio. In such situations, I would inevitably start to feel queasy and start asking myself what I was doing there, putting myself in unnecessary danger after having been in so many battles. But every time we reached a military post manned by IDF and SLA soldiers I knew that the danger was worthwhile. It was simply impossible to understand the situation along the front in southern Lebanon without venturing there. My first visit concluded at SLA headquarters with a sumptuous Lebanese meal followed by a mad race back home during which we came under light arms sniper fire.

As early as 1986 we realized that a terrorist organization known as Hezbollah was emerging alongside the Shiite militia Amal. Even when the first Lebanon war was still in its planning stages in 1982, my impression was that it had not been the subject of sufficient strategic thought. It is fair to say that Defense Minister Sharon fought the war as if it was another reprisal operation like those he had carried out in the 1950s, except on a larger scale. Throughout his illustrious career, Sharon proved to be a brilliant tactician but a weak strategist. CGS Rafael Eitan, who also began his ascent to the senior echelons of the IDF from the post of company commander in the 890th paratroop battalion, also suffered from a lack of strategic thinking in contrast to his extraordinary personal courage. The fact that we did not seriously consider the importance of the Shiites of southern Lebanon and that we did not develop our relationship with the Amal movement was another result of the strategic blindness that characterized Israel's overall implementation of "Operation Peace in the Galilee." The growth of Hezbollah, which initially did not appear threatening, quickly grew largely because of Israel's long-term presence in Lebanon. It was part of the same entanglement and should have been considered soberly and strategically.

The IDF had been in Lebanon for more than three years before the defense research and development community recognized the need to change the weapons development paradigm for the next war. Slowly but surely, and as a result of the growing number and variety of attacks on IDF forces in Lebanon, MAFAT came to understand that the 'next war' had already begun. We therefore began to focus our work on "low intensity war" — at the time an innovative concept that referred to a new type of fighting that differed significantly from full-scale wars between armies like all of Israel's wars until that time.

While defining the threats in Lebanon and searching for possible solutions, we were surprised by the fact that by and large the threats were not really new. We had already encountered primitive and sophisticated roadside bombs in the Jordan Valley in the early 1970s during the War of Attrition. The car bombs that Hezbollah began to use against IDF convoys travelling in southern Lebanon were also nothing new. What troubled me most at the time, and what I still find so disquieting today, is our lack of collective memory. Our behavior is comparable to the biblical passage "But Jeshurun grew fat and kicked; filled with food he became heavy and plump." (Deuteronomy 32:15). When threats arise on one front after a period of calm on another front, it is necessary to start the learning process from scratch as if we have learned nothing before. My past experience as a battalion commander, a deputy brigade commander, and commander of the

Jordan Valley Brigade during the War of Attrition, served me well, and enabled me to gain a good understanding of the threats facing Israel in Lebanon and how we needed to change Israel's paradigm of weapons development.

The new approach that evolved called for unveiling some of the capabilities which until that point we had been keeping under wraps until the next "big war", and starting to use them in Israel's low intensity war in Lebanon and the war against terrorist groups.

After a short period of harmonious work together, and after he was convinced that I had a good command of affairs at MAFAT, Brigadier General Yossi Ben-Hanan, the director of R&D and my second in command, asked for my help in his promotion. His next move, as he saw it, was to be appointed as the chief officer of the armored corps. I promised Yossi to assist and he eventually won the post. Even before he left his post at R&D a fierce competition began to replace him.

Eleven candidates battled over the prestigious position of director of R&D, which offered diverse fields of interest, senior status within the defense establishment, extraordinary leverage for a future in the defense industries, and promotion to the rank of brigadier general.

Successful candidates for senior positions within the IDF are selected by a small group of generals headed by the CGS, and the proposed points for discussion regarding each candidate are prepared by the Head of Staff Administration. I decided to thoroughly prepare myself for the meeting with long conversations with each of the candidates. Ultimately, I decided in favor of the ground forces candidate, reflecting my belief in the priority of ground warfare in R&D.

I was on edge when I arrived to the selection meeting in the office of the new CGS, Moshe Levi. I wasn't yet unfamiliar with the dynamics of such meetings and worried that my colleagues, the generals, might back me into a corner. I prepared a table evaluating the candidates with respect to the necessary skills and qualities, assigned a point value to each of the qualities and a total score to each of the candidates. The generals were extremely impressed by the methodical appearance of the table, which looked very professional. The fact that my table showed that a particular ground forces officer was the leading candidate quickly took the wind out of the sails of the supporters of the other candidates. After everyone in attendance made the arguments they were obliged to make in favor of their respective candidates, the CGS concluded the meeting by approving my selection. Levi understood the importance of selecting a unit director with whom I wanted to work. Relieved, I returned to my office to call Colonel Shmulik Keren, the next director of R&D, to inform him of the decision. "You won't regret it," he said after thanking me with his characteristic composure. Indeed, I never did.

AN OVERALL POLICY FOR DEFENSE R&D

One of the first issues I worked on at MAFAT was the reformulation of a new defense research and development policy. I recalled the experience of formulating and approving policy in the R&D Unit back in 1974, when the pain of the Yom Kippur War was still so fresh in our minds. Particularly, I remembered the advice of CGS Motta Gur, who told me that I would have no trouble getting policy approved as long as it did not involve allocating budgets or setting priorities. I remembered the formidable challenges we had faced back then in the 1970s even though the policy we presented to the General Staff and the defense ministry had no explicit budgets or prioritization.

I never dreamed that this undertaking would be so long, complex, arduous and involve such intense inter-departmental battles. I called a meeting of the directors of the MAFAT units: the R&D Unit, the Technological Infrastructure Unit, the Budgetary-Organizational Unit, and the Foreign Contacts Unit. I came armed with a copy of the historic defense R&D policy document from 1974. Pointing out that the issue had not been addressed for the past decade, I told the directors present that we needed to look forward and adopt a new approach to create technological leadership for the entire defense establishment. One of the most important differences between our situation in the early 1970s and the mid-1980s was our mastery of advanced technologies. By 1986 we understood that we could no longer set our sights on what was happening in the US and say that in 10 years we would possess those capabilities. Israel's progress during the past decade at that point meant that we had to look into the unknown future.

The fact that the Israeli defense establishment was so close to the front lines of technological development posed a challenge that we had never addressed in an organized and systematic manner. On that festive spring day, I set an ambitious three-month deadline by which we needed to formulate a new policy document. Little did I know that it would actually take three years. Nobody could have foreseen the innumerable obstacles we would face along the way. Compared to the 1974 plan, the major change in our new approach included budgets and prioritization — inevitably entailing a great deal of work and many phases of discussion and revision of the different document chapters.

The more progress we made the more new vistas opened up. It was important to begin with a chapter on the technological forecast that would serve as the foundation for defense R&D into the foreseeable future. The deeper we delved the longer this chapter grew. The subjects addressed in the technological introductory chapter were not particularly classified, enabling us to share the drafts with teams of academics and to consult with Tel Aviv University's Interdisciplinary Center for Technology Analysis & Forecasting. By that point, the center was headed by Baruch Raz, whom Tel Aviv University President Yuval Ne'eman and I had selected back in 1974. The vast amount of material we reviewed during our work was fascinating, and we were intrigued by studies on advanced materials for aeronautic structures and for achieving small radar cross-section capabilities. Other fascinating areas were advanced sensor capabilities that could give us a substantial advantage on the battlefield of the future if they were integrated into weapon systems, warning systems and command and control systems. All-weather vision capability in the air, on the ground, and at sea was an old and familiar operational need, and presented developers with difficult challenges. We regarded research and development of thermal vision and synthetic aperture radar (SAR) technologies as essential for the significant improvement of our weapon systems capabilities in the future.

Our work on thermal vision was based on the premise that every object emits electromagnetic radiation, the spectrum distribution of which depends on its temperature: the higher the temperature of the object, the shorter its wavelength. Thermal vision devices translate thermal radiation into images of visible light that human beings can see. The two preferred regions of light for viewing, known as "atmospheric windows," are located between 3 and 5 microns and between 8 and 12 microns. The capability of a thermal device to read radiation and produce an image based on temperature differences between various objects requires a suitable detector. At the time, the most promising direction was detectors sensitive to infrared radiation, based on indium antimonidem (InSb) or mercury cadmium telluride (HgCdTe). For years systems based on multiple detectors could not be built, and thermal vision devices used only single detectors cooled to temperatures within a few degrees of absolute zero. Images were created by a cumbersome and extremely expensive optical-mechanic system of mirrors and motors that would scan the surface at a rapid pace. But scientific research was moving towards developing multiple-detector systems that would make it possible to forego mechanical scanning. Such systems would still need to be cooled, but not necessarily to cryogenic temperatures.

In technologically advanced areas, such as the growth of unsoiled crystals for thermal vision detector systems, it was clear that Israel would need to make significant advances on its own. We already knew that the Americans would be willing to exchange knowledge with us, and perhaps also to supply us with systems based on advanced technology — but only once they were convinced that we already possessed such technology or were close to acquiring it. Policy regarding the development of future night-vision capabilities set a high priority for the production of crystals for sensors, including the capability to produce gallium arsenide crystals, which were the latest development in modern night-vision devices. The work of crystal production is close to alchemy. It requires clean crystal and a system capable of maintaining stable and precise temperature and pressure conditions to enable the ions of the substance to join the original core and produce a large crystal with a perfect crystalline structure.

For years, the Americans refused to allow companies that developed advanced detectors of radiation in the 3-5 micron and 8-12 micron regions to provide us with models. After searching all the advanced industries in the West, we learned that the French possessed the knowledge and were willing to sell models of advanced sensors for a hefty sum. The French technology was the product of research carried out in the Grenoble laboratories of the CEA, France's Atomic Energy Commission. It did not take long before the research centers of Israel's Atomic Energy Commission at Nahal Sorek and the Dimona Nuclear Research Campus also began the alchemy of growing crystals and achieved impressive results. The French crystals provided us with a shortcut in the development of advanced night-vision sensor systems by Rafael, Israel's electro-optic industry, and a few smaller companies that were the start-ups at the time.

Synthetic aperture radar (SAR) has been one of the most important inventions with relevance to remote sensing in the battlefield in all-weather conditions. The underlying principle is ingenious: instead of building a radar device with a massive antenna to achieve high resolution, the technology involves using a relatively small device to produce the effect of a much larger one. This breakthrough could only be realized only after the development of computerized processing capacities that could interpret reflected radar radiation. The technology enabled developers to achieve the effect of a gigantic radar device many times larger than the aircraft itself by sending signals during flight and amassing the data received for computerized processing. At the time, the small bits of preliminary information we had gathered on SAR technology encouraged us to incorporate it into the technological goals of the still-evolving policy. Today, 15 years later, Israel is capable of producing synthetic aperture radar for its reconnaissance satellites, using this technology to achieve differentiation and photography capabilities from space under all-weather conditions.

The second chapter of the policy document was supposed to map out our future operational needs and use them to derive the directions of future development. Writing it was as challenging as the first chapter. It required working with various parts of the IDF to learn the needs and priorities of the users of future weapon systems. The chapter also served as a means of heading off opposition and criticism later in the policy development process.

Armies are typically strict and have formal frameworks that stringently adhere to rules and procedures; they oftentimes find it hard to engage in creative and imaginative thinking. This limitation is less serious within the IDF because Israelis are creative and like to improvise. Incorporating officers trained in engineering and the exact sciences into all the corps and services of the IDF has been another dimension of the Israeli army's ability to think ahead and make leaps of logic that would be extremely rare in other armies.

Our work on the third chapter of the policy document, which dealt with priority recommendations and budget estimates, emerged as the most formidable obstacle to achieving broad agreement on overall policy among the corps and services of the IDF. The draft we distributed for comments set off a massive earthquake within the defense establishment. It was easy for the General Staff to accept the first technological chapter, which gave the impression of a general introduction requiring no commitment. It also had little problem agreeing with most of the assertions in the second chapter, which

referred to discussions conducted during our meetings with the corps
and services and the insights they generated. However, discussing
budgets and setting priorities regarding issues typically under the
jurisdiction of the individual corps appeared to be too much for the
General Staff. However, the discussion of policy turned out to be
a constructive and educational process, and we soon realized that
the bitter debates actually filled the participants with adrenalin and
helped them better understand the significance of many of the issues.
In any case, in accordance with the system in place, it was general
practice within the IDF to plan and commit to one budget year at a
time. Looking ahead was therefore important, but did not necessarily
result in commitment.

THE DEFENSE MINSTER'S ADVISORY COMMITTEE ON DEFENSE R&D

An important component of the decision-making process with regard to defense research and development was the reestablishment
of the defense minister's Advisory Committee on Defense R&D. I
recalled Dr. Ernest David Bergman, David Ben-Gurion's science advisor, and the days when (the late President of Israel) Prof. Ephraim
Katzir served as the chief scientist of the defense ministry. Ben-Gurion had a profound awareness of the importance of science and technology for a small nation with such limited resources. Because of
his undisputed authority, Ben-Gurion, who was both prime minister
and defense minister, was able to support and nurture the country's
technological capabilities and to create a national agenda that would
ensure its continued development.

When I began my work as director of MAFAT, the defense ministry had no chief scientist, and it was clear that as director of MAFAT
I was also the defense minister's senior advisor on defense-related
science. However, the responsibilities of the position and its focus on
day-to-day work with the IDF and the defense ministry meant that

the director of MAFAT enjoyed neither unfettered observation nor objective judgment when it came to the desired direction of future research and development. A meeting with Rabin was set to propose reestablishing the Advisory Committee on Defense Research and Development. "All I request, Uzi," Rabin said to me at the end of the meeting, "is that you go discuss the matter with the CGS." When I entered Levi's office he was seated behind the desk I knew so well since the days of Haim Bar-Lev and David Elazar. He leaned back in his chair comfortably with his long legs stretched out underneath the desk, almost touching mine. His brown eyes looked tired but not exhausted when he asked: "What's the issue?" I briefly explained the idea of reestablishing the Advisory Committee on Defense Research and Development, emphasizing its past influence in research and development decisions within the defense ministry. The structure I proposed incorporated not only representative figures from within the defense establishment, but highly experienced individuals from outside the defense establishment as well. The chairman of the committee, I told him, needed to be a prominent experienced scientist and, most importantly, someone from the outside.

Levi did not like the idea: "Why should we bring in civilians?" he asked, and continued as follows: "In the end, everything will get to the Knesset and the newspapers! And why choose an outside person as the chairman? Why shouldn't you be the chairman?"

"Slow down Uzi," I thought to myself, taking a deep breath. "Don't get into an argument with Moshe Levi. After all, you know him so well and this is a new playing field with which the CGS is unfamiliar. Try to explain the whole issue again in a way that alleviates his concerns." I told him the names of a few of the people I thought to include as members of the Advisory Committee: Lieutenant General Tzvi Tzur, Major General (Res.) Amos Horev, Major General (Res.) Aharon Yariv, Prof. Israel Dostrovsky, and Prof. Haim Harari. I also told him that I was recommending Prof. Joshua Jortner as chairman. Once he heard the names, Levi's opposition began to dissipate. I stressed the importance of having someone to oversee the director of MAFAT, who was deeply involved in the day-to-day work of the military and the defense industries. I expressed my faith in the experience, wisdom, and honesty of the prospective committee members, as well as their ability to maintain confidentiality. I could see that I was managing to convince Levi, who ultimately reluctantly agreed to the establishment of the committee.

Immediately after the defense minister signed the letters of appointment, the Advisory Committee began to operate. The director and personnel of the R&D Unit prepared detailed reports on a variety of subjects and their plans for research and development, as did the director of the Technological Infrastructure Unit. The material contained in these reports was fascinating for the committee members from within the IDF and the defense establishment, as well as the members who had formerly held central positions within the defense establishment and research laboratories.

The surveys presented to the committee were candid and provided a transparent presentation not only of the success stories but of the failures and the issues that had yet to be decided. At first, we were concerned that our work might be received with excessive criticism by the committee's extremely experienced professionals who had formerly held such senior positions. All our fears evaporated once the committee began meeting. MAFAT personnel surpassed themselves with the clear and thorough reports they prepared, and they now felt that they were working with people with a profound understanding of the subject at hand who asked important questions from which much could be learned. Prof. Joshua Jortner, who had a deep baritone voice and took care to make use of its low registers, ran the meetings in a skillful and businesslike manner. Jortner possessed a combination of a good temperament and the calm confidence of a person who was completely at ease in the world of science. Despite all his academic pursuits and his weighty responsibilities as the president of the Academy of Sciences in Jerusalem, Prof. Jortner dedicated much time to committee meetings and preparatory sessions. He even agreed to remain in the position for a second term, after his first term came to an end.

The subjects the committee addressed included annual and multiyear research and development programs, as well as many other issues. The defense minister regarded the committee as a body with which to consult on weighty issues, such as the Arrow (Hetz) program, the satellite program, and Rafael's conversion into a government-owned company.

The Arrow project had its ups and downs and a number of failures during its initial phases of development. The undertaking was controversial from the outset, and the Israeli military, led by the air force, was one of the staunchest opponents of the development of a missile defense system. The Israeli satellite program was also the subject of fierce debate. At the General Staff, most people lacked confidence in Israel's ability to develop a satellite on its own. Indeed, the program was unusually audacious on our part, but the defense industry teams that engaged in the work were convinced that it was possible. These teams were led by Dov Raviv in the area of satellite launching and Israel Aerospace Industries MABAT space facility personnel, the experts from the electro-optic industry who worked on the development of a space telescope. As with any other development project, there were setbacks which added fuel to the fire among the opponents of Israeli satellite development. Rabin asked the committee to undertake detailed assessments of both major projects and to provide its opinion on the chances of success and the best ways to move forward. The committee endorsed the defense R&D policy and provided us with a strong tailwind for planning of multi-year programs. However, more enlightening than the clear, concise meeting summaries were the discussions themselves, and the dozens of intelligent questions asked by the committee members.

The Advisory Committee had long discussions on missile defense in general and the Arrow program in particular. The program's administration, headed by Uzi Rubin, and the project's management framework within the Israel Aerospace Industry, headed by Dov Raviv, presented committee members with their plans, their successes, their failures and concerns, and their ultimate confidence that the Arrow missile was capable of intercepting ballistic missiles threatening Israel. The Advisory Committee's support for the development programs was important both for us at MAFAT and for the personnel of the Israel Aerospace Industry. However, its opinion was also important to the defense minister himself.

Opposition to the missile defense program within the IDF stemmed from concerns that at a certain point it would start requiring large allocations from the defense budget. As long as the funding for development came almost exclusively from the budget of the US Strategic Defense Initiative Organization (SDIO), the army's resistance was not influential. I was not surprised by the opposition from within the army. It was reminiscent of the way the air force had opposed the first air-to-air missiles developed by Rafael in the 1960s, during my days in the Weapons Development Department of the Operations Branch. It also brought to mind Benny Peled's stubborn opposition, during the early days of the R&D Unit, to electro-optic surface-to-air missiles to be launched dozens of kilometers from their targets. On the basis of such budgetary considerations, the air force had also opposed the development of "pods", mounted on the wings of aircraft to serve as advanced electronic warfare devices. Within the ground forces, which were never as monolithic as the air force, opposition was much more diffuse. Nonetheless, it too brought back memories from the past: of the opposition to the development of the Merkava tank led by Armored Corp Commanders Avraham Adan and Quartermaster's Branch Chief Amos Horev. In that instance, the balances were tipped in favor of the Merkava by the influence and persuasiveness of Major General Tal, and the tank development program continued to push forward. Israel's small navy had not acquired American naval warfare systems and was forced to secretly transport completely unarmed missile boats from the Cherbourg shipyard on the southern coast of France to Israel. The navy gratefully accepted most of the development plans which the defense industries and the defense ministry proposed. This is how the sea skimming anti-ship Gabriel missile was developed, as well as the naval electronic warfare systems that resulted in impressive successes in battles against the Soviet missile boats of the Egyptian and Syrian navies during the Yom Kippur War. Development of the Arrow missile defense program again received a green light, but was nonetheless in constant danger with every failure of an experimental launch.

At the request of the defense minister, the dilemma regarding the conversion of Rafael into a government company was also brought for discussion before the Advisory Committee. Rafael, the Israeli defense establishment's main research and defense laboratory, had come a long way. For many years, Rafael had a direct and exclusive relationship with the defense establishment. Its role was to advance military technology and develop weapon systems for the IDF. For years its primary customer was the Israeli air force, for which the Rafael developed air-to-air missiles, air-to-surface missiles, and airborne electronic warfare systems.

But like the other defense industries, Rafael had started to engage seriously in defense exports. With every reduction in the overall defense budget and the resulting reduction in the funds allocated to R&D, Rafael was compelled to search for external funding sources just to keep its exceptionally skilled teams of workers intact. Cuts in the defense budget were accompanied by an increase in the importance of American aid, and Rafael, along with the other defense industries, stood by helplessly as the United States provided Israel with weapons seemingly free of charge. The annual allocation of $1.8 billion to Israel each year so that Israel could turn around and purchase weapon systems that were developed and produced in the US was a shrewd political and strategic maneuver that kept Israel militarily, economically, and politically dependent on the US. American aid to

Israel gradually rose to $2.4 billion per year, and the single ray of hope context was a provision by which Israel was permitted to convert $600 million each year into shekels to acquire weapon systems from Israeli defense industries. This provision was compensation for Israel's 1987 decision to cease development and production of the Lavi fighter plane. Most of the funds were funneled into R&D projects within the defense industries and this funding remains an important basis of Israeli military technological development today. And so it came to pass that the defense establishment found itself with a gradually decreasing shekel budget which made defense exports to foreign customers a promising solution to the budgetary problems facing Israel's defense industries.

Rafael, still a government-owned defense laboratory, was authorized to export advanced weapon systems; one of its major successes was the export of the air-to-air Python missile. Beijing became an important customer of Israeli defense exports during the period that billionaire Shaul Eisenberg was responsible for all contacts with China.

The successful management of its missiles project enabled Rafael to continue full funding of the development of a new generation of air-to-air missiles for the IDF, thus establishing a primary principle of defense exports — that permission to export a weapon system depended upon the defense industries' ability to develop the next generation of the same system. Dr. Zev Bonen, Rafael's director at the time, was a missile man himself. He made enthusiastic and over optimistic calculations of a future in which Rafael would be able to successfully market all the weapon systems it developed. Bonen envisioned a Rafael with more than 10,000 employees, working in all the areas characterized by advanced military technology on development and production for the IDF and exporting hundreds of millions of dollars of weapon systems each year. After its success in exporting its air missiles Rafael also wanted to market the anti-tank missiles it had developed. Here, however, it encountered fierce IDF opposition to the export of such an advanced and classified system which, army officials argued, had to be maintained as a surprise weapon for future wars. The obstacle was overcome by promising that the income generated by the export of the missile systems and the associated knowledge would be invested in developing the next generation of anti-tank missiles for the IDF. This agreement was reached by Yitzhak Rabin, thus reinforcing the principle that guided us in all subsequent deliberations in the Supreme Defense Export Authorization Committee.

The greater the cuts in the defense budget for research and development and for acquiring Israeli-made systems, the greater efforts the defense industries made to export their products. The defense ministry worked with the defense industries in a number of capacities. Some of the industries were private companies, such as Elbit, Elisra, Tadiran, and El-Op, which could be dealt with based on the quality and uniqueness of the products they developed and produced. Other industries, such as Israel Aerospace Industries (IAI) and Israel Military Industries (IMI), were government-owned companies. In these companies the defense ministry was in charge of supervising operations on the part of the government, or the owners. Although the government companies were run like commercial companies, they enjoyed a special relationship with the defense ministry and their directors had unfettered access to the defense minister and the director-general. A widespread sense of responsibility for the well-being and success of these industries pervaded all ranks of the IDF and the defense ministry.

Rafael was a large government-owned defense laboratory whose personnel were state employees and whose budget was part of the Israeli defense budget. As defense exports grew and became an increasingly important basis for the existence of Israel's defense industries, competition in foreign markets intensified and became in some cases fierce and bitter. The private companies complained that the defense ministry was favoring its "own" industries and that they were in an inferior position when it came to receiving export permits and exerting pressure on the government level. But these grievances were nothing compared to the claim that Rafael, as an integral part of the defense ministry, was enjoying the best of both worlds. Both the private industries and the government-owned industries began to pressure the defense ministry to rectify the anomaly of this government-owned agency that was competing with them and at the same time being clearly favored by the defense establishment.

Since its establishment Rafael had been engaged in research and development and in pushing the technological envelope. Largely due to its status as a national laboratory and the relative freedom with which its research teams could dedicate themselves to projects without considering competition or income, Rafael accumulated a diverse wealth of knowledge...aluable asset that gave Rafael a clear advantage in the new area of competitive defense related exporting, even without the preferential treatment of the defense ministry.

Eventually, the defense ministry reached the conclusion that it needed to change the nature of its relationship with Rafael. Since it was clear that this would be a difficult task, Rabin appointed Major General (Res.) Moshe Peled to be the director-general of Rafael, trusting that his extensive and diverse experience would enable him to make the necessary changes within Rafael. Peled, a member of Moshav Nahalal who had been an armored division commander in the Golan Heights during the Yom Kippur War, finished his military service as a major general and as the commander of the armored corps. For a few years after leaving the military he served as an advisor to the defense minister on defense industries; he possessed a solid understanding of the complex problems he faced in his new position. Peled was endowed with traits that gave him a good chance of success: intelligence, honesty, the ability to speak directly and candidly to all types of people, and courage, not only on the battlefield but within the civilian arena as well.

The first challenge that Peled set out for himself was Rafael's Testing Unit, which had an illustrious history and unique organizational culture. Working for years in the heart of the Negev desert, testing unit personnel had a great deal of experience with stressful situations and with the tension of waiting. In the course of his confrontation with the unit, Peled did not hesitate to close the unit and delay tests that were essential to the development of weapon systems. The employees, however, were not alone in their viewpoint, and received the full support of Rafael's union throughout the struggle.

Defense Minister Yitzhak Rabin was aware of the intense confrontation stemming from Peled's campaign at Rafael and asked for the Advisory Committee's opinion on the matter. It was then that Jortner's committee began one of the most important and fascinating chapters in its work. It was presented with detailed reports on Rafael as a company and on the organizational reforms that Peled had initiated. These background reports contained a wealth of information on the company's specialization centers and its development and production plans for the present and the future. With the encouragement of the defense ministry, Rafael tried to operate as an economic entity in every way, and made great efforts to organize itself into a complex of profit centers, to treat its different departments as subsidiaries, and to forge partnerships with outside entities. It also maintained a technology transfer company for civilian applications, which handled, among other things, the development and production of advanced optic sensors. The defense ministry established a board of directors that tried to function like a typical board of directors in the business world, with monthly meetings that included presentations on working plans and discussions on budgetary issues. It was nonetheless clear that all real decisions were made within the defense ministry. All this information provided material for Advisory Committee discussions and for tackling the question of whether Rafael should operate as a government company. Assuming that Rafael would be permitted to become a company, other questions were whether it could be run like an ordinary business and whether such an approach would interfere with efforts to maintain the high quality technological drive that had always played such a dominant role in Rafael operations and made it so productive.

One of my surprises when I returned to the defense ministry as the director of MAFAT was the resolute position of Elbit President Emanuel Gil. A significant portion of the research and development budget was earmarked for activities classified as "exploratory R&D", which could be based on the results of basic research and make use of accessible technological capabilities. We found such initial exploration necessary to reduce the number of technological questions that required answers before embarking on full-scale engineering development with a relatively high level of confidence. From the outset, Rafael engaged in much exploratory R&D. Israel Aerospace Industries, and its subsidiary Elta in particular, also had a significant number of teams engaged in this type of work. Elbit, however, was unwilling to undertake a substantial amount of exploratory R&D. When I met Gil, I asked him why. "Uzi", he began, "You have to try to understand us. In order to engage in exploratory R&D, we need to allocate our best people to the task. You cannot ensure that every exploratory R&D effort will result in a full-scale engineering development project and continue on to a production line. Our real profit is found there, in projects that enable us to market products. That's where we need our best people. They will not, however, be available if we are committed to exploratory R&D projects. At the end of the day, we are measured by our quarterly reports and our value on the stock market. Find companies that are willing to use your budgets and work on exploratory R&D, and we will buy them when the products of the process are ready to begin full-scale engineering development, and when it is certain that there will be a product."

I remembered how shocked and disappointed I was when I heard his explanation, which I shared with my colleagues on the Advisory Committee as the discussions about how to go about the reorganization of Rafael began to heat up. In addition to the strategic considerations of maintaining the company's capacity to remain at the forefront of modern technology, there were also the more prosaic considerations of budgets and funding. Rafael's experience in beginning to undertake business-oriented financial activity and the routine of reporting to the board of directors exposed the truth about the scope of the budgets and funding provided by the defense ministry. Despite Rafael's handsome profits from weapon systems projects based on advanced technologies, it became clear to the committee that Rafael was not and would never be profitable when judged according to business criteria alone.

The committee began leaning toward the idea of converting Rafael into a company. The prevailing tone within the committee was set by men of experience, not only in senior positions within the IDF and the Israeli establishment but also in business. Slowly but surely the committee generated its recommendation, which was meant as a compromise. It called for restructuring Rafael in a way that would enable its departments and units to operate like the other defense industries and, at the same time, to maintain a critical mass of personnel and organizational structures to function as a national laboratory under the auspices of the defense ministry. This recommendation, which at the time appeared to be a balanced and feasible solution, was supported by most members of the Advisory Committee, including Jortner, Tzur, Horev and myself. Professor Dostrovsky, however, who was a physicist through and through, vehemently opposed our recommendations and argued that the compromise would never succeed. If we wanted to terminate Rafael's status as a national laboratory, he asserted, we needed to be straightforward and honest about it. Dostrovsky also maintained that Rafael should be maintained as a technological unit and that the framework that would result from the plan on the table would not ensure a critical mass of research personnel. Dostrovsky's dissenting opinion, written in the his characteristically sharp, clear style, was also submitted to the defense minister, in addition to the committee's majority recommendation. I suggested to Jortner that Dostrovsky be included in the subcommittee that would meet with the minister to present the committee's findings, conclusions, and recommendations regarding Rafael's conversion into a company. I then decided that it would be better if I did not take part in the meeting.

Rabin adopted the recommendation and Rafael continued along the path toward becoming a company. The process was not an easy one, and much of the credit for the success of the process belonged to Moshe Peled.

Today, Rafael is a well established, successful government-owned company. Professor Dostrovsky, who continued to argue passionately in favor of "the necessity of maintaining a large national laboratory, and not selling off the defense-science assets for a bowl of mess of potage," appeared to be wrong. However, one cannot always trust appearances. Today, 15 years later, I have no doubt that Dostrovsky was right, as Israel currently no longer has a laboratory for defense research and development. Dostrovsky accurately anticipated that Rafael would lose the critical mass necessary to operate as a national laboratory. In addition, the defense ministry funds allocated to this purpose are nowhere near what they once were. Rafael, which has indeed become a government company, still relies on the research foundation it built during its period as a government laboratory and sells its products to customers around the world.

After the murder of Yitzhak Rabin and Benjamin Netanyahu's subsequent victory over Shimon Peres in the elections of 1996, Yitzhak Mordechai assumed the post of defense minister. Mordechai, who was strong and muscular and a soldier through and through, knew little of the world of technology. One day, Jortner and I were summoned to a meeting with Defense Minister Mordechai to update him and receive his blessing for our working plans and the direction in which the Advisory Committee planned to move forward. We drove to Jerusalem and met Mordechai at the Beit Hachayal soldiers' hostel in the city. It was the height of winter, freezing cold. A power outage in the building left us and the minister together in a cold, dark room. Mordechai had been briefed ahead of time on the Research and Development Advisory Committee, and we tried to explain the nature and role of the body. The combination of the freezing cold and the defense minister's total lack of understanding will remain forever ingrained in our memory. When Jortner and I left the meeting we knew that the era of Yitzhak Rabin was gone forever, and that the incumbent defense minister lacked a real understanding of the issues and would be unable to guide and trust the committee.

THE OFEK SATELLITES

Israel is now a member of the exclusive group of developed nations that produce satellites and launch them into space. Israeli-produced optical and radar reconnaissance satellites displaying the Israeli blue and white flag circle the earth at low earth orbits (LEO) of 300–600 kilometers and provide Israel with the ability to see beyond the horizon in high resolution. Israel's satellite reconnaissance capabilities have also expanded to include civilian satellites, developing a commercial business that generates profits for the Israeli defense industries. Communications satellites at the high earth altitude (HEO) of 36,000 kilometers provide a diverse range of satellite communications services from broadcast stations around the world. Today, we take such services for granted but when we started the picture was not so clear. To move in this direction, we had to undertake two primary technological projects: development of the satellite itself and development of its launcher. At the time both projects looked like pipe dreams. Israel possessed academic theoretical knowledge regarding satellites but no practical experience. It was the height of audacity to think that we could begin the process based strictly on our own means.

The use of reconnaissance and communication satellites increased during the 1970s around the globe, primarily for military uses but also in the civilian market. At the time, only three countries were capable of launching satellites: the US, the Soviet Union, and France.

These three nations were subsequently joined by China and a number of other countries. In the mid-1970s, in accordance with its tradition as a national laboratory striving to reach the outer limits of modern technology, Rafael identified space as an important field for future research and development, and its personnel were sent on one-year sabbaticals to space centers around the world.

Within the IDF it was the Intelligence Branch that first specified that the ability to take photographs from space was a genuine operational need...irection reinforced by the imminent Israeli withdrawal from the Sinai Peninsula after the Israeli—Egyptian peace treaty of 1979. Intelligence Branch Chief Major General Yehoshua Sagi was virtually alone within the Israeli military leadership in his quest to achieve satellite capabilities, and only Deputy CGS Major General Yekutiel Adam supported the idea. Sagi's support for satellite development enabled Lieutenant Colonel Haim Eshed, who was appointed as a department director within the bureau of the Chief Intelligence Officer in 1979, to request Rafael and Israel Aerospace Industries to undertake a preliminary assessment of the feasibility of developing a reconnaissance satellite and launching it into space. At the time the Intelligence Branch enjoyed almost complete freedom to contact the defense industries directly and to independently commission research and development work. The defense ministry carried out the contractual agreement by means of a unit within the Production and Purchasing Administration. Rafael possessed extensive knowledge, thanks to the vision of Dr. Jonathan Mass and the company's investment in the cultivation of scientific personnel to work on space-related subjects. The scientists at Rafael reached the conclusion that an operational reconnaissance satellite could not be launched without long-term, expensive development. Rafael's recommendation was to move forward by participating in international development projects. They were correct in their assessment of the scope of the investment and time required, but they never imagined how difficult it would be to join international work on satellites.

Israeli Aerospace Industries, in contrast, submitted a confident, well-structured, convincing plan, complete with timetables and budgets. During this early phase two components of IAI work on satellites were already beginning to take shape: development of launchers, by a factory that would come to be known as Malam, and development of satellites by the Mabat factory. These were the days of the Islamic Revolution and the toppling of the Shah in Iran, and IAI was under stress because a number of projects in which the Mabat factory had been involved were cancelled...ignificant factor that motivated IAI to seek new directions and space seemed like the most promising one.

However, we still had a long, difficult road to travel before the IDF would authorize the goal of acquiring satellite photo capabilities. CGS Rafael Eitan thought there was no need for an Israeli satellite, a position based on the familiar concern that such an ambitious project would inevitably take a huge bite out of the IDF budget. Major General David Ivry, commander of the air force at the time, also opposed the project, ostensibly due to operational considerations. His argument was that aircraft could provide all the country's needs with aerial photos. Here too, however, opposition appears to have stemmed from concerns regarding the project's possible impact on the air force budget, and perhaps also from concerns that it might be detrimental to the development of advanced aerial photography capabilities. Only with his appointment as director-general of the defense ministry in 1986 did Ivry change his position, becoming one of the most important supporters of Israel's satellite program.

In mid-1981, a solution for the budgetary problems facing the Israeli space program was finally found. The R&D Unit proposed contracting IAI's Electronics Division to take the lead in satellite development incorporating Malam's launcher development program and the Mabat satellite and transmission programs.

By the time I returned to the defense ministry in early 1986, we already had a great deal of experience in satellite development. At MAFAT I met Colonel Haim Eshed, whom I knew from my days as director of R&D when he was a talented technical officer in the development department of the Intelligence Branch. Eshed was now in charge of the satellite program, which had already taken root and started to grow. As director of the program, Eshed was promoted to the rank of brigadier general, and I had the privilege of working with him and his team of devoted professionals in the space program during my entire tenure as director of MAFAT.

The process of developing launchers was a story in itself. Since the early 1960s, Israel's defense industries had amassed a substantial body of missile-related knowledge. By 1961 Rafael had already launched its Shavit II missile from a site along the Mediterranean coast just south of Acre, and the event was attended by David Ben-Gurion, Golda Meir, Shimon Peres, Tzvi Tzur, and other senior officials. Shavit II was a 250-kilogram two-stage solid fuel rocket for meteorological research that reached an altitude of 80 kilometers. To the best of my knowledge there was no Shavit I. Perhaps there had been an unsuccessful initial model that failed to launch, or perhaps the name was a public relations stunt aimed at giving the false impression of a series of tests. The launch was filmed and publicized, without any precise information about the missile itself, and made waves above and beyond what might be expected for a two-stage rocket of such modest dimensions (it was only 3.76 meters in length). The first stage of Shavit II was based on the Luz missile, and its subsequent development was transferred to IAI and also served as an important phase in the development of the Gabriel sea skimming anti-ship missile.

Israel Military Industries learned how to build large rocket engines at a factory run by Michael Schor, a charismatic engineer who later served as the director-general of IMI and chaired its first board of directors.

The development of satellite launchers was as challenging and dramatic as the development of the satellites themselves. For a number of years the program within the defense ministry was headed by Dr. Anselm Yaron, a talented engineer who was educated in Europe and was a quick and seasoned politician. Launcher development suffered from budgetary shortages, which prevented us from achieving the necessary momentum. At one point Yaron began to lose hope, and told me privately that he wanted to take a one-year sabbatical in the US and, for all intents and purposes, to resign his position. I told him that there was a chance we would acquire the budget, and that it would be a shame for him to miss a once in a lifetime opportunity. Nonetheless, Dr. Yaron thought it over and informed me that he was sticking to his decision to leave the project. One day, as if out of nowhere, a round chubby man with an almost completely bald egg-shaped head and round frameless glasses rolled into my office. His name was Uzi Rubin, and at that point I had no way of knowing that he had entered my life for good. However, the special relationship that developed throughout our subsequent years of work together endures till this day.

Uzi Rubin was an IAI aeronautical engineer who was trained at the Technion by Professor Moshe Arens. At the time of our first meeting, Rubin belonged to the recently established marketing unit of IAI. There was good chemistry between us from the moment we met. It was clear I could work with this straightforward, talented man. Our introductory meeting did not provide me with an opportunity to observe Rubin's diplomatic skills in action, and it was only later that I realized the full extent of his ability to lead large technical teams. I was glad that I chose him to lead the program.

The issue of salary, however, still remained an obstacle, as the IAI pays its workers salaries with which the state cannot compete. I promised Uzi that I would do everything in my power to have him authorized under an "A+ Research" rank, the highest rank in the government system.

In the mid-1970s the IDF instituted a research rank similar to that used by state research institutions, and decided to award it to officers of the rank of captain and higher. The IDF contacted me while I was still directing the Atomic Energy Commission and asked me to assume the chairmanship of the Research Rank Committee. I came to the meeting with branch chief Major General Moshe Nativ with a proposal to change the nature and constitution of the committee altogether. The committee, I argued, must consist of professionals from all relevant fields. It was clear that representatives of the corps and services of the IDF could not also serve as judges, and my proposal was to have representatives attend only the meetings that dealt with their candidates in order to present their recommendations to the committee and take part in discussion.

Major General Nativ adopted my proposal in full. The committee now proceeded to recruit civilians and former military personnel in a manner that ensured it could competently discuss any realm of technological development raised before it. Research rank within the IDF developed and expanded into an efficient, prestigious mechanism for encouraging officers engaged in research and development to remain in the army for the long term. The committee was independent in its considerations and decisions, and its recommendations went directly to the chief of the Adjutant General Branch for approval. During my 15 years as chairman of the committee I cannot recall even one instance in which the branch chief rejected one of our recommendations. The IDF commanders and human resource officers found it somewhat difficult to accept the existence of an independent, influential, and prestigious promotion framework. The importance of encouraging young promising officers to remain within the research and development frameworks of the military services was extremely compelling. When I returned to the defense ministry to assume direction of MAFAT, the chief of the Adjutant General Branch thought it was only natural that I continue chairing the Research Rank Committee, and I agreed to do so. The position of chair of the Research Rank Committee was held by the director of MAFAT, and this practice remains in place today.

In Rubin's case, it was a Research Rank Committee of the Civil Service Commission that provided him with the necessary rank, clearing the last remaining obstacle and enabling him to accept the position. He started working with a contagious vigor and optimism that quickly spread to other members of the project staff. Three industries worked together on developing the satellite launchers: Israel Aerospace Industries, Israel Military Industries, and Rafael. The project administrators were responsible for keeping each industry in its place, a difficult task because each partner was extremely capable, experienced, and well established, and had its own goals and ability to maneuver within the defense establishment.

Dov Raviv, a talented aeronautical engineer who knew how to work on all stages of missile system planning, was the dominant figure within IAI. He was involved in everything, and people followed him without hesitation. With thinning hair which he combed back European style and dancing eyes that took in everything around him, Raviv was slim and energetic with a persuasiveness that radiated in all directions. He was endowed with a mesmerizing sense of confidence, which at times seemed overblown but which ultimately proved to be justified, as well as full command of the technical details of the many project proposals he submitted for authorization. Raviv was born in Romania and immigrated to Israel when he was young. He picked up French during his advanced training in missile technology with the French defense industries. When it became clear that Raviv attracted projects and work orders, IAI gave him considerable freedom of operation. A special, separate missile development factory called Malam was established when the personnel working on missiles split off from IAI's Engineering Division. Only a few years after the beginning of the satellite launcher program, Dov Raviv had already convinced us and the Americans that he was capable of developing the anti-missile missile known as Arrow, an accomplishment that earned him the nickname "Mr. Arrow".

With every new success Raviv's self-confidence grew, as did his independence from the IAI administration. Uzi Rubin and I had great respect for his abilities, but we also knew that we needed to supervise his whims. Raviv's colleagues at IAI were jealous of his string of achievements and felt inferior due to the high level of his work and his administrative independence; they waited patiently for an opportunity to bring him down. Dov Raviv did indeed eventually meet his downfall, which turned out to be unbearably painful. After a series of successful satellite launches and progress in the development of a missile defense system based on the Arrow missile he had envisioned, he was diagnosed with a brain tumor. The doctors recommended surgery as soon as possible, and Raviv took time off to have the operation in the US. Later, he told me that he had been worried about what lay in store for him and that he had not been certain that he would live through the procedure. This new sense of fatality and concern that his family might find itself without a strong financial foundation compelled Raviv to use the months of waiting before his operation to provide consulting services for a Canadian company with ties to Israel Aerospace Industries. The doctors successfully removed the benign but extremely large tumor, and, aside from a facial spasm caused by a nerve that was damaged during the procedure, Raviv was soon on the road to full recovery. However, when he returned to Israel the authorities began an investigation of the consulting services he had provided to the Canadian company and the police started working on an indictment against him for accepting a bribe. Dov Raviv was still in the process of recovering when the roof caved in. More than his medical condition, he was most disappointed and deeply saddened by the reaction of IAI. It was suddenly as if he was a total stranger with everybody keeping their distance. Without warning IAI management, in coordination with the defense ministry, suspended Raviv from all projects. In 1993, after fighting the indictment for two years, he was convicted of accepting a $175,000 bribe from a Canadian company based on the consulting contract he had signed with them. The prosecution argued that, in return for payment, Raviv recommended that the Canadian company be awarded a contract to supply heavy vehicles for the IAI. "The consultation was merely a cover," concluded District Judge Amnon Strashnov, who sentenced Raviv to a fine and two years imprisonment. Raviv's appeal to the Supreme Court was denied, and his prison sentence was not commuted. When all hope was lost, Raviv's attorneys requested a pardon from the president of the state. They also made an appeal to senior officials within the defense ministry who had worked with Raviv in the past. I did not hesitate to write a letter to the president recommending that Raviv be pardoned. I sent the letter to President Ezer Weizman, feeling that an historic injustice had been committed but President Weizman was unable to pardon Raviv, who subsequently began serving his two-year sentence. I visited him twice during his fifteen months in prison, after which he was released due to the standard deduction of a third of his sentence.

Israel Military Industries (IMI), which began operating prior to 1948 while the Jewish state was still in the process of being established, boasted major accomplishments during Israel's War of Independence. In addition to its production of bullets, hand-grenades, mortar shells, and artillery and tank ammunition, it also developed the capability to produce explosives and propellants. From there to the development of rocket engines the path was short. Michael Schor had been responsible for establishing the Givon Division for the development and production of rocket engines of all types and sizes. Schor, a chemical engineer by training and a yekke (the common name for German Jews known for their punctilious nature) who remained in the village in which he was raised his entire life, was a natural leader. He was a good looking fellow who looked like one's notion of an American senator, with a gray lock of hair swept attractively across his forehead. His vulture-like nose and massive jaw endowed him with a stern countenance. Behind this stern exterior was a sensitive and at times apprehensive man who tried not to show his true emotions lest they be understood as signs of weakness.

The Givon factory was assigned to develop large engines for the satellite launchers, since it was clear the production staff possessed the necessary knowledge and physical infrastructure to do so. Although production of the solid propulsion material only required heating in large vats, it was still necessary to pay careful attention to the safety guidelines. Post-production molding of the material also proved to be an art requiring experience and expertise. The Givon factory acquired the necessary experience through years of developing and producing small engines, and gradually came to be able to produce increasingly larger engines. The ultimate test involved operating a full-size engine, which required the construction of an isolated testing facility far from inhabited areas for safety reasons. One stage of a rocket launcher engine contained a few tons of propellants, and the detonation of this material during testing posed a potential danger.

Uzi Rubin and the program administration coordinated between the overall planning of the satellite launchers, carried out by Dov Raviv and his staff, and the engine developers at IMI. We knew the IMI Givon factory possessed solid knowledge and human resources that would help meet it the challenges. However, Givon personnel also needed to be supervised and to recognize the fact that project management personnel understood the ins and outs of the project. Rubin and his small staff succeeded in getting the job done effectively with project management working with great determination and strict adherence to the timetable, while consistently demonstrating sensitivity to the different problems that arose.

Rafael's role in the project was not as large as it had hoped it would be, with a role limited to developing the third stage of the satellite launch. This, however, was an exceptionally challenging technological and engineering undertaking in itself. Weight was a critical issue because the third stage, which pushed the satellite into orbit, couldn't be too heavy. This presented a challenge to developing the ball shape shell containing the fuel for the third stage. The shell had to be strong, durable at high temperatures and corrosion resistant, which meant it had to be made from titanium.

The technological challenge of building a ball out of paper-thin sheets of titanium, and ensuring that this body would be strong enough to withstand the shock of separation during the three stages of the launch, was a gauntlet that Rafael was eager to pick up. The facts speak for themselves, and Rafael's titanium balls did not fail even once.

We decided to organize development of the entire satellite program within two parallel and coordinated projects: one for launchers and one for satellites. The participating defense industries were selected according to their capabilities and to our assessment of their ability to learn and begin working in areas of technology that were sometimes completely new. For some of the satellite launchers, IAI's Malam facility was chosen as the primary contractor; while IMI, Rafael, and a number of smaller companies took part in the project as sub-contractors. Rubin's project administration played an important role in ensuring coordinated, harmonious work among the different companies involved, which is something that can never be taken for granted anywhere, especially not in Israel. The primary contractor for satellite development was the IAI Mabat factory, where a space center was established in 1986. The sub-contractors for satellite development included the electro-optical company El-Op, which developed the telescope, Rafael, which developed small engines for satellite movement once it was in orbit, and a large number of other companies in Israel and abroad. Brigadier General Haim Eshed directed the satellite project administration from the outset, along with a handful of talented and dedicated colleagues. Both the project administration and the defense industries had to learn space technologies as the program advanced. It was an extremely unusual situation, as most projects are carried out by industries and administrations with basic prior knowledge that enables them to function as a source of technical authority and to provide effective leadership.

In this instance, imagination, creativity, daring, and in some cases audacity was necessary to counterbalance the gaps in our knowledge and the technological inferiority from which we suffered during the early years of development.

One can still question whether it was right to maintain two separate project administrations but in retrospect I think there was good reason to establish separate administrative structures to focus on the unique technologies and organizational and administrative demands of each subject area. The people involved were also an important consideration: Uzi Rubin was a whiz in the area of launchers, and Haim Eshed began to emerge as an authority in the world of satellites. Inter-administration coordination was handled by the office of the director of MAFAT, and this arrangement worked well.

From the early days of both project administrations it became clear that directing a complex, multi-partner, budget-heavy administration required skills that transcended technical and management knowhow. There was much opposition from within the IDF, whose leadership feared the project would take too much from the overall defense budget to the detriment of IDF operations. Another struggle was underway with the Budgets Branch of the defense ministry, and it was always necessary to convince the economic advisor to the defense minister and to make sure that he understood the issue and would support it. It was also necessary to stand by the defense minister and the director-general as they continued to support the program. Project directors cannot survive without deep familiarity with the Darwinian ethos of the Israeli defense establishment and without the capacity to convince senior defense ministry officials of the logic behind the plans. Directing a large program of research, development, and armament of a large weapon system requires knowing how to play chess on a number of different boards simultaneously. The problem is that unlike chess, each game board within the defense establishment has different rules, as does each player. The IDF service that will ultimately receive a system must be handled differently from the decision makers at the General Staff, the CGS, and the deputy CGS. There are even multiple game boards within the defense ministry, the finance ministry, the Knesset foreign affairs and defense committee, and even the State Comptroller's Office. Then there are the defense industries, among which the project director must find paths of compromise to ensure harmonious work between the primary contractors and subcontractors. Working with the defense industries involves keeping control of budgets and milestones, some of which have to be updated from time to time. Through all of this, the administration staff must work with enthusiasm and high spirits in a professional and well coordinated manner despite the obstacles of an ambitious development program. I frequently took part in this simultaneous chess match with either Uzi Rubin or Haim Eshed at my side. Sometimes, however, the two 'growing boys' had to handle things on their own, and as the years passed I watched as they grew into their positions, acquiring the skills and confidence that were so essential to getting the job done.

A typical example of the modus operandi was the way the project administration handed the case of the flexible nozzle. In the process of developing the satellite launcher Michael Schor of IMI stuck to the simplest planning possible and refused to get carried away with technological innovation. In contrast, Uzi Rubin thought that we were ready to integrate an advanced mechanism into the gas vent of the missile engine that would enable us to direct the missile toward the correct trajectory. Instead of four small devices emitting gas streams directing the missile, he envisioned one flexible nozzle, which would also respond to commands issued by the missile's own computer system. Rubin tried to assign the undertaking to Dov Raviv who wouldn't hear of it. Eventually, Rubin asked for my authorization to bypass Raviv and to develop the nozzle in IAI's engineering division as a separate engineering feasibility project. Like most efforts challenged by the laws of physics, our work took us three steps forward and two backward. Ultimately, we possessed the technology, but development of the satellite launchers had already reached the stage where it would be wrong to introduce such substantive changes. The nozzle was eventually used in a later program led by none other than Raviv himself — the Arrow missile-defense program. We were all pleased to possess the flexible nozzle technology for the innovative missile. Due to the high speeds at which an intercepting missile such as the Arrow must travel and the sharp turns it must make in order to strike an enemy missile, the missile defense system would not have had a chance had we not already developed the flexible nozzle.

Overseeing the administrative structures of both satellite projects and, somewhat later, the establishment of a missile defense program administration, meant entering a world that was very different from the world of pure research and development. In my past positions within the Weapons Development Department of the Operations Branch and the R&D Unit, my responsibilities had been limited to full-scale engineering development. Once this stage was complete and production began, responsibility moved to the defense ministry's Production and Purchasing Administration. When the Merkava tank development project first got underway, a Tank Development Program Administration, located outside the R&D Unit and the Production and Purchasing Administration and initially directed by Israel Tal, was established within the defense ministry. In the case of the development and armament of navy missile boats, a different solution was found — the establishment of a sea vessel administration as a separate body within the Production and Purchasing Administration, which officials were wise enough to place it under the direction of a senior Navy technical officer. The Lavi program was also run by a project-focused administrative structure led by air force officers such as Amos Lapidot, Dan Halutz, and Menachem Eini — all of whom were trained as pilots or navigators, had academic education in the fields of engineering or the exact sciences, and had experience in directing research and development projects within the corps.

Even after Prime Minister Begin approved the space program,

the development of both the satellite launchers and the satellites themselves encountered additional bumps in the road. In 1983, we received significant support from the Ministry of Science and Technology. Minister Yuval Neeman, who had been closely following progress in the field of satellite development in Israel, decided that the time had come to establish a national space agency for making use of space. Indeed, in January 1983, under Neeman's leadership, the Ministerial Committee for Research and Development decided on the establishment of the Israeli Space Agency (ISA). Neeman and I had many conversations about space when, as Director of the Atomic Energy Commission, I would visit his office for weekly meetings to update him on Israel's nuclear activities. We discussed the role of Israeli academia and its contribution to the creation of Israel's space-related knowledge and the development of Israel's technological capabilities. It was clear that the Israeli defense industries were relatively ignorant when it came to space, but that this lack of knowledge could be filled by means of focused academic research in selected areas. It was also clear that the more progress we made in academic research, the easier it would be for us to build bridges with space-related research and development efforts underway in other advanced countries around the world. I recommended that Neeman designate a significant budget within the Science Ministry to support space related work within Israeli academic and research institutions. Although the budget itself was certainly important, I maintained that commitment to the continued funding of such activities in the years to come was even more important. The Science Ministry, which from its early days did not enjoy large budgets, was a difficult ministry to run. However, thanks to Neeman's persistence and the talents of his director general, Tanchum Grizim, the ministry established and institutionalized its commitment to providing research budgets for space related work. This commitment remains in place today.

One of the most difficult obstacles had to do with the lifting capacity of the satellite launchers we were developing. The overall budget could not accommodate the budget intensive development process proposed by IAI. Nonetheless, we had to prove ourselves and to the IDF that satellite capabilities were not a dream. This could only be proven by a successful, full-scale launch. Toward the end of 1984, Dov Raviv was forced to acknowledge that launcher development, which had been led by the IAI, had stalled and he announced that the launcher would not reach the planned energy capacity by the date planned for the launch of the first satellite with satellite photography capabilities.

One of the first decisions I faced had to do with a realistic assessment of both launcher capability and the weight of the photography satellite. Efforts to minimize the weight of the satellite included eliminating a small camera that was supposed to scan a large area during the flight of the satellite and aiming the main camera in directions that promised more efficient photography. However, in light of Dov Raviv's statement, not even this reduction was enough to enable a launch on the planned date. At a meeting attended by many members of the two project administrations within the defense ministry and leaders of the satellite project from the IAI, I concluded that the weight of the first two satellites would have to be reduced. These two satellites, which we named Oz, weighed 160 kilograms instead of 250 kilograms and were planned for launch in 1987 and 1988. The launch of the operational satellite with photography capabilities was pushed back to 1993; the delay was meant to enable us to overcome the majority of the many development problems we faced. IMI had to reduce the weight of the satellite launcher without diminishing the quantity of propulsion material, and Rafael had to successfully complete development of the third stage engine of the satellite launcher. El-Op was supposed to complete work on the large telescope, which remained the sole device by which photographs were to be taken. And above all else, Malam, under Dov Raviv's direction, was supposed to provide an overall assessment and recommendation regarding the chances of a successful launch of a photography satellite weighing 250 kilograms.

Nineteen eighty-six was a year of major cutbacks for Israel's defense budget. Prime Minister Shimon Peres and Finance Minister Yitzhak Moda'i started a radical program to eradicate the triple-digit inflation that had been plaguing the Israeli economy since Yoram Aridor's tenure as finance minister under Prime Minister Menachem Begin. Defense Minister Rabin accepted the challenge and decided to reduce the defense budget by hundreds of millions of dollars. Ariel Sharon was the only other defense minister to give up such a large portion of the defense budget, and none have done so since. CGS Moshe Levi understandably believed that the IDF was facing an unprecedented budget crisis, and decided to publically voice his opposition to the satellite program. In doing so, he sent a signal to the defense ministry, which continued to support the program, that the army had different priorities. However, despite the explicit opposition of the CGS, the Intelligence Branch continued to pursue satellite photos. A foreign company was selling satellite photos at a resolution of 10 meters to anyone in need. Although this was far from military resolution, which at that time was defined as a resolution of less than one meter, it was the best that could be acquired. As a result the satellite communications station at the Mabat factory received its first operational assignment from the Intelligence Branch, and proved that it was possible to receive satellite photos and to process them for intelligence use.

On September 9, 1988, one year later than planned, the Oz I satellite was launched and entered orbit as planned. The body of the satellite was covered with solar panels that provided the energy required to operate the satellite system and to broadcast technical data to earth.

Israel had three centers for supervising satellite launches: the launch safety control center operated by air force at testing area headquarters, the IAI control center for satellite launchers in an IAI building in the test area, and a space activity control center in the IAI Mabat factory.

The space center was planned to manage all space-related activity, from tracking the satellite after it entered orbit to issuing commands to the satellite while it was in space and receiving data from the satellite in future launches. The air force center was closed to guests and visitors, and only a few select senior civilians were permitted to enter during launches. The control center operated by the program administrations at the testing area was the place to see all the drama of the launch as it happened. Permission to view launches from this location was in high demand. There was intense competition to get into the closely guarded lists of people who could get into the inner sanctum of the launch process. As a rule, the list of those who were disappointed by the selection process was exponentially longer than the list of the few lucky ones. During the many different types of launches I attended I noticed the immeasurable tension of the launch teams. For this reason, I was convinced that we must not burden them with the presence of high-level guests and convinced Defense Minister Rabin not to come to the facility to watch the launch.

Launch countdowns often stop in mid process, and over the years many tests were delayed due to weather conditions and other problems. However, as the date of the launch approached, Science Minister Gideon Pat asked to attend the launch at the testing area itself even though I insisted on maintaining our principles and not allowing VIP's inside the testing area during the launch. The evening before the launch, I visited Rabin at his home for a final briefing. Leah welcomed me and served me coffee as Rabin smoked his umpteenth cigarette of the day. Toward the end of the briefing, Rabin told me that Gideon Pat wanted to observe the launch from the test facility, and that he would not leave him alone about it. My response was that I did not think it was a good idea, but that the Science Minister could be present at the IAI space center and follow the launch from there. "Speak to Gideon," Rabin said, counting on my persuasiveness. Science Minister Pat was present at the space center during the launch, and enjoyed every moment. After the launch, I was gratified when he called me to convey his appreciation.

The launch's complete success was a shot of encouragement for us all and prompted us to give the satellite an optimistic name: Ofek (horizon). Since then, this has been the name used for all the satellites we have launched. Even though we knew that the launch of the operational photography satellite was only planned for 1993, we established a small administrative body that we referred to as a "program bureau" to lead the development of the radar for the future satellite, which would operate on the principle of synthetic aperture radar (SAR). This was a daring and perhaps slightly overconfident decision, but in hindsight absolutely right. In April 1990, a year and a half after the launch of the first satellite, Oz II (publicized as "Ofek") was launched successfully, ensuring our confidence in the launching system and our ability to put a satellite into orbit. We also grew more confident in our ability to communicate with our satellites. It was a time of intensive development and high morale for everybody.

The First Gulf War left its mark on Israeli work on satellite development. For the first time in history Israel was threatened by an enemy country hundreds of kilometers away when it came under attack from ballistic missiles launched from Iraq. All in all, Israel was hit by 39 missiles carrying conventional high-explosive warheads, but there was also concern that Iraq might launch missiles carrying the chemical warheads that Saddam Hussein had at his disposal. For the first time ever, Israel found itself dependent on another country in its efforts to locate the site in Iraq from which the al-Hussein missiles (Soviet Scud missiles that were modified and improved by Iraq) were launched into Israeli territory. Only the US with its global satellite array could give us the early warning we needed to tell Israeli citizens to enter on time into their bomb shelters or prepared sealed rooms to provide protection from the threat of chemical warfare. Unsurprisingly, after the war Defense Minister Moshe Arens instructed MAFAT to prepare an updated operational plan for reconnaissance satellites. This order, which superseded CGS

Moshe Levi's previous decision that denied the need for photography satellites, was meant to start a process of redefining needs based on the fresh lessons of the first Gulf War. Arens was not willing to wait. In October 1991, after realizing that the IDF was taking its time, he authorized a multi-year space program. CGS Ehud Barak, who was serving as deputy CGS during the missile attack launched from Iraq, reapproved the operational need for the satellite with its definitions of necessary operational capabilities. However, he was still unwilling to support full-scale engineering development and acquisition of the system after successful development.

I took part in a small meeting that included the commander of the air force and the Intelligence Branch chief in the office of the CGS. The meeting reflected the discrepancy between both services' recognition of the need for an Israeli satellite and their concern, which to me always seemed somewhat short-sighted and unwise, that the program would be a heavy burden on their budgets. Barak's General Staff remained on the fence, waiting for the defense ministry to pull the chestnuts out of the fire. This waiting reflected the IDF's desire to steer clear of blame in the case of failure, but to remain in a position from which it could jump on the bandwagon in the case of success.

These were difficult years for the space program. In addition to the opposition from the IDF there were also difficulties with development of the launcher and important components of the photography satellite. The most significant crisis was the failed launch of the first operational satellite caused by a problem with the launcher which we could not completely diagnose. When we had come to update the defense minister after our initial successful launches, his office was full, overflowing with defense industry directors and project directors. Now, when the time came to explain the failure, Uzi Rubin and myself found ourselves completely alone. Rabin did not hesitate to back us up, and even asked us to attend a meeting of the security cabinet to update them on the status of the program. Professor Jortner's Advisory Committee on Defense Research and Development also offered its opinion and supported Rabin's decision to continue the program. All this was very well, but we still didn't know why the launcher had failed; as a result, we had lost our only operational satellite. This really complicated matters because we had been unable to allocate the funds needed to build alternate operational satellites, which should have been done due to the high-risk nature of the program. During the dark hours that followed the failed launch we needed faith, optimism, and, above all else, a good sense of humor.

An independent committee of experts, consisting of the country's top missile experts who had not been working on the project, was appointed to assess the failure and recommend ways of fixing the problem. The committee found five failed mechanisms, each of which could have caused the problem. With no way of knowing which one was responsible, Rubin recommended overhauling all of them. So we started work on developing and adapting an alternate launcher. There was also a satellite problem. The only satellite we had was the experimental model, a full-scale satellite meant only for lab experiments. This model, called the QM, was similar to the operational satellite we had lost but was not meant to be launched. This intensified our dilemma. On the one hand, we needed to address all the questions about the launcher's reliability and ensure that it wouldn't fail after implementing extensive improvements. A cautious faction called for launching the improved system with a dummy 250 kilogram payload, the same weight as the operational satellite. However, this meant delaying the photography satellite. In the atmosphere prevailing in the IDF at the time this could really hurt the program or kill it altogether. A second faction said we should adapt the QM satellite and make it operational. This more daring faction maintained that the least this would give us was a dummy satellite weighing 250 kilograms, and could even provide us with an operational satellite, even if only for a few weeks. During a long complicated discussion we gained a solid understanding of all the data and the different aspects of the various options. It was extremely tempting to play it safe and prove that we had solved the launcher problem. We knew that the new launcher would be built from unused engines and parts left over from the development program and it took a great deal of conviction to persuade ourselves that we could pull it off successfully. The very idea of launching a test satellite also raised serious questions. After all, the satellite in question had been built based on the premise that it would not be launched. We subjected the test satellite to a long, arduous series of tests, which we had not dared to carry out on the operational satellite out of fear that use of the satellite systems during testing would exhaust the satellite's long-term ability to operate.

The analytical considerations and our gut instincts led me to adopt the more daring approach, and I had no difficulty convincing the defense minister and the director-general of the logic behind the decision. With this, we embarked upon a bold, high-risk emergency plan aimed at launching a satellite into space at the beginning of 1995.

The next problem we faced had to do with the radar systems of the testing facility, which were supposed to ensure that the launched missile would not deviate from its planned route. The testing area was operated by the air force, which had a number of tracking devices that offered significantly greater ability to identify any deviation from the planned trajectory and to transmit a self-destruct command in the event that the missile strayed outside the safety zone and endangered the civilian population. In addition to careful testing of all missile systems, the launcher, and the satellite, countdown protocols in launches around the world also include testing of the safety system. Optical tracking devices that work properly only in certain weather conditions play an important role in launch safety systems, which is why weather and visibility are such a sensitive issue during space launches. The testing area's large, heavy radar devices are another essential component of launch safety oversight, and the testing facility requires that at least two be in operation during a launch.

One month before the launch, when the launcher and the satellite itself were already at the testing area and we began the exhausting sequence of pre-launch tests, Uzi Rubin was told that one of the radar systems had a malfunction that could not be repaired. We immediately began performing tests and system checks in an attempt to fix the problem, but after a few days we received another discouraging report: the second radar was also malfunctioning. We had no idea what to do. The scheduled launch was one month away, and if we could not produce two functioning radar devices by then, there would be no launch. We started an emergency project that involved the use of parts that had been classified as unusable and were on the shelf in the warehouse of Elta, the company that build and operated the radars. The necessary parts were sent to the factory in Netanya and we told them to start working even though they had not yet received a contract. Within three weeks, as a result of this mad dash against time and against all odds, we had two functioning radar devices, which were carefully moved to the testing area to be incorporated into the safety system.

It was also necessary to address the standing policy of not staging launches on days when American and Russian satellites were in our area. In these circumstances, we received special authorization from Prime Minister Rabin to disregard the presence of all satellites over the region and to continue making preparations for the launch.

The day of the launch finally arrived after days of rain and heavy clouds; the clear weather made us all smile. The air force had prepared the area with all the required safety tracking equipment, and Chief Safety Officer Colonel Giora was called up for reserve duty to take part in the mission. Giora was an excellent pilot and a first-rate technician with extensive launch experience at the testing area. He also possessed an additional essential quality: steely nerves.

The satellite launcher I had visited one day earlier was now crowned with a satellite and rested on the cradle of the launching pad, ready to stand upright and commence its journey. The few fortunate visitors allowed to enter the IAI control facility were seated on the other side of a glass window to ensure they did not disrupt the engineers and technicians who were all hard at work at their respective computer screens, each with his own respective area of responsibility. Before I went in to take my seat behind the glass window, I visited the air force oversight facility in the testing area to wish Giora and his people a successful launch. Only 10 minutes remained, and the countdown continued. The room was completely silent, and the tension inside was almost unbearable. All that could be heard was the humming of computers and a voice over the intercom periodically delivering information about the countdown. "Five minutes and counting," it said, and a groan of relief could be heard as the tension continued to build. "Three minutes and counting," it said, as the moment of truth quickly approached. We then reached the automatic countdown of the last ten seconds, during which there is almost no way to stop the process. At that point, the missile was already upright, the support beam had returned to the launch pad, the countdown was being executed by the missile itself, and only the chief test director of Israel Aerospace Industries, who had his finger on the red emergency button, was authorized to stop the launch. Suddenly, voices could be heard over the air force control room intercom: "Stop! Stop!" they said. Our hearts sunk, and we tried to figure out what was happening. It was not, however, a distress call that needed to be obeyed, and the test director looked straight ahead as the final two seconds counted down. Then other voices could be heard shouting: "The missile is off!" Indeed, the screens now displayed an image of the beautiful missile, proudly bearing a white and blue Israeli flag, rising higher and higher into the sky, leaving behind a trail of thick smoke.

As the seconds passed in the air force control room, Giora displayed all his wisdom and level-headedness and did not press the self-destruct button, allowing the missile to continue its ascent. The missile separated from its first stage and continued climbing with the help of the second stage, until it was beyond the range in which it posed a threat to the Israeli population of the Mediterranean coastal plain. But tension was still in the air, and the telemetry transmitting information on the status of the missile and its flight continued to rivet us all. In the control room there was silence, aside from the quiet, laconic updates of the technicians sitting across from their screens. We remained motionless on the other side of the glass, waiting for the separation of the third stage with its Rafael-made engine. Then, the words "proper separation" could be heard from within the control room. All that remained was the final stage, which was supposed to bring the third stage to the satellite's exact window in space. After a few more seconds that seemed like an eternity, two excited sentences could be heard clearly from the control room: "We have proper separation! The satellite is in orbit!" The tension was broken, and the room erupted into joyful cheers, warm hugs, and beaming faces. I rushed into the control room to shake the hands of the heroes who had so impressively given birth to the satellite. Then, I quickly updated director-general Ivry and told him that I was on my way to his office, and that I would be there as soon as possible.

During the launch preparations we placed tracking stations along the satellite's trajectory to make sure it was following the correct path for entry into orbit and to ensure that everything was going as planned. At this early stage it was also already possible to transmit a short command to modify the trajectory in the event of a dangerous deviation from the nominal desired trajectory. At the IAI space center at Mabat, everything was ready for the satellite's first appearance over Israel.

At the director-general's office, people were visibly tense and nervous. With the help of the defense ministry spokesperson we prepared an initial short statement about the launch as we waited for word from the space center that the satellite was in orbit over Israel. I had an open line of communication with Haim Eshed, who was already at Mabat, and I heard him mumble something I could not make out. "Haim," I shouted, caught up in all the excitement, "What's going on? Is it up?" Haim told me that the satellite had appeared and that everything seemed to be in order. The news spread like wildfire and our joy knew no bounds. Still, we had to be patient and wait for the satellite to finish opening the wings of its solar panels and for the space center engineers to carry out the series of necessary tests before the satellite could begin taking photos. Twelve hours later, after Ofek had circled the earth more than eight times, we activated the satellite telescope, which had been developed and produced by Israel's electro-optical industry. Suddenly, Ben-Gurion airport, the cluster of buildings of Israel Aerospace Industries, and the group of military cargo planes parked on the runways flashed onto the screens of the space center. I was informed immediately: "There's a photo! The resolution is amazing! They're making a print of it!"

I went up to the defense minister's office. Rabin was in the middle of a large meeting, and I wrote him a short note: "Yitzhak — The satellite takes high quality photographs! I'll give you a copy of the first photo the moment it arrives." The secretaries quickly brought him the note, and I can only imagine how much it pleased him. As for me, I had to see the images on the screens of the space center control room with my own eyes. I drove straight there, and was mesmerized by the sharpness of the photos and the professionalism of the space personnel who were operating the satellite command system as if they had been doing it for many years. The prime minister, the defense minister, and President Ezer Weizman also arrived one after the other to see the miracle first hand, to take pride in the quality of the photos.

After a few days, Rabin's office sent me a moving letter of appreciation which I copied and gave out to all the directors of the program administrations and the satellite development teams. Together, they were responsible for this outstanding achievement, which positioned Israel in a respectable spot among the countries in the world that had made it to space. The letter read as follows:

19 Nisan 5755
April 19, 1995

Brigadier General Uzi Eilam

Dear Uzi,

The Ofek satellite is now in space and we are gathering its output. With every hour and every day that passes, we are increasingly amazed by this exceptional accomplishment. The reality has surpasses anything we could have imagined.

Ofek III is a song of praise not only to the technological capabilities of the country but also, and perhaps even more so, to the unique nature of its people. Only exceptional people are capable of producing such work. You are one such person, as are your colleagues.

The People of Israel are greatly indebted to you and your colleagues of all ranks. Your work is an extraordinary achievement, a human and technological wonder, and a phenomenal contribution to the security of the state.

Please accept my thanks and be so kind as to convey the gratitude of the entire country to the people behind Ofek.

YITZHAK RABIN

THE STORY OF THE ARROW PROGRAM — DISAGREEMENT AND DETERMINATION

The beginnings of Israel's missile defense program, which in its initial stages focused solely on the development of the Arrow intercepting missile, was closely linked to the US initiative to develop a ballistic missile defense system, known widely by the nickname "Star Wars". During my first days as director of MAFAT I learned that Lieutenant General James Abrahamson, director of the US defense department's Missile Defense Agency, was visiting Israel and was to be a guest of MAFAT. I was curious to meet Abrahamson, who was not only a three-star general, a pilot, an aeronautical engineer and a trained astronaut, but who had also successfully directed the F-16 project within the American air force. Israel's purchase of the F-16 brought our people into contact with this unique man, who had been invited to deliver a speech at an aeronautics conference in the country, and who had decided to take advantage of the opportunity to stay for a longer visit. The conference was organized by Israel Aerospace Industries, and David Ivry, then serving as director-general of IAI, proposed inviting Abrahamson.

I spent three days in the company of this slender, energetic, un-pretentious, soft spoken and extremely intelligent man. Abrahamson was a typical example of an exceptional kind of American military officer whose background combined broad academic education with operational and combat experience, service in senior command positions, and positions in management and administration. For four years Abrahamson had directed the international program to develop the F-16 fighter plane, which Israel was one of the first countries to purchase. In 1981, Abrahamson was appointed as deputy director of NASA's space shuttle program, and subsequently became its director.

The Strategic Defense Initiative (SDI) was launched by President Ronald Reagan in a speech delivered on March 23, 1983. Its aim at the time was to defend against Soviet ballistic missiles carrying nuclear warheads. The program was unique compared to others because its defensive array included bases not only on land but in space. The aim of the new Strategic Defense Initiative was ambitious and for many people in the United States and around the world sounded like pure science fiction.

The idea, first conceived by the researchers at Lawrence Livermore National Laboratory in Berkeley, California, called for producing x-ray length laser radiation by means of a nuclear explosion. It was Professor Teller who told President Reagan about the discovery at Lawrence Livermore. In addition to being an accomplished physicist and a Nobel Prize winner, Teller was also an actor from birth who possessed incomparable skills of oration and persuasion. Reagan's unbridled enthusiasm about the idea prompted him to make the following appeal to American scientists during his 1983 speech: "I call upon the scientific community in our country, those who gave us nuclear weapons, to turn their great talents now to the cause of mankind and world peace, to give us the means of rendering these nuclear weapons impotent and obsolete."

Lawrence Livermore Laboratories and the high-powered laser program piqued my curiosity. During one of my trips to the US as the director of MAFAT I visited their facilities for a presentation on their high-powered lasers. For the occasion, the classification restrictions on the research program were lifted according to instructions issued from the Missile Defense Agency in Washington. On the first day of the visit we met in the laser team's meeting room, and the laboratory director began with an introduction and overview of the research. An hour after the presentation began the door opened and a tall man walked in. He wore a brown overcoat that looked like a shepherd's cloak and carried a cane that was about as tall as he was. It was Professor Edward Teller, whom I'd met before and was delighted to see again. The room went silent as Teller, who for me immediately brought to mind images of Moses, calmly walked to the seat that had been reserved for him at the head of the table, right next to me. He knew about my visit and had insisted on accompanying me for the first half-day of the visit. The presentations continued, and I soon heard Teller snoring peacefully. I glanced to my left and was certain that the elderly man was fast asleep. However, the moment the speaker finished his presentation Teller opened his eyes, made two insightful comments, and asked a question that made it abundantly clear that he had heard every word. This ritual repeated itself over and over again throughout the presentations: Teller would fall asleep and snore, wake up at the end of each presentation, and, in a thundering voice with a heavy Hungarian accent, ask the terrified scientist an extremely intelligent question.

President Reagan had a warm place in his heart for Professor Teller. When Reagan launched the Strategic Defense Initiative, he was opposed by a large group of prominent American scientists for a variety of reasons. Nobel Prize-winning nuclear physicist Hans Bethe, who also played a role in the Manhattan Project, studied the idea of x-ray lasers created by a nuclear explosion and was not convinced that this was the right solution. Other scientists had political reasons for opposing the program, stemming from the fact that American achievement of full immunity to nuclear missiles would tip the global balance of power that was at the time based on the doctrine of Mutually Assured Destruction. Edward Teller provided scientific and political backing for Reagan's initiative, and the doors of the administration were open before him.

SDIO, the Strategic Defense Initiative Organization, was established in 1984, and General James Alan Abrahamson was its founder and first director. Israel followed the development of SDIO, and in 1986, after Abrahamson's visit to Israel, we began to look for ways to play a role in the initiative. The idea was not kept secret and resulted in a vigorous debate between supporters and opponents. Opponents argued that joining the Americans in such a purely strategic and clearly anti-Soviet project might cause the already anti-Israel Soviets to toughen their stance on Israel and halt all permits for Soviet Jews wishing to immigrate to Israel.

As the public debate in the Israeli media gained momentum, I was asked by the defense minister's office to appear on a television program to discuss the issue. I drove to the studio in Jerusalem, and found that it was to be a debate moderated by Menashe Raz and that Shlomo Avineri, former director-general of the Israeli Foreign Ministry and a world renowned professor of political science, would be making the case against Israeli participation in the program. I took a deep breath and focused on the technological aspect of cooperation and the benefit that such work would bring to the Israeli defense establishment and defense industries, and argued passionately that Israel was neither interested in nor capable of joining an American strategic plan for developing defense systems against Soviet nuclear missiles. We could, however, begin working in this new area of technology and develop, as a by-product, our own defense system against missiles used by the enemy countries surrounding us. As a result of Raz's graceful and intelligent moderation and Shlomo Avineri's cultured demeanor, the debate remained decisively civilized in tone. Without thinking twice, I answered the interviewer's somewhat provocative question regarding the funding that Israel expected to receive from the Americans for the project, and said that I expected it to total approximately one hundred million dollars per year. The next day, I was bombarded with questions from people who wanted to know where I had gotten such a surreal figure. My colleagues were also concerned that it would be detrimental to future support of our work. However, subsequent developments proved that my estimate was well based and over the years — after we began full-scale development, including a series of tests and production — the funds dedicated to the program actually exceeded one hundred million dollars per year. The US played a major role in funding the Israeli program from the outset, and continues to do so today.

It was clear that we would not be permitted to take part in the classified components of the program. The Americans refrained from involving foreign countries, even allies, in the sensitive area of nuclear missile defense. We therefore made efforts to begin working with SDIO on basic research in less sensitive areas, and to this end we issued calls for research proposals to relevant institutions throughout Israel. Abrahamson suggested that we try our luck with a number of general subjects, including realms of technology necessary for the remote sensing of ballistic missiles and the construction of missile classification systems that would be central to the destruction of enemy missiles. In response to our appeal, we received a significant number of research proposals which we passed on to SDIO but heard nothing back for months. Later, we were disappointed to learn that our proposals were sent on to the American research institutions, to advise SDIO of their value. The proposals had been of such great interest to them that they decided to carry them out on their own.

Abrahamson was aware of what had happened, but he was unable to fight his own people and all of American academia. However, he was still interested in the prospect of cooperation, and he actively sought ways to integrate Israel into the missile defense initiative without getting us involved in sensitive fields. The idea he would eventually propose was brilliant: "Why don't you develop a missile defense system that addresses the threats you face?" he suggested. "This will get you significantly involved and make it easier for us to convince the Pentagon that the work is legitimate. It will also make it easier for the administration and Congress to approve a defense system for you." Abrahamson did not adopt this approach by chance. It stemmed from the conclusion he and his colleagues reached after almost three years of work on the project that defense based solely on spacebases would be quite expensive and would require extensive development. In order to keep their feet planted firmly on the ground (both literally and figuratively), US officials resolved that the first phase of the defense program would rely on a land-based sensing system and a land-based missile interception system. Abrahamson had good reason for contending that the development and production of a system addressing the threats facing Israel would contribute to the overall concept and the engineering of solutions. In this integrated, riveting context, Israel began working on what ultimately evolved into the Arrow intercepting missile and the Homa (the Hebrew acronym for hetz v'ma'arekhet hatra'a, or "Arrow and Warning System") missile defense system, the world's first ballistic missile defense system to go operational.

Abrahamson and his colleagues asked us to help them by reviewing and categorizing the proposals for an intercepting missile that would address the long-range missile threats against Israel. The task was presented before Israel's defense industries, and three industries accepted the challenge: IAI, Rafael, and IMI-General Engineering. We decided to administer the contractor selection process as a tender, in accordance with general practice on development issues within the defense establishment.

The Developer Selection Committee was an established institution within MAFAT. In addition to professional personnel from MAFAT, it consisted of representatives of the IDF and defense ministry officials specializing in the fields of economics, finance, law and security. To begin the process we convened a full committee meeting in June 1988 attended all the by senior representatives.

The first candidate, IMI–General Engineering, was a unique unit within Israel Military Industries that engaged not in development and production, like the other units within IMI, but in systems analysis and planning. General Engineering's presentation included an overview of its conception of an anti-missile defense system, and nothing else.

The Rafael representatives decided to present their idea which they called the AB-10. While they were in the process of making their presentation, which consisted of a collection of sketched and handwritten slides, Dov Raviv and his associates from IAI waited patiently to state their piece. I had no doubt that Rafael's missile experts were experienced and that it would take an immense amount of work for IAI personnel to acquire the missile knowledge and scientific expertise that the Rafael teams already possessed based on previous projects and years of operating as a national R&D laboratory. At the same time, however, Rafael had developed a technological arrogance, a sense that "we know better". Later, when Rafael began its work in defense exports, this haughtiness remained a prominent characteristic of the company and impeded its ability to succeed.

Rafael's missile experts based their presentation of the AB-10, a quick-responding missile it had developed for the Israeli navy, as a significant step-up from the Gabriel missile defense system. The presentation itself appeared to have been prepared hastily and without much effort, and the system Rafael proposed was limited in its ability to intercept missiles to altitudes of below 20 kilometers, but the Rafael missile experts nevertheless argued with great conviction that this was sufficient.

Dov Raviv and his associates were the last to present their proposal before the committee. Their presentation did not consist of handwritten slides. Rather, they offered an eloquent and comprehensive presentation of a new high-powered intercepting missile with dreamlike maneuverability and an interception altitude of dozens of kilometers (the higher the interception altitude, the slimmer the chance of enemy missile penetration). Although the committee was convinced that IAI's proposal was the best, we chose not to expedite the process by choosing one successful competitor but rather to allow the missile defense experts in the US to review both proposals without concealing our preference. As a result, both Rafael and IAI sent groups to the Redstone Arsenal development base in the United States to make presentations. The Americans were also convinced by Dov Raviv's proposal, and the founding father of the Arrow missile began his work on this bold innovative ballistic missile interception system.

From the outset, this project clearly differed from all other projects we had worked on in the past. In theory, the work was done for the US

Strategic Defense Initiative Organization, which completely funded development costs for the initial years of the project. In practice, however, the customer was the state of Israel — not the IDF, and not even the air force. The reasons for this strange situation were internal struggles within the Israeli military. The IDF felt its sense of dignity was at stake because the project had not emerged from within the Israeli military but was imposed from the outside and from above. Another concern was that the project would start to eat into the overall IDF budget. The unavoidable outcome was that MAFAT served as a virtual consumer. While creating the program administration that had not yet been officially established, MAFAT now had to compose a statement of operational need and a description of the system that Israel Aerospace Industries was about to begin developing.

Under these circumstances we found it prudent to create another locus of thinking and systemic planning to serve as the planning conscience of the system under development and as the trustee of SDIO. This body would also be responsible for compiling regular reports on project progress for SDIO. The critical tender was won by Brigadier General (Res.) Micha Cohen, who had established a small but efficient consulting firm called Wales. Cohen was a former squadron commander in the Israeli air force and an experienced aeronautical engineer with a broad systemic view. Cohen came a long way after immigrating to Israel from Bulgaria as a boy, rising through the ranks of the air force's enormous maintenance system and emerging as one of its top officials. He was modest and soft-spoken, and his fluent Hebrew still betrayed traces of a Bulgarian accent. We knew we could rely on the work of Cohen's firm, and the Americans also quickly came to appreciate the reliability of the expert opinions issued by Wales. Micha Cohen joined SDIO, IAI, and MAFAT as the fourth locus of the program.

In the absence of a military customer Cohen's logic and wide-ranging analytical skills boosted our confidence in our ability to actualize Dov Raviv's vision, which at times seemed surreal, if not hallucinatory. Beginning with Yitzhak Rabin, and later with Moshe Arens as minister and David Ivry as director-general, the defense ministry provided firm support that counterbalanced the opposition from the IDF and allowed the program to move ahead. Nonetheless, questions still remained regarding the actual feasibility of using a high-speed missile to intercept a ballistic missile penetrating the atmosphere at a speed of Mach 6, especially since the weapon had to be exceptionally maneuverable at those speeds.

The two first launchings of the initial model of the Arrow missile were aimed at testing its flight capability and maneuverability, and the missile failed in both departments. Defense Minister Moshe Arens decided to observe the launching on site, and his attendance did little to improve the state of mind of the test directors and engineers seated in front of their tracking screens. The missile's failure was the result of planning. We considered how to go about analyzing the stream of data transmitted from the testing system telemetry, and we had no hesitations about swallowing our pride and asking the Americans to appoint a blue-ribbon team to assist us, which they typically did whenever in-depth technical investigations were required. A number of veteran missile developers from the US army examined our model and discovered that the small openings on its body were large enough to allow scorching heat (which envelops all bodies moving at 6-8 times the speed of sound) to penetrate the missile and to cause a malfunction in the steering mechanism. This realization proved particularly useful to our development teams, whose future plans were flawless in this respect.

When the Arrow missile development reached the stage of testing against an actual target, we used an Arrow I missile as a target. The Israeli navy also participated in the test using a boat from which a target missile would be fired directly upward. Much later we began developing a different target which we referred to as "Black Sparrow", which bore a closer resemblance to a quickly approaching ballistic missile that had already passed the zenith of its trajectory.

For this purpose Rafael proposed developing a missile based on the experience and expertise it acquired while developing air-to-surface cruise missiles. The target missile was supposed to be launched from a plane and then ascend to a higher altitude before turning downwards and simulating an almost perfect ballistic trajectory.

The more progress we made the clearer it became that the project needed to be run by a program administration within the defense ministry. Uzi Rubin was already running the satellite launcher program for which IAI (Malam), headed by Dov Raviv, was the primary contractor. Rubin was worried about management problems with the operation of two separate administrations — one for satellite launchers and one for the Arrow missile project — with Dov Raviv maneuvering between the two. Rubin had volunteered to direct the Arrow program in addition to the satellite launcher program, and I could see the benefits and savings in salaries that would result from effective coordination between the two programs. After a long series of meetings with Rubin, I was convinced that he could do both jobs simultaneously. We brought the proposal to director-general Ivry who did not like the idea but had no choice but approve it. We now needed to establish military and civilian norms for staffing the Arrow program. Despite our assurances that the entire budget would be provided from the US we still had a long road to travel within the IDF and the defense ministry. Rubin quickly learned the secrets of negotiating and persuading the authorities, and provided me with invaluable support as I constructed the program administration.

With the assistance of Wales and the unfailing logic of Micha Cohen we began to lay the groundwork for the central structure of the missile defense system. Cohen showed us that intercepting an enemy ballistic missile required more than simply developing the Arrow missile. It also required advanced warning that an enemy missile had been launched and was travelling toward us. The enemy missile needed to be physically located and tracked, and the Arrow missile needed to be guided to the optimum location for detonating the Arrow warhead and destroying the enemy missile. Our analysis and tests, and the fact that we would clearly not be defending ourselves against one single missile, meant that the system would consist of multiple launchers and a large number of missiles. This also meant that it would also need to incorporate a command and control system.

We had no idea how to detect the launch of enemy missiles from hundreds of kilometers away and tried to obtain the assistance of our friends at SDIO in persuading the American authorities to lift the ban on selling early warning systems, which were considered strategic in nature and highly classified. We tried to develop a system design based on American early warning radar, a less developed form of the strategic radars, and also on an Israeli-developed system that tracked missiles at closer range. Unfortunately, our pleas and the political pressure we exerted were unsuccessful. In the end we decided to continue developing a warning and tracking radar that had been started by Elta of Israel Aerospace Industries. By this time we had established a complete program administration with technical branches and a financial branch.

During the First Gulf War (1991), Iraq launched dozens of long-range al-Hussein missiles at Israel and Saudi Arabia, creating an unprecedented threat to both countries. There was no real solution for the threat of a warhead-bearing missile with a range of 600 kilometers. The Israeli air force began to arm itself with batteries of Patriot anti-aircraft missiles, and additional batteries were rushed over from Europe along with their American operating teams. The Patriot missiles were important in terms of morale, but on a practical level neither our Patriots nor the model used by the Americans was capable of intercepting al-Hussein missiles. Even the US and British air forces, which enjoyed complete control of Iraqi airspace, were unable to take out even a single missile-launching vehicle.

Throughout the war MAFAT maintained a constant presence in the Command Center, and this provided us with access to everything the military knew about where incoming Iraqi missiles had struck. One night, after the sounding of an air-raid siren indicating an incoming missile, my family and I entered the sealed room in our home like the rest of the Israeli population. Three minutes later we heard a thundering explosion, and the officers on duty at the General Staff called to tell me what I had already gathered...issile had landed in my neighborhood of Savyon. My daughter Noa was upset and frightened, and I suggested that we go see what had happened. Hand in hand, we walked through the empty streets of Savyon until we reached the site of impact. The home of our good friends Eli and Rivka sustained a direct hit and was almost completely destroyed. The only undamaged part of the house was the piano room, Then suddenly, from out of the smoky, dusty ruins, we heard music. It was Rivka, whose house had just been destroyed before her very eyes, playing the piano. "Why are you playing?" we asked her, "Why now, of all times?" "Is there anything better to do at a time like this?" she said. The real damage from the missiles was the economic loss that stemmed from the temporary destabilization of the Israeli economy, as well as the sense of anxiety experienced by many Israelis.

It quickly became clear that the Patriots, designed to intercept aircraft, could not intercept long-range missiles. Raytheon Company, which developed and produced the Patriot system, had a public relations department that did impressive work. During the war, it hosted President George H. W. Bush and received international recognition when the American president praised the success of the American Patriot defense system in intercepting the Iraqi missiles launched against Israel and Saudi Arabia. When we visited Raytheon many months after the First Gulf war, we were still walking on eggshells and were unable to tell the whole truth about the failure of the Patriots.

The unilateral missile attack provided us with pieces of al-Hussein missiles that broke apart when they entered the atmosphere and landed in Israel. Some of the missiles were almost whole and were collected and stored on a military base in central Israel for the country's top experts — Rafael, IAI, IMI, Micha Cohen's consulting firm, and MAFAT — to analyze. Of course, the information obtained was also shared with the Americans.

The First Gulf War served as a powerful motivating force for the personnel of the Homa administration (also known as the Israel Missile Defense Organization, or IMDO) and the Israeli defense industries working on the project. They worked around the clock, often paying no attention to the periodic sirens indicating that Iraqi missiles were about to strike Israel. This momentum was sustained after the war. Many more people, within the IDF as well, began to recognize the severity of the ballistic missile threat and the importance of developing a suitable response.

The Berlin wall had been torn down and the Warsaw Pact had crumbled along with the Soviet Union, and it was clear to the Americans that the Russians had thrown in the towel in the technological struggle for control of space. SDIO searched desperately for a foundation for its continued existence. By that time the Americans already knew about the failure of the Patriot system, and new ideas were emerging such as an upgraded model of the Patriot missile and the completely new THAAD missile (acronym for "Theatre," and subsequently "Terminal, High Altitude Area Defense.") A pulse of activity could again be felt in the veins of the Missile Defense Agency. We regarded this as a welcome development because of the exchange of ideas and the almost equal sense of partnership between the Homa Program and the American regional defense programs. The new THAAD missile was planned to be lighter and more compact, and for this reason the Americans thought it would operate on a hit to kill basis with no need for an explosive warhead. The radar that was supposed to track the enemy missile and guide the intercepting missile to a direct hit with extreme precision was also supposed to be light and compact. For the Americans it was important to be able to easily fly the defense system to any part of the world in which they or their allies were in need, so the system was designed to fit into a C-130 Hercules aircraft that could land on short airstrips and straight stretches of hard ground. We were interested in the challenges the Americans presented to their defense industry, but we also knew that we were not in a position to undertake such ambitious plans. So we retained the principle of a directional warhead that would detonate tens of meters from the enemy missile. We didn't have to develop a light, compact missile, and the new Arrow missile, an advanced version of the Arrow I, was also quite heavy and could not be rapidly distributed by plane into an operational array.

The radio frequency used by the warning and guidance radar was also selected based on considerations of time and budget. We decided to develop a radar system we referred to as Green Pine that operated at the L-band, an ability that had been developed by Elta during its work on the radar for the Lavi fighter plane. At that time the Lavi program had already been grounded, but like other high budget projects, it had left the defense industry with a legacy of many new skills including radar technologies. We deliberated over the type of radar required and decided to base development on L-band radar models that Elta had already developed and could immediately begin producing. We still had a long way to go before development of the full radar system but from the start Elta was able to assemble a few dozen models. They placed the experimental radar system on the roof of an Elta building and used to it to track everything that flew through the sky, from civilian and military aircraft to missiles launched from the air force testing area. Tadiran was selected to lead development of the command and control mechanism, the third component of the Homa system, as a primary contractor. Tadiran had significant experience in developing command and control communications systems for field forces, and it justifiably won the tender to head up development of the Homa control system.

The overall concept of the system had not yet been developed. Micha Cohen's people at Wales prepared many studies on the subject and we also had increasingly clear data about the feasibility of all three components of the system. Although the development process was at its height, it had still not generated an overall concept. As it turned out, the concept would not evolve naturally but was to be born under stress. It all began during a relatively routine trip to Washington for a meeting with SDIO officials at the Pentagon, during which we were scheduled to present the progress of the project. The situation was somewhat different during the trip in question, because this time we were attempting to convince our friends at SDIO to support our request for increased funding for system development and additional Arrow batteries. I was joined for the meetings in Washington by Uzi Rubin and a small team of Homa personnel, as well as Moshe Kochanovski, director of the defense ministry delegation in New York, and by Major General Giora Rom, our defense attaché in Washington. When Rubin and I arrived in Washington, Rom told us that he had managed to schedule us meetings with Defense Secretary William Perry at the Pentagon, with the Deputy Secretary of State at the State Department and with Martin Indyk of the National Security Council at the White House, who would later serve as the US ambassador to Israel.

We suddenly found ourselves in an unexpected situation without a fully developed and authorized operating conception for the full Homa system. It would be a folly to pass up an opportunity to present Israel's complete anti-missile defense system concept to the Americans and to significantly shorten the process of gaining support and acquiring budgets. But not only had we not finished developing the concept at home and won approval at the ministerial level and from the General Staff, we did not even have a presentation to show our plans. We had 24 hours before the first meeting in the office of the Secretary of Defense. Working with Homa administration Director Uzi Rubin and his people, and with the help of the military attaché's personnel at the embassy, we worked late into the night on slides that would effectively convey the information we knew we needed to present. By the time we arrived for our meeting at the Pentagon we were able to effectively present the deployment of missile and radar batteries in Israel, the defensive arcs that covered all parts of the country, and the estimated number of radar sites, missile launchers, missiles, and control systems required to adequately defend the entire territory of Israel.

Defense Attaché Rom and I had a private meeting with William Perry. I had met Perry when he was serving as undersecretary of defense for research and development in the US Defense Department in 1974 when I ran the Israeli R&D Unit and we were analyzing the technological lessons of the recent confrontation between Soviet and Western weaponry. When the three of us entered the meeting room where Rubin and his people were waiting with senior SDIO personnel, Perry was pleasantly surprised to see Rubin and shook his hand cordially. During the 1980s, before he returned to the Pentagon to fill a senior post in the administration, Perry headed a strategic studies institute at Stanford University. In 1989, Rubin spent a sabbatical year at Stanford, where he impressed his American colleagues with his global understanding of strategic missiles and the possibility of intercepting them.

Our presentations before this high-level forum were successful, and we could see the enthusiasm in the eyes of our colleagues at SDIO when Perry voiced his approval of the system's conception and issued instructions to support it. The meeting at the State Department was less difficult for us, as we were able to build on our initial presentation at the Pentagon. At the White House we met with Martin Indyk, deputy chairman of the National Security Council, who greatly impressed us with his intelligent approach and his support. The only suitable room they had for our presentation was the inner sanctum of the classified meeting room. There were technical glitches of the NSC presentation system and the air conditioners were not working. Our welcome to the White House during that visit was a warm one in more ways than one.

We returned home from this visit quite worried. Uzi Rubin asked me how we would tell the director general and the defense minister that we had already developed an overall missile defense concept and presented it to the Americans without their authorization. I was able to calm his nerves, but not my own, and as soon as we arrived I requested a meeting with director general Ivry to update him. The report covered a wide variety of issues, including the unexpected need to present the logic behind the Homa defense concept that emerged during our visit. Without such an explanation, we maintained, there would have been no basis for American support of the continued funding of the project. The director general accepted our report without any problem and instructed us to be ready to present the same report to the defense minister. And so it came to pass that the strategic conception underlying the Homa missile defense system was born. It was a strange process with a rushed outcome that stemmed from in-depth consideration of the system components and the issues related to the array required to defend Israeli territory. Although we were relieved that we did not have to change the concept we knew deep down that the defense ministry could not introduce changes once it had already been accepted by the Americans. Today, I am still convinced that evolution of this concept, unusual as it was, was based on solid, rational consideration of the three components of the Homa system, as well as on the strategic system analyses we carried out with the assistance of Micha Cohen and the Wales firm.

PROFESSOR EDWARD TELLER, THE MIRACLE LASER, AND THE NAUTILUS PROJECT

The idea of using high-powered lasers against Katyusha rockets which constituted the foundation of Project Nautilus was linked to Professor Edward Teller. Senior Israeli physicist Yuval Neeman had close ties with the scientific community in the US, including a personal relationship with Prof. Teller. In the early 1980s, Teller visited

Israel, and Neeman asked us to organize a meeting of researchers of the Israel Atomic Energy Commission for Teller to address. The hall was filled to capacity before Teller took the stage, and during our short conversation in my office before his lecture I was completely captivated by this tall man, with his thundering voice and mischievous eyes. In the lecture hall, Teller easily mesmerized the audience for the entire hour, and could have easily continued speaking for a few more, had he wanted to.

We hosted Teller at our home for dinner, and my wife Naomi was tense and worried about whether the Hungarian professor would like her goulash. The Israeli paprika passed the test, and Teller awarded Naomi's Hungarian kitchen three stars.

By Teller's next visit to Israel I was already the director of MAFAT, and I was pleased when Neeman told me that the professor had asked to meet with me. He was staying in a spacious suite at the Tel Aviv Hilton, and I came to meet him at noon, as scheduled. We sat in the conversation area of his spacious suite, and my eyes were fixed on an enormous bowl filled with fruit, overflowing with yellowish-greenish bunches of grapes. Teller invited me to join him in this healthy feast and we began discussing missile defense. "I know that you are developing a missile to intercept ballistic missiles launched at Israel," he began, "but that's only one defensive layer against the threat." "Uzi," he continued, "What do you think about the idea of adding a second layer of missile defense? I suggest you consider integrating a high-powered laser for shorter distances." He then proceeded to tell me that a high-powered laser facility had been activated at the US military testing area at White Sands, New Mexico, and that the laser had already proven effective in intercepting air-bound objects during testing. "You can ask the Pentagon to lend you the laser," he said. "It's called Miracle, and you can use it to run tests in the arid, dusty conditions typical of Israel and the climatic conditions of the Middle East." As he spoke, I thought about how appropriate the name of the laser was for us Israelis, who hoped for new miracles on a daily basis.

After years of support for the development of a missile defense system Teller enjoyed a special status at the Pentagon and the White House, and I knew we could rely on his support in a time of need. During my next visit to the US we asked to visit to White Sands US military testing area. Testing areas in the United States are highly classified, and obtaining permission to visit involves a complex bureaucratic process. Moreover, entry into a testing area does not necessarily ensure entry into the facilities they contain, and stern sentries are stationed at every turn to make sure that the rules are followed. This time, however, the process was quick and smooth, perhaps due to the fact that we were the guests of SDIO, and perhaps due to Teller's recommendation.

White Sands had become an enormous laboratory for the critical stages of missile development by the US military. This work required the construction of large, complex radar systems to gather data about each launch. Over the years the developers built up the capacity to operate a high-powered laser guided by advanced radar systems which proved to American military engineers that it was possible to disable and shoot down unmanned air targets.

Intensely curious, we arrived at the base and received a royal welcome and a comprehensive overview of base operations that had clearly been tailored to our security clearance. We were taken to the site of the high-powered laser in the afternoon. The weather was extremely hot and dry, and we felt right at home like at the Rafael testing area in the Negev desert. We had no idea what to expect, and when we approached the area we saw a group of huge buildings. We watched films of tests and concluded that the system, which could identify targets flying by at high speed and track them by radar until the decision was made to fire the laser, had great potential. The range of laser beams depended on the weather. When there was no dust, fog, or water vapor in the air the range could reach up to 10 kilometers. However, it was clear that not even the magic of Professor Teller could convince the Americans to lend us the system, and we knew we had no chance of bringing this technology to Israel.

We returned from our trip to the US with the image of the giant laser shooting down quickly maneuvering helicopters and destroying experimental rockets. We knew that the films documented only the high powered lasers' success stories and not its failures, but what we saw was sufficiently convincing. Before long Katyusha rockets attacks from Lebanon on northern Israel began with increasing frequency. Operation "Accountability" (din v'kheshbon), which Israel launched in July 1993 in response to the firing of Katyusha rockets against the border town of Kiryat Shmona, ended with a memorandum of understandings that was meant to ensure quiet along Israel's northern border with Lebanon. By then we already understood that we would need to find another way to address the threat of rocket fire from Lebanon, preferably based on active defenses. We began discussing the idea of using high-power laser beams to destroy rockets in mid-flight. Our initial work in this direction was modest, and was limited to asking the Americans to allow us to test the laser's ability to penetrate the body of a Katyusha rocket.

Katyusha rockets presented a number of challenges. Developed and produced by the Soviet Union with the massive engineering style common to all Soviet systems, the body of the rocket was made of 10 millimeter-thick steel. The rocket was designed to revolve around its axis to increase flight stability. This was good aerodynamics with an additional advantage that could not have been foreseen by the Katyusha's designers. Even if a radar locked on the missile the laser following the radar's guidance would not be focused on one point but rather on a ring created by the rocket's revolving motion.

With the support of our friends at SDIO we received permission to begin testing at White Sands. We did not need to use the full strength of the Miracle laser. During the static tests, which began with un-armed warheads and ended with the complete destruction of explosive warheads, we already knew we were on to something important. To assess the laser's ability to intercept rockets in mid-flight, we had to import rockets and a launcher to the American testing area from Israel. As the Americans were not willing to assume responsibility for maintenance or the safety issues involved in the tests, MAFAT had to bring army munitions personnel with experience preparing and launching Katyusha rockets. The day of the first test arrived, and the tension in the Miracle laser control room in the testing area ran high among Americans and Israelis alike. The rocket was launched and rose carelessly into the sky. On the screen, a blinking light suddenly appeared on the warhead, and then, a few seconds later, we saw an explosion on the screen and the Katyusha disappeared. We now had two reasons to celebrate: not only because of the success of the development process, but more importantly because we crossed an historic threshold proving the feasibility of intercepting rockets in mid-flight.

Project Nautilus, or THEL (Tactical High Energy Laser), was now underway, but its difficult beginning must be understood as part of a longer road lined with challenges. The US Army did not like the idea and was not prepared to cooperate in developing the system and understandably was not eager to spend tens of millions of dollars on the project. As a world superpower, the US is not willing to arm itself with systems that cannot operate anywhere in the world under all-weather conditions. The overall conception of the US military called for the use of compact, mobile vehicles that could be transported in large cargo planes to any place on earth. Congress, however, exerted pressure on the Pentagon, and the US Army continued to cooperate with the project against its will.

In 1996, the United States and Israel signed an agreement to develop a laser system to intercept rockets. For Israel, it was urgent to deploy two experimental systems in Kiryat Shmona, even though we knew that they would initially not be mobile. Calculations based on test data indicated that two such experimental systems would be sufficient to effectively — but not completely — defend both the town and a large portion of the Galilee panhandle. This was not the first time Israel went operational with a weapons system that was still in its final stages of development. In this instance necessity dictated principle, and we quickly realized that being able to observe the system in operation under realistic conditions was a great advantage, as it would significantly shorten the development process. We carried out dozens of tests in which Katyusha rockets were intercepted by the Miracle laser at the White Sands testing area, and our success was compelling. However, there were still many obstacles, such as the toxicity of the laser's chemical substances, the need to reinforce the laser fuel tanks against sabotage and damage from artillery shrapnel; and, above all else, the budget, which had to come not just from the US but from Israel as well.

After Israel withdrew from southern Lebanon, the general feeling was that the situation had changed completely and the threat of artillery rockets against the Galilee had decreased substantially to the point that there was now no rush to finish developing the system. The homemade Qassam rockets used by the Palestinians in the Gaza Strip were considered primitive weapons, and even though hundreds had struck the city of Sderot and other localities around the Gaza Strip they were not classified as a serious threat. Israel's development of the Nautilus project was halted in 2004, and, needless to say, the US Army did not continue working on it alone. It took the painful blow of the second Lebanon war in which barrages of short-range Katyusha rockets fell on localities throughout northern Israel for Israeli decision makers to realize not only that the missile threat still existed but that it was more dangerous than they had thought. The firing of Qassam rockets over the years, which continued and intensified after the withdrawal of the Israeli military and civilian presence from the Gaza Strip, is proof that the efforts undertaken to develop a means of addressing the threat of enemy rocket and missile fire that began in the early 1990s were justified.

TENDERS, STRUGGLES, AND DIFFICULT DECISIONS

In May 1993, the Mandatory Tenders Law went into effect throughout Israel, and, despite its efforts to bypass the law, the defense ministry eventually fell into line. R&D defense projects had always maintained a decision-making mechanism to help make the right choice when it came to developers. It was relatively easy to transform this mechanism, known as the Developer Selection Committee, into a tenders committee. There were cases in which I had no choice but to get into the thick of things and chair the committee. During the process of selecting the primary developer for the Arrow missile program, discussed earlier in this chapter, MAFAT enjoyed the additional support of the US Defense Department's Ballistic Missile Defense Organization.

Between 1992 and 1995, when Yitzhak Rabin was both prime minister and defense minister, MAFAT reached another important and difficult decision. For a number of years we had been assessing the feasibility of a new revolutionary weapon system that consisted of UAV platforms, intelligence and control and command systems, and different types of payloads carried by unmanned aerial vehicles. After proving that we possessed the technology to address the operational need and that a solution was within reach, we received a green light to begin work. During its early phases the project presented formidable technological and engineering difficulties, and its cost was estimated at hundreds of millions of shekels. For the major defense industries, it was both a challenge and an aspiration. We realized very early on that we would not be able to avoid carrying out a tender, and the professional departments of the R&D Unit began preparing the thick book containing the specifications. After the first round, two competitors remained in the running: the first was Elbit and the second was IAI, which already dominated the field of UAVs.

Some years earlier, however, a former air force officer with an innovative idea for light-weight, high-performance platforms established a small company in partnership with the Federman family.

The Elbit Company recognized the latent potential of this small UAV company and added it to the list of companies competing within the aerospace industry to win the major contract.

IAI's sense of confidence led it to designate Elta as the company responsible for the chapter on electronic command and control. The result was a proposal that was much more expensive than the plan proposed by Tadiran as part of the Elbit-led consortium. At a very late stage in the competition, after realizing that it was not at all certain that IAI would win the tender, IAI Director-General Moshe Keret made a last-minute proposal to significantly reduce the price in hope that this would tip the scales in IAI's favor.

The evaluation was to be undertaken by three separate teams that addressed technical aspects, financial implications, and suitability to operational need. I decided not to involve director-general Ivry or defense minister Rabin in the process while it was still underway. Due to the potential sensitivities surrounding the tender, I thought it prudent to keep the entire process entirely in the professional arena and to inform the directors only after a final position was reached.

The committee examining the proposals found that the Elbit proposal possessed significant advantages over the proposal submitted by IAI. However IAI would gain significant assets from the project, as it was designated to perform close to 50% of all future work on the project. When Elbit was selected to lead the project the IAI suffered a massive blow to its self-esteem. Reflecting his usual wisdom and caution, Ivry had no desire to get involved with the issue after the decision was made, and Rabin also chose to steer clear of the issue.

IAI's reaction was intense and tumultuous, and its all-powerful union soon began voicing harsh criticism of the decision and exerting pressure aimed at annulling the outcome of the tender. IAI management decided to take the defense ministry to court. This step was not only unprecedented but also turned out to be unproductive for IAI, which was unable to appeal. The court ruling did little to calm things down, and the pressure of the politically powerful union continued.

382 | Eilam's Arc

One day, the defense ministry's legal advisor contacted me and asked me to consider resigning as a member of the IAI Board of Directors. Rabin was obviously behind the request, and it was clear that he was under intense pressure. My response was that I had no reason to resign and that if Rabin thought that I did, he should tell me himself. Soon after, during a routine working meeting, Rabin awkwardly and hesitantly tried to point out the conflict of interests between my role as director of MAFAT and as a member of the IAI Board. I looked up at Rabin and told him that to the best of my knowledge, the process by which civil servants were appointed to boards of directors of government companies had not changed. "With regard to the decision of the Tenders Committee," I continued, "all I know is that I acted without bias, that I regret nothing, and that my conscience is clear. If you choose not to reappoint me after I complete my present term, I will of course respect your decision." Rabin did not insist, and the matter was dropped.

INTERNATIONAL CONTACTS AND R&D AGREEMENTS

As a small island in a sea of hostile enemy states, Israel has always aspired to build productive military and defense relationships with other countries. The experience acquired through our contacts with foreign countries and agencies in the course of the work of the Weapons Development Department, the R&D Unit, and other bodies was important, but in the mid-1980s we began to feel the need to transcend our exclusive relationship with the US and to begin establishing ties with Europe and the Far East.

After the Six Day War, Israel's relationship with the US intensified. France and England made political decisions to impose an almost complete embargo on the sale of weapon systems to Israel. Even Germany, which remained politically and morally supportive of Israel, was limited in terms of the types of systems and parts it could allow itself to sell to us. Our leanings toward the US in the defense arena had a number of manifestations, which were supported by American political backing in the international arena. In addition, the Americans' brilliant idea of providing Israel with grants, which continued to increase in value until the current level of more than $2 billion a year, obliged Israel to purchase weapon systems produced in the US. In many cases purchases were made through the technical-financial agencies of the American armed services, resulting in a diverse network of personal connections between officers of the IDF and the American military.

The ingenious aspect of American aid was that it made us extremely dependent on the US and created a situation in which all parts of the IDF and the Israeli defense establishment grew addicted to ongoing arms acquisition from the Americans. The human element also played an important role. The fact that all Israeli high-school graduates know English to some extent still helps Israelis to easily adapt to academic and business environments in the US. The US offers a full range of courses and training programs for Israeli military personnel, which have also served to increase pro-American sentiments in Israel. Local support for Israel's pro-American policies was strengthened by countless opportunities in American higher education, including sabbaticals for academic scholars and the personnel of research labs and the defense industries.

During the 1960s and 1970s, Israeil ties with other foreign armies were based primarily on Western countries' interest in the experience gained and lessons learned from our battles against Soviet weapon systems. As time passed and as Israel made more progress in our own independent R&D we realized that we also possessed technological assets that could be shared with friendly nations with whom we enjoyed trustful relationships. However, the more aid we received from the US, the less funds in shekels the Israeli defense establishment allocated to the development and production of Israeli weapon systems for IDF acquisition. This dynamic forced the defense industries to consistently increase the extent to which they engaged in defense exports.

Defense exports continued to expand, and the increasing international competition for weapon system markets resulted in mounting demands by the defense industries to allow them to market increasingly advanced and classified systems. The pre-export authorization process involved three primary considerations: political factors, security clearance, and, most importantly, technological factors. The professional units of MAFAT were responsible for preparing and assessing the arguments for and against issuing export permits for products in classified areas. Both the defense ministry and the IDF recognized the need for a supreme coordinating body to determine the position of the entire defense establishment on questions of export permits. The task of chairing this committee, known as the Supreme Coordinating Committee for International Contacts, naturally went to the director of MAFAT. The committee consisted of the heads of the relevant branches of the defense ministry, senior representatives of the General Staff and the services of the IDF and the directors of the IDF's information security units. For a few years there was an increase in the amount of work assigned to the technical units of MAFAT and the other agencies involved with preparing the material for committee meetings. This in turn increased my workload but I had no doubt that it was important to invest the necessary time. Reductions in the shekel-based defense budget for IDF armament were at their height and the defense industries reinforced their international marketing teams just to keep their capabilities and their well-trained professional personnel. The results were quick to come. Not long had passed before the defense establishment calculated that only 20 percent of the work of Israel's defense industries was being undertaken for the IDF, and that the remaining 80 percent was dedicated to export.

Defense R&D professionals found themselves being drawn into a new area of activity. Within just a few years, defense R&D emerged as a force that could play a pivotal role in establishing and maintaining defense-business related relations between Israel and other countries, and in paving the way for Israeli defense exports. As such, from the mid-1980s MAFAT became increasingly involved in the complex process of cultivating a new type of foreign relations with a unique dynamic of its own. The defense industries needed to come up with new projects to develop and market while the defense establishment recognized that the reduction in the IDF's shekel-based acquisition budget required a different kind of effort to enable the defense industries to survive.

France

France was and remains an important technological and industrial power and a leading force in Europe with its own global aspirations. Before the Six Day War France was Israel's main supplier of military technology but President Charles de Gaulle imposed a total embargo on all arms exports after the war. The embargo was ostensibly to all combatants but was soon lifted for Arab states but applied rigorously towards Israel. This meant that we needed to find creative solutions to renew the relationship.

The DGA(Direction générale de l'armement) is staffed by civilians and military personnel. The officers, who at the time consisted mostly of graduates of the École Polytechnique state-run engineering school held the ranks of munitions officers. We initiated contact with DRET, the French Military Research Agency, which was headed by General Marçais, and resolved to base our renewed relationship on modest endeavors with low security clearances. MAFAT decided to establish a joint administrative and supervising body over which Marçais and I presided and to meet on an annual basis (meetings alternated between France and Israel) in order to follow the progress made on the issues of common interest. Victor Marçais was a tall, bald man with a courageous, resolute character concealed by a shining, smiling face. I came to appreciate his courage, which enabled us to forge partnerships in increasingly sensitive development projects that posed risks that he took upon himself.

During the initial phase of our renewed relationship it was clear that we would need to begin with issues involving no security risk by selecting purely civilian unclassified areas. I had no hesitations about moving forward in this direction, because I understood that it was the only way to cultivate the relationship. I hoped that the joint work would generate the trust necessary to begin work on classified subjects and the joint development of defense systems.

Five years later, after making slow progress in the process of gradually removing the secrecy-related obstacles to our collaboration, we reached the point of being able to write a draft agreement for French–Israeli cooperation in the realm of defense R&D. By this point General Marçais had already retired. He was replaced by another general specializing in armaments who was also an engineer and a graduate of École Polytechnique: Paul-Ivan de Saint-Germain, a thin and bespectacled officer with a pointy face and laser-like brown penetrating eyes. He managed his personnel sternly and decisively, and it was only after I got to know him better that I came to appreciate his softer side. With energy and vigor, he set to the task of improving Israeli–French relations, and within no time a draft agreement for cooperation in the realm of defense R&D was ready to be signed by the Israeli and French defense ministers. We waited for Defense Minister François Léotard's visit to Israel as the guest of Defense Minister Rabin. At the meeting with the French minister's delegation, I was asked to make a short presentation on the status of joint research and development activity. With audacity that I am still unable to explain today, I decided to give the presentation in French. Rabin and Léotard signed the agreement, which provided a strong tailwind for future ongoing joint work and which is still alive and in full force today.

French–Israeli cooperation in the realm of defense technology has known no dramatic developments. Rather, the ties between the Israeli and French defense industries have been based on an ongoing process of the gradual establishment of relationships and mutual trust between people. In the years that followed this sturdy foundation facilitated an expansion of the French–Israeli agreement, which was signed in 1999 by then defense minister Ehud Barak and French Defense Minister Alain Richard during a visit in Israel. This relationship also resulted in the exceptional development of limited but significant French procurement of Israeli weapon systems and ammunition.

Germany

Ever since the signing of the 1952 reparations agreement by Prime Minister David Ben-Gurion and Chancellor Konrad Adenaur, Israel has enjoyed friendly relations with Germany. On the basis of our past experience, which began with Mr. Belkow and Dr. Held's visit to the battlefields of the Sinai Peninsula following the Six Day War, we had no difficulty understanding the approach of our counterparts in the German Ministry of Defense, the Germany military, and the impressive German defense industry. After the Yom Kippur War the relationship between the two defense establishments was formalized and institutionalized, and evolved into a routine of regular meetings between senior officials, as well as a great deal of practical lower level work in the field.

During the 1980s the Israeli defense industries already possessed advanced technologies in diverse areas of electronic warfare that interested Germany during the previous decade. The key figure in the German Defense Ministry was Peter Runge, a talented, intelligent, and dominant engineer whose support was required for all new undertakings. Runge instilled fear in the personnel of the German Defense Ministry, as well as the Israelis who met him. I was fortunate enough to have been able to find my way into his good graces, not without drinking countless glasses of beer and listening patiently to the many stories he told in his loud, thundering voice. The high-level annual meetings between the director-generals of the two defense ministries continued, providing important assistance to the cooperative efforts that continued throughout the year. One of the high points in the relationship between the two defense establishments was Chancellor Helmut Kohl's decision after the First Gulf War to provide the Israeli navy with two modern submarines almost free of charge. For years, a large team of Israeli naval and technical officers were stationed in Germany, in the capital city of Bonn and in shipyards in the north, to work with the Germans on the construction of the submarines.

The Germans knew that I was scheduled to finish my work at MAFAT in 1997 and invited me to make a formal official farewell visit. Fortunately I was allowed to bring my wife Naomi; however, both of us were somewhat taken aback when we stepped off the plane and were received by a formation of officers and soldiers of the honor guard dressed in elegant ceremonial uniforms. Runge and his wife went to great lengths to make the touristic parts of our visit pleasant for us. Throughout our entire trip there was a police presence in all the areas we visited by car, and we were escorted by police cars and motorcycles to clear the way and provide protection. At that time Germany was already in the practical stages of integrating the East and West parts of the country, and at my request my hosts also arranged a visit to the East German defense industry, which was still having trouble reaching the efficiency levels of Western industries. In East Germany we visited the city of Dresden, where our host one evening was a well-known politician with great influence in Bavaria. This talented and experienced man, I had been quietly informed, had been caught embezzling money and was sent into exile in East Germany, where the Germans expected him to rehabilitate the floundering East German defense industry. During the day we visited the Zeiss optical industry, which had been the pride of the German defense industry prior to World War II. We also visited a factory for growing gallium arsenide crystals meant for optical products for the defense establishment. During dinner our host delivered an emotional speech about the obstacles he faced in his efforts to rehabilitate and upgrade the East German defense industry.

Britain

Britain's defense relations with Israel grew chilly after the Six Day War, primarily for political reasons. During the golden age of British–Israeli relations before 1967 Britain supplied Israel with its first submarines (including the Dakar, which sunk in the Mediterranean while en route from Britain to Israel) and collaborated with Israel on the development of the Chieftain tank. We tried but did not succeed in finding ways to resume collaboration even if only on a limited scale and without entering sensitive and classified areas. On a formal level, everything was fine: we had a respectable embassy in London with economic, commercial, and military attachés, and there was no official policy of a British arms embargo against Israel. In the field, however, there was no activity whatsoever. Even the war against terrorism, from which Britain itself started to suffer not only from the IRA but also from Arab-Islamic terrorists, did not bring about closer relations. Neither did the downing of the Pan-Am passenger plane above the city of Lockerbie, the assassination of Israeli ambassador Shlomo Argov in London (which served as the pretext for the outbreak of the first Lebanon war), and a long list of other terrorist attacks. Indeed, at the height of the first Intifada, the British refused to authorize Israel's acquisition of Land Rover jeeps, stating that we would undoubtedly arm them and use them against the Palestinians in the occupied territories.

Relations between the two countries were suddenly transformed after a meeting with the chief scientist of the British Defense Ministry, who was a mathematics professor with great experience in research and development. I met him at the annual conference organized by the US Defense Department's Strategic Defense Initiative Organization. At the conferences, which were usually held in the United States, Israel was always treated with great respect, which was justified because we truly were pioneers in the development of regional defense systems against long-range missiles. The British, the French, the Germans, and the Japanese took interest, received information, established teams to consider the issue, but never initiated substantial development operations and never committed to purchasing American systems.

This was one this reason why the Americans made sure to periodically hold the conference outside of the US. We attended such a conference in June 1995 in Britain. In addition to our missile interception technologies and an analysis of our practical test results, we were also able to present an overall concept of missile defense. Our Green Pine radar, which could detect an enemy missile in flight and guide missiles to intercept the threat, captivated everyone's attention. The principles of erecting an array of batteries and command and control junctions were new territory for most participants and were also the subject of great interest. SDIO personnel traditionally hosted a lunch only for delegation heads. During the lunch in Britain I was seated next to the chief scientist of the British Defense Ministry, and an unconstrained and natural conversation developed between the two of us. He had not been aware of the progress we had made in defense technology and our work on missile defense systems both impressed him and piqued his curiosity. This led to a second meeting later in the conference during which I invited him to visit Israel. He agreed and said that all that remained was to set a date. It was clear that such a high-level visit would require government authorization, and I hoped that curiosity would help make it happen. Indeed, one year later a British delegation headed by the deputy chief scientist of the British Defense Ministry arrived in Israel. The delegation included experts from a variety of disciplines, and we went to great lengths to make their visit as impressive as possible.

The next step was to secure a reciprocal visit of an Israeli delegation to Britain. R&D Director Brigadier General (and subsequently Major General) Isaac Ben-Israel led a MAFAT team to Britain, creating a positive dynamic of communication and information exchange. We selected areas that would be of interest to both sides and began doing the groundwork for drafting a written agreement for British-Israeli cooperation in defense R&D.

Over the years we had learned that signed agreements have significant influence because they provide a framework that can easily be filled with content and can be changed from time to time when the need arises. The importance of formal agreements becomes particularly clear during periods of political tension, since such accords are typically only annulled after extremely serious crises. Agreements provide a means of ensuring that when a political storm subsides collaborative work can be easily resumed without starting over from scratch. In partnership with officials of the British Defense Ministry we succeeded in drafting an agreement that was meant to be signed by the British and Israeli defense ministers. At that crucial point in the process, defense officials and their legal advisors were asked for their comments on the agreement. From the perspective of MAFAT, the requested modifications in wording regarding information security and legal matters seemed minor and almost petty, but for the sake of smooth working relations at home they needed to be addressed. However, during the time it took for us to complete the revisions the political climate in Britain changed and British officialdom decided not to sign the agreement. We were now forced to wait for a more opportune moment and a change in the political climate, which finally occurred after Prime Minister Benjamin Netanyahu signed the Wye River Memorandum in 1998. Although by this time I was already on sabbatical in Paris, I encouraged MAFAT to get to London as quickly as possible in order to sign the agreement — an agreement which is still in effect today and which provides an open framework for cooperative work on defense technology in the future as well.

Switzerland

Cooperation with Switzerland evolved through a process that had no precedent in the history of Israel's foreign defense relations. Switzerland was and remains a unique country, with its policy of neutrality which entails maintain a substantial military force and a mandatory draft for a short period of compulsory military service followed by reserve duty. The Swiss defense concept called for an advanced air force, and an armored corps based on the acquisition of German Leopard tanks and a broad array of artillery. For many years, an Israeli military attaché was stationed at the embassy in the Swiss capital of Bern, but the result was limited to mutual visits out of formality and minimal Israeli acquisition of Swiss-produced weapons systems such as Oerlikon anti-aircraft cannons.

One day I was told that Yekutiel Federman wanted to speak with me. Federman was a known hotelier who had entered the world of defense industries as a partner in El-Op and also had business connections in Switzerland. I had already met Federman a few times, but we never had a close working relationship. Federman, a man of German extraction and European outlook, was short, energetic, and extremely enthusiastic...an whose brain was quicker than his ability to express himself in words. As a result, he always sounded as if he was stammering. When I picked up the phone, he lost no time in getting to the point: "Uzi," he said excitedly, "you have to go to Switzerland! There's an opportunity to start working with their army and defense ministry — now! Get a team together and go next week. I've spoken with people there. They're waiting."

I chose not to show my astonishment at the nature of the call. All I said was: "Yekutiel, things like that don't happen immediately. I need to check out the situation, and if it is decided that we should go, we will still need to make the necessary arrangements for the meetings."

Without missing a beat, another stream of intermingled words flowed loudly out of the telephone receiver. "No, no, no, no!!" he insisted "Everything is already prepared. I told the Swiss that we would conduct a seminar for them on the issue of technology! They're interested in bringing over the senior leadership of the army and the defense ministry!"

Our military attaché in Bern was Arieh Alon, a red-haired, feisty, unconventional lieutenant colonel from the intelligence corps. I called him immediately and learned that something was actually coming together there, and that, by organizing a technological seminar, we now had a chance to meet directly with the senior echelon of the Swiss defense establishment.

The gauntlet had been thrown and I saw no reason not to pick it up. We decided to plan a seminar on electronic warfare...ubject that Alon insisted was at the top of the Swiss agenda. We obviously faced difficult questions while planning the seminar, such as the extent to which we could reveal sensitive and classified information to the Swiss. We did not doubt their ability to keep a secret, and we knew we could trust them. Nonetheless, we still felt uncomfortable. Our contact at the Swiss General Staff and the moving force behind the evolution of our relations was General Paul Rast, deputy CGS for planning and training. Before joining the General Staff, Rast had served as the Swiss defense attaché in Moscow. We arrived in the capital city of Bern for a two-day seminar and a third day of visits to Swiss military installations. When we arrived we learned that the seminar would be attended by the entire leadership of the Swiss army and defense ministry, including the CGS, who opened the event himself and hosted lunch on the first day of the event.

The Swiss participants listened attentively to the focused presentations delivered by personnel of MAFAT, the IDF's communications and intelligence corps, and the Israeli air force. During the two-day seminar they asked a large number of questions that were clearly more than just polite questions posed for the sake of etiquette. Before the seminar ended Alon began quietly advocating the idea of holding a follow-up seminar. Indeed, when we returned to Israel we had a series of meetings to begin the process of selecting a suitable subject. It was decided to focus on issues related to command and control, and we succeeded in persuading Ehud Barak, who was then OC Central Command, to participate in the conference and to give a lecture on the overall conception of command and control systems on the modern battlefield. Federman was delighted and told us that we had made a marvelous impression on our Swiss counterparts and that the second seminar was a success as well. We were already familiar with the dynamics of such seminars and with the most effective ways to convey messages and emphasize specific points to the Swiss army officers. We learned about the Swiss defense establishment, and came to understand that although its civilian component was small, it nonetheless controlled decisions relating to acquisitions for the Swiss military.

Almost naturally, and as a result of the two seminars and the mutual benefit recognized by both sides, we successfully established a joint coordinating body. Israel's aim was to help the Israeli defense industries market their products in Switzerland. Switzerland's aim was to institutionalize its relationship with Israel and to institute oversight of all activity between the two defense industries. The Swiss team was headed by the Swiss deputy CGS for planning and training and included senior representatives of the purchasing apparatus of the Swiss defense ministry. We thought that the Israeli team should include the director of the Defense Export Assistance Branch, the director of MAFAT, the assistant chief of the Operations Branch as a representative of the IDF, and director of the defense ministry's Foreign Contacts Unit. It was only logical that our team be headed by Export Assistance Branch Director Zvi Reuter, as our primary aim was to promote defense exports. Reuter unwilling to take this responsibility upon himself and asked me to head the Israeli team in his stead.

Our work with the Swiss taught us an interesting lesson in organizational culture. It taught us to respect and appreciate agreed upon schedules and to begin insisting that meetings begin on time. It was a new approach for us, as we were used to the casual improvisatory nature of Israeli organizational culture, which is perhaps best epitomized by the typically empty assurances "Don't worry — it'll be fine" and "trust me." I identified naturally with this aspect of Swiss culture and worked hard to persuade my colleagues in the defense establishment to be precise and punctual when it comes to dates and time. The Swiss–Israeli cooperative work supported by the coordinating committee had impressive results, including the export of advanced Israeli systems to Switzerland. After learning the principles of the Swiss defense concept, it was easy for us to instruct our industries on how to provide solutions for the needs of the Swiss army. General Rast retired from the post of Swiss deputy CGS for planning and was replaced by General Paul Müeler who, although very different from his predecessor, nonetheless maintained the openness, trust, and enthusiasm for collaborative work that had come to pervade the Swiss military leadership.

While wandering through the music shops of Bern during one of our first visits to Switzerland, I found a pocket trumpet. On the last evening of our visit there was a dinner at the home of our military attaché in Bern and I played a number of yodels and traditional Israeli folk songs for our Swiss hosts. It turned out that the Swiss secretary of the joint-committee knew how to play the guitar, adding a musical dimension to the Swiss–Israeli coordinating meetings. At the last meeting I attended, held in Switzerland in 1997, my colleague General Müller knew that I would soon be leaving my position and prepared a surprise. After two days of meetings, the Swiss hosted a celebratory dinner at a palace in Bern. After dinner we began the speeches and gifts that had become customary during our meetings with the Swiss. Müller began by praising the positive and stable relationship between the two countries, and when it came to the time to begin presenting gifts he proposed reversing the order, beginning with members of the Israeli delegation. One after another each member of the delegation was presented with a tie bearing an embroidered symbol of the Swiss army. "And for Oussi," my friend Müeler continued, "today I have something different." Then, he formally presented me with a small green instruction booklet for learning how to play the trumpet in the Swiss military orchestra. I leafed through the booklet while thanking General Müller, and jokingly asked for an exemption from the visit scheduled for the next day in order to study the booklet. At that point, the General's assistant crept up behind my back and placed a large case in front of me. When I opened it, I discovered that it held a shiny silver trumpet! My heart pounded as I picked it up, and I realized that it was a Bach Stradivarius trumpet made in Elkhart, Indiana by the world's top company for high-quality trumpets. I was speechless. The only words I could get out were: "I'll forego what I had planned to say, and instead I'll just play." I placed the beautiful Bach Stradivarius to my lips and, without warming up, began with a light rhythmic Swiss yodel. I then told the group that I would play an Israeli song, and the first one that came to mind was "Jerusalem of Gold." It was a touching and extraordinary ending for the period during which I was deeply involved in Swiss–Israeli joint-defense activities.

Asia

Israel's relations with Asia constitute a unique chapter in the history of Israeli foreign relations. I had the privilege of being instrumental in some aspects of these relations. My connections with the Far East and with Southeast Asia began during a seminar for Asian student leaders in 1959 when I was studying at the Technion in Haifa. During the five weeks I spent in the Malaysian capital of Kuala Lumpur with student leaders from other Asian countries, I found a warm place in my heart for Asia, which remains with me today. Years later, while on my way back to Israel after a special program for university lecturers in the field of business administration at California's Stanford University, I passed through Taiwan, the Philippines, Singapore, and India and visited a few friends from my university days. Martin Bonoan of the Philippines was then working as a professor of business administration at the University of Manila and would later be appointed as director-general of the national airline of the Philippines. Prof. Paul Fang, a Chinese-born economist who moved from China to Hong Kong with his family when he was a boy, relocated to Singapore, where he was appointed as a professor of economics at Nanyang University. Paul and his wife spared no effort in making my stay pleasant. After Singapore declared independence in 1965 the country's legendary prime minister, Lee Kuan Yew, commenced his efforts to unify the people of the country and to lead them on a path that would transform Singapore into a major economic, commercial, and political power within Asia and in the international arena.

The budgetary problem posed by the high cost of developing advanced weapon systems for the relatively small market of the IDF intensified as the years went by. To put things simply, Israeli defense industries faced difficulties providing the IDF with the systems it needed because the army's armament outlays did not cover the cost of development. The number of systems that the IDF could afford was nothing compared to the quantities that a superpower like the US or the larger European countries could afford. In recent years European Union countries such as France, Britain, and Germany have also started to face the problem of limited purchasing versus high development costs as defense budgets have been cut.

Israeli decision makers reached a point at which there no choice but to work towards the establishment of large collaborative projects for weapon systems. When we started working towards this direction we had no idea how important this would be for the future of Israeli defense export policy. Israeli defense industries were proposing ingenious solutions to the challenges of future wars in the air, at sea, and on land. But there was no chance of getting the budgets to develop these systems from domestic Israeli sources. The only option was to persuade our counterparts in Asian countries to purchase the systems before they were actually developed. This started a very complicated process in which the Supreme Coordinating Committee for International Contacts was asked to authorize the provision of information about the future systems abroad while the relevant corps of the IDF were asked to commit to purchasing the systems upon the successful conclusion of development. These elements were a precondition for our foreign partners to decide to arm themselves with the systems. It was also necessary to obtain the support and authorization of the IDF General Staff and the director-general of the defense ministry. In some cases we were forced to reach compromises that appeared impossible to execute. However, when we finally reached the point of signing agreements, we knew we were heading down a new path. It marked a breakthrough that would lead to hitherto unimaginable modes of work, levels of partnership, and budgetary resources. This format of partnership based on projects beginning with engineering development was so successful that we returned to it at every possible opportunity. Indeed, in Israeli defense exports today, a substantial share of development costs are paid for by the foreign countries who intend to acquire the system. This enables the IDF to save on development costs and to reach the phase of arms purchases with little financial difficulty. Involving the Israeli customer in the process from the beginning allays concerns of foreign customers by reassuring them that every project is under professional supervision to ensure its suitability for operational needs. The involvement of IDF officials also secures the interests of the Israeli customer.

India

From my highly personal perspective, Israel's special relationship with India also had roots reaching back to the 1959 Kuala Lumpur seminar for Asian student leaders. Another personal factor was my participation in the special course for lecturers in the field of business administration at Stanford University in 1965–1966, where I had eight Indian lecturers as classmates. I was impressed by the Indian participants' ambition and their drive to succeed. I learned about their national pride and their desire to prove to everyone that India is a world power. They were intelligent, well read, hard-working individuals, and more than anything else, they were ambitious. They had come from different parts of India — from Calcutta and New Delhi to Mumbai — but despite the many differences between them, there was also a discernible common denominator.

When the process of institutionalizing the relationship between the Israeli and Indian defense establishments got underway, I made plans to fly to India to initiate contacts in the area of research and technological development. The man I was to meet was named Dr. Abdul Kalam, who occupied the top position in the massive hierarchy of military and defense R&D activity in India. Defense Ministry Director-General Ivry, who had met Dr. Kalam during a visit to India, described him as a closed, indecipherable man, and did not think we could benefit from a relationship with him in any way. I embarked on my trip with no expectations, but with a great sense of curiosity. First on the agenda was a private introductory meeting with Dr. Kalam.

Abdul Kalam...hort, thin man seated behind a gigantic desk piled high with books and papers — stood up and shook my hand warmly. Within a few minutes it felt as if we had a common language and the chemistry between us evolved effortlessly. We talked about Israel, and the way both countries had blazed their own trails to techno- logical independence. We talked about the challenges facing Indian research and development and about the almost complete embar- go the US had imposed on India after the first Indian nuclear test. Dr. Kalam was a talented aeronautical engineer and was born and raised in the Tamil state of Nadu. This modest Muslim man, who looked like a true ascetic, was also endowed with a powerful, capti- vating personality. His role in developing India's ballistic missiles and his deep involvement in India's nuclear program made Dr. Kalam, a Tamil Muslim, one of the most admired personalities in India.

With great sensitivity and understanding, Dr. Kalam did not raise the nuclear issue even once during our meeting. We both knew about each other's role in this area. During all the years of the American technological embargo, Abdul Kalam was the moving force behind India's struggle for technological independence. In 2002, after a long, glorious career during which he led India's defense research and development community, Dr. Kalam was elected president of India.

During that first trip we visited research laboratories and ambitious projects and bore witness to the Indians' efforts to develop missiles of all types and sizes. We learned about the major efforts they had been making to develop electronic warfare systems and were impressed by their knowledge of metals and advanced materials and their mastery of computerization and advanced applications. Dr. Kalam also insisted that we visit universities and meet professors and students of the natural sciences. He has always been interested in education and inspiring the younger generations, and he still is today, even after his resignation from the post of president and all other official positions.

At the time of my visit, the Indians were highly ambitious but faced a relatively long road towards their target of developing all necessary capacities on their own without help from the outside. At the conclusion of this instructive, jam-packed visit to India, the most suitable approach appeared to be to establish a cooperative program and to let them understand that they were leading the project. The agreement we reached with Dr. Kalam and his associates called for maintaining a framework of regular meetings that would alternate in location between Israel and India. Issues that were important for them and possibly for us were identified. Nonetheless, in Israel we were only beginning to consider the risks of security exposure and suspicions regarding our new partner's ability to maintain the confidentiality of shared information. Dr. Kalam made only one request during our first meeting to which I had no choice but to respond with a definite "No" — the Arrow missile. Although Kalam's request, which was aimed at shortening the process of acquiring a system to defend against long-range Pakistani missiles, was certainly understandable, I was forced to tell him in no uncertain terms that the Arrow missile was being developed in partnership with the Americans and was receiving massive American funding; there was no way Israel could supply India with the system without the express authorization of the Americans. I also knew that more modest help — analysis of a missile defense system that was not from an American source, including its various components — would also require consultation and coordination with the Americans. In short, we clearly understood that any help Israel could give the Indians in the strategic–political area would require assessing American sensitivities on the issue. I told Dr. Kalam that I estimated that we would have to invest approximately two years in the partnership before we would be able to help them in the area of missile defense. By this point it seemed to me that he had a clear understanding of our political and defense oriented limitations. During our ongoing relations with the Indian we came to understand that it was actually our direct and honest negative response to their Arrow missile request that established a bridge of trust which still supports large numbers of technology-laden, high budget complex cooperative projects.

Later, when I was already leading the delegation in Paris, my special personal relationship with Dr. Abdul Kalam brought about a quick trip to India. The trip was sparked by concern within the defense ministry that Israel was entering a period of crisis in our relations with India, which could jeopardize our joint projects. Within less than three days, I flew to Israel to get brought up to speed on the state of relations, continued by plane to India for talks with Dr. Kalam and his associates, flew back to Israel to report the results of the meetings, and then returned to Paris to my responsibilities as head of the defense ministry delegation in the country. When I arrived in New Delhi, Kalam's office informed me that he would like to meet with me at my hotel. He came alone without assistants, and his bodyguards apparently remained at the entrance to the hotel. Three hours and two pitchers of fresh squeezed orange juice later, we had resolved the entire issue. However, we still needed to meet his senior weapons development and procurement associates for dinner at the fanciest restaurant in town, where we had been reserved a quiet private room. Dr. Kalam's calm and captivating leadership left his associates unable to do anything but agree with everything he said in his quiet melodic Tamil accent. After dinner, Dr. Kalam's official car drove me directly to the airport for my flight back to Israel. Our relations and collaborative work returned to normal, and I was pleased to have been able to play a part in maintaining the momentum in Israel's ongoing relations and collaboration with India.

The United States

During my 12 years at MAFAT, our relations with the military and government defense institutions and agencies in the United States were based on the foundation laid in the 1970s. The diverse work and extensive dialogues that took place following the Yom Kippur War regarding the war's technical and tactical lessons enabled the Israeli defense ministry to establish strong ties with the Pentagon. My 10-year absence from the defense ministry posed no problems for me in reestablishing close contacts within the Pentagon and the services of the United States military. By that time, the status of the MAFAT representative in Washington was well established, alongside the Israeli defense attaché and his assistants on air, naval, and ground-related matters. When the Arrow missile defense program got underway we added another representative to the embassy in Washington, an official who worked only with SDIO at the Pentagon. In May 1993, shortly after Bill Clinton entered the White House, the Americans decided to change the name of the Defense Department agency responsible for the program to the Ballistic Missile Defense

Organization, or BMDO. In August of the same year, Major General Malcolm O'Neill was appointed to direct the agency and was promoted to the rank of three-star general (lieutenant general). During my first visit to BMDO, which was located in a well-guarded basement deep beneath the Pentagon, I was greeted by O'Neill with the enthusiasm of a long-lost brother. He had told his colleagues that he would never forget the gracious assistance I provided him during a visit to the US in 1991, immediately before the hostilities in Iraq and Kuwait. At that point, O'Neill held the rank of Brigadier General and was the commander of the development laboratories of the US military. Our visit was part of the ongoing close cooperation Israel maintained with the American army during the war. After the Iraqi army seized control of Kuwait, during the period of readiness that preceded the war itself, the Americans were troubled by what awaited them in Iraq. The laboratories of the US military prepared themselves for accelerated emergency work on weapons development for the ground war in Kuwait. The period before the attack was too short for any major projects, and the Americans were impressed by the open manner in which we answered their questions and the willingness with which we provided them with technical information. They were also extremely appreciative of our effort to share with them some of our experience in anti-tank and special forces weaponry. During our visit to the laboratories, which O'Neill hosted, we were provided unprecedented access to the quick reaction projects undertaken by the labs during the period of readiness that preceded the war. During this window of opportunity we were treated to a one of a kind display of new systems for night vision, mine detection, electronic warfare defense, and special-forces operations.

General O'Neill had a Ph.D. in physics. He was also a paratroop officer who had been trained as a special-forces combat soldier and who received citations for bravery and leadership under fire while fighting with the Green Berets in Vietnam. I felt a strong affinity with him from the moment I met him, but I never suspected that our paths would cross again, certainly not at a juncture as important as the ballistic missile defense system. In this course of his career O'Neill moved from combat positions to positions in R&D administration and back to combat positions, all the time rising in the ranks. A thin muscular man who maintained a regimen of physical activity that included long-distance running and hours of weight training in the Pentagon officers' club, O'Neill's brown eyes always made direct eye contact revealing curiosity, warmth, and a trace of mischievous humor. I was happy to see that he had reached such a senior position that was of such great importance for American– Israeli cooperation in the area of missile defense. O'Neill's approach permeated the personnel in his command, who provided the Israeli program with open, effective, and encouraging assistance. We were also now let in on the more secret aspects of the American missile defense programs, such as their misgivings after the failure of the Patriot system during the Gulf War. Raytheon's post-war PR campaign in praise of the missile system they had developed could not change the disappointing fact that the anti-aircraft missile system was ineffective against al-Hussein missiles. O'Neill led the complex development program that included the PAC-2 project, through which Raytheon attempted to improve the Patriot missile, and an effort to develop the capability to intercept Scud missiles from the sea, which would subsequently be incorporated into the advanced defense system of Aegis naval cruisers. I looked on in amazement as O'Neil created new sources of support for missile defense within the defense industry, the services of the US military, and the Pentagon. He knew just how to talk to the different parties in order to turn them into allies. The crowning achievement of the American quest for a suitable solution to the missile threat that had become so apparent during the Gulf War was the development of a new and original defense system known as THAAD — Theatre High Altitude Area Defense. The idea behind the program was ingenious: a light, compact missile that would destroy enemy missiles through direct contact, with no need for an explosive warhead. The system was meant to cover an outer perimeter of missile defense, intercepting enemy missiles at ranges of 150–200 kilometers. For shorter ranges the Americans designated the upgraded Patriot missile, known as the PAC-3 (Patriot Advanced Capability 3). The new system for guiding the intercepting missile to its target had stringent radar requirements that dictated a light missile weight and a small missile volume. The system was designed to be transportable by C-130 Hercules military cargo planes, which are capable of landing on short improvised landing strips.

Development of this light, quick missile encountered numerous difficulties and a series of failures during its initial years, and O'Neill asked MAFAT to send over a team of Israeli experts to provide an assessment. We regarded this as the highest form of compliment possible for our development personnel. It provided us with an opportunity to repay the Americans for their crucial assistance during the early phases of developing the Arrow missile. We sent the best team we could assemble and committed them to strict secrecy due to the security sensitivity of the project, the need to maintain the reputation of the industry, and our desire to help ensure Pentagon and Congressional support for the future of the THAAD project.

When it comes to procuring weapon systems, the Americans abide by one sacrosanct principle: not to acquire systems that were not developed and produced in the US (NIH, or "Not Invented Here"). This principle, which overshadows all others, prevented the Americans from even considering purchasing the Homa defense system, even for use during an interim period. But then the miraculous occurred: at a time of need, when hundreds of millions of dollars were being spent on the effort and the Americans lacked a clear, sure-fire plan, some elements of the Arrow missile began to be integrated into the THAAD. The heat-sensitive device used to facilitate the Arrow's final interception found its way into the American system, as did the principle of using a sophisticated explosive warhead to destroy the enemy missile.

Shortly before O'Neill's planned retirement from the military, I visited Washington and gladly accepted an invitation to his home one Sunday afternoon. It was summer, and, as I usually do, I woke up early to take an hour-long morning run through the still quiet streets of the city. I had completely forgotten that O'Neill had suggested that we run and work out at the Pentagon officer's club. I was sitting in the hotel lobby rehydrating myself with a glass of fresh-squeezed orange juice when he arrived, and only then did I remember that I had promised to go running with him. Not wanting to disappoint a friend, and not daring to tell him that I had already run five kilometers that morning, I joined him. We drove to the Pentagon, changed into our running clothes, and started running. The sun was up and it was already hot, and O'Neill kept the quick pace of a deer darting through the woods. That Sunday morning run with O'Neill was a test of my endurance and determination that I will never forget. I can only imagine what O'Neill's wife was thinking after we arrived to their house as she watched me gulp down glass after glass of ice water.

O'Neill was replaced by General Lester Lyles, another exceptional man. Lyles was the first African American general with whom I had close ongoing contact. Lyles received a first degree in mechanical engineering and a Masters degree in mechanical and nuclear engineering. He began his career in the US air force and quickly climbed the ranks as a result of his considerable talents. By 1991, Lyles was already a brigadier general within the logistics center of the American air force, and in 1993 he was promoted to the rank of Major General. After his appointment as director of the BMDO he was promoted to the rank of Lieutenant General. Despite his height and his broad shoulders, which served him well when he played college basketball at Harvard, Lyles was a shy and sensitive man with a soft, almost hesitant handshake that seemed inconsistent with his size. Above all, his talents, sharp mind, and analytical abilities were unmistakable, and he had a charisma that was different from that of his predecessors, Abrahamson and O'Neill. In the case of Lyles, still waters truly ran deep. He brought with him vast experience in technical administration that he acquired during his service in the US air force and quickly established his leadership within the BMDO. During his work with MAFAT he knew how to distinguish between the important and the tangential, and the relationship that developed between the two of us was an important asset. Lyles worked hard to increase American support for the construction of additional Arrow missiles, enabling us to deploy the full array for defense of the entire country without having to make impossible budgetary outlays. Like his predecessors and many of the senior officers under his command, Lyles saw us as a vanguard in establishing the concept of regional missile defense and the Homa system as an important asset for ensuring the continued government support of the BMDO.

A special relationship evolved between MAFAT and the Defense Advanced Research Projects Agency (DARPA), the small US Defense Department agency (employing less than 100 people) responsible for pushing the envelope in the development of new technologies for military use. DARPA had an annual budget of more than two billion dollars, but equally as important was the agency's complete independence in selecting its areas of activity and setting its working program. DARPA tended to set its sites 20 years in the future. A prominent example of this long-term approach was its development of Arpanet, the concept of a decentralized network based on packet switching that ultimately evolved into the Internet.

DARPA was established as a closed and highly classified agency that is impenetrable by outsiders. In the early 1990s, during Dr. Victor Reis's tenure as director of the agency, we were provided with a rare opportunity to learn more about DARPA during a visit that was classified as a courtesy call. Dr. Reis was willing to listen to our assessments of the future technological needs of the Israeli defense establishment and even shared his own views on the future. Our suggestion of cooperation was met with the polite but reserved response, "We'll check it out and see if something concrete comes up in the future"; we had no illusions about our chances of success. Still, we never gave up on the idea of somehow participating in the fascinating work of this unique organization through cooperative projects, even if they only dealt with specific, well-defined topics. Dr. Reis was replaced by Dr. Gary Denman, whose legacy included the institutionalization of joint annual meetings in which views were shared on various issues, but which still had no real content. At this point, we decided to change tactics and to make DARPA an offer it could not refuse.

In the early 1990s, we began a comprehensive multi-focus effort to develop an advanced defense system for armored vehicles. The project was still in the stage of exploratory development and the quest for possible technologies for providing passive and active defenses for our tanks. During the Yom Kippur War, we had been surprised, among many other things, by the threat which Sagger missiles posed to our tanks. Many tanks were also hit by RPG-7 rocket launchers, which were actually a Russian duplication of the Panzerfaust (German for "tank fist") personal anti-tank rocket launcher, which was developed by the Germans during World War II. This development, in addition to the development of American anti-tank missiles such as the TOW and European missiles developed by Germany and France, emphasized the increasing vulnerability of our tanks. Although there had been impressive achievements in the development of active armor, it was clear that both the thickness of the armor and the weight which tanks and other armored vehicles could carry were limited. We had technological solutions based on passive defense against missiles and rockets of all kinds. We were also able to address the threat of missiles armed with smart fuses and tandem warheads, which detonate one charge after another in order to penetrate even the most advanced armor.

We had also thought about active defenses against anti-tank missiles and dreamed of defenses against kinetic warheads such as tank shells, which had become faster and more penetrating over the years. At that stage we did not need to request authorization from the ground corps or from the Merkava tank program administration, over which Tal still had complete control, even though his official title was as a consultant.

We debated amongst ourselves whether to share these ideas and decided to try to pique DARPA's curiosity regarding future defenses of tanks and other armored vehicles. We invited DARPA Director Gary Denman and his associates to visit Israel, and they accepted our invitation. The bait worked well, and it was decided to establish a secret joint team to exchange ideas about existing defenses and what could be researched and developed in the future. Denman's three years as director of DARPA passed, and his successor, Larry Lynn, continued to support the cooperative relationship that had evolved between the two bodies. However, when we began discussing active defenses against kinetic bullets and demonstrated that we knew what we were talking about, the curtain suddenly closed and we could no longer move forward. Our conclusion was that this was an area in which they themselves were working and they did not want to involve Israel. The moment we realized that discussion on these issues would be uni-directional, we decided we would no longer provide information to pique their curiosity without receiving something suitable in return.

After the attack on the World Trade Center, and the resulting change in US priorities in the war on terror and the creation of the Department of Homeland Security, there was something that DARPA wanted from us. The agency's focus had been redirected from 20 years in the future to a much shorter horizon. DARPA was aware of the major Israel investment in the field of anti-terrorism and sought to renew cooperation with us on that basis. This was testimony to our achievements in anti-terrorism methods, but it also reflected the importance of institutional frameworks for cooperation that can be easily filled with content when the need arises. Our cooperative framework with DARPA now joined the ranks of our relationship with the BMDO and our much older technological agreements with the United States, dating back to the development of means for securing Israel's borders in the 1960s.

Although my final trip to the US as director of MAFAT was very much a business trip, it was also a farewell of sorts. A few days before the trip we were contacted by the office of Dr. Paul Hoeper, assistant secretary for research, development, and acquisition: "Would General Eilam agree to play tennis with Dr. Hoeper at the White House?" I immediately went out to buy a suitable tennis racket and a tennis outfit worthy of the occasion. I also asked a friend to play a few sets with me in order to work the rust out of my game. I first met Paul Hoeper when he was appointed to his senior position in the defense department. He was a friend of Bill Clinton but was given the job based on merit. Unlike many of his predecessors who were trained in engineering and the exact sciences, Hoeper was a doctor of law. His managerial and business experience resulted in a quick and smooth appointment. During our first meeting, Hoeper suggested that we eat lunch at a fish restaurant on the bank of the Potomac River. As we talked, I came to appreciate the intelligence, curiosity, and friendliness of this young, long-legged man. Even then I knew that he was a dedicated tennis player, but he also told me that he had been playing the piano since he was a boy. We discussed work-related matters and priorities from Israel's point of view, but we also had time for more personal conversations, which gave me the opportunity to tell him that I play the trumpet. We also joked about playing music together and about the possibility of a tennis tournament between our respective agencies. Now, all of a sudden, we were going to have that tennis match.

Paul Hoeper had connections with President Clinton and the White House staff which allowed him to reserve the only White House tennis court for a farewell game with me. On the appointed afternoon, Hoeper picked me up at my hotel, and his driver dropped us off by the southern entrance of the White House. Everything had been arranged in advance, and we quickly passed through the security inspection, where one of Clinton's secretaries was waiting for us. With camera in hand to commemorate the two sets we played, she never once left the side of court. On the way to the White House, Hoeper told me that he was sorry that the president was out of town. "We could have arranged a trio," he teased, "Bill on saxophone, you on trumpet, and me on piano." Despite all my preparations and my best efforts, Hoeper was simply the better tennis player. I may have only managed to score a few points, but I enjoyed every moment. During his kind words at the dinner he arranged in my honor later that evening, he mentioned that we even found time to play tennis at the White House. In response to a guest who asked "Who won?" Hoeper, an experienced diplomat, answered: "We both won, and we both enjoyed ourselves."

I kept in touch with Paul Hoeper during my time in France as well, and I even met him once at the Le Bourget Air Salon in Paris. After the Monica Lewinksi scandal and Bill Clinton's escape from Congressional impeachment, I felt the need to write a few words of encouragement to the president.

It was particularly important for me to commend him on the fact that despite the impeachment campaign against him, he nonetheless mustered the resolve and energy to continue his work on the Middle East peace process. After I finished the letter, I asked Hoeper to personally deliver it to the White House for me.

One Paris morning approximately two weeks later, my secretary Sima Perry greeted me at my office flushed with excitement: "You received a letter from the United States embassy in Paris," she said. "It's a letter from President Clinton!" Indeed, I had received a large official envelope containing a personal letter from Clinton (pictured below), on which the President had taken the time to add a few words of appreciation in his own hand.

On September 12, 2001, Hoeper called me from the United States to tell me that the plane that had crashed into the Pentagon had hit

THE WHITE HOUSE

WASHINGTON

March 31, 1999

Dear General Eilam:

Thank you for your letter that our friend
"Page" Hoeper delivered to me. I
appreciate very much your kind words of
support. It has been helpful over the
past year to have the encouragement of so
many from around the world.

There is still much to do on the peace
process, and I look forward to progress on
a matter that is so important to the
region and indeed, the world.

Again, thank you for writing.

Sincerely,

Bill Clinton

Your letter was very moving — thank you.

General Uzi Eilam
Ministry of Defense
Embassy of Israel
120 Boulevard Malesherbes
75017 Paris
France

the wing in which his offices were located, and that the casualties included a number of his employees. I was speechless. I suddenly felt deeply connected to the tragedy, and I told my friend that I had been worried about him and that my thoughts were with him. In retrospect, when I think back on that conversation, I am struck by the way collaborative work has the potential to turn total strangers into close friends. Indeed, I have remained close with many of the people in the US with whom I have worked over the years, despite the distance between us and the passage of time.

Another American official with whom I enjoyed a positive relationship was Dr. John P. White, who served as deputy defense secretary between 1995 and 1997. When President Clinton decided to appoint Deputy Defense Secretary Dr. John Deutsch to the post of director of Central Intelligence, White was appointed to fill the vacant position. John Deutsch and John White were two very different people. Deutsch was a Jew born in Brussels who immigrated to the US as a child. He became a professor of chemistry at MIT and then held senior positions in the US Department of Energy, which was also responsible for the military development of nuclear energy. Deutsch was an abrasive and determined man who instilled terror in officials throughout the Pentagon. Once, in an effort to acquire broad support for continued American funding for the Arrow program, David Ivry, then director-general of the Israeli defense ministry, attended a meeting of the US National Security Council without the knowledge of the Pentagon. Deputy Defense Secretary Deutsch was furious, crudely informing his director-general, "Next time I will cut his balls off!" We learned our lesson quickly, and the next time Uzi Rubin and I visited Washington for a briefing on the Homa missile defense system, we began with presentations at the defense department and only then, after coordination carried out by Giora Ram, our defense attaché in Washington, did we make our way to the State Department and the National Security Council.

John White, in contrast, was a quiet, pleasant man with understanding and good will that could always be counted on. He was an economist by training who had served as a young officer in the Marines and who possessed long-term experience in business and the defense industry, including nine years as a senior official of the Rand Corporation and three years as assistant defense secretary for manpower and reserve affairs. Once during a private meeting between the two of us, he offered important insight on American–Israeli relations within the defense arena: "Uzi," he explained, "you must understand that 50% of the people in this building [the Pentagon] may be your friends, but the other 50% are your enemies. Now, when the winds from above are positive, everything looks rosy. However, the moment things change, your enemies will come out of the woodwork."

During my last trip to the US as director of MAFAT, White hosted me at his home for a special farewell dinner. Early in the evening, his official car picked me up at my hotel to take me to his house. I had no idea what to expect, and I was captivated by the long, winding drive through thick forests on the outskirts of Washington. The night was dark, and the only light we could see was the flicker of the headlights against the thick trees lining the road. Eventually, another light could be seen through the trees, and we pulled up in front of a lone large wooden house at the center of a clearing. John greeted me and introduced me to his wife, who soon retired to her bedroom and left us alone. We went out onto the large patio and I joined the deputy secretary for a glass of select whiskey. At the edge of the patio stood a grill on which White had already started preparing fish and seafood. He did everything quietly and congenially, which enabled me to overcome my sense of embarrassment at being cooked for by the US deputy defense secretary. It was a quiet evening, and the calls of night birds and the constant chirping of crickets provided pleasant background music for our meal. Although our conversation was the continuation of conversations we had in the past, this time it assumed the air of a farewell discussion. I was touched by the gesture of being hosted in such an intimate manner. I found it much more meaningful than a meal with a large group of people in a fancy restaurant. The private setting was more conducive for meaningful conversation about sensitive issues and gaining new insights. At the end of the meal, White presented me with a fancy, ornamental pistol from the Civil War era which will always remind me of him.

THE TALPIOT PROGRAM

Any chapter on MAFAT would be incomplete without mentioning the most important component of scientific and technological research — the people. Without a doubt, one of the most prominent achievements of MAFAT is the Talpiot program. The program was established after the Yom Kippur War, which had a destabilizing effect on all Israelis involved in the military and defense, and prompted a process of checking and rechecking our aims and understandings. This process often involved seeking out new approaches in all areas of concern. Two professors from the Hebrew University in Jerusalem, Felix Dothan and Shaul Yatziv, came up with a new and innovative way to cultivate high-quality human resources trained in science and technology for the IDF and the Israeli defense establishment. In 1979, after many discussions and consultations on the subject, the two professors submitted a detailed document to CGS Rafael Eitan, which read as follows:

> ....he proposal described here is the summary of thoughts and ideas we first had a few years ago that became more developed after the Yom Kippur War. Concern for the future of the country in general and the desire to do everything possible to minimize the number of Israeli casualties in future wars has inspired us to submit the proposal in writing. It is based on three points of departure that are not reflected in any of the country's research and development institutes: firm recognition of the fact that the state of Israel must make an effort to develop weapons that are as modern and innovative as possible and

that are not unknown to other countries; that in order to achieve this goal, we must make planned utilization of creative human faculties, which are at their height at a young biological age, when people are in their twenties; and that the ability to invent requires creative imagination, great knowledge, and an intensive approach, which can be encouraged by posing challenges and creating a lively and inspiring atmosphere in which every practical effort and contribution receives recognition and encouragement. As one way of achieving this goal, we propose an intensive and systematic effort to invent and develop effective new weapons, "new" in this case meaning that it is not used by other armies, even those of the superpowers. The core of the program must be made up of extremely talented and dedicated individuals who also have a suitable background in the natural sciences and weapons technologies.

Eitan was convinced and approved the program, which, within just a few years, took shape and began training exceptional high-school graduates for service within the research and development facilities of the Israeli military. Overall oversight of the program, including budgetary responsibility, was assigned to the R&D Unit, which was soon incorporated into MAFAT. The Hebrew University in Jerusalem agreed to provide the program with space on its Givat Ram Campus. There, a military base was constructed especially for the Talpiot students, complete with dormitories and classrooms.

When I first arrived at MAFAT in early 1986, the program curriculum was already in place, with mathematics, physics, and computer theory constituting its primary foundation. We initially limited acceptance to 25 young male and female students each year, but the number later rose to 50. The entire training program, including its military components, was ambitious and impressive. Within three years the students had to complete the requirements for their Bachelors degree, to complete courses in squad commanders training and officers training, and to get an idea of air, naval, and ground warfare through other special training programs. I was impressed by the motivation of the students and by the team spirit and unit pride that the dedicated program commanders inculcated in them. We needed to appoint class officers and commanders for the program, and we decided to use Talpiot graduates for this purpose as soon as possible. This process was institutionalized within a few years, and today's Talpiot commanders and class officers, who implement all the courses and function as elder siblings and tutors, are program graduates.

From the outset the aim of the program was clearly not just to train the participants to be good researchers. Emphasis was also placed on combining technical knowledge with a deep understanding of operational needs. We worked to overcome obstacles which we thought could prevent students from fitting in and contributing from the moment they were assigned to units. During the first years of the program, fear of the Talpiot students was widespread within the IDF. The concern was that they would be too independent and would outshine their commanders. It took a great deal of patience and persuasion to bring about the Talpiot students' integration into the corps. Integration was relatively smooth within the air force, the navy, and the intelligence corps, but was more difficult within the ground forces.

For many years the program was flexible and willing to implement changes based on lessons learned along the way. Lessons were learned at all levels, including the selection and training process and graduates' service within the IDF. Hard work was ongoing in a number of areas: the academic work, which required maintaining a high level of instruction; effective management of the program and the military–civilian campus; and student motivation and team work. Important work also had to be done outside the classroom to ensure the program's present and future existence. Institutional and bureaucratic systems find it difficult to contend with exceptions, and Talpiot was one of the most exceptional programs in the IDF. Ten years after the program's establishment, it was still fighting for its life.

It was sometimes even necessary to meet with the Adjutant General Branch chief himself in order to make sure that steps would not be taken that would harm the young program.

As part the need to improve the program, we came up with a special track consisting of a few years of service in command positions within combat units followed by a return to positions in the field of research and development. The model we adopted was somewhat similar to my own experience, and combined command positions in combat units and administrative units in the realm of R&D. Not all of the students in the Talpiot program possessed the characteristics necessary to succeed in command positions in combat units, but some students did complete this track successfully in the field corps, the navy, and the air force. Brigadier General Ofir Shoham, who completed the naval officers' training course and reached the position of missile boat commander, is a good example of one of these students. Shoham subsequently returned to the realm of R&D and rose through the ranks until he reached the rank of brigadier general. Today, he is serving as the director of MAFAT — the highest position in the field of defense R&D.

During my time at MAFAT I kept a soft place in my heart for the Talpiot program. I maintained regular contact with participants by lecturing in their classes, speaking with students, listening to student presentations of development projects as exercises throughout their studies, and holding a discussion with each class just before the end of the period of service, aimed at convincing them to continue their service. The more Israel's high-tech industries grew, the greater the temptation for Talpiot graduates to return to civilian life quickly and not to extend their service. Nonetheless, over the past quarter of a century the program has created a sizable critical mass of high quality human resources within the IDF and the defense establishment, leaving no doubt regarding its contribution to the long-term security of Israel.

13

On Sabbatical at the French Foundation for Strategic Research (FRS)

MY FINAL DAYS AT MAFAT

Although I found the job of director of MAFAT interesting, challenging, personally satisfying and critically important to Israeli national interests it was never my intention to continue in the post for the twelve years that I did. Certainly, I was happy to have another opportunity to work with Yitzhak Rabin as prime minister and defense minister beginning in 1992. As usual, he gave me the feeling that his door was open to me and that he was always willing to give my ideas serious consideration. When I voiced my opinions during the meetings he convened on major development-related issues, I always felt like I was being listened to. Rabin dedicated a great deal of time to his responsibilities as defense minister, and to us at MAFAT it seemed that he enjoyed this job much more than the job of prime minister.

Although I first began thinking about leaving MAFAT after six years on the job, such thoughts were typically overshadowed by the sheer magnitude of the tasks at hand and my feeling that I could not just abandon my position for no good reason. It was only in 1995 that I began to feel comfortable with the idea of planning my departure. The Homa missile defense program was already well established and had a series of successful tests of the Arrow missile under its belt.

The satellite program had entered space with astounding success, and Ofek was already in orbit, producing and transmitting high-quality satellite photographs. The IDF had also finally recognized the importance of the project and was enjoying its products, which continued to stream in. Project Nautilus, the program for developing high-power lasers to shoot down Katyusha rockets, had proven its ability to destroy Katyushas in mid-flight. As a result, a Project Nautilus Administration was established at MAFAT and, in the face of Congressional decision on the issue, the US military was forced to assign teams and allocate funding to the project.

I requested a private meeting with Prime Minister Rabin to inform him of my intentions and to seek his advice in deciding on a new post. I had actually started to take interest in the position of chairman of the Israel Electric Corporation, which was vacant at the time, and I anxiously awaited our meeting, scheduled for Monday, November 6, to discuss the issue. But business as usual for me and the rest of the country came to an awful halt when Prime Minister Rabin was tragically assassinated on the evening of Saturday, November 4. I was devastated. Words cannot describe the feelings of shock, disappointment, indignation, and helplessness Israelis experienced that night, and in the weeks and months that followed. It took me another year to be ready to continue planning my departure from MAFAT, now with a new defense minister, Yitzhak Mordechai, and a new director-general, Ilan Biran.

The most important task was to find a replacement. Of all the options considered, the most suitable candidate was R&D Unit Director Brigadier General Itzik Ben-Israel, who had been working under my direction at MAFAT for four years. Ben-Israel sought promotion to the rank of major general, which meant that CGS Shaul Mofaz and Defense Minister Mordechai had to be persuaded to recommend giving the director of MAFAT the rank of major general on a personal basis without creating a precedent that would attach this rank to future directors of MAFAT. Ultimately, it was decided to provide Ben-Israel with a temporary rank of major general for a three-month transitional period, after which he would be discharged from the military and become a major general in the IDF reserves. When all the parties involved finally reached an agreement, the tight schedule according to which Ben-Israel needed to begin functioning as director of MAFAT and the special arrangement regarding his rank left us no time to lose.

The defense ministry proposed that I assume leadership of its Paris-based delegation to Europe in the summer of 1998, and I agreed. At that point, I suggested what to me sounded like an ideal solution: vacating my position as soon as possible and spending the time that remained on sabbatical in France. Professor Baruch Raz, scientific advisor at the Israeli embassy in Paris, provided me with energetic assistance in exploring the possibilities, and he soon summoned me to France for a meeting. I knew that my old friend General Paul-Ivan de Saint-Germain was the current director of FRS — the French Foundation for Strategic Research — which was linked to the French ministry of defense. This French think-tank was based outside Paris on the campus of École Polytechnique, the renowned state school of engineering that has trained generations of engineers and directors for service in the French military, the French defense ministry, and the French defense industry. General de Saint-Germain, a graduate of the École Polytechnique with extensive experience in directing defense technology development for the French defense establishment, had recently been appointed to head FRS.

Before I left Israel for my meeting in Paris, Raz informed me that FRS was interested in undertaking research on non-conventional terrorism and would be delighted to have me lead the project. At the time, Western countries, including Israel, did not dare to broach this subject openly, and instead limited themselves to classified assessments carried out by intelligence research bodies. I set a meeting with Shabtai Shavit, former director of the Mossad and chairman of the recently established Institute for Counter-Terrorism at the Interdisciplinary Center (IDC) in Herzliya. A young doctoral candidate named Boaz Ganor, who had been charged with the task of setting up the Institute at the IDC, took part in the meeting, during which I proposed carrying out a joint study on non-conventional terrorism under the auspices of three different research centers. I also discussed the plan with Dr. Yair Sharan, director of Tel Aviv University's Interdisciplinary Center for Technological Analysis and Forecasting, who was also eager to take part. I hoped that MAFAT would agree to allocate the relatively small sum required to fund the work at the two research centers in Israel, and it ultimately did. I intended proposing to the French that each partner bear the expense of the work done under its auspices, and I prepared a project outline that was received enthusiastically by Shavit and Ganor at IDC and by Sharan at Tel Aviv University. With a sizable dowry, I was now ready for my meeting at FRS.

LEAVING MAFAT

There were still two more things I needed to do before leaving for Paris. The first was to remove my personal papers and belongings from my office, and the second was to take my leave from the defense minister and the director-general. I knew that the large safe in my office held dozens of files that had accumulated in the course of my service with the IDF, the Israel Atomic Energy Commission and MAFAT. However, I really had no appreciation for how much written material there actually was. The Israel Defense Forces and Defense Establishment Archive were willing to provide space to store my personal documents, and without the dedicated assistance of the secretaries in my office, I would have never been able to sort through all the documents and organize them by subject and chronological order. The most valuable find was a few thick notebooks containing chapters of a personal journal I had written at critical junctures during my career over the years. It was all packed up in cardboard boxes and sent to the archive for safe keeping.

My meeting with Defense Minister Mordechai took place in his office at the defense ministry at the Kirya government campus in Tel Aviv. As I walked into the office I knew so well my ears rung with the echoes of the past. I could hear Moshe Dayan ruling on the dispute between the IDF and the defense ministry, which ultimately resulted in the establishment of the R&D Unit. I could hear Shimon Peres authorizing submission of the Treasure list to the Americans after the Yom Kippur War. I could hear Defense Minister Ezer Weizman resolving to launch the Lavi fighter jet program in his characteristically determined and decisive manner. And I could hear Defense Minister Moshe Arens, with his heavy American accent, approving the complete missile defense program. I remembered the feelings of disappointment and uneasiness I felt when telling Defense Minister Rabin of the failed Arrow missile and satellite launchings, as well as my joy and elation upon reporting the success of the Ofek launch. Defense Minister Mordechai was friendly and upbeat as he offered me his gratitude and wished me success, and my meeting with Director-General Biran was also quite positive.

I was determined to prove to the minister, the director-general, and myself that there were new things to do with the defense ministry delegation to Europe. I was also aware that the research project I would be leading at FRS during my sabbatical was something I had never done before. With these two tasks before me, I knew that an interesting and challenging period lay ahead.

GENERAL DE SAINT-GERMAIN AND FRS IN PARIS

Raz and I made our way to the French Foundation for Strategic Research, which was housed in a modern, practical building on the grounds of the École Polytechnique. The building offered a vivid example of modern French construction, which was decisively different from the traditional grand walled palaces that housed government ministries and other national institutions. When we arrived, General de Saint-Germain and his colleagues were seated around a conference table, and I was already able to speak freely in French albeit to a limited degree.

The discussion quickly took a goal-oriented direction, and I presented the FRS leadership with the proposed chapters for the final report to be submitted at the conclusion of the study. I was aware that they had funding for their work, but I reassured them by telling them that the Israeli portion of the project, to be carried out at the IDC and Tel Aviv University, would be funded by the Israeli defense ministry. The proposal was accepted without comment, and few hours later I was already meeting with Dr. Jean-François Daguzan, who had been charged with heading the French research team, Dr. Gérard Chaliand, the team's terrorism expert, and Dr. Olivier Lepick, a brilliant and charming young man who had just completed his Ph.D. on the use of chemical warfare during World War I. Dr. Daguzan had visited Israel before, and had on numerous occasions expressed his admiration for our achievements. Dr. Chaliand came from an Armenian family that immigrated to France in the early 20th century.

When I grew to know Dr. Chaliand better, I came to understand how the history of his people had had a decisive impact on his path in life. He had spent more than 15 years in terrorist training camps in Libya and the Lebanon Valley, not to mention the training camps that sprouted up throughout Afghanistan during the 1980s. He had developed an explicit sympathy and support for these terrorist groups, to which he insisted on referring as "freedom fighters". Chaliand was a prodigious author, and his books included titles such as *Guerrilla Strategies; The Atlas of Diasporas; A People without a Country: The Kurds and Kurdistan;* and *The Art of War in World History.* Although he and I had many arguments, we remained friends and I admired his independent thinking, his ability to encompass broad issues without lapsing into shallowness, and his capacities as a writer and speaker.

General de Saint-Germain had hopes that transcended our study of non-conventional terrorism, which started to take shape at FRS and the Israeli research institutions concurrently. The French were intrigued by the IDF and the Israeli defense establishment due to their unique technological accomplishments, and I was immediately accepted by the think-tank's senior faculty members. Our meetings, which focused primarily on lectures and reports, also included the non-formal component of group lunches in the campus cafeteria. Saint-Germain went to great lengths to enable me to take part in the discussions, and initially made sure to speak slowly and clearly so that I could understand his French. For me, every group meal was a double test: first, of my ability to address the substance and questions raised by my colleagues on issues that were still only in outline, and second, of my ability to communicate in French. From the outset, I insisted on speaking only in French, which was difficult at the beginning. During our conversations we planned a program that consisted of a series of lectures in which I would share Israeli perspectives on strategic, tactical, and technological issues with FRS faculty members and their guests. Saint-Germain asked me to prepare a list of subjects for the lecture series, and made clear intimations that the faculty would be particularly pleased if I would also address the nuclear issue. I deftly dodged the nuclear issue by not including the subject on my proposed list of lectures.

My lecture topics included: the American Revolution in Military Affairs (RMA) as seen through Israeli eyes, technological trends and their effects on the battlefield of the future, the war of information, and the challenge of maintaining technological capacities in an environment of budget cuts. After FRS publicized the topics as part of its "Working Breakfast" lecture series, there was no turning back. I had no choice but to adopt a regime of lecture preparation. My French teacher, Dominique Cottard, was forced to roll up her sleeves and go over the papers I wrote in French during the process of preparing my lectures.

FRS breakfasts were widely attended by the personnel of various government agencies, from the DGA — the development and acquisition body of the French Defense Ministry, through the Strategic Department of the Defense Ministry, to the CEA, the French Atomic and Alternative Energies Commission. Every hour-long lecture was followed by another hour of questions and answers. I was always prepared for the lecture section of the meetings, but I was unable to prepare myself for the Q&A, during which those in attendance would ask questions in a straightforward and unbiased manner, showing no mercy. Saint-Germain sat next to me, and sometimes helped me by more clearly rephrasing the questions asked.

The research on non-conventional terrorism was still underway when my sabbatical year came to an end, but I did not let the researchers at FRS and the two research centers in Israel rest until the work was complete. During the study the French team made visits to Israel, which were joined by Saint-Germain himself, and the Israeli researchers made two trips to Paris. At the end of the study two classified reports were written — one in France and one in Israel — and distributed to the two governments. An unclassified report was written in English.

For me, directing an international research project carried out by three research institutions staffed by talented and ambitious people was a new experience that provided a deep and comprehensive understanding of the different terrorist groups. It was also the first time I had heard the name al-Qaeda and comprehended its destructive potential. None of us imagined just how non-conventional al-Qaeda could become by using simple means to hijack airplanes and turn them into gigantic passenger-filled bombs to attack the World Trade Center and the Pentagon. The technical material and the historical survey of chemical and biological attacks, like the one carried out by the Japanese terrorist organization Aum Shinrikyo, were instructive and important for the formulation of the report.

The study provided readers with an assessment of the factors motivating terrorist groups, the many different organizational forms they employ, and the possibility of their making use of chemical, biological, or radiological substances in attacks in the future. The Israeli and French experts wrote a chapter with detailed information on all the substances that could be used for this purpose and analyzing their implications for defensive measures. Special emphasis was placed on analyzing individual attacks, such as the Sarin gas attack on the Tokyo subway. Emphasis was also placed on drawing conclusions and generating forecasts regarding the use of non-conventional materials in future terrorist attacks. Our assessment was that the chance of a terrorist group succeeding in acquiring a nuclear weapon for use in a terrorist attack was extremely low. We also assessed that while radiological weapons using radioactive waste were not particularly effective, chemical and biological materials were much more likely to be put to use by terrorist organizations. The results achieved by using chemical and biological materials, the report emphasized, would stem more from their potential to cause mass panic than from any actual damage they might cause. The anthrax envelope scares in the US shortly after September 11, 2001 clearly illustrated the potentially immense psychological effect of the threat of a biological terrorist attack.

FRS also asked to publish the lectures I had delivered during the think-tank's Working Breakfasts. I placed everything I had written in the trustworthy hands of Saint-Germain, who did a miraculous job editing it all. The resulting publication, which also appeared on the think-tank's internet site, consisted of four articles written in excellent professional French, along with a number of articles in English I had written on my own.

Throughout my tenure as director of the defense ministry delegation in Paris, I remained a welcome friend of the FRS and attended many of the events it organized. During this time I learned to appreciate the elegant and effective way the French raise subjects for discussion over working breakfasts, and I was even able to convince a few members of the defense ministry delegation to attend the meetings as well.

14

The Defense Ministry Delegation to Europe — Paris

It was only when I started my job as head of the Defense Ministry Delegation in Paris that I realized what an excellent introduction my time at FRS, and particularly my participation in its 'working breakfasts', had been for my work with the delegation. Suddenly, people throughout the French defense ministry woke up to the fact that there was an Israeli defense ministry delegation in Paris, and doors were opened up to us, seemingly on their own. My insistence on speaking only in French, which I started at the FRS, also proved helpful in maintaining my contacts throughout my tenure as delegation head.

The series of introductory meetings I scheduled upon beginning my job brought me to the office of Jean-Claude Mallet, director of SGDN, France's National Defense Secretariat. Mallet, a tall man who moved like a panther ready to pounce, had served as director of strategic affairs in the French defense ministry between 1992 and 1998. In this capacity he had led the French team during the French–Israeli strategic dialogue, which is where I first met him. When I referred to the meeting as one in a series of introductory meetings as I began my new job, Mallet stopped me abruptly. "You need introductory meetings?" he asked with a smile. "But you already know the whole city, and everyone knows you!" Two years later I took advantage of Mallet's open door to request authorization to export parts of a weapon system that the Israeli defense industry had not succeeded in purchasing in France. Mallet came to the meeting well prepared, familiar with the details of our request and the reasons behind the refusal to authorize them.

The delegation in Paris had a long history. Its golden age was in the 1950s and 1960s, until the Six Day War. Everyone knew it as the "acquisition delegation", and I had to work hard to convince people that the delegation's tasks involved much more than simply purchasing arms and hosting the defense ministry elite each year for the Paris Air Show or the Ground Systems Show at Le Bourget airport. To this end, I emphasized the contacts between the Israeli and European defense establishments in research and development, strategic dialogue, and defense exports to Europe in general, and to France in particular. The new name of the delegation was Mission Européen de Ministère de la Défense — the Defense Ministry Delegation to Europe.

My sabbatical year at FRS made me increasingly aware of the importance of cultivating personal relationships and provided me with the motivation and confidence necessary to work in this direction. It was clear that our home could offer a good meeting place for forging ties in an unofficial and informal atmosphere. The time we spent in the neighborhood of Marais in the city's 4th arrondissement during my sabbatical motivated us to look for a place to live there. We found an enchanting apartment on Île Saint-Louis — spacious, and made up of two smaller apartments in a house with foundations dating back to the 12th century. From the fifth floor we could see the River Seine and most of the Latin Quarter on its Left Bank. The view from the narrow balcony, with its iron-cast balustrade, was breathtaking, including the Eiffel Tower in the west, the Pantheon Dome, the Church of Notre Dame and the French Ministry of Finance in the east. This gem of a home quickly emerged as wonderful location for small intimate dinners, larger dinner parties, and musical evening programs in our large parlor.

One evening, composer and Tel Aviv University professor Yechezkel Braun gave a fascinating lecture in French during which he played selections of his own music and explained his approach to music. My friend Professor Joshua Jortner, president of the Israeli Academy of Sciences, gave a lecture on the opening up of the sciences in Israel. When Prof. Elie Barnavi arrived in Paris to take up the post of Israel's Ambassador to France, he told me that he had heard about our cultural evenings and offered to speak at one. After inquiring into his academic background, I suggested that he speak about religious wars from the Middle Ages onward. Although this was before al-Qaeda's attack on the World Trade Center and the Pentagon, radical Islam was already in the midst of worldwide expansion that was causing considerable concern. Ambassador Barnavie gladly accepted the invitation, and the wide-ranging lecture he delivered was attended by a large French audience who came especially to hear him. After his lecture he was encircled by a crowd who wanted to hear more. A few days later the new ambassador was scheduled to have an introductory meeting with French Defense Minister Alain Richard, and he asked me to join him. The meeting was also attended by Marc Perrin de Brichambaut, director of strategic affairs at the French Defense Ministry, and Jacques Audibert, political advisor to the defense minister. Both men had also been at our home for the ambassador's lecture, and the resulting sense of familiarity lightened the mood considerably.

Lionel Jospin's socialist government came into power in June 1997, and from the moment I began functioning as head of the defense ministry delegation we began trying to bring Defense Minister Richard to Israel for a visit. We were assisted by Audibert and de Brichambaut, who were two key members of the defense minister's inner circle. During my first meeting with de Brichambaut, the new director of strategic affairs, I was accompanied by my deputy Dr. Stefan Deutsch and Military Attaché Brigadier General Avraham Asael. Before the meeting, I read up on de Brichambaut and learned that he too was a graduate of the ENA, the National School of Administration. De Brichambaut was thin and bespectacled and had the look of a shy schoolboy. During our first meeting he did not reveal the true power of his personality. He had a brilliant career in the service of his country. At the age of 34 he was appointed as chief of staff of Foreign Affairs Minister Roland Dumas, and was later dispatched to the US to serve as the cultural attaché to the French embassy in Washington. After his return to France in 1988, he was appointed chief advisor to Defense Minister Jean-Pierre Chevènement.

"What should I call you?" de Brichambaut asked me at the beginning of our first meeting, "Mister representative? General Eilam? Or perhaps Mr. Eilam?" "Call me Uzi," I said almost instinctively. "That's what my friends call me." Although my colleagues were shocked by the manner in which I began my relationship with de Brichambaut, which was highly unorthodox according to French standards, they remained silent. Later, they told me that they were also surprised when de Brichambaut ended the meeting with the words: "Thanks Uzi, I'll see you soon." This meeting was the beginning of a wonderful friendship, which I still enjoy today.

Jacques Audibert, the defense minister's political advisor, also spent many years in the French Foreign Ministry before receiving his appointment at the defense ministry. My chemistry with Audibert was apparent from the moment we met. Later, he told me that he was Jewish, that his family was from Alsace, and that many of his relatives had been killed in the Holocaust.

Together, we started planning the French defense minister's trip to Israel, aware of the special sensitivities regarding the political implications of the places he would visit and the people he would meet. When I met with Audibert in the defense minister's office to coordinate the substance of the visit, he asked, in the name of the minister, what Richard would gain from the trip. That is, what would he be able to present as his unique contribution to French–Israeli relations? I was not prepared for such a direct question, but I picked up the gauntlet and offered an analysis of the relationship between the two countries' defense establishments. There had always been strong and stable intelligence cooperation between the two countries. There was already an open door for military meetings and a continuing, well-established French–Israeli strategic dialogue was in place, with professional and forthright meetings held in a positive atmosphere. Furthermore, an agreement for cooperation in the realm of research and development had been signed by Defense Minister Rabin and Defense Minister François Léotard in 1994. All that remained, I told Audibert, was to create a framework that would encourage cooperation between the French and Israeli defense industries. The next day Audibert phoned me and asked if I could jot down a few words to briefly summarize the issue. We worked hard within the delegation during the next few hours writing up a short text that declared both countries' intention to encourage cooperation between their respective defense industries. The text was specially delivered to Audibert's office the same day. At the same time, I translated it into English and Hebrew and wired it to Yekutiel Mor, who was responsible for foreign relations at the Israeli Ministry of Defense, and noted that it could serve as an agreement that could be signed by the ministers. I waited anxiously for a response from both defense ministries, and the positive responses for which I was hoping soon arrived. Both the French Defense Ministry and the Israeli Defense Ministry agreed in principle that the text we had formulated would serve as the agreement to be signed by Defense Minister Richard and Defense Minister Barak.

A two-day visit requires precise timing and close attention to every detail. Our goal was to squeeze in as many important issues as possible, while at the same time working in the requests of the French Defense Minister. Richard had requested a meeting with Israeli intellectuals, and the French ambassador had taken it upon himself to invite prominent Israeli academics and figures from Israeli industry to a gathering at his home, which would include dinner. Due to the constraints of Prime Minister Ehud Barak, we were forced to schedule the official Israeli meal, a large, well-planned event, for noon the next day. I found myself as the host of the event, during which I spoke freely and comfortably in French. The morning after the guests arrived, I came to the French Defense Minister's hotel bearing an English version of the text which the ministers were set to sign. I was anxious that we might have missed something that might prevent Richard signing sign the document before the ink on the final text had even dried. Ultimately, however, my worries were in vain. When Barak and Richard were sitting in the defense minister's office at the Kiriya government campus in Tel Aviv, after the honor parade and the blasting of trumpets, the two ministers signed the agreement for cooperation between the French and Israeli defense establishments without the slightest hesitation.

The French defense minister also asked to speak with Israeli soldiers and to get a first-hand impression of the experience of serving in the IDF, and their feelings about serving in the occupied territories in particular. The soldiers selected for the purpose included a representative cross-section of French-speaking combat soldiers from the Armored Corps, the Paratroops, and the Artillery Corps; the minister's direct interaction with the soldiers made for a dynamic and extremely successful gathering. For Richard, it was one of the most meaningful and moving parts of his visit.

Before boarding his plane, Richard thanked me graciously for the visit, which he said he would never forget. He emphasized his positive discussions with the Israeli defense minister and his belief that the agreement they signed would result in cooperative endeavors. He also stressed how much he had learned from his conversations with the soldiers. Finally, he thanked me for the manner with which I had conducted the visit. When Richard departed, I knew we had a friend in the French government. I also knew and that the defense ministry delegation in Paris would now have even greater access to government officials than they had previously.

The agreement signed by the defense ministers was declarative in nature, and it was still necessary to draw up a detailed document to be signed by the director of the French Direction générale de l'armement (DGA) and the director-general of the Israeli Defense Ministry. We prepared the material for the meeting of the directors, which usually took place during the Paris Air Show, and a detailed agreement institutionalizing cooperation and charging the directors with supervision of implementation was signed as well.

The French–Israeli agreement for defense industry cooperation was tested sooner than expected, in the context of an unmanned aerial vehicle project. MATRA, a French company that had earned an international reputation in the field of missile development, including its well-known air-to-air missiles, had a good relationship with IAI. Toward the late 1990s Israel was considering a joint project for developing an advanced UAV (unmanned aerial vehicle) system capable of covering large geographical areas. The system was meant to be a poor man's satellite system of sorts, but the more the project crystallized the clearer it became that the poor man in question would actually need to be quite rich. To the French–Israeli defense industry partnership, IAI contributed its considerable knowledge in developing complete UAV systems that had already gone operational. From its part, the French defense industry could boast an ability to deploy a satellite network to command UAV movement within large geographical areas. In the midst of this ambitious and expensive project, a golden opportunity arose in the form of a serious matter discovered by a small wealthy state in the Persian Gulf. Iraq's invasion of Kuwait and the First Gulf war led this country's leadership to resolve to develop a strong military. In 1999, MATRA and IAI concluded a proposal to develop the Eagle heavy UAV. The fusion of the French industry's political and industrial power and Israel's operational experience and technological expertise in the field of UAVs proved to be a winning combination, and by the end of 1999 the joint venture received the authorization of the French and Israeli governments to market Eagle UAVs to the third country.

In the late 1990s Germany and France established EADS (European Aeronautic Defence and Space Company), a large aerospace and defense corporation which also incorporated the Spanish aerospace corporation CASA (Construcciones Aeronáuticas SA). As a result of its long-time work with MATRA (Mécanique Aviation TRAction), IAI suddenly found itself in partnership with a new massive company. Somewhat belatedly, the Israeli and French partners resolved to try to convince the French Air Force to purchase first models of the heavy UAV and to use a UAV command and information transmission system. However, the French Air Force, which recognized the future importance of such systems, had already done its homework and had decided to purchase the American Predator UAV, a system that had been developed by General Atomics of San Diego, California. In order to make their company relevant, EADS personnel concluded that the first thing they needed to do was to change the decision of the French Air Force.

To this end, EADS and IAI requested a coordinating meeting with the Israeli Defense Ministry delegation in Paris — an unprecedented move at the time. The French personnel of EADS were aware of the French–Israeli agreement for defense industry cooperation and thought we would be able to influence the defense minister to help bring about the change in direction they sought. It was also clear that our maneuvers vis-à-vis the French Air Force would need to be sophisticated and could only be carried out by the Israeli Air Force. Within a few days I assembled IAI personnel and the EADS's vice-president of commercial development and his team in my office for a focused strategy meeting. For the Israelis, the hands-on meeting with EADS personnel was a golden opportunity to get a first-hand look at the way the enormous corporation operated. The meeting lasted three hours and produced a clear and realistic situation assessment as well as a division of tasks and responsibilities for all those involved and an integrated plan of action with clearly defined time-tables. According to the plan, French Air Force officials would be invited to Israel to learn about how the Israeli Air Force was using UAV systems at the time. We took it upon ourselves to induce the director-general of the Israeli Defense Ministry to write a letter to the director of the DGA asking him to assist in the process. We also agreed to persuade Prime Minister and Defense Minister Ehud Barak to write a letter to Defense Minister Richard at the appropriate moment, asking him to authorize the introduction of the French–Israeli UAVs to the French Air Force for study and assessment. It was clear to all of us that we could not let the American UAV establish itself within the French Air Force, even as an experimental model.

A few months later I paid another visit to the office of the French defense minister to meet with my friend Jacques Audibert who told me that the minister had made a decision and that the French Air Force would fall into line, reverse its previous decision, and purchase the Israeli UAV.

Victory in such an important and complex battle was important. It was encouraging to see that the French–Israeli agreement, which had been expanded upon and institutionalized by the directors on both sides, was now firmly in place. The agreement also afforded us a key strategic accomplishment within Europe as a whole, as the process of European unification made pan-European defense establishment partnerships much more common and easier to achieve. In practical terms this meant that every Israeli partnership with a French defense company opened the doors to a broad spectrum of partnerships with other European countries as well. This was clearly demonstrated by the heavy UAV project and the resulting partnership with EADS. Moreover, as an agreement between two sovereign countries, the French–Israeli partnership cannot be annulled due simply to minor problems that may arise in the relations between the two countries. It was clear to all of us that taking full advantage of the agreement's potential was largely up to us.

I was mesmerized by the new Europe that was slowly but surely emerging within the framework of the European Union. In the political arena, Britain, under the leadership of Tony Blair, had also started to move closer to the continent. I listened closely to Blair's speech before the National Assembly, and I was particularly impressed by his decision to deliver it in French. Blair's summit meeting with Chirac at Saint Malo, and the two leaders' declaration of the European Union's obligation to remain autonomous and to support this autonomy with European military might, paved the way for the two countries' leadership role in the effort to establish a European military force. Later, it was the British–French–German triangle that facilitated EU intervention in the conflicts in the Balkans.

Europe's handling of the Kosovo crisis highlighted the continent's fundamental weakness and military and political helplessness. In the end, the EU was forced to ask the US to assume leadership of military operations in the region. Charging NATO with contending with the crisis was an elegant solution that provided the only means of incorporating the American military into the operations.

The growing movement of countries joining the European Union at an ever increasing rate made it abundantly clear that Israel was now facing a very different Europe. Competition with the American defense industry, which was growing stronger and gaining increasing economic influence within Europe, pushed the Europeans to unify their industries, as exemplified by EADS. This dynamic also motivated the Europeans to enact new laws and install new regulations to enable their industries to compete in the international arena.

With all of this in mind, I thought it only made sense for the representatives of the Israeli defense establishment stationed throughout Europe to have a stronger network. It was not enough for the military attachés, the individual defense ministry envoys to European countries, and the members of the defense ministry delegation to meet once a year in Paris for the Air Show and Ground Systems Show at Le Bourget Airport. To improve coordination, I discussed the matter with the director-general of the defense ministry, the director of foreign relations, and the director of SIBAT (the Defense Export and Defense Corporation of the Israeli Defense Ministry) to get their authorization to set up a "European Forum". We resolved to meet once a year in Paris for a special conference in which defense ministry representatives would share reports with their colleagues, including reports on developments within the continent as a whole. All the representatives were enthusiastic about the establishment of a new open communication network that would carry a regular flow of information which they themselves would generate. Most information, we realized, could be sent via the open internet, and we found an alternative arrangement for conveying classified information based on the communication system of the Israeli Foreign Ministry. The Paris delegation assumed responsibility for setting up a European information center to collect, process, and disseminate the information provided by the representatives.

After I returned to Israel and joined the Jaffe Center for Strategic Studies at Tel Aviv University, I decided to explore defense issues as they related to Europe. This new direction was based on the fact that so few people in Israel truly understood what was happening on the European continent, despite is size and close proximity to Israel. In this capacity I was invited by NATO to make a trip to Kosovo, which included meetings at NATO headquarters in Brussels followed by a few days in the Kosovo region itself. The trip provided an extremely valuable addition to the information I had already gathered on the war in Kosovo, and proved what I already knew about the military power of the US. However, it also provided me with a first-hand look at the political–military lessons of the EU's involvement in a war it was simply incapable of fighting on its own. My extensive report on the subject, published by the Jaffe Center under the title L'Europe de la Defense, contains an assessment of the manner in which the European Union dealt with the lessons of the war. It calls for joining forces with Europe in a number of ways: from ongoing cooperation in research and development, through expansion of the agreement for cooperation between the Israeli and European defense industries, to seeking as much of a formal relationship as possible with NATO. The article also highlights the need to fight terrorism around the world and in Europe in particular, and emphasizes the unique contribution that Israel can make as a result of its longstanding confrontation with phenomenon. To be sure, Israel's assets for future warfare are becoming increasingly based on advanced technologies, whose development relies on experience and insight on the battlefield of the future as opposed to the battlefield to which we have grown so accustomed in recent decades. Nonetheless, Israel's ongoing experience with anti-terrorism operations, low-intensity warfare, the war of information, and the threat of short and medium-range rockets, and long-range missiles, provides a common denominator and a broad foundation for Israeli cooperation with many other countries.

15

The Israel Security Prize

During my time as director of the R&D Unit, I was asked by the Israel Security Prize Selection Committee on many occasions to offer my assessment of various issues. Although each year the defense minister would appoint a new three-member committee, the principles and procedures followed by the committee were part of broader standing defense ministry procedures and were passed down from generation to generation by the committee secretaries.

The deep soul-searching we all experienced after the Yom Kippur War also left its mark on the Israel Security Prize Committee and the process it employed. In the wake of the war, I assembled all the material documenting committee discussions and defense ministry procedures to assess the ultimate outcome of each of the weapons systems that won the prize. My findings were disappointing. The main criterion for awarding the prize was the originality of the technological concept underlying the weapons system in question, and not its likelihood of being integrated into the IDF order of battle. One case in point was the roller-bridge, which was awarded the Israel Security Prize just a few months before the outbreak of the Yom Kippur War and which was still in the midst of development when it was rushed to the Suez Canal after the outbreak of the war. Ultimately, the bridge turned out to be a major disappointment and was only used after the fighting came to an end.

Based on my findings, I prepared a paper on the discrepancy

between the projects to which past prizes were awarded and their actual contribution to the IDF. I therefore recommended changing the selection criteria by only awarding the Israel Security Prize to systems that had either proven themselves in battle or been integrated into the fighting forces of the IDF. This recommendation was adopted and is still in effect today.

In addition to outstanding weapons systems, the prize bylaws enabled the committee to recommend long-time contributors to Israeli defense to be awarded a lifetime achievement award in recognition of numerous contributions made over many years. In this area, prize committees have always been strict and cautious and have awarded very few lifetime achievement awards. The prize, traditionally awarded at the President's Residence in Jerusalem, was named after Eliyahu Golomb, a pioneer of the concept of a Jewish defensive force; he was a major figure in the establishment of the Haganah, and a member of the Haganah national command between 1931 and 1945.

A few months after my return from Paris and my retirement from public service, Yehuda Engel, the long-time secretary of the prize committee called and with a voice trembling with excitement, told me that the prize committee had approved a recommendation that I be awarded the 2002 Israel Security Prize for Lifetime Achievement. Although I was overjoyed, I still had a hard time believing it. I knew that some of my acquaintances had begun gathering material to recommend me for the prize, but, based on what I knew of the history of the committee, I never thought it would actually approve the recommendation. It was only a few days later, when I received a letter making it official and requesting the names of family and close friends to invite to the ceremony, that I realized it was going to take place. Although I gradually grew accustomed to the idea, the news filled me with an undying sense of excitement and gratification that remains with me today.

At the ceremony in June 2002, I was asked to speak on behalf of all the Israel Security Prize recipients for 2002. Here is what I said:

Mister President, Minister of Defense, Chief of the General Staff, Director-General of the Defense Ministry, Chairman of the Israel Security Prize Committee, honored guests, family members, and, of course, fellow recipients of this year's Prize. I was asked to say a few words on behalf of the recipients of the Israel Security Prize for the year 5762 (2001–2002), a task which I see as a great honor.

Once a year, for one brief moment, a tiny window into the defense establishment opens, shining a light on a small portion of the accomplishments achieved by the immense ongoing effort underway within. Those familiar with the diverse work of defense research, industrial development, and the assimilation of new systems during the process of armament, know that this is just the tip of the iceberg (although considering the amount of energy generated within it, it might be better referred to as a volcano).

Three weeks ago, after the Ofek 5 satellite was successfully launched into orbit, I asked the director of the defense ministry satellite program to convey my congratulations to all those who played a role in the undertaking. I reminded them that when we breathe in the fresh, crisp air on the high peak of success we tend to forget the thick, stifling air of the dark depths of failure (where we usually find ourselves alone...), as well as the misgivings, the struggle for righteousness, and yes — the struggle for funding as well.

This, ladies and gentlemen, is the name of the game for every defense establishment development project. It is not only a test of creativity, talent, and valor, but also of determination, the courage in civilian life, persuasiveness, and the ability to lead and direct a project along the stormy and difficult road to its successful completion.

Behind each of us — each and every recipient of this prize — are countless others who provided their assistance, and without whom we could have never achieved success. Each one of us has a family –parents, husbands and wives, children (and even grandchildren, at least in my case) — whose support over the long and demanding years has enabled us to dedicate all our energy to the sacred work of defending Israel. Without this sturdy foundation, we would not be standing here today at this impressive ceremony.

We still have a long road to travel before we reach the peace for which we yearn. We still face different types of threats — the remote threats of weapons of mass destruction and more immediate threats such as various monstrous forms of terrorism. Contending with the challenges we face demands a high level of creativity, innovation, resourcefulness, and uncompromising focus on the goal at hand. Success also requires a great deal of belief in oneself, unqualified optimism, and, most importantly...ision!

Decades ago, the research and development community picked up the gauntlet, and these are the results. The Israel Security Prize encourages us all to be better — to persevere and work hard, to persevere and succeed!

On a more personal note, I see many people in the audience with whom I travelled long roads and who stood beside me at critical moments. Thank you for being here, and thank you for your partnership.

I would like to thank my dear family: Naomi, Osnat and Ron, Nimrod, Noah and Ofir, and my grandchildren Amitai and Toam, to whom I owe so much.

I would also like to thank the defense establishment and the Prize committee for selecting us as worthy recipients of the 2002 Israel Security Prize.

Finally, I would like to thank all of you for being here at the President's Residence to encourage and give honor to all those engaged in the security of Israel. Thank you very much.

After the prize details were made public I was flooded with congratulations. The close friends who stood by me at different points during my career in public service showered me with warm, heartfelt words. Of all the letters I received, I have chosen the letter from Shimon Peres to include here. It would have meant a great deal to me had Yitzhak Rabin also been able to congratulate me, in his deep, baritone voice.

The Office of Deputy Prime Minister and Foreign Minister

Jerusalem
June 24, 2002

Dear Uzi,

I was delighted to hear that you were awarded this year's Israel

Security Prize for Lifetime Achievement.

I am a great admirer of your abilities in the field of defense research and development policy, which have enabled you to achieve success in the positions you have held over the years. You have succeeded in applying a standard of excellence and professionalism within Israel's extremely complex security reality, and in this way you have made an important contribution to our progress toward a goal that still stands above all others: the existence of the state of Israel.

Our work together during your tenure as director of the Atomic Energy Commission provided me with a first-hand opportunity to observe your unique contribution to scientific research and made me an admirer of your great ability to assimilate advanced technologies within the defense establishment. Israel is presently enjoying the fruits of your efforts to develop human capital, and will continue to do so in the future, in fields other than defense as well.

For all these contributions, it is our privilege to honor you with this award.

In friendship,

Shimon Peres

EPILOGUE

How Can a Small Country Pursue Large Technology?

Israel has come a long way since its days as "a state in the making", and the country's impressive development over the past six-and-a-half decades has by no means been a foregone conclusion. The moving force behind Israel's technological development has been inextricably linked to its quest for survival. The 20th century was characterized by advancements in military technologies which governments regarded as urgent development priorities to counter the major military threats that emerged throughout the century. Although the drive to develop ever more advanced technologies has continued into the 21st century, there has also been a major change: the decreasing influence of military concerns and the growing importance of civilian economic considerations. The evolving Israeli state's initial efforts to acquire advanced technologies were linked to its quest for a strong foundation for national defense. In those early days, the defense forces had only light weapons, hand-grenades and explosive charges. The Science Corps consisted of a group of young scientists and science students, including the Ephraim and Aharon Katzir-Katchalsky brothers, most of whom studied at the Hebrew University of Jerusalem.

Before the establishment of the state, and even before the outbreak of the War of Independence, David Ben-Gurion, Israel's first prime minister and defense minister, understood that we would need to make use of our qualitative advantage to secure our existence. For him, it was clear that statehood required not only the ability to defend ourselves physically but also the capacity for economic development. His policy called for placing an emphasis on development of the country's scientific and technological capabilities.

In a speech before the first Knesset in 1949, Ben-Gurion said the following:

The third factor that will bring about the miracle is the scientific and technological power with which we carry out our work. Our generation is currently witnessing perhaps the greatest revolution in human life on the face of the earth — the revolution by which man is seizing control of the strong forces of nature, the power of the atom, the conquest of air and space, and the secrets of the universe. Our intellectual and moral capacities are equal to those of all other peoples.

Between the end of the War of Independence in 1949 and Operation Kadesh in late 1956, Israel had made a number of strides with important aeronautic developments, most importantly Rafael's first surface-to-surface missiles. During this decade, Israel relied on the political and military support of France, which enabled us to import substantial French knowledge and technology. This was the beginning of the heyday of French–Israeli relations, which played a far-reaching role in laying the human foundation for Israel's achievement of technological capabilities in a number of fields. One crowning achievement was Israel's development of the Uzi submachine gun, a product of the hard work, talent, and exceptional resourcefulness of Uzi Gal, a brilliant technician and a serial inventor.

The second decade of statehood, from Operation Kadesh through the Six Day War, was characterized by two developments that played an important role in shaping Israeli efforts to acquire advanced technologies. The first was the onset of Soviet military presence in the Middle East — in Egypt, Syria, and Iraq. The Soviet weapons systems with which the USSR armed Israel's enemies motivated Israel to find an integrated tactical and technological solution. The second was the intensification of Israel's 'French connection', which stemmed primarily from French strategic and political considerations vis-à-vis its war in Algeria and provided Israel with welcome opportunities for defense cooperation. Indeed, the nuclear research center near Dimona was constructed under the supervision of French nuclear scientists.

Another influential factor during Israel's second decade was a growing concern with border security and the struggle to prevent border infiltration and attacks in border settlements. Border defense provided a legitimate and effective basis for the emergence of techno-logical cooperation with the US. The initial result was the provision of capabilities which the Americans had developed for their war in Vietnam. It began with a sparing supply of first generation night-vision technologies, such as infrared floodlights and starlight amplification goggles. We also learned about border penetration warning devices and were encouraged and motivated to develop electronic warning fences. We were not, however, provided with advanced technologies for planes, tanks, and ships.

The period between the Six Day War and the Yom Kippur War was characterized first and foremost by a widespread sense of euphoria, the result of the stunning victory that led to the hubris of preventing us from learning the lessons of the war. Today, all we can do is express remorse at our arrogance and our refusal to second-guess success. Today, we know that mistakes are made even during successful wars and military operations, and that we therefore need to analyze and learn from our successes as well as our failures. Soon after the end of the Six Day War, Israel began to fight the War of Attrition, which differed in form on the two fronts where it was fought: the Suez Canal and the Jordan Valley. The main focus of the Israeli Air Force during operations in the Suez Canal Zone was the threat of the Soviet SA-2 and SA-3 missile systems that had been deployed by Egypt. On the ground along the Canal, the main challenge was defending our combat soldiers against Egyptian sniper fire and artillery shelling along the Bar-Lev Line. Along the border with Jordan, in contrast, our main goal was to seal the front line with warning devices, ambushes, and manhunts in which we achieved a high level of operational success. A major development during this period was our loss of British and French military–technological support, and our sudden and almost complete dependence on the acquisition of American-produced weapons systems. Our increasing dependence on the United States, which stemmed from political considerations and from the generous military aid with which the US has provided Israel, sparked an ongoing reduction in Israel's development and production of weapons systems for the IDF. The greatest beneficiary has been the Israeli Air Force.

Israeli reactions to the trauma of the Yom Kippur War were extreme, and resulted not only in a fierce hunger for quantitative armament but also in an effort to achieve a clear technological advantage over our enemies. The "treasure" lists we submitted to the Americans included weapons systems based on the most advanced technologies in the fields of night vision; encoded communications; missiles (including Lance and Pershing missiles); and technologies for air-delivered landmines. Although the Americans refused to supply us with systems which they deemed as overly sensitive from a technological perspective, this was actually a blessing in disguise. We quickly realized the principle behind the Americans' response: they would agree to provide us with technologically advanced weapons systems only if we could prove that we either already possessed the technologies in question or that we were at an advanced stage of acquiring them. Israel learned its lesson well, and the result was a determined effort to develop advanced technologies on our own. These efforts were extremely successful and ultimately resulted not only in the ability to market Israeli weapons systems, but in American and European willingness to enter into equal partnerships with Israel for the development of advanced weaponry.

Israel's unique advantage in technological research stemmed from

450 | Eilam's Arc

its pool of talented technicians and technological scientists serving in the corps and services of the IDF who were trained primarily by the IDF Academic Reserves program. Over the past three decades, the Talpiot program has also emerged as a producer of high quality scientific human resources for the IDF and the country's technology sector. A major advantage of the Israeli defense establishment lies in the fact that many employees of the country's defense industry have military experience not only in training but also, and perhaps most importantly, as soldiers in war.

It is difficult to escape the troubling conclusion that the challenge of developing the technological capabilities necessary to support Israel's many varying operational needs is almost impossible to meet. One way of meeting this challenge has been through bilateral cooperative projects. In order to enter into such partnerships, Israel needs to display a sufficiently high level of technological acumen. In addition, our cumulative experience of warfare with Soviet weapons systems from Operation Kadesh through the Yom Kippur War provided us with a wealth of tactical, technical, and technological information that the countries of the West could not have accessed otherwise. This experience provided the IDF and Israel's defense industry with a unique form of enticement during its dialogue with the armies and defense industries of the West.

In order to effectively generate advanced technological capabilities, it was important to support the momentum provided by large-scale development projects. A major project, we learned, is like a comet: the project itself is the nucleus, and its tail contains the technologies which we could never allow ourselves to develop without the project itself, as well as the professional skills acquired during the development. One example is an air-to-air missile development project, which provided us with new capabilities in aerodynamics, homing warheads, and missile navigation technologies. A second example is the Merkava tank project, which generated capabilities in the realm of tank-fire command-and-control systems and advanced armored defenses using various substances and complex electronic and mechanical systems. A third example is the aborted Lavi fighter plane project, which provided us with advanced aeronautic and radar technologies that were applied in the Homa and Arrow missile-defense systems. A fourth and final example is Israel's satellite programs, which provided us with capabilities in the fields of satellite launchers, advanced observation systems, and synthetic-aperture radar (SAR) for satellites.

Throughout the history of these developments, upgrading the foundations of these systems, which could not be changed, was achieved through the transplant of technologically advanced components and sub-systems. In planes, this included armament with advanced air-to-air missiles and air-to-surface homing missile counter-measures which could not have been assimilated without adapting the plane's programming.

Tank development also involved efforts to upgrade to higher caliber cannons and to adapt the system to accommodate more accurate and deeper penetrating ammunition. Installing fire-control systems in already existing tanks necessitated a complex transplant that proved to be a technological and engineering challenge. Isareli specialization in carrying out transplants with relatively modest budgets enabled the Israeli defense industry to offer its expertise in the field to many other countries seeking to upgrade their older weapons systems.

An important consideration in the establishment of frameworks for cooperative technological-engineering projects with friendly foreign countries has been the classification level of the material in question. We always had to feel confident that information regarding the systems under development revealed in the course of joint work would not leak out or be passed on to a third party.

But today, the playing field has changed. First, we no longer enjoy the advantage of having fought against the weapons systems and technologies of the Soviet Union, the West's principal opponent.

Second, the IDF is no longer a major consumer of the products of the Israeli defense industry. Rather, the defense industry today exports four times of what they develop for the IDF, and the argument "If it's good enough for the IDF, it's good enough for you" can no longer be used when marketing abroad. At the same time, however, Israel's experience still carries weight in the war against terrorism.

Toward the end of our extended presence in Lebanon after the first Lebanon war, Israel began making use of technologies which were initially developed to provide us with an element of surprise on the battlefield of the next "major war" in the war against terrorism. This move was based on recognition of the fact that the next war had already arrived: It was a different type of war with a dynamic nature, rapid changes requiring heightened alertness, and rapid responses in the realm of technological development.

It is reasonable to assume that Israel, which has succeeded in achieving such a high standing among the world's technological powers, will be able to contend with the challenges posed by the war on terrorism, in all its forms. This will require a readiness look anew at the way things are done and a new approach to decision making.

Israel's success in joining the ranks of countries that command today's most advanced technologies has been the result of human effort. Working on technologies that verge on science fiction requires people who are gifted, talented, and creative. However, they must also be motivated. In the past, such motivation stemmed from a sense of dedication to the survival of the State of Israel against the threats posed by neighboring countries. Today, it must be recognized that there are a number of motivating factors. The strategic threats posed by long-term missiles and the use of non-conventional weapons are threats to Israel's survival. Terrorism also presents a strategic threat, although it is actually composed of a massive collection of tactical threats. Today, however, the efforts of the Israeli defense industry to continue enhancing its ability to compete on the international market is as important a factor driving technological advancement as is the current threat to the existence of the state.

Israeli decision makers, however, must not content themselves with the technological advancements stemming from competition on the global defense exports market. They must also pursue policies of allocating budgets and setting priorities to facilitate the development of technologies designated exclusively for the security of Israel.

With President Reuven Rivlin

CPSIA information can be obtained
at www.ICGtesting.com
Printed in the USA
BVHW041815020419
544395BV00015B/208/P